breaking in

breaking in

HOW 20 FILM DIRECTORS
GOT THEIR START

NICHOLAS JARECKI

Broadway Books | NEW YORK

The interviews in this book were completed from direct transcripts of meetings held with each director. They have been edited for clarity and organization.

Broadway Books titles may be purchased for business or promotional use or for special sales. For information, please write to: Special Markets Department, Random House, Inc., 1540 Broadway, New York, NY 10036.

PRINTED IN THE UNITED STATES OF AMERICA

BROADWAY BOOKS and its logo, a letter B bisected on the diagonal, are trademarks of Broadway Books, a division of Random House, Inc.

Visit our website at www.broadwaybooks.com

Library of Congress Cataloging-in-Publication Data

Breaking in : how twenty film directors got their start / [interviewed by] Nicholas Jarecki.—1st ed.
p. cm.
Filmography: p. 297
1. Motion pictures—Production and direction. 2. Motion picture producers and directors—United States—Interviews. I. Jarecki, Nicholas, 1979–

PN1995.9.P7 B646 2002
791.43'0233'092273—dc21

2001037418

ISBN 0-7679-0674-8

10 9 8 7 6 5 4

For My Parents

"The reasonable man adapts himself to the world; the unreasonable one persists in trying to adapt the world to himself. Therefore, all progress depends on the unreasonable man."

George Bernard Shaw

CONTENTS

ACKNOWLEDGMENTS

I would like to thank the people without whom this book might not exist.

My mother Marjorie Heidsieck not only gave me the initial inspiration for this project, but also perhaps for becoming a filmmaker when she bought me a videocamera for my tenth birthday. She has tirelessly supported all of my endeavors and been a deep reservoir of strength. Henry Jarecki is the best father I could have hoped for and gave me a great deal of insight and encouragement on the text, including several late-night editing sessions. Janice Kaplan believed in this project from the beginning, and went out on a limb recommending me to her friend Esther Newberg, who became my agent. Esther found the publisher for this project and took a chance on an unknown who had little more than an idea and the will to see it through. She is a pleasure to work with.

Joshua Rubin, a talented screenwriter, helped me wade through hours of interview tapes and made countless phone calls to track down the directors in this book. Anna Fogg spent endless days assisting me with text editing and organization of the material. She is a terrific writer and friend.

Gerry Howard and Ann Campbell at Broadway Books believed in my abilities and agreed to publish this book having seen only a few sample interviews and a proposal.

Xander Charity, Michele Civetta, Bryan Newman, and Michael Zaro are my friends from film school who share in this mad love of movies with me. They all not only collaborated with me on my projects both in film school and after graduation, but also helped me think about what makes a director successful and noteworthy.

Ralph Acosta, Alexis Arkus-Duntov, and Christopher Calnek are three of my closest friends who spent many hours listening to the stories the directors told me and providing their critiques on the material. They have always believed in me and supported me to no end. I am lucky to know them.

Nicholas Loeb provided me with amusement, accommodations, and insight on the interviews during my trips to Los Angeles.

Roger Ebert wrote a brilliant introduction for this book. He is an intelligent, kind man who has a vast knowledge of film and a keen insight.

I thank the directors I interviewed for their grace and introspection. They were very generous with their time and honest about their lives. I enjoyed being with every one of them.

Thanks also to: Richard Batka, Jim Cairl, Eric Corley, Ari Danes, Bruce Fancher, Brian Gay, Sam Pollard, and Ivy Supersonic.

There is a certain age when you believe you can ask a successful person, "How did you get your start?" and they will tell you and the answer will be helpful to you. There is another age, not much later but after some hard personal experience, when you realize that the answers are always autobiographical, and autobiography does not transfer. You have to get your own start.

That doesn't mean the answers are not interesting. I have interviewed a fair number of successful filmmakers over the years, and seen their eyes glaze at the routine questions and then seen them quicken again when asked . . . how they got their start. They are describing the movie of their lives, in which the first scenes are unique and individual, before the broad contours of the movie industry began to shape and guide their careers. They remember someone who helped them. Someone who did them more of a favor than was necessary. Someone who gave them a break. Harvey Weinstein remembers that when he was a kid at Cannes, trying to get into a screening, Clint Eastwood saw him and held the door open and grinned. So every year Harvey makes it a point to help someone sneak into something.

More than anything, filmmakers telling their stories remember their own loneliness and resolve, at a time when they *insisted* on writing a screenplay, making a film, being a director, in the face of overwhelming indifference. It is a career you have to make for yourself. The studios don't send recruiters to campuses to hire young film directors. The film schools turn out hundreds or thousands of graduates a year, and if you want to make feature films there are no jobs and no openings except the ones you make yourself. Kids at film festivals tell me, "I want to become a movie director," and I tell them, "That's your first mistake—to word it that way. Say, 'I am a movie director.' Give yourself the title. No one else will. Then go off and make your movie."

This book by Nicholas Jarecki was waiting to be written, and I am glad he has written it. He is honest enough to say it grew out of his own desire to become a film director. He asked directors, "How did you get your start?" and realized they all had answers they were invested in, and he thought of collecting them in a book.

No one reading this book will get their start in the same way anyone in the book did. That is in the nature of things. This is not an instruction manual. It is more of a source of hope: If this improbable mob all became movie directors, anyone can, even though (statistically) hardly anyone does.

I had heard some of the stories myself, from directors like John Carpenter or James Toback. Others I turned to quickly because I had seen their first films and wanted to know where Ben Younger or Neil LaBute came from. As an admirer of *Zero Effect*, I assumed Jake Kasdan had been helped in some way by his father's success in the business, but I wasn't really surprised to learn that Jake was on short rations at the time and more or less made his own breaks. Nepotism may get you a job as a second assistant director, but it will not get you a job as a director, because then people are investing real money and want to know who *you* are, not who your father is.

A thread that runs through most of these stories is a love of movies. Younger talks about how he and his father rewound *Planes, Trains and Automobiles* to look at their favorite scenes over and over again. Not a masterpiece, you may think, but I have seen it many times and will insist that it works and holds up and gets better over the years. Their taste was sound. I looked through Edward Zwick's interview hoping for a mention of his father's video store, but found none; he leaves the story of his father after a string of business setbacks and a divorce. But I knew Allen Zwick when he ran Video Schmideo on State Street in Chicago. That was the storefront business he wound up running after the merchant banking and the clothes stores, and I suspect it reveals a love of movies that he shared with his son.

Another thread that runs through the stories is single-mindedness. It takes self-confidence, perseverance, and a kind of ruthless determination to become a film director. You have to be able to impose your will on large numbers of other people—on those who do not want to finance your film, on those who do not want to act in it, on those who do not want to be your crew or follow your directions, on those who do not want to distribute it, and eventually on those who do not want to exhibit it, praise it, or attend it. Compared to this personality type, a symphony conductor is a pussycat.

I will give you one story. Every year at Sundance I am assaulted by human waves of would-be filmmakers trying to press their videos into my hands. I am attending a festival where dozens of films are being shown every day, and each of these films has been selected from among dozens of others by skilled programmers, yet these supplicants believe I have nothing better to do but sit in my hotel room and look at their video on a VHS machine, which in any event I do not have. I hurt their feelings, I am sure, by refusing to even accept their offerings, but what good would it do to return home with dozens of videos that I will never look at? I am not the first port of call. By the time a film sails into my harbor it should have been through some kind of preliminary selection process. I see five hundred films a year as it is, not counting classics and film classes. It isn't my job to process films that have not been able to find distribution or a festival berth, no doubt for excellent reasons.

But on the opening night of the 1999 festival, I could see the hurt in the kid's eyes when I made a kind of anti-vampire cross in the air as he attempted to give me his film. I explained, as I just have, why it is not my function to view every film anyone cares to hand me. He said he understood, but his film was "really good." They are all really good, I said. He disappeared into the crowd. I could tell he did not understand. He took my general point, but he felt, of course, that he was the exception.

Four or five days later, I was in the coffee shop of the Yarrow Inn, where ESPN was on the big screen on the wall, when a voice in my ear asked me to watch the TV. It was the same kid from opening night. His name was Stuart Acher, and on the screen was his fifteen-minute film, *Bobby Loves Mangos*. He had bribed the manager to put it on. Check and mate, I thought, and sat down to look at it. "This is really good," said the actor Paul LeMat, who was sitting next to me. It was. And so I wrote about Acher, and we have kept in touch, and on the basis of his film he got an agent and some jobs doing commercials and now, he says, he is about to do a feature.

That film, in turn, may be really good or perhaps not. The point is that Acher has the stubbornness, even the divine obnoxiousness, necessary to press himself upon the industry—to insist that he is a movie director. All of the stories in this book resemble his in one way or another, although to see that you have to look beneath the details to the underlying structure. And they all provide the following helpful suggestions:

It doesn't matter if you go to film school or not, or which film school, or what you study. It doesn't matter if you work on film or video, or what kind of camera you use. It doesn't matter if you write in the morning, or at night, or on yellow pads or on a Macintosh. It doesn't matter if you work as an intern or an apprentice, in Hollywood or Austin or anywhere else. It doesn't matter what movies you watched or what books you read—as long as the answer is "a lot of them." What matters is that you called yourself a movie director, and you made a movie. How did you make a movie? As Malcolm X once said, and Spike Lee once quoted, you did it "by any means necessary." I am reminded here that I also heard Lee advise film students to "liberate" a camera if necessary, but that is another story, and another book.

breaking in

At its core, this is a selfish book.

The idea for this project came to me when I was in the midst of pursuing my own "break in." Like many young people, I had been interested in film from an early age. I grew up in New York City and movies were always a big part of my life. I was going to the movies as far back as I can remember, and films always had a big impact on me. I liked many different kinds of films and was interested in how a movie could explore character, how it could bring you into the world of people different from yourself and enable you to share in their joy and sadness. I felt enveloped by the cinema, transported into an existence that was so vastly different from my own, yet touched nonetheless on the same life issues that I dealt with. My mother gave me a videocamera for my tenth birthday, and I started making short films with my friends, playing around and trying to figure out how to make interesting movies.

I was also fascinated with computers while I was growing up and was a quick study of their advanced workings. This helped me to get my first real film job when at the age of fifteen I was hired as a technical consultant for the MGM/UA film, *Hackers*. Having been a hacker for many years and having learned all about the ins and outs of computer security, the producers thought that I might be helpful in advising them on the "realism" of their film. I worked for a week on the production, and met and talked with the actors, director, and screenwriter about the reality of the script, and even worked with the prop master to help build some hacking props for the movie.

Around this same time, I read Sidney Lumet's fascinating book, *Making Movies*. It provides great insight into the filmmaking process and details the making of all of Lumet's films, starting with his origins and continuing up through his most recent film at the time of publication. The first chapter is titled, "The Director: The Greatest Job in the World." After reading Lumet's book, I was convinced that it was.

I enrolled in a six-week filmmaking course that the New York Film Academy held at Princeton University and made my first serious films. We shot short subjects on black-and-white 16mm film and assembled the movies to screen for our peers. It was a wonderful experience; after that I was hooked. I had written short stories since I was young, but now I started trying to write short scripts, determined that I would begin to make real movies.

After high school, I attended NYU film school and worked hard on my student projects, trying to prepare myself for the films that I would make after graduation. At school they didn't teach us much about "The Industry." We focused on our films and the production process of making them. I knew that it would be difficult to become a director, but I hadn't really figured out how I would do it other than by working hard at it.

Due perhaps to my precocious nature, I was not interested in "working my way up." I wanted to tell stories and I wanted to direct movies. Getting a PA (production assistant) job, moving to key PA, then to second-second assistant, then to second assistant, then to first, then to unit production manager, and so on seemed like a ten-year process, at least. And I was increasingly finding that this path didn't necessarily lead to directing. Who was to say how those transitions between jobs would come, and even if they would come at all? And what did they have to do with directing? What did running for coffee, organizing call sheets, calling helicopter pilots, and picking up movie stars have to do with actually making movies? How did these "apprentice" jobs teach me anything about art, about storytelling, about being good at what I wanted to do? Were these simply the dues I had to pay?

At first, I wasn't sure. However, it seemed to me that the only way to make movies was to make movies, just as I had done in film school. I felt that my writing wasn't yet at the level where I could produce a filmable script, so I thought that I should do something where I could gain directing experience outside the high-stakes world of feature filmmaking. I focused my attention on making music videos, which was a form that interested me both because of the short format and also because it was heavily focused on the visual aspects of filmmaking, something that had always appealed to me. However, breaking into directing music videos wasn't any easier than breaking into directing feature films. After I finished directing my first video (which I did by splitting the cost of the production with an unknown band and getting friends to work for free), I sent it out to thirty music video production companies along with a nice note and a copy of my resume.

I'm not quite sure what I expected, but at the end of three months, I had received two rejection letters and absolutely no response from the twenty-eight others I sent the tape to. I did my research as best as I could, but what I heard back from most people I talked to was that the only way to really get into the music video business was again to "work your way up" the industry food chain, starting out getting coffee for someone and maybe five years later swinging a boom pole. What kind of world was this? Was it all based on nepotism or "working like a slave to become a master"? Was this the price I had to pay? Was I really going to be somebody's schmuck?

I was.

My now-darkened view of my future prospects came mostly from the advice I had solicited regarding my career and the people I had solicited it from. On the whole, I had been out to talk to business people about film. As they would tell me, film is a complicated business that is mainly based on nepotism or years of hard and unrecognized work. I should start at the bottom, steal studio time to do my own work, and then hopefully end up as "Director of International Sales" at a media conglomerate. But I didn't want to be "Director of International Sales" when I was forty-five. I wanted to tell stories. Could I really believe that this was how filmmakers got their start, working as development or sales executives? I had read articles about filmmakers, but the origins of their careers were never really that clear. It always seemed that they were just "geniuses" who were discovered one day, usually early in life, and from then on the world was their oyster.

As I sat at home one day in frustration, I thought about what I would do if I could do anything. If I could have access to any information I wanted about how to become a filmmaker, where would that information come from? It occurred to me that the best thing to do would be to sit down with twenty successful filmmakers and to ask them how they became filmmakers. What did they do when they were in my position? How did they deal with frustration, how did they break through the seemingly impregnable wall that surrounds the film industry to become directors and tell their stories? How did they get their first real deal, their first shot at making a film that would be widely released and seen by people outside of their immediate families? How did their careers come together, and how did the journeys affect their personal lives?

That was what was behind the impetus of this book: a simple, selfish motive for me to find out the "truth" behind the origins of filmmakers and their careers. The goal was to answer the question, how do filmmakers "break in"? Come with me now as I try to find out.

Edward Zwick | ABOUT LAST NIGHT

EDWARD ZWICK *was born in 1952 in Wyneck, Illinois. He attended Harvard University and began publishing work at the New York Observer and other publications by the time he was twenty-one. During a year abroad in France he met Woody Allen, who gave Zwick his first job working on a film. This exposure pushed Zwick to begin developing his own material. At the age of twenty-six he became producer of the television show "Family." He went on to direct his first feature,* About Last Night, *starring Demi Moore and Rob Lowe. Subsequently he created the television series "thirtysomething," and directed and produced many more films including* Glory *and* The Siege, *starring Denzel Washington and Bruce Willis. He also produced the Steven Soderbergh film* Traffic. *Zwick lives in Los Angeles with his family.*

I grew up in Wyneck, Illinois, an affluent, middle-class suburb of Chicago. I went to a public high school, but it was a very progressive one, called Nutrier High. It's a bit odd, but a disproportionate number of people from this school have gone into the entertainment business, mostly as actors. I can't necessarily say why, but they have a very good drama department and I think it's that combined with the privilege of the suburb. Growing up there you're exposed to a number of artistic things as a child and indeed are given the presumptuous notion that you can go out into the world and succeed. There may be some sense of entitlement that comes from growing up in that particular way.

My mother had once been the assistant director in the high school class play. That was the extent of her theatrical involvement and yet it struck a chord in her. She loved the theater. She loved films. My father had loved film too, and it was important to my mother that we go see movies and important to my father that we go see them the first night. He was very into the glitz and allure of it and I think she was more aesthetically interested in the films themselves. When I was a kid I was initially very drawn to the theater. I first worked on a school play in fifth or sixth grade. By the time I was in eighth or ninth grade I was directing these little productions and acting in them and lighting them and doing all the things that somebody does when you're that age. We lived in a little split-level house that had three bedrooms. I have two younger sisters, and when they no longer wanted to share a room, I moved out of my bedroom and into the den of our house. In the den there was a television set, and although it was scandalous to have a television set in your room, particularly at age twelve or thirteen, I was now in the den, where it was somehow okay. That meant that I could stick a towel under the door so the light wouldn't show and turn the sound down and keep watching. When they thought I was asleep I could watch late-night movies.

It was about 1965 and at that time in the Midwest the late show was a wonderful venue for watching older movies. I remember seeing some of the real American standards such as *The Maltese Falcon* or *Red River* when I was supposed to be sleeping. It was a guilty pleasure, and one that I was passionate about, but not one that I ever really thought I could partake of.

WHAT WERE YOUR PARENTS' PROFESSIONS?
My father had several professions over time. He initially went to work for my grandfather in the dress business. Then he was a mortgage banker, which is someone who puts together financing for larger business projects. Then in the midst of one of those projects he chose to open some clothing stores. He had three different incarnations over the course of his life. Each business had a spectacular rise and an even more spectacular fall, and by the time I went to college he was in the midst of the most spectacular fall of all. I think he owed the government a lot of money. My mother took care of us while we were young, and then she and my father divorced when she was forty. She began to work, starting out at Harcourt Brace, a publishing company, and then went on to become director of entertainment at a geriatric hotel as a kind of a recreation director for eight hundred senior citizens.

I had been watching films since I was young, but didn't really ever think that I would be making them, so when I went to college at Harvard University, I didn't study film but instead was an English major, although theater remained central to my life. As well as doing all the things that one does at a liberal arts school, I also spent an inordinate amount of time in the theater.

SO YOU WERE DEFINITELY LEANING TOWARD AN ARTISTIC PATH.
You're getting to a very watershed moment, which is that after working so much at the theater, I began writing. I wrote for *Rolling Stone* while I was in college and later for a magazine called *The New Republic*. I also applied and was accepted to Harvard Law School. Certainly law school was a more conventional choice, and one that my parents thought more legitimate. I'll say though that my mother, because she harbored this very secret love of the arts, was encouraging about the idea of me being in theater, and my father, who was at the time in the midst of his business collapse, had lost some moral authority in the argument.

At the same time that I got accepted to Harvard Law, I received a Rockefeller fellowship to go to Europe and work with some local theater companies. It offered a year of grace, a year not to have to decide, and so I took it. It was cash really and tax-free cash and so I took it and went to France.

While I was there, I was very lucky in that when I had worked with *The New Republic* I had corresponded with Woody Allen because he'd written a number of short humor pieces for *The New Yorker*. But there were a number of pieces that William Shawn had not published, and Marty Peretz, a professor and a friend of mine from college, had solicited Woody to give those pieces to *The New Republic*. So I had had a brief correspondence with him throughout that process. I had heard that he was making a movie in France, and so when I actually saw him one day walking Saint-Germain des Prés, I did something that I would never do now. I was twenty-one and brash, and so I walked up to him and introduced myself right there on the street. He was remarkably kind and open. He professed to recall the correspondence, although I'm not quite sure he did. I told him I was in France on a fellowship and asked if I could hang out at the set and see what that was all about. I didn't even know if I was interested in doing that, really, because as I always felt like the technical aspects of film were daunting. I was well aware of film's relationship to what I did in the theater in terms of storytelling and directing the actor and things like that, but I felt that I needed to know all the technical side. Then at this encounter Woody invited me to hang out on the set, and work as a kind of a half-assed assistant. I spoke some French, so I could help out, and they didn't have to pay me much.

I could tell very quickly that Woody was not technically inclined, but rather was an artist, a writer with a vision, and that he had surrounded himself with a number of people whose job it was to interpret that vision. Whether it was a cinematographer, or Kurt Gallow as an assistant director, or Paul Feyder, Woody had all these wonderfully talented people surrounding him. Although this was before he made what I consider to be the extraordinary breakthrough of his career, stylistically, which was *Annie Hall,* he had only made a couple of movies at that time, and was now filming *Love and Death.* I worked on that movie for six weeks in France and then we went to Hungary for two or three weeks and then back to France. Ultimately I got bored because I wasn't doing anything truly interesting, but rather holding a walkie-talkie in the rain or doing office work. But the experience of the filming was revelatory.

HE WAS KIND TO YOU.
He was generous. I don't know how else to put it. He was very important, and yet he honored my idiotic questions and really was a big help to me at that time.

For the rest of that year that I lived in France I would go to the movies often. Paris is about the best place in the world to see movies. There are twenty (or at least there were at that time) revival houses going at any one moment including the cinemateque where they're showing every movie by Vittorio De Sica, Roberto Rossellini, Pier Paolo Pasolini, any Italian director, and at the same time they are doing a retrospective of John Ford and Preston Sturges, along with Jean-Luc Godard and François Truffaut. It's a remarkable place to get a cinematic education. I spent a lot of time going to movies, mostly because I was lonely, bored, or scared or uncertain as to what my future might be. The movies have always been a lovely refuge for those who want to escape for a couple of hours in the dark, and I wanted to do it for at least twelve hours every day if not more. The difference though was that I began looking at movies as a possible mode of expression whereas before I'd only looked at them as entertainment, or a kind of diversion. During that year in Paris, I also began to write much more seriously. I had written some bad plays in college, but alienation and disenfranchisement are a really good prompt to becoming a more internal writer and I began to do that.

I had always thought that when I started to run out of money I would go to New York, as I had had some offers to work in the theater there. But ultimately, and I can't remember how I heard about it, I decided that I wanted to go to the American Film Institute. I was about twenty-two at this point, I had finished Harvard and my year of rest, and so I wrote for the application and sent it in to the AFI. I didn't have a film to show them so instead I sent them some reviews of a few plays that I had directed, some music and songs that I had written, some articles I had written for magazines, and an essay, and on the basis of that I got an interview and was accepted.

WHAT KIND OF FILMIC INFLUENCES OR AESTHETIC TASTES WERE YOU DEVELOPING AT THE TIME?

I know that I had already been influenced by the things that touched a boy in the mid-1960s—by John Sturges, Sam Peckinpah, John Huston, and all the very muscular American directors. At the same time, I will never forget the moment when I sat and saw *Lawrence of Arabia* for the first time, or the moment that I saw *Seven Samurai*. They were just indelible. Once I went abroad, I think the influences were more sophisticated, and a bit more intellectual, and so it was about seeing Ingmar Bergman movies and the films of more contemporary European directors as well as the more venerated ones. What I didn't know, and wasn't able to figure out till years after, was that working with Woody was really extraordinary for me in a very unexpected way—later when I read the first script of *Annie Hall*, I saw aspects of Woody's life mirrored, transmuted into art. His breakup with Diane Keaton, some things that I knew about him personally, were lifted up onto the screen, and the autobiography of it was quite striking.

YOU MEAN THE IDEA OF INCORPORATING A PERSONAL EXPERIENCE INTO THE WORK.

Yes. Something began there which didn't really flower in my own artistic life until we did "thirtysomething" or "My So-Called Life" or even the projects I work on now. I think that the more personal, anecdotal things that I've done in television actually date back to that moment with Woody. What I learned is that I find myself through film.

LET'S TALK A BIT ABOUT YOUR EXPERIENCE AT THE AMERICAN FILM INSTITUTE.

It began in September of 1975. The first year, there were about twenty-five of us invited there as directors. What you do is you make short films on videotape, and you shoot them single camera, as if you were shooting film-style. After this process, the class is narrowed down to about six or seven students who are invited back to make a thesis film in their second year, which I did. It was at AFI in that second year that I met Marshall Herskovitz, and therein really began a kind of dialogical relationship about film and storytelling that continues to this day. He had also been invited back to do a film and we worked with each other on our projects. It was not in any way a formal collaboration, but it was the beginning of what would become one.

CAN YOU TELL ME ABOUT THE FIRST SHORT FILM YOU MADE?

Not with any great pride or desire for it to ever reach the light of day. It was a father-son story, a twenty-five-minute short, and it had some nice actors in it. Bobby Carradine, Melanie Griffith, and Michael Conrad were in it. They all worked for nothing. Melanie had done *The Drowning Pool* with Paul

Newman at the age of sixteen. She was about nineteen then. Bobby hadn't done much, I don't think. It was an allegorical story told about a kid and his father. The kid is a forest ranger who meets a biker. The title was "Timothy and the Angel" and that referenced a biblical story called "Tobias and the Angel," about a visitation into a life and how that changes the relationships of the two protagonists. The film wasn't very good, it was just all right, although it did win a couple of student film competitions.

I also shot an original script by a young woman named Claire Townsend, who later went on to be a film executive, as well as an adaptation of a John Guare play called *Something I'll Tell You Tuesday*. Those three were the pieces that I did that first year; all naturalistic, all about human behavior and emotion, nothing stylized or genre-esque.

SO THIS WAS YOUR REAL FORMAL FILM EDUCATION?
Yes, and it was an interesting one. There were three extraordinary people there. There was a woman named Nina Fouche who still teaches acting there. She had been a starlet and contract player in the 1940s, and I think she was even once nominated for an Oscar. A wonderful teacher, she ran the class on directing the actor. Then there was an artist in residence named Ján Kadár who was a Czech director who had been at the Prague film school and had done an extraordinary movie called *The Shop on Main Street*, a real touchstone movie for those who know Eastern European film, and then a movie called *Adrift*. A truly great director, he had first been imprisoned by the Nazis for being a Jew and then by the communists for being a socialist. He had emphysema and was not well, and was not an entirely pleasant person either, but a very strict European conservatory type of a teacher who believed that there was a way that things should be done, that there might be one place to put the camera that was best and that there was a way to best tell a story, and he was quite pedagogical about it. Finally there was Tony Vellani, who was the dean of the AFI for many years, who had been an assistant to George Stevens, and was very steeped in the tradition of narrative American film. Between the three of them, they ran a very rigorous program and you were beaten down and torn apart and humiliated and brutalized for the sake of reinventing yourself.

To me, it wasn't until a number of years later that some of the things that they were talking about began to coalesce in my mind. I had to get out there. It was just not my nature to be able to learn things academically that way. The actual process of storytelling is one that did not initially sink in and it was not until many years later, after I had made mistake after mistake and only in the mortification of what I had done, or rather what I had not done, that I really began to grow as a film director. I look at the lives of directors that I know. Larry Kasdan is somebody who I know and *Body Heat* was his first film. They were the first two hours of film he ever shot and it is so stylish and so accomplished that I marvel at somebody being able to do that. I was much more like the guys must have been in the twenties and thirties who shot fifty-two-reelers before they ever knew what they were really doing. That's what George Stevens did, that's what John Ford did, it's what most of the early directors did. They needed to shoot film in order to understand film, and for me, the first episodes that I directed, or the first TV movies that I made were like making crepes—they tell you to throw the first couple away because the pan isn't seasoned yet. I needed to be in the process of shooting film before I really came to understand what shooting film meant, and the leap between my first film and my second was accomplished by virtue of the sixty hours of television that I shot or produced or wrote or cut in between the two of them. That somehow was my learning curve.

An important thing for me stylistically was to find a way to integrate that which I already knew with that which I was learning. I was really steeped in the theatrical tradition, the classical tradition of the well-made plays of the thirties and forties or Shakespeare or Molière or Sam Shepard and all those things.

BUT YOU HAD A PREOCCUPATION WITH REALISM?
That's right, I did. On the other hand, I also had this secret adolescent love of the epic and the muscular "movie movie" that I had watched and loved as a boy, and it took a while for those things to be integrated.

TELL ME A LITTLE BIT ABOUT THE CLIMATE AT THE AFI.
It was very competitive. It was very pernicious. You really felt in competition with your peers as to who would survive, and in that was a microcosm of what would be expected once you got out. I suspect all film schools are diabolical in that particular way, and not entirely healthy. The alliance that Marshall and I formed was very important. It gave us a certain feeling of comradeship amidst this environment, but there were also some very talented people there. John McTiernan was in my year, and Amy Heckerling and Marty Brest were a year or so ahead of us. David Lynch was a couple years ahead. It was a fertile group and we were aware of each other. I think I was under the delusion that once I finished my film I would immediately be besieged by competitive studio or TV bids, people wining and dining me and trying to hire me, but of course it didn't happen. The climate had changed. When Francis Ford Coppola did *Dementia 13* or when Steven Spielberg did the *Amblin* short, the appetite for young directors was so extraordinary that if you owned a Bolex you had a chance of getting a job. But by 1974 that had started to change, and it was not coincidental that the thing that got me my first job was my writing.

After school, I took a bunch of crummy jobs just to pay the rent. One thing I did that was invaluable to me was work as a reader for a film studio for about a year and a half. I read hundreds of bad scripts for $25 a piece and wrote synopses and criticism of them. It was an extraordinary way to internalize the form of screenplays, and to break them down and analyze them was—however deadening to the spirit—very, very helpful later on in terms of having a real sense of how the mechanics of the film script work. I had not learned that in film school. We didn't really do a lot of feature scripts. It was more about directing than writing, and this was a beginning for me of understanding the form. So I did that for a long time. Also, in that half-assed schmeister way that you hear about things and get things, I wrote a script for a couple of guys from Kentucky who wanted to be in the movie business, but didn't want to pay someone in the Writers' Guild. They had somehow gotten my name and paid me $1,000 a week to write a movie about the Kentucky Derby, but wouldn't send me to Kentucky to learn about it. So I wrote an imagined script about the Kentucky Derby and they stiffed me on the last two weeks' payment and took off with my script and vacated the rented house that they had used to say that they were producers in Studio City, and that was the last I saw of them. Then there was another job for American International Pictures for Samuel Z. Arkoff for an adaptation of a book called *The Way of an Eagle*, which was a biker movie and a Christ parable that they paid me for under the table. I did anything and everything to get by and get work.

BUT YOU WERE A PAID WRITER.
I was a paid writer, however illegally and tax free, but it all was part of the preparation for doing it for real. I suppose it was for real except that it was so half-assed.

AFTER THIS AFI SHORT AND THE REALIZATION THAT HOLLYWOOD WOULDN'T BE IMMEDIATELY BEATING DOWN YOUR DOOR, HOW DID YOU VIEW YOURSELF? DID YOU CONSIDER DOING ANYTHING ELSE?
It's funny; I actually still have the letter of acceptance from Harvard Law School on my wall. It haunted me, because there I was three years later, and friends who had made the more established choice were graduating and taking very significant jobs working for Supreme Court justices or going to work for big corporate powers or doing good social work. But I wasn't. I was reading shitty scripts for two hundred bucks apiece and figuring out how I could repair my car and get an agent. There were all sorts of doubts.

There was a group of people who befriended me at the time. There was a producer named Michael Phillips, a screenwriter named Nick Meyer, a screenwriter named Jeffrey Fiskin, and a director/producer named Tony Bill. Those guys took me under their wing. They were about four or five years older than me, and they invited me to their nice houses when I had no place nice to go and fed me when I really couldn't afford a nice meal. It never was about employment, it was more about feeling like a part of a place. Through them I would get invited to a screening or meet a girl or two, and I had little moments where I felt a little more inside than having my nose pressed up against the glass wondering how I was ever going to get in. But there was something exquisitely painful about that too, because here were Tony and Michael having produced *The Sting* and about to do *Taxi Driver* and there was Paul Schrader doing that and there was Nick Meyer having written *Seven-Percent Solution* and Jeffrey Fiskin who was working with Jackson Browne and they had this life and they were excited about it. I was desperately hungry and had to hide that hunger in some way to be included. To know that you're not really legitimately part of that orbit brings with it a certain bittersweetness. So I felt at the time, in retrospect inappropriately I think, that if I could only get a chance to show what I could do, then it would really mean something. When indeed I began to get chances, what I did wasn't up to the level where I would have liked it to be, and it felt like it took forever to get anywhere. That said, I worked on a television show by the time I was twenty six and I started making movies around thirty, but it seems at the time to be endless, hugely frustrating, utterly painful, and humiliating. But it wasn't; it just seemed that way because that's what it feels like when you're in your early twenties. I was enormously precocious, which was not surprising, because I had had things happen early. I published a book when I was twenty-one. I had written articles, I was always the youngest kid picked for the varsity. But precociousness is a burden, and I had to reckon with it.

HOW DID YOU ULTIMATELY FIND REAL WORK?
There's a little tom-tom that beats among your friends like, "This agent is looking and this one you'll meet," and somehow the script for my AFI short film got to a man named Jeffrey Sanford, a very literate, kind man, who was looking to take on young clients. He said, "Yeah, I'll take you on." I'm sure it was conditional, but he sent the script to the producers of a television show called "James the Fifteenth," and a young producer there, a man named Richard Kramer, read the script and asked me for a meeting. It was my first meeting. Soon I discovered that Richard was about to be fired as it turned out and the show was about to be canceled. But what came from that was that Richard and I became friends and Richard said, "Well, I've written a script for this television show called 'Family' and they would probably like your work." So he sent my script to those producers and they did like it, and they invited me to come in for a meeting. I did some homework, had seen the show a few times before I went in there, and by virtue of the meeting

they invited me to write a script. So, suddenly, having had no money and no legitimacy, just by virtue of that meeting, they were saying yes. That was $15,000 or $20,000 and a job, and I was suddenly a professional writer.

At the time the story editor of that show was a man named David Jacobs, who was about to leave the show because he had written a pilot about these rich people from Texas. The pilot was "Dallas," and so by the time I turned my script in, David had gone off to become a multizillionaire television producer and his job was open. The producers really liked the script that I wrote, and on the basis of that script they invited me to come on staff as a story editor. At that point I had the good sense to say, "You know what I really am is a director," and they said, "Oh yeah, sure." But I said, "No, I have this short film, let me show it to you, just to prove that I have some sense of what the process is, and if you want to hire me as a story editor let me direct an episode." So they said, "No, you can't direct an episode but what we will do is set some conditional terms by which if you make it through ten weeks as a story editor and if at the end of the thirteenth episode it all works out and we still think your work is valuable to us, we'll let you direct the last episode of the season." I think the premise was that if I hung around enough and observed carefully, then by the end of the year I might be ready to direct. And that's how it happened. I was able to direct my first professional job on that television show that I had been on for a year, "Family." And that was a very nice way to have an introduction to directing, because I had spent a year getting to know the people, getting to know the actors, getting to know the crew. The episode turned out well. They liked it. Then, to my astonishment, Nigel and Carol McKeand, the people who had given me the opportunity and were very good to me, announced that they were leaving. They said that they had burned out on the show and they wanted to do other things. So I was left to produce the show myself at twenty-six years old. The executive producer, Len Goldberg, said well, why not try it. I immediately hired all my friends. I hired Marshall. I hired a woman I went to college with. I hired my friend Richard Kramer, who had gotten me the job in the first place and then I produced the show for another year.

WORKING IN BOTH MEDIUMS LATER ON, CAN YOU TALK A LITTLE BIT ABOUT THE DIRECTOR'S ROLE IN TELEVISION AS OPPOSED TO THAT IN FILM?
I have to analogize it to writing an imitation of poetry when you're in college. Your professors say that they want you to write in a certain rhyme scheme with a certain scansion and form. You're constrained by a certain set of limitations. That's what television directing is like. The question is, given that set of limitations of form, of time, and of money, how inventive or creative can you be? What's remarkable is that even though you realize that it

is prescribed, you can look at episodes by ten different directors and you will see the difference: There are those who are able to bring something personal or dynamic to it, and then there are those who are not. Initially I was not. But I was watching dailies every day. I was writing the scripts and seeing how everybody did them, how they did them well, and how they did them badly. I would become inspired when they elevated them and I would become furious when they trashed them. It was a process that was not only going on in those times where I would get on a set and direct an episode, but it was going on every day.

I continued directing while I was producing, but I don't think I made any significant leaps. I think I began to understand the form, but I wasn't really making great strides, and the show ended after another year. Based on the relative success of the show, I had made a deal to write and direct a movie for a studio, but then the project died, so I got hired by several people to write for them, primarily Michael Douglas, who had liked some of the work that I had written. I did two separate projects for him; one was an original screenplay and one was a rewrite on a movie called *Starman*. I was living the life of a screenwriter. All the while I wanted to be a movie director, but I was earning a living by writing by that point.

PRODUCING THE SHOW HAD GIVEN YOU . . .
Some legitimacy. It opened certain doors, and I began writing other scripts as well. One I wrote on spec was about a man going to Tibet in 1952 when the Dalai Lama was about to flee. That script got a lot of attention. Nobody wanted to make it, but it was a good writing sample. I began to accumulate a body of work that I could show to people.

HOW LONG DID IT TAKE YOU TO WRITE SCRIPTS?
Three to four months. I used to think that five pages a day was a good day. That's after I did all the hard work of beating out the story, and that could take anywhere from one to three weeks. The scripts that I was writing were pretty catholic in their differences. One was an action/adventure movie. One was about the first year of coeducation in a dormitory. One was about a small town in Texas and the importance of a football team.

THERE SEEMS A COMMONALITY AMONG THEM IN THAT THEY WERE MASS-MARKET THEMES.
Yeah, I think I was interested in trying to do things that were more adventurous, while still being for a commercial marketplace. That concept began and still remains at the center of what I'm interested in doing. I'm not interested in exploitation, and I'm not interested in things that are insulting to the intelligence, but I do want to exist in the context of popular culture. I

think the movies that I'm drawn to have a lot to do with the movies that I try to make in two regards. They do have people at the center, and they focus on the moral dilemmas or the emotional odysseys of those people. But each of them in some way also has greater ideas. They are meditations on something that is important to me. I like to think that a film can actually have both of those things in it, as well as the obligatory components, like action and excitement and emotion.

I THINK IT'S EASY TO CRITICIZE TELEVISION BY SAYING IT'S LIMITED OR IT'S NOT REALLY AN ART FORM. WHAT'S YOUR TAKE ON THAT?
It took me eight years to get *Shakespeare in Love* made. It took me seven years to get *Legends of the Fall* made. Things that are ambitious in film, that cannot be boiled down to an obvious, collapsible one-line description, that are not slam-dunk marketing opportunities, take for-fucking-ever. In television, I've written about very personal concerns in a way that I don't know how I could have ever have written about them in films. To be able to do it every week is such an astonishing opportunity. For someone to say, "Here's a million and a half dollars every week, do what you want with it. We'll give you no notes. It's your idea." That's what our experience has been for eleven years now. "We'll give you no notes. You'll cast who you want. You write it the way you want. You cut it the way you want and we will release it for 11 or 12 million people every week just as you have written it." I'm sorry, but that would be a very difficult thing to piss on. It has value for someone who is trying to have a life with a family and would like to be able to stay at home for a year or two at a time and not go off to these adventures in far-flung places with very self-important people, where everyone narcissistically believes that the movie is about them and for them, and you're right in the middle of the unholiest of crossfires all the time. There's never a movie that doesn't have politics in it. There is never a movie that doesn't have competing agendas. And in television, we're just trying to serve ourselves, to do the work. TV is very different in that.

SO HOW DID YOU GET TO BE INVOLVED IN DIRECTING YOUR FIRST FEATURE?
First I did a couple of movies for television. Marshall and I came up with this very odd notion for a TV movie called *Special Bulletin*. It was shot on tape and done as if it was taking place as seen on TV news, and it was very radical, and turned out to be very successful. It created a huge controversy and won seven Emmy Awards. Sydney Pollack, who is a very talented director, saw the movie and invited me to this new film studio that was just started called TriStar. First, Sydney had called and asked if I wanted to direct a movie that he was producing. I think it was called *Songwriter*. I didn't and he was somewhat put off that I would say no to a feature, but I ex-

plained to him that I was more interested in doing my own things. So he said, "Okay big shot, come over here and we'll let you see what you can come up with," and they made a deal for me to have a year or two to come up with something. By the end of that time Sydney was long gone (he had left to make *Out of Africa*) and the executives didn't want to do what I wanted to do. But then I read an adaptation of the David Mamet play *Sexual Perversity in Chicago* that had been floating around town and said, "Well, with some work this would be a wonderful movie." They said, "Yeah, but that's been around forever and no one wants to do it." So I said, "But it's very contemporary and if you tried this and this it would be a movie." They said, "Well, we don't know, but if you can get Rob Lowe to be in it, we'll let you make it." So I met Rob and thought that if I surrounded him with a very strong cast, he would be able to pull it off, and the executives agreed and let me do just that.

It was very straightforward after I got past the "Yes, we'll let you do this and how much will it cost" part, but I tested about nine actresses opposite Rob, and it wasn't until I saw Demi Moore's test that I found someone who could really do that part well. Jim Belushi had done his part on stage in Chicago six or seven years before and I heard that he had been good in it, so that was easier. For Betsy Perkins, this was her first film. She had been an actress at the Cligma Theater and knew some friends of mine from Steppenwolf in Chicago so she came to the door during our casting session, and I thought she was right for it.

WHAT WAS THE BUDGET?
Eight million dollars. We had forty shooting days. We went to Chicago, which is where I'm from, so I felt that I knew that world. I knew that bar scene, I knew those people, and we went back to Chicago and made the movie.

To have forty days seemed so luxurious. Of course what you discover is that your ambition forces you into a situation where you're shooting at the same rate and intensity as if you're shooting an episode of television. Bigger scenes, more people, more production value, more camera moves, size of sets, all those things come into play. We rehearsed, and that was a blessing. We spent a week in real rehearsal, and had I not done that I don't think that the movie would have been as good. Jim Belushi and I had some real trouble the first couple of days. He was very nervous, and he was very unsure about me. We got into a big fight the second day of shooting, but we came out of it in the best way possible. Having measured our dicks we realized that it was not who was more of a man but who was more scared to be in that particular moment. They were all good to me during that process and I hope I to them, and it was one of those situations where I showed the studio my first cut of the movie and they just adored it. They said, "Well, let's preview this," and so we went up to a mall in Paramus, New Jersey, to do it. During that first preview, the reels were switched, so the movie was playing out of order. And so I went up to the projecting booth and I'm screaming at the guy, saying, you've switched the reels, so he got all flustered and stopped the film and then he changed over from one projector to the other but he had jiggled the projector, so when it started again, the film was now projecting down into the audience. He had changed the angle of the projection system and it was just an utter disaster. But we did it again the next week and then it went very well and the movie succeeded beyond anybody's imaginings. By today's terms it would be a huge success. It was made for $8 million and made somewhere close to $40 million, which is proportionately a very big return. So it was a very happy result.

HOW DID MAKING THE FILM CHANGE YOUR VIEW OF YOURSELF?
It gave me pause, and time to reflect on my technique. I had finished that film, it had done well, and then Marshall and I had a deal to try and do some television. We came up with "thirtysomething" right at that moment, while I was still finishing the film. And the network wanted to do a pilot for it, which we were convinced no one was gonna watch, but we went ahead and did it anyway and all of a sudden it took off. It turned out to be a godsend because I was able to really stop and think about the kind of film I might want to make for my next movie and to wait and reflect and shoot hour after hour of television that we were writing, so by the time I ended up making my second film, it was a quantum leap from my first. *Glory* was my second film and although we only had $19 million, the ambition of the film and its mastery was so different than that of my first film, and I think that's a result of the television that I did in between.

WHEN YOU LOOK BACK AT YOUR EARLY BODY OF WORK AND HOW IT CAME TO BE, WHAT DO YOU THINK WAS MOST INSTRUMENTAL IN MOVING YOUR CAREER ALONG?
The writing. Writing exists. It goes out before you, it can precede you in some way. It's not about how you behave in a room; it's not about how people perceive you. Writing either succeeds or fails on its own merits. I think that was the key for me. The hard part came later, once I began to get those opportunities and in fact discovered that I was unable to necessarily realize the vision that I had in my head. It took some time to understand how to do that. But launching my career had everything to do with the writing.

I would also say that a director's career (not just one film but a career) is made or broken by virtue of your ability to work with material as a writer whether you are one or not. To develop material, to rewrite material, to re-imagine material that already exists in a different way, to select material, to understand the principles of dramaturgy and structure and writing: that's what gives a career longevity. It's making five and six and seven and eight and nine things, all of which are of a high standard. Its not about being able to shoot something well. I think the certain exceptions, those who shoot well, and only that, end up having much less interesting careers than those who actually are invested in the theater of ideas and think about movies more deeply and understand the traditions from which they come and all that they aspire to.

DO YOU THINK THAT WRITING IS SOMETHING THAT YOU DEVELOP WITH EACH SCRIPT YOU WRITE?

I think that every great director is a writer, profoundly. I think you write the film. The choice of camera, the choice of cut, the working of the script; each decision is one of writing. You have to have authorship. It's a fatuous notion to think that a director is not in some way implicitly involved in the actual writerly creation of the film, whether in tandem with a writer or alone. And I think you'll find that most of the directors that you love are writers. I think you'd be hard-pressed to think of one who isn't.

WHAT DO YOU THINK ABOUT THE IDEA THAT ONE MUST HAVE DETAILED LIFE EXPERIENCE TO WRITE, GIVEN THAT YOU WERE A WRITER AT SUCH A YOUNG AGE?

One reason why my work didn't become very interesting until I was in my late twenties is because I lacked life experience. I had to go through a lot of turmoil and some heartbreak, chaos, even tragedy, to understand how I fit into the world and how I could open up and let the world into my heart. I wasn't able to do that right away. I wasn't ready, really ready to make interesting art till I was in my late twenties or even thirties. I could critically talk about it, I could presume to understand it, I just couldn't do it. It didn't involve going off on a merchant marine ship, it didn't involve working in the Peace Corps or as a day laborer or on a swing gang, but it did involve the death of parents or the birth of children or disappointment in love or betrayal by friends or a certain amount of experience that had to mark me.

WHAT CAN YOU SUGGEST TO THOSE WHO WANT TO MAKE FILMS, GIVEN THAT THERE IS THIS PLETHORA OF PEOPLE WHO WANT TO DO IT, THIS SEEMINGLY INEXHAUSTIBLE SUPPLY AND A LIMITED DEMAND?

It depends on the access you have or the money you have to some degree. The availability of funds is certainly part of it, but you can literally make a movie with a laptop and a digital camera now. You can write and produce and cut movies for nothing. The technology is available to learn that process.

I don't mean to say anyone will look at that and hire you, but you can begin that mastery. Every screenplay that anyone writes in television or film is available to everybody. You can find it on the Net and download it in five minutes. So the resources of imitation are available. Really it's about breaking down the inner obstacles to your creativity, to understand who you really are and what legitimately interests you. Because finally only when you write those things that reflect some deeper chord in your person—and I don't mean necessarily biographical. It could be about science fiction and aliens, but there is science fiction that is personal too or horror movies that are deep and personal that reveal obsession, that reveal fear—only when you touch those things that are really of you can you hope to do something that will be of interest to anybody else. And I think you just do it over and over until you get better or accept the fact that you have no talent. Most of the extremely talented people who I know have found that with a certain amount of perseverance, talent can't help but be recognized. At the same time, there are a lot of moderately talented people who are rightfully not given opportunities because good is not good enough. You have to be great. It has to be great or else it has no place in an economic imperative, which is unfortunately what the film business remains, what it is, was, and always has been.

HOW DO YOU RELATE TO THE "HYPE" OF HOLLYWOOD, OF THE SEEMINGLY SPECTACULAR RISE OF THE GLAMOROUS YOUNG GENIUSES OR THE SO-CALLED "GLITTERATI"?

It always terrified me. I was always convinced that those people who seem of it, with it, and for it were going to get ahead. Maybe initially they did, but I think that always reveals itself. I think when you can't deliver then you fall by the wayside. I think attitude and chic and pretension is a mask of insecurity and that, finally, among those who actually do the hard work, there is only humility. There is only the genuine recognition of how hard the game is, how grueling, how arduous, and how frustrating it all is, and how often at a certain level even when you succeed you fail. How many times you get it wrong when you're trying to break a story, how many times you think you got that scene right and then you shoot it and it's wrong or the first cut doesn't work. I think that the people whom you genuinely admire will all finally say about their films that all that they look at is what doesn't work. All they remember is how hard something was that then failed, that they deal with fear and despair and insecurity every day of their lives no matter what their level, and that it's the adaptations that you make to those obstacles that defines you. You hope you're not too self-destructive in how you deal with them, but it's almost as hard to make a bad film as it is to make a good one. Every single film is hard to make. Increasingly it's harder to get a film made, what with the economics being what they are and the stakes being as high as they are. It's a potentially very heartbreaking and sometimes rewarding game. The truth is, having had a life in film, what is ultimately rewarding as much as the films themselves are the relationships that I have developed and held over the time. That's what takes on more and more meaning.

WHY DO YOU MAKE FILMS?
Since the youngest age I have had a deep need to organize my experience in some way for myself and others and to express those feelings holding a mirror back up to the world, to make a joyous or a hateful noise, to shock or embrace people. The experience of being in a relationship with an audience and creating a theatrical moment has been the most seductive, constantly vital, sexiest, potent feeling that I've ever known, and it remains so.

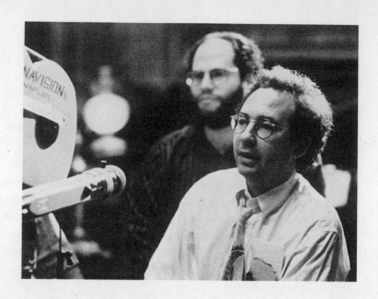

Barry Sonnenfeld | THE ADDAMS FAMILY

BARRY SONNENFELD *was born in 1953 in Upper Manhattan, New York. He attended college at New York University and Hampshire College, in Massachusetts, and returned to graduate studies at NYU film school. After graduating, Sonnenfeld purchased a 16mm film camera and began shooting industrial films for corporate clients. A chance meeting with Joel Coen at a dinner party would win Sonnenfeld the job of cinematographer on Joel and Ethan Coen's critically acclaimed* Blood Simple *and an introduction to the Hollywood film industry. After working as a cinematographer for many years on some of the highest-budget films made, Sonnenfeld directed his first feature,* The Addams Family, *at the behest of producer Scott Rudin. Since then he has directed numerous big-budget, highly grossing films such as* Addams Family Values, Get Shorty, Men in Black, *and* Big Trouble, *starring Rene Russo and Tim Allen.*

I was born April 1, 1953, in Upper Manhattan in Washington Heights at 174th and Broadway. I grew up as an only child. My dad sold theatrical and architectural lighting for a company called Century Lighting that supplied spotlights and other equipment to Broadway shows, so I grew up going backstage. At a very early age my dad bought me a little dimmer board, which I used to light school plays. My mother worked as an art teacher at the elementary school I attended.

I had no interest in movies at all when I was a kid, but I would still sometimes go to the local Loews theater at 174th Street. The first movie that I ever remember seeing was *Jason and the Argonauts* and I was so scared after seeing it that I didn't want to go to the movies ever again. Eventually I did return to the theater with my father sometimes, and we would watch movies together. But film was not a passion for me at all; it was not something that really ever interested me, even up through college. I had no idea what I was going to do when I grew up.

My mother was very protective of me and she didn't want me to go to "sleep-away school," so I attended college at New York University where I was a political science major. I hated NYU so much that I only took courses that would meet on Monday, Wednesday, and Friday between the hours of nine and two, so that I had to spend as little time there as possible. The school just really didn't suit me. But my parents were very supportive of my opinions about my education—they were not the typical overprotective Jewish parents and since they themselves were in the arts they never said that I should be a lawyer or a doctor. My dad used to tell me not to worry about a career, but to simply try to figure out what I wanted to do with my life and somehow I would make a living doing it. Throughout college I really didn't have a clue what I was going to do, but I did know that I would eventually figure it out and that I would be successful at whatever I decided upon.

After three years at NYU, the school sold the uptown campus, and I was told that I would have to attend school downtown. I really didn't like that idea, and it hadn't been part of the deal when I had signed on, so I refused to go. The school acquiesced and said that I could go to any college for my senior year and transfer the credit to NYU, graduating with an NYU degree. So I applied to a couple places and I was accepted at Hampshire College in Amherst, Massachusetts. Hampshire was a great place where I basically hung out for a year and spent all my time doing still photography, which had become an interest. I did take one film course while I was there as well. At Amherst I met a bunch of people who eventually became very successful in the film business. I took film class with Ken Burns, and my next-door neighbor was Casey Silver who ended up running Universal for many years.

When I finished college, I felt like I had a real interest in photography and writing. After I graduated, I drove around America for a while trying to figure out what I could do that would combine my two interests. I thought about doing a photo book, imagining a sort of Jack Kerouac piece with photos inlaid. Ultimately I found that I didn't have the discipline for writing, and I returned home from my journeys. When I got back, my mother was afraid that I would leave New York again, so she suggested that I go to film school at NYU. For lack of anything better to do, I applied and was accepted, pretty much on the basis of my photographs and an interview. Unfortunately, once I got into the program my mother and father announced that they couldn't afford to pay for school, so I took out massive student loans and had to live off of my credit cards.

WHAT WAS YOUR NYU EXPERIENCE LIKE?

I was at NYU from 1974 until 1976. I tell people who are interested in film school that the worst three years of your life will be the time that you spend there. It is a weird place because it is you against your fellow student who wants to keep the camera one extra day instead of returning it when it is your turn to use it. At the end of the first semester there were about one hundred students in the class and half of the class received letters saying that their first films weren't good. They were told that if their next two films weren't better, then they wouldn't be invited back to finish the last two years of the program. Even though I didn't receive the letter I thought that this was outrageous. I couldn't understand how a school could judge if a film was good or not and make subjective determinations about people based on that. It was a system that totally discouraged students from taking chances and trying something and failing; it begged for the status quo and the safe decision, which bred mediocrity. In protest a bunch of us took over the school auditorium during a speech by Mel Harris, who was the head of the school at that time. When he tried to talk to us we would interrupt him and confront him on the policy.

At the end of the year Harris failed to ask the teachers who should get scholarships to continue the program, so he had to review the list of students himself. If he remembered your name, he gave you a scholarship. Well he remembered my name, but fortunately he didn't remember that that was because I was part of the protest that tried to make a fool out of him, and I got a full scholarship for the second and third years of my studies. I completed the full three years of the program, but I was not one of the better students and I was certainly not one of those guys that everyone expected to become a successful director.

WHAT TYPE OF FILMS WERE YOU WATCHING AND MAKING WHILE AT SCHOOL?

The graduate and undergraduate schools at NYU had different sensibilities. The graduate school tended to be more about angst and less focused on commercial value, and I suppose my films reflected that. My early movies were about a guy living in the East Village who was trying to get laid because that was what my friends and I were all doing. My films were pretty straightforward and not very well done. One good thing about school though was that I was able to try out a lot of different things. In this process I discovered that I was very good at lighting and cinematography so I became one of the two guys at school who everyone wanted to shoot their movies.

The other guy was Bill Pope, who later shot *The Matrix*. Since he was more talented than I was, I was his assistant and we developed a reputation as the best cinematographers in the school. During school I saw very few movies but the movies I really liked were Martin Scorsese's and Bernardo Bertolucci's, so I was watching *Mean Streets, Taxi Driver,* and *The Conformist.* I was never a movie buff and I'm really film illiterate even to this day. I have no knowledge of film history or any of that stuff. In the past two or three years I have started to watch more movies and I am more interested in them now that I have a screening room in my house in East Hampton. So on a Saturday night I invite friends over to watch a film, but that is only a recent phenomenon.

WHAT HAPPENED AS YOU WERE COMING TO THE END OF YOUR TIME AT SCHOOL?

I never felt in any way that I would be successful as a filmmaker. When I was at film school I felt that the closest I would ever get to the Brill Building (where everyone edited and did sound work) was as a FedEx delivery man. When I got out of film school I felt that my best chance of working in the business in some capacity was to be a cinematographer, so I bought a used CP 16 Reflex 16mm camera with another student from school named Bob Chappell. I hit the pavement and started trying to get work. One of my first jobs was as cinematographer on a documentary called *In Our Water,* and two years after shooting it was nominated for an Academy Award. I started to shoot industrials (little films for businesses) and did some work for the *Wall Street Journal.* They were small jobs, but they were hiring me because I owned a camera, and I would work cheap, so for the camera rental rate they got a guy to go along with it. Thankfully I was making enough money to pay the rent for my apartment in the East Village.

One night I was at a party and I met a guy named Joel Coen. We sort of gravitated toward one another since there weren't many Jews like us at this very WASP party. We talked and he told me that he had just graduated from NYU undergraduate film school. Wim Wenders' film *American Friend* had just opened and we spent a lot of time talking about that. Joel Coen and his brother Ethan had just written a script for a movie called *Blood Simple* and they intended to raise money for the film by shooting a trailer for the movie even though they hadn't made it yet. They wanted to show the trailer to investors as a sort of demonstration that they could make the film, so that they could get enough money to actually do it. Because I owned a camera, and maybe because we got along, Joel hired me that night to shoot the trailer. They paid me $100 for four days of work and I assumed that nothing would come of it. I convinced them to rent a real camera and shoot the thing in 35mm because I thought that having shot something in 35mm might help me down the road. I taught my cousin Kenny to load the camera and he was my assistant cameraman; Ethan Coen was the gaffer. We shot it over President's Day weekend because we could rent the camera for one day and use it for four days since the rental house didn't charge for holidays and weekends. Joel and Ethan cut the trailer after we shot, and we soon became good friends. Amazingly, they managed to raise $750,000 by showing people the script and the trailer. I found $100,000 from some investor I knew, and all of a sudden we had the money to make the film.

One year after we shot the trailer all the money was in place, and we began to make the movie. The first day that Joel, Ethan, and I had ever been on a feature film set was for *Blood Simple*. Joel was directing, Ethan was producing, and I was shooting. We made the film in Austin, Texas, because Joel had spent a year there going to graduate film school at the University of Texas. He wrote the script around specific locations, and we went out there to shoot them. The night before production started, I had the assistant cameraman come over to my apartment to show me where the on/off switch was because I had never seen a 35mm Arriflex camera before. I had never been an assistant cameraman or a production assistant before, and I literally went from shooting little industrial films to being a cinematographer on a real feature. I never worked my way up the ranks of assistant cameraman or any of that stuff.

HOW DID YOU LEARN TO CONSTRUCT A VISUAL IMAGE?
Joel, Ethan, and I spent about three months in Austin storyboarding everything. We had very similar sensibilities about designing shots. A lot of the ideas were from Joel and Ethan, but some of them were mine. The lighting just came to me. I was figuring out how to light things from an early age with my dimmer board from elementary school. Now, having shot nine feature films, I have developed specific feelings about lenses and camera moves. I have theories about how to shoot comedies that are a combination of my own ideas and stuff I learned from watching screwball comedies like *His Girl Friday, Bringing Up Baby*, and Preston Sturges movies. I don't know exactly how it happened, but I just developed my own way of seeing things as a cinematographer and, more recently, as a director. I really got into film accidentally, and I saw it as a way to pay the rent. It was never a lifelong dream to be a film director. I had no plan. I still don't view what I do as anything other than the way I earn a living. I feel that I have to be responsible and do as good a job as I can. I don't feel that I'm an artist. I look at all the movies I've shot and directed and somehow they all feel like I did them but I don't really understand why. At film school I discovered that I could want something to look a certain way and I was able to achieve that. What I saw in my mind I would see in dailies and it would look like what I imag-

ined it to look like. The most control I have ever had in my life was when I was working as a cinematographer where I actually had an image in my mind and I was able to re-create it on film. That is something you can rarely do at other times in your life.

WHAT HAPPENED AFTER THE RELEASE OF *BLOOD SIMPLE*?

Blood Simple took a year to edit and when it came out it received a lot of recognition, and I received a lot of attention because the visual style was so self-conscious and specific. That got me other jobs shooting other films and that's how I got into the film business. The success of *Blood Simple* was really thrilling and unexpected. A guy named Frank Perry was going to direct a movie called *Compromising Positions* and I was being considered as the cinematographer. He asked me to send a videotape of *Blood Simple* to him so he could review it. I didn't want him watching it on videotape because I thought it wouldn't look good, so I told his people that he had to see it on film. Of course they said that Frank was very busy and he would only have time to see it on tape. I felt that if he saw it on tape he wouldn't hire me, so I told them to forget it. I've always believed in taking chances like that. Surprisingly enough he agreed to see it in a screening room and he liked it and he hired me to shoot the film. That was great because the film was shot in East Hampton, where I was living, and it was done with a real New York crew. After that I shot *Raising Arizona* for Joel and Ethan, and after that everything snowballed and since one thing led to the next, I never had to look for work again.

DID YOU BECOME INTERESTED IN DIRECTING WHILE YOU WERE WORKING AS A CINEMATOGRAPHER?

I had no interest in directing whatsoever. I always viewed myself not only as a cinematographer but more as a "Friend of the Director." In that capacity I was the cinematographer but something more. I did whatever it took to make the film work, and I would often design the shots and in some cases I would work out the shot list myself. In other cases I would work with the director, but I never felt that I should be doing something rather than the director doing it. I was very happy being a cinematographer. I had total control over my craft and I liked it that way. I remember working on *When Harry Met Sally* when we were shooting on West Broadway and lighting a whole half mile of New York City with 210-foot condor cranes and lights on roofs and generators that were a half mile away. I remember thinking about how great that was.

I remember being in Los Angeles doing preproduction for *Misery* with Rob Reiner, which was the last movie I ended up working on as a cinematographer. Then I got a call from the producer Scott Rudin, who asked me to direct *The Addams Family*. I read the script, which was not very good at that point, and I told him that I had no interest in directing. He convinced me to have breakfast with him to discuss the project. So I told him all the reasons why the script was no good and he said, "Those are the reasons why you would be a good director, because you can figure it out." He asked me if he was able to get Orion to hire me, would I direct the film? Since I thought there wasn't much chance of that, I agreed. And then of course, he got me the job.

HOW DID YOUR EXPERIENCE AS A DIRECTOR DIFFER FROM YOUR EXPERIENCES AS A CINEMATOGRAPHER?

The main advantage of being a cinematographer was having control of my craft. As a director you have much less control because you rely on many more people. As a director I'm relying on a cinematographer to light something, and they may not light it the way I would have imagined it. I must also deal with actors, who may not see a line the way I see it or interpret something in the same way I would interpret it. As a director I make many more compromises.

I decided that the way to be a good director was similar to being a good father and that it was all about consistency and love and hugging. All directing really is is having an opinion about everything, and through this you create tone and style that makes it seem as if you had a plan from the start. Directing is about making choices on who you cast or picking the red book instead of the green book for a shot or telling an actor to say something flatter. No matter what you are working on at a given moment, you accumulate thousands of answers a day from everyone in your various departments and it is through this accumulation of answers that you create tone and style. Directing is ultimately about having an opinion and making sure that your opinion is consistent. All of my movies look like the same guy directed them. It is not that I am the author of the movies I have made but it is apparent that I had an opinion about everything, and that I made choices about how things were done. It is the consistency of these choices that has dictated my particular style.

HOW DID YOU CAST *THE ADDAMS FAMILY*?

Scott Rudin and I agreed that we wanted Anjelica Huston and Raul Julia to be the stars of the film. Orion wanted Cher to be Morticia, but Scott and I stuck with our choices and I realized that it was better to have a strong opinion and be willing to walk away than to just give in to stuff you think is wrong. Christina Ricci was cast as Wednesday. I remember that Scott Rudin preferred another actress who looked more like Raul Julia and had bigger, baggier eyes. But I held out and was able to convince Scott that Christina was a better choice.

It was horrible. We shot for over one hundred days and we went twenty days over schedule. Scott Rudin and I didn't get along at all, even though we liked each other very much and ended up making another movie together later. To this day I have tremendous respect for him regardless of that experience, which was most unpleasant. On the set things were very tense and directing the film was a horrible process. To complicate matters I was in Los Angeles and my future wife was in New York. We were going bankrupt because the house that I was renovating went over budget and I had no other source of income. It was a very difficult time in my life and making the film made everything going on in my life even more unpleasant.

WHEN YOU FINISHED THE FILM WAS IT ANYTHING LIKE YOU HAD ENVISIONED IT WOULD BE?

It ended up being exactly what I wanted as far as the tone of the film and it looked the way I wanted it to look. After I became a director I began to look at the work of other cinematographers who had become directors like Gordon Willis, who directed a movie called *Windows;* John Alonzo, who directed *FM;* and Bill Fraker, who directed *Legend of Lone Ranger*. They were all top cinematographers who ended up not having success making the transition from cinematographer to director. One of the things they did was to move their camera operator up to cinematographer instead of hiring from the outside and to me that meant that they weren't willing to give up the camera completely. Rather than hire a cinematographer they still wanted to be the cameraman. I felt that if I was going to have any success as a director I had to give up the camera. I needed to force myself away from that to deal with what I didn't feel comfortable doing, which was being around the actors. I hired Owen Roizman, who is a brilliant cinematographer. By hiring someone of that talent I was forced to get as far away from the camera as possible. I think that helped tremendously in terms of forcing me to learn how to talk to actors, because there was nowhere else I could hang out. Owen did all the lighting, but I designed all the shots and picked all the lenses. During the years I spent doing still photography I could only see things in wide angle and to this day my movies are shot with very wide-angle lenses. Owen was willing to let me select the lenses as long as I stayed out of the lighting.

HOW WAS THE EDITING PROCESS?

I was very lucky to work with one of the top editors, a woman named Dede Allen. In fact, her son Tommy Fleishman is mixing my current movie in the next room as we speak. Dede was incredibly smart and loyal and she taught me a great deal about editing. She called it the dialectics of film. Sometimes if the editing isn't working it has nothing to do with the ending of the film, it has to do with the middle. She taught me that if you change the middle then it affects the end. If one scene doesn't work, instead of losing the scene, it is often better to lose the previous scene. Editing is like a jigsaw puzzle. I enjoy editing the most because you can fix problems. You may have many ideas for your film, but when you go to shoot, due to a hundred logistical problems, they don't work. When you get into editing, you have the time to correct things and try to make things play the way you had envisioned they would. You get to separate the wheat from the chaff.

HOW DID THE STUDIO REACT WHEN YOU DELIVERED THE FILM?
They were very nervous before I delivered it. I had started making the film at Orion, but they went bankrupt halfway through shooting and sold the movie to Frank Mancuso at Paramount. Then once my film was finished Frank left and a new studio head, named Stanley Jaffe, replaced him. Jaffe watched dailies of the film and hated it. He announced that the movie could not be cut in a way that would work and that it was unreleasable. The last six weeks of making the movie were a nightmare because the people at Paramount hated it and couldn't figure out what to do with it. Everyday they would call me and ask really scary questions like, "Barry, you only shot one angle with Fester and one angle with Wednesday, but there is no angle with both of them together. How do we know that they are in the same room? We don't see them both in the same shot." Idiotic questions like that kept popping up. When I finally screened the rough cut for Jaffe, he simply detested it. I remember that no one in the screening room laughed because Jaffe wasn't laughing. Dede Allen called me after the screening to ask me how it went. I told her that it went terribly and Dede, who is a very proper woman, said, "Fuck them. Fuck them all!" Then I was called in to see the head of production, Brandon Tartikoff. I was preparing for the worst, but I went in to see him and he congratulated me, saying that he and everyone else loved the movie and that it would be a big success. And it was.

HOW DID THE RELEASE OF THE FILM AFFECT YOUR FUTURE CAREER PLANS?
The success of this film immediately increased my salary, which was a good thing because at that moment in my life I was on the verge of bankruptcy. I took a movie in New York City that would pay me a lot of money and keep me in New York. It was a romantic comedy called *For Love or Money*. It didn't do well at all but I still really liked the movie and that was probably the best experience I had directing a film. I love working in New York, where the technical crews are exceptional.

HOW DO YOU FEEL NOW ABOUT CINEMATOGRAPHY?

I am a director now and that is what I do for a living. I don't shoot anymore. I was a cinematographer but now I'm a director. My becoming a director was an economic decision for me. I couldn't in a million years go back to anything else because it pays really well. If it paid the same I would definitely go back to shooting because it's a much easier job where you feel much more in control of your craft. Directing is really hard. It is not as hard as being a mother or a schoolteacher but within the world of film it's the hardest job you can have. If they paid me my directing rate to shoot, then I would shoot for Joel and Ethan Coen and I would shoot for Danny DeVito. Basically, I would shoot for a handful of friends who are directors, but of course it's all a dream because no one is gonna pay me the same as they do now just to shoot films.

HOW RELEVANT IS THE WRITING PROCESS FOR YOU?

Even though I don't consider myself a writer, I feel that the script is incredibly relevant to the film, and I work closely with writers. I know what I like and what I don't like. When it comes to the script I'm very specific and I cross out words and phrases and I make a lot of notes, but in no way am I a writer. I really like working with writers and I've been lucky to work with Scott Frank, who wrote *Get Shorty*, and Stephen Schiff, who has written two scripts for me. Barry Fanaro was at film school with me and he became a writer and producer and has written several things for me. I love having relationships with writers that I can come back to.

WHAT DO YOU THINK ACCOUNTS FOR YOUR SUCCESS AS A FILMMAKER?

I have a very specific tonal point of view and I believe that the tone of a film either works or it doesn't. I think that that is the hardest thing for the director to maintain. I feel that I am able to do that and to remain focused. However, I don't consider myself an artist. Joel and Ethan Coen are artists. Martin Scorsese is an artist. I am a craftsman and I am proud to be one.

The process of becoming a film director can be very discouraging and there is no one way to make it happen. Sydney Pollack started out as a dialogue coach. Other people were editors or writers before they got into directing. Since I made the transition from cinematographer there have been others who have done what I did. It is daunting because you are not told to take steps A, B, C, and D and then you have a career. But what is great is that you can get to a directorship from anywhere and from anyplace. I think that the best way into the business is through writing a script, because that is the one thing that is unique to you. If you own a script that you have written and you say to a studio that if they want to buy the script they must let you direct it, then you have a decent shot if the piece is really good.

That's your single biggest weapon. Either you write or your best friend writes or he produces and you direct. That is how Joel and Ethan got to direct *Blood Simple*. And they went one step further: Because they are so smart, they raised the money for the film themselves. There is no right or wrong way to become a director. I didn't think I would ever become a director and I wasn't looking to direct and I didn't have an agent looking at scripts for me to direct. I was just in the right place at the right time when I met the Coen brothers. That was my huge break.

You have to be willing to have strong opinions and not just say, "I don't care, what do you want to do?" Right or wrong, whatever you do, have an opinion. Another thing is that you should be willing to walk away from the table when negotiating. I've always been willing to walk away from a project and whenever I felt that I cared about a project too much, I knew I was in danger because I might lose control. If they had made me put Cher in *The Addams Family*, then I would have been out. It was not because she's not a talented actress, but she wasn't right for the part. As long as you are willing to walk away, then you are in control, but if you love a project too much then that is a recipe for disaster and the studio can just take over and manipulate you however they see fit.

DO YOU HAVE ANYTHING THAT YOU ARE TRYING TO ACHIEVE NOW WITHIN YOUR WORK?

I learn with each film that I do, and with each film I find a few more actors I would like to work with again. Eventually I hope I can develop an ensemble cast that I will be able to work with over and over again. In movies that I direct I am always learning things, trying ideas, and seeing what works and what doesn't work. I just hate that there is so much pressure with every film because it discourages people from taking chances. I like being under the radar. When I was making *Men in Black*, the big movies that year were the sequel to *Jurassic Park* and *Batman and Robin*. Nobody even knew we existed until the film started to get ready for release. I wish that I could operate in that situation again. The movie I just finished, called *Big Trouble*, is a nice little movie and it is entertaining, but it is not going to change anyone's opinion about life or death. I hope people don't see it as anything other than what it is. Expectation and publicity make this business hard. There are times I wish I could be invisible again.

John Schlesinger | A KIND OF LOVING

JOHN SCHLESINGER *was born in London, England, in 1926. After a four-year tour in the Royal Engineers, Schlesinger began making documentary films on a shoe-string budget. Eventually he became a director of television documentaries for the BBC. His first feature was* A Kind of Loving, *starring Alan Bates. His fifty-year career in the cinema has spawned such classic films as* Midnight Cowboy, The Day of the Locust, Marathon Man, The Falcon and the Snowman, Pacific Heights, *and many others. He also directed* The Next Best Thing, *starring Madonna and Rupert Everett, and in the fall of 2000 mounted an opera production in Los Angeles. He lives in Palm Springs, California.*

I was born the youngest of five children. My parents were middle class, and we were reasonably comfortable. My father was a pediatrician and my mother had no profession, though if she had one, it would have been that of a violinist. They were highly musical and tried to instill a love of music in us children and succeeded very well. I played the piano, the oboe, and per-cussion instruments in the orchestra while I was growing up.

We lived in a suburb of London until the war broke out when I was thir-teen. We were all at boarding schools at the time and I would say it was at this point that I was starting to develop a healthy interest in the theater, as well as entertaining certain fantasies about it. My fascination was with the sets themselves and what was behind the curtain. At the time I wanted to be a designer, so I studied it theoretically, reading books on it, realizing I would have to go to an architectural school to get a basis in architecture in order to be a designer. I was also slowly getting interested in film in a general way, though I'm not very well educated in it and never went to film school. I'm entirely self-taught, because I've always thought the best way to learn is to do. I was given a movie camera when I was quite young, about eleven, and made films from an early age. Most of the film we shot was of Granny in the back yard and that sort of thing. We were severely rationed as children, so we would not be spoiled. That said, my parents were always in support of any and all creative endeavors, and encouraged my brothers, sisters, and I to put on our own plays, shoot movies on birthdays, and attend the theater at Christmas. Before I was thirteen, I was given my first projector.

WHAT TYPE OF FILMS WERE YOU EXPOSED TO AT THE TIME?
Because of the period, most of the films I saw were German Expressionist films. Hitler was in the news, and Germany was feared and exploited. I remember the earliest film experiences I had were of seeing pictures by Leni Riefenstahl and things like *The Cabinet of Dr. Caligari*.

It wasn't until I was thirteen that I started getting seriously interested in the idea of directing. I started working on theater productions, acting, and eventually won a play competition by directing a shoe-in piece by Thornton Miles called *The Happy Journey from Trenton to Camden*. It was a fascinating play and fun to do, although my interest in theater didn't happen immediately, but rather grew over time. It wasn't like, *boom*, now this is my life, I'm wedded to the theater. But by this point, I loved acting, and was quite sure I wanted to be an actor in some form. Whether I was any good or not is another matter altogether.

Knowing I would have been called upon eventually, I volunteered when I was nearly eighteen to join the Royal Engineers and build bridges. Soon after, I worked briefly as an architect in France. I found designing lavatories was just too much for me and that put an end to my architectural ambitions. But I still traveled quite a bit in those days. I spent my twenty-first birthday in Singapore and remember it very well. There were all these trashy whores about saying terrible things like, "Wanky, wanky in the mouth one dollar." Needless to say, I didn't experience it, but found it all fascinating. I guess you could say that as a result of witnessing things like this, I started to become interested in the idea of recording real-life stuff, in telling and directing my own stories on 16mm film. Because we couldn't afford to finish our films properly, my friends and I turned ourselves into a mobile cinema, touring the local villages, giving performances to raise money for finishing costs.

Eventually, we decided to make a film called *Black Legend*. It was my first real taste of experimenting with film. At one point during the filming, I tried to hang the camera on a two-by-four to achieve a point of view, but it dropped off and broke the motor, and in the middle of shooting I had to rush up to London and get the camera mended. These were the years of great borrowing and stealing. We had to go to people who owned timber businesses and say, "Could we trouble you to build us some tracks?" It was after the war so everybody had a lot of blackout cloth to use or get rid of, and we got all the local vicars' wives to issue a plan for using blackout for skirts and blouses and things to approximate costume. We staged a public execution, which all the locals were terribly interested in, and I guess that's how we started making films.

WERE YOU CONFIDENT IN YOUR ABILITIES AT THIS POINT?
I knew I was quite good at it. A friend of my father's, a man in Parliament, suggested screening the film in the House of Commons, where they had a party room. It was a rather fashionable, smart address for a film screening, so I decided to invite one of the main British pretties, Dyllis Powell, a most elegant woman film critic for the *Sunday Times*. She wrote a glowing review headed, "Brains not Money," and Michael Bolton, who ran a film studio, read it and said to his staff, "You must show this film to your directors. It truly is an interesting show of what can be done for nothing."

Here I was, finishing university, thinking my film was a shoe-in into the business and that I was going to get a job very quickly. Of course, it didn't happen that way. I was rather disappointed when I got a letter from Michael Bolton, who wrote, "Thank you for coming and showing us your *amateur* film. We appreciated it very much." After that I wrote him asking him for a job, but I never heard back. At this point, I decided to put directing on hold and become a professional actor. I was becoming somewhat established, mostly playing Germans because of my name. I had a nice little tenor voice, so I eked out a living working in film and television. I realized my limitations and nearly gave up, though thinking back, I don't know what other job I would have done. I lived at home to save money and my father, a very positive man whose motto was "Never take no for an answer," said, "You mustn't give up yet, you haven't tried long enough, for God's sake. Don't think of other things!" And I took his advice and I didn't.

During this time, I hadn't completely given up filmmaking. I went on to direct a sort of facetious documentary called *Sunday in the Park*, with my then agent, who wanted to be a film producer.

It was more or less a distillation of things I'd seen in London's Hyde Park. We eventually managed to screen a heavily cut version of the film one Sunday afternoon on the BBC. It started a sort of interest at the BBC, and another film producer friend of mine saw the film, said he thought I was talented, and asked if I wanted a job doing small pieces for a magazine program called "Tonight Show"—no relation to the American version—and I did. After that, I was hired to do a short film a month for £8.

The producer and I didn't like each other because I was entirely self-determined and didn't like the idea of a program that passed your raw material to an editor-in-chief without your input. I couldn't conceive of a program that assembled and dubbed your work for you, had music that was chosen by somebody else, had cuts you didn't approve of. I detested that and insisted on doing my own editing and mixing, with every intention of putting my stamp on it. I think one of the most important lessons I've learned to this day is: Do it yourself and supervise it yourself. That's the only way you'll ever be satisfied that it'll come out right. Of course the producers didn't like this because the process took longer, and let's just say that by the end of the year the producer said no more work for you. Luckily I found another magazine program, called "Monitor," to work for where the producer was an extraordinary man who I adored and learned a great deal from. There I managed to do a few longer films and was eventually given my own program to do full-length documentaries.

DID YOU HAVE THE FREEDOM TO CHOOSE YOUR OWN PROJECTS?

We would get together at the beginning of every month to discuss what musical or art events and exhibitions were coming out and decide which of these we'd like to make films about. Our team would meet with the producer, who was also the presenter, and he would listen to our suggestions and give us feedback. All in all, it was a wonderfully free situation. I was perfectly happy and definitely not frustrated, though I did have the idea in mind that I would like to at some point make a feature. This was in no way based on an ambition to go to Hollywood or anything like that. I was just learning a great deal about documentary filmmaking and the idea that things exist in the world, and that your job as the director is to in some way place subtle abstractions on reality, and to view things in a personal light. This really interested me. One idea I read about and borrowed was to explore the underside of seaside piers. What we observe is no more than a veneer of a lovely resort pier. Underneath, it's entirely sinister and dark and strange. I did all sorts of subjects, one of which resulted in "Celebrating 50 Years of the English Repertory System," where I followed a weekly repertory company who were given one week to prep and perform a play. Really, they were quite theatrical, the subjects I chose.

Documentary feels very free because there is no script and no structure except for the one you prepare yourself. When you're telling a story and you've got actors, it's very different. I hadn't really gotten to that stage. It was never my intention earlier in life to be a film director; that came later.

Of course, when I found I could do it and developed confidence, that made all the difference.

By this point I was in my early thirties, and I decided I needed to learn even more, so I pulled back from "Monitor" and the safety of the BBC. I started making commercials and things of that nature, and also became part of a team working on a television series about Winston Churchill, largely doing interviews with the generals and admirals of the Second World War. I wasn't paid properly and was getting disheartened about having to ask for more money. I remember gardening with my father in London and we were discussing the pay situation, and he thought I was out of my mind, insisting that I should be grateful to meet these great war heroes and to work for next to nothing. I guess, even at this point, I knew my time and talent was worth something.

DID YOU HAVE A GREATER SENSE OF SECURITY KNOWING THAT YOU WERE ABLE TO FIND WORK, A FEELING THAT YOU WERE PART OF THE INDUSTRY?
I was getting regular work by this time. One of my first professional jobs in the industry was researching a documentary about British cheese, called "Mousetrap Is Out!" I toured all these farms and interviewed cheese-making experts. I wrote up my findings and, because I wanted to get into the union, begged the company to get me a job as an assistant, so that I could qualify for membership. I did end up getting the job and did quite well, I remember. The director asked me to come into the cutting room, and when he'd left the room, I started making all these suggestions. Unfortunately, the mistress of the boss of the company overheard my efforts, and needless to say, I got the push once again.

British society can be tough in that way. I remember years later when I was making my third feature, there was an electrician who was terribly interested in all of our work around the camera. He used to hang around when he wasn't up in the gantry doing the tasks of a head electrician. The gaffer basically told him to get lost, that he was sure that the electrician had things he could be doing instead of just hanging around the camera. The thing is that I genuinely believe that he was a guy interested in learning more about film and he was written off as lazy and a burden. I think he lost his job over that.

WHAT WAS YOUR NEXT STEP AFTER THE WAR SERIES?
At this point most of the films I was doing were for the BBC, particularly documentaries for "Monitor." A man named Edgar Anstein who ran British Transport Films asked me if I would like to show them some of my work and talk about it, and so I did. British Transport ran the rail station in Britain at the time, and they were curious as to what kinds of projects I was

interested in doing. I told them about this idea I'd had to document a day in the life of a big railway station. After a while, the project—called *Terminus*—was approved, and I spent the next few months at the railway station doing research. We shot on 35mm and I was able to dramatize incidents with actors or with friends. The narrative structure was more in the form of things like interviews with people who lived at the station, prisoners going off in handcuffs and chains to the west coast, and coffins being unloaded. I enjoy the oddities of life, so I tend to focus on them in my filming, really getting into the reality of it.

Because of the budget, we only had two weeks to shoot and a few months to cut. When we first edited it, I remember very distinctly being terribly depressed and not liking the first cut. I did go on to refine it and recut it, and eventually when it was shown it won a big documentary film award at the Venice Film Festival. It was also the supporting film at the opening of the London Film Festival. Although I think it was generally pretty well received, a lot of critics were quite snide about it.

AFTER THE FILM'S PREMIERE, DID YOU HAVE A DIFFERENT SENSE OF ACCOMPLISHMENT THAN ONE GETS FROM TELEVISION WORK?

Absolutely. It was a big scream and I loved it. I've never liked television, even though I've worked in it and continue to do so. I've always said that I prefer my films to be seen on the big screen instead of on video. I don't like that small screen or the fact that you make something for television, and it's seen by millions maybe, but it's not seen in nearly the same circumstances as a feature. It just doesn't have the same regard, the same attention given to it. Even though it's communicating with many more people maybe, I don't feel it's treated seriously.

Nevertheless, I have continued to make films for television over the years. When I made *Cold Comfort Farm*, the fact that it had such a success on the big screen was very important to me. I had fought like crazy to get a commercial release, which the BBC, who financed it, just wasn't interested in. Since we shot it in Super-16, we were capable of making a 35mm print for theatrical release, but they didn't want to do it. It just didn't appeal to them and they didn't think we could get a distribution deal. I asked them if they might reconsider making one print if I would pay half, and finally they agreed. I should have renegotiated my contract, of course, but didn't. I paid for half the process to blow it up to 35, and then we were able to screen it at festivals like Telluride and Montreal. Eventually we got distribution, and I patted myself on the back.

AFTER THE SCREENING OF *TERMINUS*, WHAT WAS YOUR NEXT MOVE?

At that point, I was still working for "Monitor," doing the whole program, and was subsequently introduced to a producer, Joe Allen, who I'd asked to come see a screening at the National Film Theater of two films, *Terminus*, and another "Monitor" film that I'd done. I was later summoned to his office, where he said, "I'd like to discover you," and I said, "Well, be my guest." And so I started working a little bit for his commercial company. Meanwhile, he was working with the Reich organization on two possible feature projects, *Billy Liar* and another film for which he had the novel rights called *A Kind of Loving*. I begged him to let me test to direct one of his films and he agreed and let me shoot an eight-minute test scene for *Billy Liar*. I was confident that I could shoot the scene, but didn't know if I could do it in the time allotted. That's always the challenge in a test. I guess I must have done all right because when it was over he decided to hire me.

The first film that he put into production was *A Kind of Loving*, starring Alan Bates. It turned out to be a great success, received very good reviews, and won the best film award at the Berlin Festival. I guess you could say it set me off.

HAVING NOT DONE A FEATURE FILM BEFORE, DID YOU HAVE ANY RESERVATIONS?

I was terrified. I remember driving up on location for the first day of shooting, with Alan Bates in the car, and I saw these lights with wheels and the trucks and the crew gathering. I was supposed to run this machine. I felt very much like saying, "Drive me back to the hotel, I'm going back to London." I was absolutely terrified.

The budget was about £170,000, which allowed us an eleven-week shoot. At that time, that amount of money was substantial enough to buy me the time and opportunity to make a decent film. It wasn't kickball and scramble like it is now.

HOW DID YOU GO ABOUT CASTING FOR THE FILM?

We tested various men for the lead role. I knew Alan Bates and thought he was a lovely man and a terrific actor. I'd seen him in *Look Back in Anger*, and felt he embodied that sort of, though it sounds cliché, angry young man in school.

WHAT WAS IT ABOUT THE MATERIAL THAT INTERESTED YOU?

I was drawn to this material in particular because I was interested in exploring the subject of guilt and the idea of standing up for one's individuality in the face of total prejudice from a mother-in-law. The story was about a man who gets a woman pregnant and marries her, but can't afford a place to live.

He moves in with his bride's mother and is stifled by her in all ways. He is ripped of his freedom, sexually and otherwise. His bride is very uncomfortable in the situation, but is too attached to her domineering mother to demand to move away. Ultimately a changed, happier, couple that lives in their own apartment emerges from the turmoil.

The seeming reality of the story intrigued me. I thought it was a beautiful model and furthermore, I believed it. And in a way, I guess the atmosphere was right at the time. The audience was going to see films about working-class people and people from industrial backgrounds. The idea, the attitude that if you got her pregnant you've got to marry her, while it may seem old-fashioned, particularly now, at that time wasn't. Even though these people were of a somewhat different social class, I felt I could still relate to them and could portray their story. The climate was right for making films with that sort of atmosphere.

My grandmother came from the north of England, and although she wasn't exactly working class, I felt perfectly at home with the northerners, with the sort of lower-middle class. Later in my career I was offered films that I felt wrongly cast to direct like, *Coming Home.* I felt like a stranger dealing with Vietnam vets and didn't think I would ever be able to understand them or talk the same language as they did, so I ended up giving it to Hal Ashby. I was also offered *One Flew Over the Cuckoo's Nest,* as well as Robert Redford's Watergate thing, but I really believed an American would end up doing the subject matter and script a higher justice.

WHAT OTHER FILMMAKERS WERE INSPIRATIONAL TO YOU AT THE TIME?
There are European filmmakers that I admire tremendously. The social realism of Italy left a lasting impression. I still consider Vittorio De Sica a God, and so is, in a way, Federico Fellini. I take a lot of my work from them. Fellini was a master of camera work and I based a lot of the shot construction of *A Kind of Loving* on Fellini. At the time I was making the film, I didn't really know how to tell a story with the camera or break a scene down in terms of the editing. The fact that I had helpful people in that department was terribly important. I would say that after time, and a good deal of help and suggestion, I did learn how to break scenes down in terms of camera, as well as achieve a certain fluidity of the shots.

As far as working with actors, when we started the filming, I didn't even know what an objective was, and therefore was basically unable to talk in those terms. My assistant finally said, "You're not giving them objectives." He explained what that meant, and so I learned. It was a terrific first film because nobody was questioning whether or not I could direct actors. They accepted that I did a good job and that the performances were well played. The learning process on that film was enormous for me.

It's only much more recently that I've felt difficulty getting subjects off the ground. The great thing about those days was that people weren't frightened to try things like they are now. I guess this has a lot to do with the lower costs. I'm quite sure the films I made at that time, like *Midnight Cowboy* and *Sunday, Bloody Sunday*, wouldn't get off the ground today, no way. Attitudes have changed in the past few decades as the cost of production has risen. People aren't willing to take those sorts of risks anymore. They want to know that their investment is reasonably secure. I don't know what I would encounter if I was starting my career now.

YOUNG PEOPLE STARTING OUT WANT TO BE ABLE TO PRACTICE AND LEARN TO MAKE FILMS. WHAT DO YOU THINK ARE GOOD AVENUES FOR ACHIEVING THAT?

I think that there are a lot of people who say they want to make films and have no idea how to get into it. My answer is that what we're short of is good writing. The way to approach getting into film is to write something, direct it, and shoot it by whatever means possible, even if that means you have to go out with a video camera and do it yourself. You've got to have something to show that may surprise people. It helps a great deal to approach your scripts as if they were short stories, and to write them with a great deal of enthusiasm—where the story is literally jumping off the page. If you've got executives sitting there reading your work, it's about keeping them engaged, allowing them to feel that they are sitting there watching something live and fully unfold.

One mistake is to say, "Hey, I've got twenty-five copies of this film I made, I'll do a mass mailing." You've got to present your work personally and let them see the whites of your eyes, the determination. That's what they'll be impressed by. Presentation is crucial to impressing someone. I think if you just send out work without being there, then there's really no way of knowing whether or not they'll look at it, and it's a lot harder to get them to commit to it over the phone, and that's a problem. The fact that they've met, seen, and heard you talk is more important than undoing a parcel.

I'm disheartened when people say the film industry has changed since our younger days, but I guess I would tend to agree. I've worked with a lot of men, past and present, in executive positions who've always seemed to exist in a constant state of battle to get something that they want made through the bureaucracy of higher executives. What's the answer? Unfortunately, I think you've got to battle away and use your head as a battering ram. When you believe in something enough and a lot of executives are thinking about whether they want to invest some money in your movie, they begin asking all sorts of questions that we were rarely asked in the earlier days. I imagine it is a bit disillusioning and disheartening. How do you convince somebody? I don't really know the answer. You just keep trying.

But I'm coming from a place that has mixed results, and I would have to say that I'm not terribly interested in commercial success for its own sake, except that it gives you a little more rope to hang yourself with. I've been lucky because I've made some successful pictures that have made a lot of money, and I've been able to coast on them for some time. *Midnight Cowboy* was an example, not just because it made money, but also because it's associated with being a profitable picture as a whole. Take somebody like [Steven] Spielberg, who's clever, but has a very different approach to filmmaking. I don't think he's ever shown himself to be somebody that's a great supporter of films that say something, but he has made films that have been hugely successful almost all of the time. He's not had many flops, which is wonderful because he's associated with success. But ultimately, he's rather different from me.

I don't know quite where to place myself in the industry, mostly because I'm coming to the end of my professional life, partly through my own will, having found filmmaking very exhausting recently. I like working very much, but the game has become really tricky. The attitude of film today is totally different from when I was in my heyday. Although I've made films that I'm disappointed in, I'm really quite happy about the way things have gone, and wish I had the energy to pick up a book like *Midnight Cowboy* and to make a film like that again. The truth is, this business requires an enormous amount of application and patience, and I don't know if I have that anymore. There are certain subjects and scripts I would love to make, but I realize the difficulty in getting them off the ground.

IF YOU WERE STARTING OUT TODAY, KNOWING WHAT YOU KNOW NOW, WOULD YOU DO SOMETHING ELSE?

I couldn't give you that advice because after all, everyone is different. I've come up for air and then sunk, and then come up for more air, and sunk again. I don't know that I've always chosen wisely. Even if the recent films I've made and like are for television and not the cinema, I'm still pleased that I got the opportunity. With the success of *Midnight Cowboy*, I could have gone on to accept assignments that were very well paid, but I chose not to. Instead I had to work on *Sunday, Bloody Sunday*, which I believe is my most personal film to date, and the one I'm really glad I got to make, even if it didn't do my career any good commercially. I then made *Day of the Locust*, always an iffy project, but again, I'm glad I made it. Not only did it make money, it also let me make a certain genre of film I'd never really tackled before.

If a film has not realized any particular ambition then there's not necessarily anything wrong with that. Sometimes a film is just there to entertain. But the films I make and would like to make must have interesting scripts. I usually know going into a project that it may not be a huge commercial success. So I guess my definitive answer is, if I was in your shoes, I would still make the same choices I've made.

I look back on a career full of interest and excitement and things that I think have worked, as well as plenty that didn't. I don't regret the failures and must say I'm glad I've continued to make an occasional film I'm proud of. I guess as long as one's got that, it's worth it. Once you have a first-run film that you're proud of, it all seems worth the effort. You never know where something is going to give you that pleasure in life.

So keep your head down, knock down the walls, and use anybody you can to gain admittance to a chance at doing something. Directing television isn't the answer, but it is an answer, and so is successful television filmmaking. But don't bother working in it unless you've got an opportunity to make something really interesting. It's garbage mostly, and an insult to people's intelligence, though nobody seems to care about that. The struggle is eternal. I don't think it will ever let up, even when you're there. That's my desire, to have my epitaph read: "You're never there until now."

Ben Younger | BOILER ROOM

BEN YOUNGER *was born in Brooklyn, New York, in 1974. During childhood he attended yeshiva and went on to Queens College. After working as a film industry grip and electrician, Younger made a short film and began writing what would become his first feature,* Boiler Room, *starring Giovanni Ribisi and Ben Affleck.* Boiler Room *was produced by New Line Cinema and opened to critical and box-office success in 1999. Younger is single and lives in Brooklyn, New York.*

My family moved quite a bit when I was young. When my parents split up we lived in Brooklyn and Staten Island, and when I was fifteen we moved to New Jersey, where my mother and stepfather finally settled. My family was of Hungarian Jewish descent and I spent my formative years studying at a yeshiva. When I turned eighteen I moved back to New York. My mother is a psychotherapist and my father was an accountant. He had colon cancer and passed away when I was nineteen. I have three brothers and two sisters; steps, halves . . . all mixed up. I have one natural brother, David, who is an actor and is in *Boiler Room*. The rest of my siblings are younger than I am and none of them are in show business.

My childhood was a little tumultuous after my parents split up and later when my father passed away, but looking back, those events definitely helped shape who I am now and what I am doing with my life. I didn't have a sheltered childhood like so many people who I have met where they may have come from money or may never have had to deal with a death in the family, things like that. It's funny, you would think that that is what you would want, but I am convinced that you almost need to experience events like these to toughen up. I don't think a perfect childhood environment exists. The reality is that life is full of hard knocks.

WHAT ARE SOME OF YOUR FIRST MEMORIES OF THE MOVIES?

From the time I was eleven until I was seventeen, I lived between Brooklyn and New Jersey. I watched movies with my dad whenever I would visit him. I distinctly remember seeing *Return of the Jedi* for the third time with my grandfather. I remember watching his reaction to the Ewoks because I knew he was going to love that shit. Don't laugh, but I remember seeing the first Steven Seagal movie, called *Above the Law.* I was a sophomore in high school at the time and I remember my friend Jeff telling me to see it, so I cut school and went by myself. The opening sequence struck me because it had a real documentary feel to it; it focused on Seagal's character growing up as a child in Chicago with film footage and still photographs from when he was a kid. The film actually had an interesting plot, believe it or not. For some reason, after seeing this movie, I stopped to think for the first time about the process of filmmaking. It was a bit of a revelation because I thought, Holy shit! Someone actually creates these movies. That was the first time I was swept away by a film. That's what turned me on. I never considered going into filmmaking as a profession because I went to yeshiva my whole life. Coming from yeshiva, you don't go into filmmaking, you go into a real profession. You have to be a doctor or a lawyer, so filmmaking was just something I hadn't considered. It wasn't even a possibility in that environment.

After seeing *Above the Law,* I didn't yet equate "Directed by" with that feeling I had watching it; I hadn't made that connection yet. But I did know that I loved going to movies. I really loved it. I didn't grow up with a camera in my hand like [Steven] Spielberg or some other people; I grew up as a viewer. I especially liked comedies. My dad and I would watch *Planes, Trains and Automobiles* with John Candy and Steve Martin and we would just rewind it to watch our favorite scenes over and over again. My love of film was there, but I just had no idea what it meant and how it would affect me in the long run.

My interest in comedy carried into my real life too. When I was seventeen I did stand-up comedy for three years. It was a big deal because my parents were like, "What the fuck are you doing?" It was at the end of my senior year of high school. I loved it, man, I loved it. I still don't know where it came from because now the idea of getting on stage seems preposterous to me. I certainly wouldn't do it now but at the time, I don't know what it was, I just had a need to do it the same way I have the need to make movies now.

DID YOUR EXPERIENCE WITH STAND-UP AFFECT YOUR VIEW OF ACTORS AND PERFORMANCE?

Definitely. I have a lot of respect for performers because theirs is a very hard thing to do. Standup is harder than acting in a sense because it is your own material and you are not just the actor, but the actor and the writer. In a movie you don't know if there are going to be those reactions right away. It is certainly not like live theater where people are going to clap when the show is over. When you do stand-up the audience isn't going to laugh because they feel bad for you. That's the one reaction that human beings can't do if they don't feel it. No one is going to laugh if they don't think it's funny, so you know right away if your writing and performance works or not. It's fucking rough, man. I had really bad nights as well as some amazing nights when the highs were higher than anything I had ever experienced, even higher than what I feel now when directing films. I think that it is the instant gratification that is so visceral when you say something and people laugh. That's pretty amazing.

LET'S TALK ABOUT YOUR COLLEGE DAYS.

I went to Queens College but I didn't take any film classes even though they had them in the curriculum. I was fortunate to have an amazing professor named Alan Hevesi, who was a New York assemblyman. He taught political science, which ended up being my major. Alan was a really charismatic guy who took me under his wing during this very difficult time in my life when my father got sick. He was the best professor I had through those years at college. He set up an internship for me as a legislative aide in his office in Albany. I think a big part of why he pushed for me to do it was my dad's death. This was my brief foray into politics. By the time I turned twenty-one I was running a political campaign, the youngest campaign manager in New York. I was working at the comptroller's office during the day and going to school at night. I was very, very busy.

HOW DID THE MOVE FROM POLITICS TO FILM COME ABOUT?

There were two events that put me over the edge. The first was when my friend Phil wrote a screenplay and the second was when I worked as a production assistant on a film. When I saw that Phil was doing it, actually writing a screenplay, I realized that I could do it too. I was seeing so many films at that point in my life, sometimes four or five each week, that I figured that

I could write one too. The PA thing came through a girl I was dating at the time. I didn't even know what "PA" stood for, but I worked for one day on the set of a film being shot in Williamsburg, Brooklyn, where I now live. I can't even remember the title, but I do remember feeling that I knew I was going to live my life in film. I knew it the moment I arrived on the set that day. I liked the people who were involved, and I was very impressed with all of the equipment and all the behind-the-scenes stuff. From watching movies I just didn't know what took place and how it all happened. I don't know if I can articulate that feeling, but there is something inherently exciting about being on a set, and after that first day I knew I had to do this. I had never experienced anything quite like it before. I had just run a successful political campaign, but in the process I became totally disenchanted with politics and my job. Working on the film was the catalyst that pushed me out and I decided to quit politics.

Before I actually quit, I had agreed to PA on another film called *Ripe*, which was being directed by Mo Ogrodnick, a friend of my girlfriend, Sarah. I quit my job and the day I was planning to leave to work on the film I got a call saying that the film had been temporarily canceled. The production was shut down because the film was going to be shot on a military base. The military got a copy of the script and didn't like the content because there were some homoerotic scenes involving military personnel. When the film fell through I got really nervous thinking that I had made a mistake by quitting my job. My mother was supportive of my decision but not ecstatic. When you actually quit you are faced with the reality of having to support yourself. This forced me into finding a job so I could pay the rent.

At that time I knew this kid who was driving a brand-new car, and he told me that I could make a couple million dollars in one or two years working as a stockbroker. This sounded good to me. I didn't have anything to lose and I thought I was interviewing at a real brokerage house so I went to check it out. My philosophy is that I will take any meeting once. I knew it was a boiler room the minute I walked in the door. I spent the day there, but of course I didn't take the job. There's a scene in the beginning of my film *Boiler Room* where Ben Affleck is yelling at all the new recruits. I sat through thirty minutes of a guy screaming at me like that. I was like, I'm outta here, but I also knew that this was going to be my first script. That is how I fell into that world. Before this I had had other script ideas, but I never started writing them because I knew that they just weren't going to be up to par. With this I had found a world that hadn't been explored on film and I felt the need to write about it.

I started reading filmmaker magazines, I joined the Independent Feature Project, and I immersed myself in the independent film world. My girlfriend at the time was also into film and she was very supportive, so when I got around to making my short film *L&M* sometime later, she produced it. My friend Phil and I also spent a lot of time together, and Phil, Sarah, and I felt like we had a bit of a collaborative community.

DID YOU START WRITING IMMEDIATELY?

No, I wasn't that hungry. I don't know what the word is. I just didn't get on it right away. I knew I had to do tons of research so I started having the guy who invited me for the interview over to my house and we became friends. He needed a place to stay for a while so he actually moved in for a short time, and that was great because I would speak with him every day. When he would come home I would turn on the tape recorder and bother him until he would tell me everything about his day at work. It felt much more like I was making a documentary than a feature film. This interviewing process went on for a couple of years with him and with other brokers I met.

I still needed to make money to live so I found a way to support myself working as a film grip. I knew this guy Will Arneau who I was going to work with on *Ripe*. He was a grip, and at the time I didn't know what a grip was. I knew I was going to be working with him and he felt so bad for me that the movie got canceled that he hired me to work with him on a Wu Tang Clan video as a third grip. I was very excited to be working, but I had no idea what I was getting myself into. Essentially a grip is a kind of electrician. So I was doing all the electric work. When Will asked me to come work with him, it never occurred to me that it would be technical work. When I worked as a PA, I ran and got people coffee. The first thing Will asked me to do was to get some sandbags and I didn't know what the fuck he was talking about. If you don't know what a sandbag is you're not going to know what anything is. That's the only piece of grip equipment whose name actually represents its actuality. "Go get me a butt plug." I was like, "What?" I started to get nervous fast, very fast. I was in big trouble. I worked a fifteen-hour day not knowing what I was doing, but I loved every moment and I made it through. He didn't hire me again for two years and it was only after he heard I was gripping that he called me again. Now when I think about the experience it is really funny. They told me they wanted to do a chandelier hanging and they wanted it rigged. It took me an hour and a half to do what I can do now in five minutes. That was my entry into the world of gripping. I just learned by doing and spent the next three and a half years doing it. I had to make a living while I wrote my screenplay, and I figured why not do it in the industry and learn something, so that is what I did. That was my film school.

I worked on videos, commercials, and a feature film called *Walking and Talking* with Anne Heche and Liev Schreiber. I got that job through another person I had met who called and said they needed a swing grip for the film. I immediately said yes. That is a big part of how I got to where I am today, I always said yes right away. I would say, "Yes, of course I know how to do that," even though I had no idea what I was getting myself into. This was key. I had to learn somehow, and I am convinced that that is the fucking key in any business. You need to put yourself into those situations so you can be in a position to do things you haven't done before. You need to learn somehow, and unfortunately sometimes you have to lie a bit in the beginning or you will never get the opportunity.

WERE YOU WRITING DURING THIS TIME?

I was still interviewing brokers while I was working. I had never written a screenplay so I didn't really know how to begin the process of writing. I was terrified to sit down at the computer. Partly because I was trying to avoid writing the feature, and partly because I wanted to learn more about production, after I worked on *Walking and Talking* I decided to make a short film. It was called *L&M* and I wrote it over a couple of weeks. It's a story about a con man and how his addiction to cigarettes goes beyond the nicotine. He starts using them as a social crutch and this ultimately leads to his downfall. He gets a classic Jaguar from a dealership but doesn't really lease it; he rents the car for a weekend and puts an ad in the paper that the car is for sale. Then a yuppie buys the car from him with false paperwork. Later that night he goes to the yuppie's house with a spare key and drives it away. At the end of the movie, the con man returns the Jag to the dealership, but the yuppie shows up with a bunch of Jaguars. He's a collector who's bringing in one of his cars for service. And there is the con man standing next to him, smoking.

The whole con man concept is fascinating to me. I guess it goes back to my father. He was a CPA but it seemed like he was always on the make no matter what situation he was in. He would cut the line and sneak deli sandwiches into the movie theater, or take me out of school for the day to go to Great Adventure and tell the school that I was sick. He was very much about beating the system. It was mostly on a day-to-day level, but he was always getting over in some way, though not maliciously of course. He found another angle to any given situation. They say in Hungarian—which is my ethnic background—that he was "Somebody who walks behind you in a revolving door and comes out in front of you." That was my dad.

In terms of making films, aside from saying yes to everything, one other important thing is to befriend everybody and listen to people rather than talk to them, not in a fake way but really listen and learn from people you come in contact with. I surrounded myself with people who knew what they were doing and, when it was at all possible, I made friends with them. When it came time to shoot *L&M*, I was able to call all the crew from *Walking and Talking* to ask for help.

The truth is that a short film is not going to do shit for you unless you make some Academy Award–winning thing, so you should view it as a learning experience more than anything else. That is the mistake that so many people make and they waste time, money, and effort doing something for the wrong reasons. My advice is not to spend a ton of your own money on a first project thinking it will be your masterpiece. I spent $20,000 to make *L&M*. I had saved money from work as a grip and I maxed out my credit cards to do it. I epitomized all of the clichés that you hear from filmmakers trying to get things done. I was in the poorhouse for a few years after that.

TELL ME ABOUT THE PRODUCTION PROCESS OF THE SHORT.

It was amazing, exciting and challenging, and very enjoyable, even with the day-to-day unexpected obstacles that we encountered. Believe it or not I liked the process. It was so reactionary. Every day you had thirty new problems to solve for one great end result. I liked being so busy and hectic. It's a great feeling.

I hooked up a crew and placed an ad in *Backstage* to find my actors. I had the responses sent to my mother and stepfather's home in New Jersey and we got boxes and boxes of mail. That was so unbelievable. The shoot was for only five days and it still cost $20,000. That is a lot of money when you don't have much, but it was twenty minutes of movie and it was worth it. We had a lot of cars, including a Jaguar which I got for free, but transporting the Jag cost $1,000. That was crazy because it was five percent of my budget being spent on one car only because the owner wouldn't let me drive it. After we started shooting the film, I immediately felt a sense of accomplishment. During those five days when I was directing, I remember almost every aspect of it, every shot. When it is your own money you are so conscious about everything you are doing. I knew then that those were the five best professional days of my life. Even to this day I know that because I have found that directing a feature is really no different than directing a short; the same issues come up, the same results derive. Those were days of discovery for me in learning that I loved directing and realizing how much I wanted to do it. It is an incredible feeling; it's almost indescribable. I loved it, and I knew then that this was what I was going to be doing for my life and there was not a doubt in my mind about it.

Unfortunately, editing the film was a big disaster. This producer I knew had promised me a Steenbeck editing machine and he didn't follow through. I had no money, no job, and it was winter in New York and I kept waiting for the call about the Steenbeck. I was so depressed that I didn't know what to do with myself. I was coming off the high of this wonderful experience and I thought the Steenbeck was coming any day. I couldn't think about getting a "real job" because it was coming. Everything depended on that Steenbeck. Day after day I waited and that went on for at least two months. I think I was in denial about everything in my life that was not going well and I just waited for nothing. I eventually realized that I would never see that Steenbeck and paid to rent one.

If you would ask me what I think of the end result of all of this, I would say that the film is actually a good director's piece but the problem is that the acting is subpar, and that of course is my fault entirely. I had to fire the lead actor two days before we started shooting and I hired another one at the last minute. If the acting were great I really think it would be a good piece because the writing still stands up. I cut my teeth on it. I don't suggest to anybody who is planning to make a short that they view it as a ticket to big-time directing. It is definitely more of a learning process than anything else. You learn from your mistakes.

AFTER THE SHORT WERE YOU FOCUSED ON MAKING A FEATURE?
I knew I had my movie in the boiler room interviews that I had been doing. I was definitely energized to write from my experience making the short. I got out the transcripts of all the interviews that I had done and I started writing them, figuring out what stories were going to be good for the movie. I began figuring out the plot, the characters, and the interaction. Just as I was getting excited again about making a film, my personal life fell into shambles. My girlfriend kicked me out of her apartment, as she should have at that point. I was depressed, I had no job, and I had no money. I ended up getting a shitty apartment with no sink in the bathroom and, believe it or not, I'm still there. I needed money so badly that I started getting grip jobs again. I got a computer and a screenwriting program and I started to write *Boiler Room*. This was about three years ago. Out of all of the bad things going on in my life, writing felt good.

TELL ME ABOUT THE WRITING PROCESS.
I couldn't get the writing done while I was working as a grip and that was a real problem. The writing process proved to be so all-consuming that I just couldn't do both at the same time. I really tried, but it was too hard to do them simultaneously. I needed a couple days of down time before I could even get into writing mode. Things weren't working out and I knew I had to find a different job. It was disappointing because at that point I felt that I knew gripping and I understood it and could do it. I just couldn't write and do it at the same time. I was in this apartment by myself barely able to make fucking rent, which was only $600 a month. I had nothing and I was dirt poor. I was also at least $20,000 in debt. Things couldn't have been worse in that respect. Out of sheer desperation I decided to take a job as a waiter at this place called Steak Frites on Sixteenth Street in Manhattan.

Two weeks after I started waiting tables a guy named Steve Kerper walked into the place with his mother. I didn't know who he was at the time, but he is an incredible writer who does a lot of work for HBO. I waited on him, and during the meal we started talking, and he asked me what I did. We had a really good rapport and by the end of the lunch he asked me if I had anything he could show to his agent. I told him about my short film and he suggested I send it to Adrianna Abingetti at Endeavor. This complete stranger that I met waiting tables just decided to help me out. This was unbelievable! And I sent her my short film. Later she would become my agent.

Three days later, Steve Harris, a cinematographer I had known from my grip days, walked into the restaurant while I was serving lunch. He was quite surprised to see me there and asked me how much money I had made that day. I told him about twenty-six dollars. He literally told me to walk out at that moment and that he would make sure that I kept working. He was willing to take a chance with me because he knew about my writing and believed in the script. He really wanted me to do it. I mean when I think about that now it's just mind-boggling. The guy knew me for a couple months and he kept his promise. I quit my waiting job and he kept me busy with work that took me all around the world. We did industrial commercials in Europe, we did work in New York—he just believed in me and took me in. I credit him for teaching me how to shoot a film. When he started getting double booked on jobs, he booked me. Once he started doing that I was making about $1,400 a day. All I had to do was work two days a month and I had enough to live. And that is how I got my screenplay done.

If you can write and work at the same time, then by all means do it. I cannot. I needed to have that time all to myself in order to write something good. My advice to others is to either save a bunch of money and take some time off or find a job that allows you the freedom to work a few days at a time. Steve Harris is the reason I was able to write my script. Meeting him opened up a door for me to have that freedom to write. I was able to pay off some of my debts and to write the script for real.

Although I was now unhindered, it was still very difficult to sit down and actually do it. But I did start the process and from there it took about six months of sitting down at the computer every day. Although in terms of actual real writing work, I'll bet you it really only happened in a month. It was a slow process for me. There could be nothing for one month, and then thirty pages in three days. That's the way it works for me. When you are on, you are on. It is un-fucking believable how that can happen. Once a friend and I wrote a script in seventeen days. It was a piece of shit, but we did it in seventeen days and that's something. If you can bang out 120 original pages and it bears any resemblance to a story, I think that that is impressive, no matter how long it takes you.

When I finished the script I sent it to Adrianna, who knew me as "the waiter guy" through Steve Kerper. It was an early rough draft, and she had never returned my phone calls from the short I had sent her, but it was satisfying to put it in the mail anyway. That concrete act fills you with hope that there is some chance that someone might read it and I needed to know that there was that hope. So I mailed it out. She was the only person I sent it to and believe it or not she called three days later and said she had read the script and liked it. I couldn't believe it; I was literally jumping up and down while having the conversation. Here I was in my underwear making pasta for the hundredth day in a row and suddenly I get a call from an agent who likes my work and is talking about representing me. It was freaky. That's essentially how I got found. The irony in this is that in all of those years of meeting producers on sets while working in film, it ended up being the guy in the restaurant who really opened doors for me.

Even though there is that element of luck in my story, I sincerely believe that if the product is there and you have a good script, you are eventually going to get it made one way or another. I really believe that. I don't think my script was unbelievably great, but I do think that I wrote about a world that was unknown to people and that is what they responded to. No one had seen that boiler room world before on film and that is what I presented to them. It is increasingly more difficult to find these "new worlds" to explore in film because everything seems to be covered in some capacity. It is about finding the psychological context within the physical context of the environment and pulling that out on a human level. I think I knew that I had that much with the father-son thing element of the film even though we have seen that over and over again. I tried to do my own take on it and I must say that I am happy with how that came out in the film. As far as the boiler room aspect, that was there for the taking. I knew people were going to respond to that regardless of the father-son subplot. If you have something like the boiler room, the film is going to get made. It is too compelling not to.

The easiest and most direct route to success in this business is to write a script. I truly believe that that is the most straightforward route to directing feature films. If you try to get there by making videos or commercials, it could be a very long road. You have to get different jobs and you have to put a reel together. So many things need to happen and you have to meet the right people. Not every music video director has a shot at directing a feature film, but if you write a script, you own something. A written work is a commodity and you can barter with that. That is what I did; I leveraged my position in that capacity. I said if you want this, then I am attached to it. It was all or nothing for me.

AFTER THE AGENT SAID SHE WOULD REPRESENT YOU, WHERE DID IT GO FROM THERE?

Two weeks after Adrianna called, I flew to Los Angeles, where I had my first meeting with her at Endeavor. It was a great meeting. From the start we had a real connection and I realized that I had found the right agent. I knew that then and I'm happy with her now. She wanted me to meet everyone at Endeavor so I would feel more comfortable, but I knew that I was at the right place without even meeting them. I just knew. Adrianna had given me positive creative script notes and I made the changes. I was never afraid to take advice about possible changes. That was something that helped me a lot, too. I could always listen to criticism even if I didn't like it. I might say, "Okay, thanks," and ignore it, but why not listen to it because sometimes you get great ideas from other people's perspectives.

Endeavor sent the script out with me attached as the director. I was in Houston doing an industrial job when I got a phone call from Adrianna saying that the script was out and that some people had passed because I was attached as director. She mentioned that there was some interest shown by a company called Artisan. So they sent another script to them on a Friday, and the following Monday Artisan made a formal offer. Bill Block was the head of Artisan, and he called me and was very into the script. He said they were excited to have me directing and they were going to make the movie for $3 million. That was fine with me since I had always imagined making it in New York by myself for $1 million. He told me that they wanted me to come to L.A. for casting. I went to L.A. and we started casting. I immediately cast Nia Long, Giovanni Ribisi, and Ben Affleck. It was a big deal that I was getting actors of that caliber. Since I was a first-time director, I had to meet with them because I thought that we should hit the big points and discuss the script in detail. As I found out, communication skills are very important when you are a director. You must also have the ability to manipulate people for different situations. Knowing how to talk to a studio, knowing how to switch gears and talk to an actor, knowing how to convey your visual images to a director of photography, they're all very important; the game is about communication.

Unfortunately, Artisan was unable to secure the financing for the film because they couldn't successfully pre-sell the foreign rights. I wasn't privy to how everything went down, but I think that they paid too much for some of the actors and the budget didn't fit the $3 million dollar paradigm anymore, so the foreign negotiations that they were having wouldn't make the film happen. They told us that they were selling the film in turnaround (which is where one studio will sell the rights to a film to another for the amount they have spent on it to date). By this point I had already hired producers, so this whole thing was a major blow. But luckily my producers, Jennifer and Suzanne Todd, had a first-look deal with New Line Cinema. New Line had passed on the script in the initial round, but now Jennifer asked them to take another look at it bearing in mind the excellent actors I had attached to the project. By this time I had also been to a lot of meetings with studio heads and studio execs, so I was somewhat more known at that point. New Line thought about it a little bit, and then said that they would finance the film, and gave us a budget of $7.5 million. It is amazing to think that all of this happened as quickly as it did. From the time I got an agent to the time the movie got made was basically one year.

HOW WAS THE DIRECTING PROCESS?

It was incredible, really amazing. We rented a big production space in Manhattan, down on Canal Street, and set to work. It was a lot different than directing my short, due primarily to the size of the film. I was a little more nervous, and I froze the first morning on the set. We walked in to take the first shot, and I literally froze. Here I stood with thirty people looking at me, and I lost the power of speech. But I recovered, and one hour after that horrible moment, I was completely into it and remained that way for the whole thirty-day shoot. I was quite happy with the finished product with the exception of the ending. It was changed after we did a test screening. That was the only loss because the original ending was a bit more complicated and dealt more with my themes of chance and odds. But it was a small price to pay.

WHAT EVENT WAS MOST SIGNIFICANT TO YOU WHEN YOU THINK BACK ON THE EXPERIENCE?

The premiere of *Boiler Room*. The premiere was the most significant event for me because all of the people that I loved were there in New York City at the Ziegfeld Theater, which is my favorite theater of all time. I actually let myself enjoy and savor the moment that night, and I didn't get caught up in all of the other stuff that was going on. I didn't talk to the press and I didn't hang out with a lot of Hollywood types after the screening. At the party I was with my friends next to the DJ booth, and we danced the whole night. For one night I let myself really enjoy my success. That feeling, of course, is gone now and I can't watch the movie again; I hate it. There are so many things I hate about that movie.

HOW RELEVANT DO YOU THINK LUCK IS IN THE ENTIRE PROCESS?

I think not very because the product can only come from one source, and there is no luck involved in whether the product is good or not. Either you are going to make it good or you are not. You won't get lucky with one screenplay. Luck does come into play with who you bump into and the con-

nections you make. In that sense there are many possibilities. But I also believe that if it's not going to be one person you meet it may be another. You
may call it luck, but I prefer not to. For me all of this happened the way it
did and it seems lucky, but I know it would have happened eventually. It
may have happened differently, but it would have happened. I know that the
script would have ended up somewhere else. It just worked out that I happened to serve Steve Kerper lunch that day. It is a great story, but I stand by
the product over luck theory.

**SO SOMEBODY COMES TO YOU AND SAYS, "BEN, I WANT TO BE A DIRECTOR."
WHAT IS YOUR ADVICE?**
If you can write, then I say write the screenplay. That was my route and
look how quickly things happened for me. I'm sure there are music video directors out there who say, "Go do some music videos. That was the easiest
way for me." From my perspective, writing is the answer. It is the prospect
of owning a property and having something tangible to leverage yourself
with even though you are a nobody. I liked the idea that people wanted that
script. Before we made the Artisan deal, we had an offer for $800,000 for the
script if I would walk away as a director. Of course, I declined it, but I recognized that the script had power. It was the power of the product, and I
knew it then and I know it now.

IS IT EASIER NOW TO DO THE NEXT FILM, GIVEN YOUR RECENT SUCCESS?
No, it's harder to do the next film. You always think, "Oh, if this goes
through then . . ." and it just never works out that way. Now I'm terrified
that I must go through this process again. How am I going to write another
script like *Boiler Room*? How am I going to do this? I guess I can't avoid
those thoughts. Sometimes I think that I want to direct material written by
other people. You can just drive yourself crazy and I do. Just look at the fact
that I hate my own movie—it's just incredible. It makes no sense, really. I
can't even watch it and that is not just because of the ending. There are
other parts that just don't work and I keep saying to myself, How did you
not know that this didn't work when you shot it? I don't think I am being
hard on myself because there are mistakes in that film that I wouldn't make
again. There were days when we were filming and I felt a time crunch and
I was like, "Okay, let's just move on." In retrospect I see that we should not
have moved on, absolutely not. It shows in the final result. But, again, that is
all part of the learning process.

BUT DESPITE YOUR OWN CRITICISM THE FILM HAS PERFORMED AT THE BOX OFFICE AND BEEN QUITE WELL RECEIVED.

Yes, that is amazing to me. For a couple of days it works. You get a good review, you're like, "Yes, this is good." Then it just disappears and the doubt comes back in and you don't give a shit. If I really loved the film and I was so happy and content with it then I know the next movie would suffer because I would be taking everything for granted. The next one has got to be better than the last one. It's about staying hungry. I took out my camera yesterday and started shooting cool shots of stuff around the city. For me that is a good sign that things are starting to happen again.

In this profession I would say that drive is more essential than talent. I say drive because the bottom line is that film is a business more than an art form. If I were a painter, I would much rather have 90 percent talent and 10 percent drive. But film is not that pure, and it doesn't have to be that pure an art form because it is a huge business. Although you must have talent to sustain, you must have drive to push it. In business, drive is more important than talent.

Within myself there is not only self-doubt, but hunger, such hunger. There were many moments when I thought that I couldn't do this and I didn't think that I was a good writer, but at the same time I was incredibly motivated. Whenever I feel I can't write I'll just make up for it and hustle. It is those two elements that actually feed off each other. And in the end, everything has worked out really well. If I didn't have confidence and drive, then I'm glad I had self-doubt and drive because that is a good combination too. It doesn't make for a happier personal life, but it gets you to where you want to go. And then things start to get better, as they always will.

Kimberly Peirce | BOYS DON'T CRY

KIMBERLY PEIRCE *was born in Harrisburg, Pennsylvania, in 1970. She attended the University of Chicago, but had to leave after one year due to financial difficulties. She traveled to Japan, where she lived and worked for several years before returning to the university to finish her degree. After college Peirce proceeded to study at Columbia film school, where she began developing a film project about the murder of Brandon Teena. After partnering with renowned independent film producer Christine Vachon and six years of struggle, this project ultimately became the spine of Peirce's Academy Award–winning film,* Boys Don't Cry. *Peirce is single and lives in New York City.*

My parents were fifteen years old when they had me so after I was born they went in different directions. Growing up, I lived with a lot of different people in a lot of different places. For a part of my childhood, I lived in a trailer park. I bounced between New York, Florida, and Puerto Rico. I am the only child that my parents had together but I have half brothers and sisters who are much younger. Throughout my childhood I had a rather nomadic existence. I became attracted to stories about people who could reinvent and redefine themselves, and this later became a theme of my work.

When I was growing up, Disney films were pretty popular in the theaters and I saw many of them over and over again. I was interested in animation and comic books and I was always wondering how comics were animated. When I was eight I got a Super-8 camera and I began to make animated films. I would write stories, draw cartoons of them, and then photograph them with my Super-8 camera to try to make little movies. I thought that maybe one day I would be a cartoonist. I was living in Florida near Disney World and my big dream was to be like Walt Disney. I would go to Disney World for birthday parties and field trips, and I was always obsessed with sneaking in the back doors to see how everything worked. I wasn't really interested in the rides themselves but in the mechanics of them.

Making images, shooting them, and seeing how they looked when they were developed was the thing that made me most happy when I was growing up. I didn't know that there was a job called "director," this was just something that I did to amuse myself. When I was about ten, I joined a special program where one day each week I would leave school and work on plays. I had to plan a play out from start to finish, and I immersed myself in the process. I think that that early experience planted the seed for what would become my love of the filmmaking process. I loved being on a set creating character and emotion that made sense and worked in a narrative structure. I feel that that appreciation is kind of like loving math. You love math because you like all the steps, not because you like the end result; the end result is sometimes less relevant than the process.

DID YOUR HIGH SCHOOL ENVIRONMENT FOSTER THIS INTEREST IN DRAMATIC ART?

I was fortunate to have taken special Advanced Placement classes that were sophisticated, and I participated in debate classes where I spoke a lot. But ultimately, I think that my home environment had more of an impact on me than school did. I lived in Miami, where there was an influx of Puerto Ricans and Cuban refugees. My family was part Puerto Rican, and I think that the stimulus of the Miami environment along with my search for an identity within that world contributed a lot to my becoming a filmmaker. It wasn't that I had a great film class that inspired me or that I had access to anything sophisticated, because I didn't. Miami lacked cultural sophistication and in that sense I was deprived of a cultural education, although through that deprivation I learned about the culture of Miami.

I was very rebellious as a teenager and I wanted to get out as much as possible, so I was out around Miami getting into trouble and fantasizing about getting as far away from there as possible. Overall my environment did not encourage educational aspiration. I suppose that I was like most kids in that I felt that I was "doing my time" at high school, and there would come a moment when I could leave and finally be free. What I would do with that freedom, I didn't yet know, but I had a desire within me to do "something."

WHERE DID YOU GO TO COLLEGE?

After I graduated from high school, I applied to top colleges like Brown and other schools, and ultimately was accepted at the University of Chicago. I enjoyed it, and was a very good student (I got straight As), but I had to drop out after my first year because I lost access to my scholarship. In order for me to get the money for the scholarship, my family had to sign off on it because I was a minor, and they refused. People in my family hadn't finished high school and weren't very well educated. I think that they had a lot of resentment about my getting into such a good school, and they made it impossible for me to return. I knew then that I would have to work to support myself, and I didn't think that I wanted to do it in Chicago. I felt that it was time for a change.

I had heard that you could make a lot of money in Japan, so my girlfriend and I packed up and went to Tokyo. We arrived there in the middle of the night after twenty-five hours of air travel. We had no idea what to do. We didn't speak the language; we didn't know the streets. We were utter foreigners without the vaguest notion of a plan. That I went there like that seems crazy when I think of it now, but ultimately we figured something out. We had one friend in Tokyo who we stayed with for a few days when we first arrived. Then I decided that I wanted to see "old Japan," so my friend suggested that I go to Kobe. My girlfriend and I got on a train without really knowing where we were going, and of course we quickly got lost, so we spent the night at a train station in the middle of nowhere.

That was the moment in my life that I felt most free. It was a moment of total unaccountability; I was anonymous and nobody knew where I was or where I was going, and nobody cared. I was just kind of burrowing through the landscape. All that mattered at that moment was that I was on a train looking at a rice field. It was like I had been incarcerated by my life up to that point, and I was now shedding the prior society that hadn't satisfied my needs and allowed me to find what I was looking for. That feeling was a pure sensory experience; everything felt very clear and vivid. I knew that I was on the right path.

When we arrived in Kobe we stayed with friends of friends until we got an apartment and set ourselves up with jobs. We had to put down ¥800,000, which was about $8,000, in order to rent an apartment. It was called "key money," and we didn't have it, so we had to borrow money from companies that we were going to work for and we basically became indentured servants for a brief while. I got a job teaching English to some Japanese lawyers who represented the Yakuza, the Japanese mafia. They had all been educated at Todai, the Japanese equivalent of Harvard or Yale. These guys were really cool because they spoke English and they just wanted me to read *Catcher in the Rye* to them. They wanted to speak in English to improve their conversational skills, and they also just wanted to hang out with someone from American culture. Sometimes they would take me out at night to hostess bars, where gorgeous women would serve us drinks. It wasn't sexual at all, but it was a big deal to them to take a teacher out. I was good at the job and I continued doing it for two years, during which time I made quite a bit of money, as it paid very well.

While I was in Japan I was renting as many movies as I could find and I was also going to the theater to see Japanese films. I was in love with movies in that same way that I was in love with the experience of living in Japan. I would sit in the theater and become overwhelmed with the beauty and emotion of the films that I was seeing—I was in a culture where I didn't speak the language, and since all the words of drama were taken away I could simply sit and watch the people on screen. This was a great study of performance, and how it contributes to the overall result of a film.

WHAT DID YOU DO AFTER YOU LEFT JAPAN?
I came back to New York and got an internship with *Time* magazine for two years. I thought for a while that I might be a photojournalist. I began to become homesick for Japan, so I returned there and spent one year studying Japanese. I traveled all over Thailand and Southeast Asia on a motorcycle. I was enjoying life, floating around thinking that I could do anything. It was then that I had a serious motorcycle wreck.

I had gotten into a Japanese university right before the accident. I was quite dramatically injured, but I still had to make up my mind about whether I wanted to go to university there, or whether I wanted to return to the United States. I decided to go back to the U.S. I went to the bank and withdrew all of the money that I had been saving, which amounted to $10,000. I stuffed it into my sock, got on a plane, and returned to the University of Chicago, this time with enough living money to finish school. I also was now able to get scholarship money because I was older and I didn't need a parent's signature. Looking back, I think that leaving school and later returning turned out to be a great thing for me. My experience in Japan didn't detract from my education; it added to it. I was more eager to be in school the second time around.

DID YOU WATCH A LOT OF FILMS WHEN YOU RETURNED TO COLLEGE?

The University of Chicago had a film library called Cobb Hall, and nobody ever used it, so I was able to go there and watch films as much as I liked. My friend worked there as a projectionist and he would screen any film I wanted in the auditorium; I basically had my own screening room. I really started falling in love with film in the same way that I had fallen in love with animation when I was younger. I dove into movies and I saw everything by Sergei Eisenstein, D. W. Griffith, Akira Kurosawa, and Martin Scorsese. I was consumed by whatever films were at the library. I was really into violence, structuralism, and formality. I was also getting very interested in how camera movement affected story and character.

WHEN DID YOU THINK THAT YOU MIGHT WANT TO BECOME A FILMMAKER?

During the time that I was in Asia, I had been taking a lot of pictures, and since I had a dark room I would spend entire days developing them. When I came back to the U.S., I took a photography class at the same time I started watching all of the films at Cobb Hall. I had not yet come to the realization that it was possible to become a director, but I was still very stimulated by film. The desire to be a director was probably always underlying, but the understanding that I could do it didn't come until just as I was about to graduate, one of my English professors suggested that I go to film school and become a filmmaker. In retrospect, it was probably obvious that was the direction I was headed in, but it didn't occur to me until someone else said it.

I submitted my portfolio of photographs, an autobiography, and an essay on movies that I really liked to the graduate film programs at NYU and Columbia and I was fortunate enough to get scholarships to both places. It was my dream to go to NYU to follow in the footsteps of Martin Scorsese and Spike Lee, but when I compared the two schools, Columbia seemed better suited to helping me achieve what I wanted. At Columbia you work with actors and write scripts, and the emphasis is more on story and character and less on production. I was twenty-two years old when I started film school at Columbia, and I felt that I was ready for the experience.

I learned a ton and I ended up studying acting and writing there for three years. The program was for three years, but I finished in six. I just kept delaying graduation because I was still learning, and loving the experience. The first year I made a lot of video projects. I shot tons of stuff, I messed around and made mistakes, and I worked hard on ideas that I had. At the end of the first year I made a short film that played at many film festivals and was well received.

DID FILM SCHOOL MEET YOUR EXPECTATIONS?

Columbia had a great program. I would not know how to direct had I not been able to attend it and deconstruct all of the aspects of directing. I also worked as a projectionist at school, so I was able to watch movies all the time. That was where I got my heaviest doses of film. Living in Japan I had seen many films and I had acquired a real love for foreign films, but I didn't know much about American films until I was at Columbia. American filmmaking struck a vein in me, and I fell in love with the films I was being exposed to. The films I really liked were by D. W. Griffith, John Ford, Nick Ray, John Cassavetes, Martin Scorsese, Francis Ford Coppola, Robert Altman, and pretty much all of the filmmakers of the 1970s. For me the seventies were a period in time where filmmakers were the most reflective of a cultural eruption.

HOW VALUABLE ARE THE RELATIONSHIPS THAT YOU DEVELOP IN FILM SCHOOL?

I think relationships are crucial because they help you to develop a common language. All of the students at film school are thrown in together, to work together, to learn together, and the more you surrender to the fact that you don't know anything and recognize that you need to learn along with your peers in order to express yourself, then the better off you will be. It is like when you travel and you don't speak the language. The Japanese that I learned most quickly came when I needed to order food or when I needed to get a place to sleep. It is the same thing in film school. Those relationships that I found in school were great because I was able to find smart people and we worked together for a common goal.

WHEN YOU WERE AT SCHOOL WHAT TYPES OF FILMS WERE YOU INTERESTED IN MAKING?

I thought I'd be an experimental filmmaker; I never thought I'd make features. I watched all the silent films and loved them a great deal, so the first film I made was silent. I never said, "I want a big Hollywood career." I worked at the level I was capable of, and I guess that level grew as my ambitions grew. *The Last Good Breath* was my first short film. It was a fifteen minute silent, black-and-white piece shot on 16mm. The film detailed a story of two lovers who spend eternity separated from one another. I shot it on a beach and constructed it with fragmented, dreamlike images. I was very inspired by Luis Buñuel.

When my writing professor saw my dailies and script she told me to see *La Jetée*, so I went down to the library and watched the film over and over. It was amazing how Chris Marker took dream images and created a narrative with them. Seeing this film helped me figure out my film's own underlying narrative structure. I hadn't started with story or narrative; I had started with images. Now I needed to figure out how to connect them together. Ultimately the film was "experimental" and it moved toward a narrative that made sense to me but was confusing to everyone else. To most people, it was the emotional impact of the film that was clear. Everybody had an intense feeling watching it, but they couldn't exactly tell you what it was about. I was working in that mode throughout school, but during my third year narrative structure started to make more sense to me. I began to be able to look at my favorite movies of the seventies like *Mean Streets* or *The Godfather* and to recognize the commonality in them. I could see in them the arc, the dramatic conflict, Act One, Act Two. Suddenly I was able to see the structure of the films. Coming into film school I had had no idea how to read structure; now I could see things more clearly.

HOW DID THE BRANDON TEENA PROJECT DEVELOP?

After my third year of school the structural stuff started really kicking in. I had been working with actors for three years and I suddenly understood acting, writing, and directing and how they related to each other. Aristotle's *Poetics* became much clearer to me. Things were converging. I started working on a screenplay set in the Civil War which was based on a true story about a woman named Pauline Kushner who was one-eighth African American. Confederate soldiers were locking up anybody with African American blood. Pauline had friends who said they would protect her if she worked for them. They told her that she would have to pass as a white man and work as a spy. I got all these old books on her life and I was completely thrilled with the idea of the story. But the more I worked on it, the more that I saw that Pauline was passing as a man in order to survive; dressing up as a man didn't fulfill her fundamental life need—it fulfilled her survival need. In April 1994 I read an article in *The Village Voice* about Brandon Teena. Brandon was a girl who passed herself off as a boy and seduced many different girls. She fell into a group of kids who discovered her secret and she was raped and killed for it. I realized that on a narrative level Brandon's character was exactly the answer to what wasn't working with Pauline Kushner. Pauline Kushner wasn't dramatic; Brandon epitomized the drama of this character. He was a kid who would ask girls to marry him after only a few dates and he would buy an engagement ring with the girl's own credit card and tell her he did it because he was in love.

WHAT WAS YOUR ATTRACTION TO THE GENDER IDENTITY QUESTION?

I think I identified with it because I am queer and at that time I was living in the East Village where a lot of my friends were girls who passed as boys. Some of my friends were transsexuals, and that community was one that I was both familiar with and attracted to. I had an uptown life at Columbia and I had a downtown life with my gay buddies. When I read about Brandon, I realized that a lot of people were interested in his story. The story got a lot of press and I subsequently read an excellent article about Brandon in a 1997 issue of *The New Yorker* by Gregory Dunne. This character fascinated people, but nobody really understood who Brandon was. My friends and I read the story and we understood Brandon because we knew people like that. It became my task to reveal Brandon, to try to explain who he was.

I went to Nebraska with a group of fifteen transsexuals to attend the murder trial. I interviewed a lot of people involved in the story and I completely immersed myself in his world and culture, which was really foreign to me. I knew that if I was going to represent Brandon then I needed to understand his girlfriend, Lana, and her friends, and everyone involved. I needed to understand the mechanics of what had happened there.

This then became my graduate thesis project. I was developing it as a short film. I soon realized that nobody who was writing about Brandon was getting his character right and that he was the whole emotional center of the story. I had to get Brandon's character to work in order to understand the characters surrounding him. I also had to make his character work because he was really an antihero and that's complicated; you can't just make the antihero the good guy. There has to be depth to his character. I ultimately shot scenes of this film for my graduate thesis, but the inherent limitations of doing this as a short quickly became very clear. I realized that I needed to shoot this film in the Midwest and that I needed to film the rape scene. I needed to tell the whole story. The project became a feature, and I got into the writing and directing lab at the Sundance Workshop. That was hugely influential and it really enabled me to make the film that ultimately became *Boys Don't Cry*.

WHAT WAS THE SUNDANCE EXPERIENCE LIKE?

In 1995 I shot a version of the short, which I submitted to Sundance, and I was accepted into the writing lab in 1997. I worked with Frank Pierson, who wrote *Dog Day Afternoon*. He was an amazing person and a great help to me. When he talked about his character Sonny, he explained him in terms that helped me think about Brandon's character. The greatest thing about the Sundance lab was that I was surrounded by other writers, people who could help me find the answers to the questions I was faced with in writing the script. I needed to figure out how to construct Brandon so that he worked as a movie character and could drive the movie. That was unexplored terrain for me and here were these people lined up who were taking me into that darkness. I felt some strange allegiance to Brandon and therefore I could not screw the film up. Here was a person who was brutally raped and killed, and I knew that I did not have the right to make a movie about him unless I brought him to life in a way that made sense.

I wasn't at Sundance because I thought I would get the film made. The idea behind Sundance was to get the screenplay working; the notion that people would later give me millions of dollars to shoot it was just not a reality. That was a miracle that was over the horizon. At Sundance I gained the ability to distill the underlying emotional truth of the narrative. I had ten thousand pages of court transcripts, interviews with everyone involved, lots of biographical material, and it was all very overwhelming. But Sundance helped me cull the story from all of these things. My time there was extraordinary. I went to the writing lab and then I went back for the directing lab for one month. It was an amazing experience overall.

HOW WERE YOU SUPPORTING YOURSELF AT THIS TIME?

I worked as a projectionist and I started working part-time as a temporary administrator. I got a job working for a vendor to the Department of Defense doing space stuff because I was good with computers and I could troubleshoot. I started working there in the summer and they really liked me and gave me a full-time job. The great thing was that I had a computer and a phone and I could do the job, troubleshoot, and then go back to my computer and rewrite my scripts while I was working. I made good money there but the job ended, and I took a job at a printer working the night shift. I'd go in at midnight because on the late shift you made more money, and I would work until 8 A.M., stagger out, and go to class completely exhausted. I was earning a lot of money that allowed me to finish my movies at school. I also worked as a floater at a law firm. They loved the fact that I was making movies and they paid me really good money, with benefits.

HOW DID YOU ULTIMATELY MAKE YOUR BRANDON TEENA SHORT INTO A FEATURE?

I was working full-time, but also working on my screenplay at night. I took time off to go to Sundance and I also went to Nebraska to do research. My whole life was focused on getting information for the film. I had access to Lexis/Nexis since I worked in a law office, and I was able to get things like Brandon's police records and all kinds of research that I could have never afforded on my own.

After I finished the short version of the film someone suggested that I show the project to Christine Vachon, an independent producer who was working in New York. My friend Rose Troche, who directed a film called *Go Fish*, introduced me to her. Christine was familiar with the story and was happy to meet with me about it. When I started to tell her why I thought it should be a feature she asked me what I thought about her trying to raise

$200,000 for me to make the film. I almost fell out of my chair because that was more money than I had ever imagined I would have to work on the film. She sent me to a film market in Rotterdam in the Netherlands called the Rotterdam Cinemart, and she set up meetings with people where I would tell my story in the hope that they would give me money to make the film. I had never been to a pitch meeting before and I didn't know anything about it. I showed people footage of the dailies that I had shot and I felt that I got a genuinely good response to them. Then people would ask me who was going to direct the film and I told them that I was going to do it. They asked me what else I had directed and I told them a short and nothing else.

Ultimately I didn't raise any money from Rotterdam. People thought that the directing in the short film was good, but they didn't think that the girl passed as a boy. I think that they were also skeptical about my ability to direct the film since I had never made a feature before. I came back from Rotterdam and knew that I had to rewrite the script, but I also knew that I needed to find a girl who could pass as a boy as much as Brandon did. As painful as it was I had to replace the actress who was in the short.

I continued working with Christine trying to put the film together, and our budget kept increasing. First it was $200,000, then it was $300,000, then $500,000, then $1 million. The budget was always increasing, but we were never bringing in any money. Four years went by and I didn't think that we were ever going to get the money. I was still working at the law firm when I got a telephone call saying that the project had been given a green light by a studio and that I had to go to L.A. for some meetings. So I quit my job and went off to Hollywood. I met with people, everyone was very enthusiastic, and then a month went by and nobody called me back. Then I was told that the project was dead and not going to be made. Thankfully I got my job at the law firm back since they liked me so much and probably felt sorry for me. Then I was called again and told that the project had a green light, and then again I was told it didn't, and then I just kind of gave up on it. I figured that since I had a decent job at the law firm, I should just continue working there and start another screenplay. The week I made that decision Christine called me up and told me that the film was really gonna happen. And that time it did.

CAN YOU TELL ME A LITTLE BIT ABOUT THE CASTING PROCESS?
Finding a girl who could pass as Brandon on screen was key, and when we found her it was an event. We needed someone who had the charm and charisma not only to pass as a boy, but to gain entrance into people's lives. I was getting tapes from all over the country from people who were transgendered and transsexual that could pass as boys, but couldn't act in the way that I needed. There were actors who didn't want to take the role because in

1996 it was considered taboo. But by 1998, somehow the cultural tide had turned and it was now cool to be queer and I was flooded with people. But I was getting tapes from so many girls who didn't have an ounce of masculinity in them insisting that they wanted to play the role. Then there were others who were very effeminate, who would never give a thought to passing as a boy or being tomboyish and they would try to convince me that they could do it.

"Lower your sexuality. Find a dick. Find your masculinity. Find your desire to be dominant." This became my mantra. These girls spent all this time in front of a mirror acting like boys, stuffing their pants, but they still didn't have any butch in them. Once we were green-lit, after three years of looking for a lead actress and all the ups and downs of the project, I went into Christine's office seven weeks before shooting and I told her that I didn't think we could find anyone to do the part. It was then that we received a tape of someone named Hilary Swank. Her smile won us over and we knew we had a candidate. She flew herself out to California and she passed as a boy to the guard of our office building downstairs. The guard called up and said, "Louis is here." So Hilary walked in and sat down next to me to ask me what I thought, and I thought she was pretty damn good. I brought her into a room with seven people and she blew everyone away. I thought that we had found our girl, and I hired her and I took her to get her hair cut.

After they cut her hair we had this gorgeous teen icon before us who was a cross between Matt Damon and Leonardo DiCaprio. I thought, Oh my god, we can shoot the movie right now and we will have all of the fifteen-year-old girls completely in love with this character. I knew that if Brandon had blond hair he would have gotten beat up as a fag. So I had them dye Hilary's hair a chestnut brown color. I sat very nervously as people were drying her hair. She was staring back at me; I was a nervous wreck. All of a sudden they were done, and I looked at Hilary. It was the first time I saw the Brandon that I was thinking about. Then Hilary stared at me and she got really cocky for the first time, because up until then she had been kind of self-deprecating and unsure. She said, "You didn't think I could do it, did you?" At that moment my Brandon was born because Hilary was so self-confident looking at herself in the mirror and she knew that it was gonna work. Then I had her go off and live off as a boy for six weeks. During this time she changed physically and became this new entity in the world that was kind of a combination of Hilary and Brandon. I think that passing as a boy brought out a deeper beauty in her.

Brendan Sexton was always my choice for Tom. I loved him. The hardest part to cast was Lana. By now we had Brandon and you'd think that that would be the hardest thing to get. Once you get the boy who passes as the girl you would think it would be easy to find a girlfriend since they are a dime a dozen. But we couldn't find anybody who had the qualities that Lana had in real life. Everybody either seemed phony or too put together. Hilary was half of the equation and the other half was Lana. None of the girls that I had seen had the depth that the character needed.

I heard that Chloe Sevigny had wanted to play Brandon. Then after we cast Hilary, Chloe wanted to be Lana and she kept petitioning for the role, but I didn't think it was quite right for her. Finally I was out in Texas location scouting, and Christine called me to say that Chloe had been telling everyone that she got the role. And I said, "It is not her role and this is not some cool downtown movie; this is somebody's life." I didn't even want to hear about it. I had offered the part to Sarah Polley, but she turned us down, saying she didn't think she was right. And everyone was saying that I should let Chloe do it. When I finally asked her to come in to audition she said that she didn't want to audition. I told her that she couldn't be considered unless she auditioned. She relented, and we scheduled her to fly to Texas, but she canceled at the last minute. This was getting quite frustrating. I asked her agents to send me all of her work since I didn't meet with her in person, but I knew I had to consider her seriously. In *The Last Days of Disco*, there is a moment on the train when music comes on and Chloe dances with a very seductive look in her eyes; that was Lana's character. She was a shy innocent girl with a tough exterior who could appear powerful, but really was scared of intimacy and needed to be led through it. I hired Chloe based upon the tapes. When it came time for the first rehearsal I had all of my characters. Hilary had been passing as a boy for six weeks and she looked like a boy. Chloe had become Lana.

LET'S TALK ABOUT PREPRODUCTION AND THE FILMING.

We received the financing for the film in July of 1998, but it was a bit of a complicated situation since we didn't get all of the financing at once. We were on a very expedited schedule, and I was in the middle of a rewrite trying to make a few things work. I had been making the margins wide and the font really small since I wasn't using a standard script format and I didn't know any better. Everyone was telling me the script was too long, but my page count said 120 pages. Since it was improperly formatted, in reality it was 145. People kept telling me to cut the script because I would only have one month to film it, but we weren't cutting it.

We began shooting, and for a week everything was going really well, but then a mandate was given that I could only shoot twelve-hour days. The second day I went fourteen hours. But the problem was that a crew needs turnaround time, or down time between when we stop shooting and when we start again, and that was mandated at ten hours for the crew and twelve for the actors. What this meant was that the more overtime we racked up, the more delay there would be in starting again. So after a while, we wouldn't start shooting until the middle of the day, and we'd have to shoot day scenes at night, so the schedule got out of control.

It was then that I was told that I had to do an interview with the Independent Film Channel. They were going to fly down to the set and watch me direct. I told everyone that I didn't have time, but then I learned that the IFC had just given us a million dollars. I was a bit confused about why we needed the money, but it was then that I learned that we had never had enough financing in the first place, and that production was about to be shut down. IFC had seen a set of dailies and put up the money needed for completion. Needless to say, I was astounded. The shoot proved to be murderous, and we lost 25 percent of the scenes we had planned. I didn't think the movie was gonna make it. I loved the story and I would have died for it, but the process was excruciating.

WHAT WAS THE POSTPRODUCTION PROCESS LIKE?
I was surprised at how much I had actually filmed given the insanity of the shoot. I was taken to a nice lunch, and then my producers showed me the schedule. They wanted my first cut in five weeks, which is quite impossible to do. I went home and sat down with forty hours of dailies and watched all of them. We didn't get to watch dailies on set because we didn't have the money, so this was the first time I was seeing the footage. From that I started making a rough cut in my head. The first cut I turned in was four hours long. Then I got to a point where the film had run out of money for post, yet the movie was three hours and forty-five minutes long. People were pushing me to release it, but Christine said it had to be under two hours. We had to get additional funds to complete it, but Christine said that the only thing I could do to make this happen would be to work double shifts and edit all day and all night to cut together a trailer. Then they would try to pre-sell the film to certain territories based on that trailer.

I came up with a twenty-minute trailer and we sent it to Sundance. I knew that this trailer was the lifeline of my movie, and if we didn't pre-sell the movie that I would get kicked off of the project. One day I got a call from Christine and she told me to leave the editing room because she had to tell me something. Fox Searchlight had bought the film for $5 million. I was of course ecstatic, but I was also concerned that they might object to the violence and gay material of the film and try to tone it down. Christine was very honest and said that there were no guarantees. I was now working with a studio and the best thing I could do was to get to know them and make them happy. That was a moment of real terror for me because suddenly it wasn't my movie anymore; I didn't have control. That happened in January of 1999 and the film came out in October 1999. It was a difficult nine months but, in the end, Fox did protect my work. In a strange way that experience was just like going to film school and just like going to Sundance. It was never my ambition to be a studio film director, but my movie had been acquired by a studio, and I had to learn all the language of negotiating with a studio to protect it.

HOW WAS THE FILM RECEIVED?
The film went to the Venice Film Festival in September as well as Toronto and New York. The first time we saw the film we were all together in Venice watching it. We were given a standing ovation. Everyone in the audience looked up at all of us in the balcony and we all started crying. When I think back to why I did this, why I made this film, I think that I did it because I love the character and I love the story. That screening at Venice provoked the most emotional experience I've ever had, and I suddenly realized that I had touched people and that Brandon was no longer mine. We hadn't yet gotten our *Variety* review (which is the one that sets the precedent), but we were sitting at lunch and one of our producers gets on the Internet and downloads it and starts reading it aloud. That review was laudatory and basically put the film on the map.

The film opened on two screens. Roger Ebert and David Denby really supported the film and they acknowledged Hilary's performance. We started picking up good reviews, and then we started picking up Oscar buzz about Hilary after the New York Film Festival. I went to all the Fox people to thank them and to tell them that this had been the greatest experience of my life because I thought it was over. But the film stayed in theaters from October until June. Eight months of play time is very rare. I think that it was because Hilary and Chloe did a lot of press, the studio really pumped the film, and the critics really kept it alive. I went all over the country promoting it in major cities and then I went all over the world.

THE OSCAR AWARD FOR HILARY . . . HOW DID IT FEEL TO HAVE CREATED SOMETHING LIKE THAT?
What was crazy was that I had never given much thought to the possibility of winning an Oscar or any of that stuff. I lived in an insulated world of creating the character and nothing else. Hilary won every single critics award and she was just on a fabulous winning streak. Then the nomination was announced, and that was just amazing in and of itself. It was extraordi-

nary to be invited to the Oscars and to attend it. I was walking along the red carpet and Joan Rivers asked me about the movie and I said, "I interviewed every butch lesbian and every transsexual . . ." and all of our cell phones went off because I had just said "butch lesbian" and "transsexual" on the red carpet. My friends were calling to congratulate us for bringing that to mainstream television. Then when I heard, "The Oscar goes to Hilary Swank," I remember my knees went numb. I felt the same as I did in that anonymous moment in Japan when I was on the train. I had done a lot of work, but now the thing was beyond me. It was as if they had given Brandon the Oscar. I thought back over the past six years to when I fell in love with Brandon Teena, who was a kid in a trailer park who didn't have any money and didn't have any role models. I never thought that people would ever really understand or identify with his story, even though it was always my aspiration to make them do so. But the Oscar was a great seal of approval, and I just thought that now Brandon was in the history books.

TO WHAT DO YOU ATTRIBUTE YOUR SUCCESS?

I believe that you are born with a certain will. The emotional truth of the journey that I went on always made sense to me. I fell in love with Brandon, and knew I had to make a movie about him, and from then on it was simply about pursuing that goal, whatever the obstacles that I endured in the process: The obstacle of the studio that said yes and then bailed; the obstacle of not finding Hilary for a long time; the obstacle of getting the script right. Those were real obstacles but they led me on a deeper journey. I couldn't have foreseen the footsteps that I have taken, but my success makes sense because it is part of a deeper thing. Being queer and having the type of education and upbringing that I had was so intense that there was such a need for me to seek out my own identity and I was always in line for making movies. As a cultural product I make sense. I am a cultural product of the times and a conduit for this story to be told. There is a miraculous logic to it and there is also a lot of good luck in it. Even though there are times when I think that it is too good to be true, I realize that it all makes sense in a strange way.

It is important for me to be true to myself. I have a need to express my own identity through film character. I think that all of those filmmakers that we love are personal filmmakers—they tell a story about themselves through their work. *Mean Streets* is Scorsese erupting through the time and place that he was born. You can say the same thing for Nick Ray. I think that this is what accounts for success. You have to be in a constant struggle to express your deepest inner life, and translate that into the characters you create. I needed to make *Boys Don't Cry* in order to come closer to my true identity, for my own well-being and sense of self-understanding. There was an urgency for me to make the movie that wasn't based on possible success in Hollywood. It was based on my need to express myself. Success was a by-product of the result; if I had simply pursued success alone I don't think it would have worked.

WHAT ADVICE DO YOU HAVE FOR ASPIRING FILMMAKERS?

You must be really clear about what turns you on about movies, and I think that is what studying film did for me. You need to figure out what you respond to because that will likely dictate where you can create. If you constantly educate yourself, then that will help bring you more in line to what you are drawn to and what you're capable of. Learn everything you can about dramatic conflict, working with actors and story and character so that you have a handle on the process. If you make good work you can succeed. It depends upon how you define success, but if you make work that is satisfying to you then you are already successful. After I leave here today, I'm going to go home and work on my new screenplay. Even though I have a studio deal, and many great things in place, today is successful if I end up writing a good scene. You can't focus on external success, you really just have to focus on the mechanics of your creation. Did I make that character clearer today? Did I make that story clear? Am I passionate about this? Will other people be passionate about it too? If you make a good film then everybody will want to see it. When you entertain people they are satisfied.

I think that writing is crucial to the process of directing. You won't walk onto a set and make a great movie if you don't have a great character and a great structure in place. It all goes back to Aristotle, dramatic structure, three acts, etcetera. There is a certain momentum that you need for a film in the same way that your car needs an engine. The more you study screen-writing and the more you study acting you will see that.

Young artists tend to get so caught up in that question, "Am I talented? Do I have it?" That can be the most damaging question of all. You can't focus on that. It has nothing to do with the work. Who's to judge whether you have talent or not? Only time will do that. You may make a movie and it might not work. Then you make another movie and it might be wildly successful and have nothing to do with the first movie. These are irrelevant distractions; it is important to be truthful to what is satisfying to you. If it is meant to happen it will happen. If the work is good, then it will find its way into the world because that is what happens with good work. If you work hard and you are good at what you do, then people are naturally going to want to work with you and they will seek you out. As far as social connections go, they will just happen naturally. There is an extraordinary amount of shared passion about this medium. I was just on the set of Martin Scorsese's film *Gangs of New York*. Not only was it a privilege to watch him direct and hear his passion for film, but also there was a shared passion for film among everybody on the set.

I feel extraordinarily lucky to be able to do what I do, and I think that film is a great medium. I think that there is a cultural rebirth happening right now in filmmaking and hopefully it won't get snuffed out. Hopefully the artists who are making exciting films now will keep following their passion to represent their desires and questions on screen because film is only exciting when something is really different. The experience of walking into a movie theater and going somewhere you didn't expect to go—that is what I hope to create with my films. I make films because they make me happier than anything else in the world. I feel lucky to be alive during this time because had I been alive one hundred years before now, I wouldn't have had movies.

Vincenzo Natali | CUBE

VINCENZO NATALI *was born in Detroit, Michigan, in 1969 and grew up in Toronto, Canada. He dropped out of Ryerson film school to work as an animator at Melvana Studios for a few years, until he applied to and was accepted at the Canadian Film Center. While there he made the short film* Elevated, *which led to the financing of his first film,* Cube, *a smart science-fiction thriller released in 1998 to a warm reception from both critics and the box office. Natali is single and lives in Toronto and Los Angeles.*

I think of myself as a Canadian since I spent my entire life there. Toronto is a very clean, efficient, and well-run city but it's not the most adventurous place in the world. I think that one of the reasons I became interested in making movies was because it was a way to escape to a creative fantasy world. My dad was a photographer and my mom was a nursery school teacher and painter. I have two half-sisters and one brother from my father's second marriage. My parents divorced when I was very young and my mother moved to Toronto, where I grew up. I have this very Italian name but I grew up with my mom, who is a British-Canadian WASP; I was a little bit disenfranchised from my Italian roots. But it was a great environment and I had a really happy childhood. Many of the people I work with now on my films were childhood friends of mine.

WHEN DID YOU START GETTING INTERESTED IN FILM?

You could consider me a *Star Wars* baby because I'm one of those kids who saw that movie and was heavily influenced by it. I think that that was the movie that really made me want to make films. I also grew up at a time when Super-8 was popular, and I really got into the filmmaking process just playing around with such a great camera. When I was eleven I made my first Super-8 short film with my friend André Bijelic, who later became the cowriter on my film *Cube*. He had a Super-8 camera and he wanted to make a James Bond movie, so we started playing around, filming stuff on the weekends. When we got to our teenage years we began to take things really seriously, and every summer we would make a movie. We were nerds in the truest sense of the word; we didn't socialize much and we just wanted to make films.

WHAT WERE YOUR INITIAL THOUGHTS ON HOW TO PURSUE FILMMAKING AS A CAREER?

Because I was fairly young when I realized I wanted to make movies, I had a lot of time to think about how to get into that field. I knew it would be very difficult. There are just about as many movie theaters in Toronto as there are in New York, but at that time not a lot of film production existed in Toronto. Canada certainly did not have a reputation as a country that produced movies. The only reputation Canada really had at that time came from the National Film Board, which exclusively made real-life documentary films. There really wasn't a template for me to follow, there was no one really to look around at as a role model.

I thought a lot about how I might be able to make my first film. I only wish that there had been a book like this one available because everybody at some point wonders how to do it and it would have been really helpful to see how others have done it. This is nothing like becoming a doctor or a lawyer because there really isn't a specific process that you can follow that will guarantee you a job as a film director. It became evident to me early on that there was no one way to do it. I think part of the decision about how I chose to get into film was based on the type of movies I wanted to make. I always knew that even though I have relatively mainstream tastes, I wanted to make films that were a little bit left of center, films that were "independent" for lack of a better word. I thought about people like David Lynch and the Coen brothers, filmmakers that I admired. David Cronenberg, who is based in Toronto, was also a big influence on me. He is a very independent filmmaker who makes the kinds of movies that I am interested in making. It seemed to me that all of them got their break by making low-budget movies that made enough of an impression on people that they could slowly build their careers. There are people like Lawrence Kasdan who made their reputation as a writer first and then were given an opportunity to direct, but I thought that the most direct approach to becoming a filmmaker was to make a film. That's ultimately what happened, but it was a very circuitous and tricky path that led me to that point.

My impression of how to get into the film business is that you have to be tenacious and willing to suffer a lot to get the resources that you need to make a movie. You just have to persevere. For me it seemed pretty obvious that there was no easy answer and that there was no simple way of doing it. I knew going into it that it was going to be a long haul and it still is.

There was no doubt in my mind that I wanted to go to film school and that is what I did. I studied at a film school in Toronto called Ryerson. It was a very hands-on polytechnic school. I wasn't very interested in film theory—I just wanted to get my hands on a camera and start shooting. Ultimately I was disappointed by the experience. I felt like we weren't doing enough work and that some people in the program were there playing the role of a filmmaker rather than making films. They seemed more interested in their image as a filmmaker than in films themselves. I left the program early after a year and a half, and I ended up working at an animation studio for five years to support myself.

I worked as a storyboard artist at a studio called Melvana that did a lot of Saturday morning cartoons. As a storyboard artist I would take a script, and break it down into shots and block it. Essentially I was directing except that I had the advantage of working under a director, so I could present my work to him and he could give me input on what I had done. I learned a lot about classic narrative storytelling through this experience. With Saturday morning cartoons you had to be as concise and simple as possible in the way that you blocked the action because cartoons are limited animation and you can't do very expressive or complicated things. You have to get an idea across in a way that won't be too complicated for the animators. That was useful because it taught me how to convey something cinematically in the most economic way. It also helped me learn how to translate words from a page into shots, and that's what a director does. That is one of the most important skills you can learn, particularly if you are a narrative director. If you are telling a classic narrative story, then there is a real language that goes along with that kind of storytelling. I have found that this is important to know even if you don't use it. That job was a form of film school for me, and it was great because I was paid to do it, and I was able to use that money to finance a couple of short films that I had been working on.

I made a few simple short films that I finished on 16mm, and I submitted them to the Canadian Film Center, an advanced film school that was started about ten years ago by the Canadian director Norman Jewison. CFC was modeled after the American Film Institute. Getting accepted was a lucky break because it carried a certain prestige in Canada, and it was an opportunity for me to meet a really great group of like-minded filmmakers. It also gave me the opportunity to make another short film with a professional crew in a professional situation. Up until that time I had only made films with my own money using whomever I could bribe into participating. This was a chance to really make a professional piece of film. So I applied to make a short film and was accepted.

WHAT WAS THE SHORT THAT YOU MADE?

It was called *Elevated*. I had already written the script for *Cube* at the point, but I didn't think anyone was gonna make my feature yet. I decided to take some of the ideas from *Cube* and put them into a short. The result was that after I finished *Elevated*, people at the Film Center really liked it, and through this film they began to understand what *Cube* was about. This short was really the deciding factor that made them ultimately say yes to the feature.

WHEN DID YOU WRITE THE SCRIPT FOR *CUBE*?

I had the idea in 1990 but I didn't have a draft of the script until 1993. The concept came from a few different places. First of all, it came from the need to shoot in just one space, which is what I knew was all I would probably be able to afford for my first feature. I was trying to compose a story that would take place on one set with a few characters. The challenge for me was in doing a film that wouldn't feel like a play. I'm a visual person, and I wanted to tell a story that had movement in it. So it occurred to me that one set could double as many. That led me to think of a room that is composed of identical rooms, and that made me think of a maze, a mathematical maze like an M. C. Escher type of environment. At the same time I was interested in telling a story that took place in Hell, and I thought it would be interesting to write a story that entirely took place in a hostile environment for which there was no context. We didn't start in the real world; we just began the film in this nightmarish realm. It took a long time to devise a story that would sustain as a feature-length film in that kind of environment.

When I initially wrote it on my own, it was more whimsical and mythologically based. It was very much like *Alice in Wonderland* or like Terry Gilliam's work, with more fantasy and less science fiction. Unfortunately the script had problems, and it wasn't working because the story was too complicated. I showed it to my roommate Andre. He read the script, and he knew exactly why it didn't work. We decided to work together rewriting this script. Andre found the core of the story and brought it out. He really streamlined the script. The film became much more about the mathematics and less about the fantasy. It took us about six months to rewrite.

DID YOU WRITE *CUBE* BECAUSE YOU WERE INSPIRED OR BECAUSE YOU WANTED SOMETHING THAT COULD LEAD YOU INTO DIRECTING?

There were moments of inspiration, but my motivation was really based on the fact that I wanted to make a feature film. That's how the idea started and that's what really pushed me through to the end of the process. I could never write a film that I wasn't excited to make, and didn't think that I would make. I have yet to have a day where I wake up and I am suddenly seized by an idea that is so brilliant that I have to translate it into a screenplay. The way I work is fairly disciplined. I sit down in an empty room and I start thinking and writing ideas down. That is just the way it works for me.

LETS TALK A LITTLE BIT ABOUT THE SHORT FILM AND THE PROCESS OF CREATING THAT. YOU HAD THESE IDEAS FROM *CUBE* AND YOU WANTED TO EXPRESS THEM. HOW DID THAT COME ABOUT?

I was interested in taking a confined space and treating it like a vast landscape. There are surprisingly a lot of interesting visual opportunities in a very confined environment. You don't see people make use of them very often in movies. I was really intrigued by the image of a group of people trapped in a box. My short film takes place in an elevator, so I was really able to play around with what seems to be a very mundane environment by giving it a slightly skewed treatment. You can do that when you are in a confined space because you are able to establish the space very quickly. The people watching the film understand the geography of an elevator very fast, so that gives you license to start doing unusual things with that space visually without it becoming confusing. With *Elevated* I threw in the kitchen sink—I added every crazy visual idea that I had into one little movie.

WHICH DIRECTORS HAVE INFLUENCED YOU VISUALLY?

I'm influenced by comic book artists and painters as well as filmmakers like Alfred Hitchcock, David Lynch, Peter Greenaway, and Stanley Kubrick. Kubrick I think is the one who really affected me visually. Certainly there are a lot of great oldies that I'm sure everybody references like Federico Fellini and Ingmar Bergman, but from the time I grew up there were the Coen brothers, James Cameron, and Ridley Scott. All of these directors have done films that I admire.

The short was a great learning process. But I think that each subsequent film continues to be also. One of the wonderful and terrible things about filmmaking is that you are always a student and never a master. There is just too much to learn. Every time I make a film it is a quantum leap, and my struggle has consistently been to get the film made. Sometimes I feel like I have failed miserably and I'm not prolific at all. It has always been difficult for me to get my films financed for a variety of reasons. I would really like to make more films because every time I make a film I feel like I improve dramatically as a filmmaker. The irritating thing about being a filmmaker is that it is expensive. A painter or writer can always practice his craft. Filmmaking, even for the smallest film, is an expensive process and a logistically complex undertaking that requires an enormous amount of energy. In many respects, I think the film directors of the Golden Age were a lot more fortunate than we are now because they would just crank stuff out. They all made fifty or more movies during their careers. Making a movie in Hollywood these days is very difficult because it is so expensive and risky. Fortunately there are new avenues opening up every day, like digital technology. That's very exciting because you can shoot a film and edit it on your home computer. I'm really excited about that prospect.

WHAT HAPPENED AFTER YOU FINISHED *ELEVATED*?
I made *Elevated* right after I graduated from the directing program. I think the film was well received because it was not typical of the type of film that the Film Center made at that time. It was a flat-out horror movie. Most of the stuff that they made was more drama and character based, so I think my film stood out for that reason. The film's warm reception was the best thing that could have happened to me because it opened the door to getting *Cube* financed. I submitted the script for *Cube* to the Feature Film Project at the Canadian Film Center. At that time they were doing three films every two years. I had submitted *Cube* twice before, but they had turned me down both times. Everyone had a difficult time visualizing the film. The common complaint was that it would be visually monotonous to watch a group of people trapped in a series of cubes for an hour and a half. But once they saw *Elevated* they really understood what I wanted to do, and that opened the door for me to do the feature. I was enormously lucky. Although we didn't have much time and money, I had complete artistic control, and I'm sure I will never have that again, at least not to that degree. Most people don't get to make their first feature that way.

WERE THERE ANY PEOPLE WHO WERE PARTICULARLY HELPFUL IN MAKING *CUBE* HAPPEN?
Norman Jewison was really supportive of me. He has always been good to me as well as to a lot of other people who went through the program. The artistic director there, Dejous Madeyar—who used to be the artistic director at the AFI and who I believe is now back at the AFI—was also really helpful. When the film was finished we invited David Cronenberg to come see it and he was really supportive as well. He gave us some wonderful quotes, which we used to help sell the film. Overall Toronto is probably one of the best places for a filmmaker who is just starting out. In Canada the govern-

ment and the film industry itself are incredibly supportive of filmmakers. Now there is actually quite a substantial catalog of feature films that have been produced in Canada over the past ten to twenty years, and I feel fortunate to have been a part of that system.

HOW DID YOU CONVINCE THE BOARD TO GREEN-LIGHT THE FILM?
I worked hard to impress them. I built a model of the cube, and I made a proposal that was full of images, drawings, and storyboards. I wanted to make the strongest impression that I could. There wasn't any formal process to apply other than giving the Feature Film Project your script and crossing your fingers. I was tenacious and I probably irritated them enough that they finally got sick of hearing from me and let me do the project. It's a very unique situation and I don't know of any program like that anywhere else in the world.

The financing was complicated because half of the film's costs were given in the form of deferrals. This meant that the equipment houses, lab, cast, and crew deferred part of their salaries to help make the film. Our cash budget was somewhere in the area of $350,000 Canadian. I'm sure that if we had paid for everything it would have been over a million, but because everyone donated their time it was well under that. This was an extremely difficult movie to make given those budget parameters, and quite honestly it was not a pleasant experience. It was the hardest thing I have ever done in my life and it almost killed me. This seems crazy because you think, How hard can it be to shoot a movie in a box with six actors? In actuality it was very difficult and psychologically trying as well. Being in that confined state was worse than it appeared in the movie, because in the film there were six people trapped in the cube but in reality we had thirty six people trapped in the cube. It was made under great duress, and we did not know how we were going to finish the film after we started shooting. We knew going into the project that we didn't have enough money or time to do what we wanted to do, but we also felt that we had a great opportunity and that we should make the most of the situation. Because of all of the people who helped us out we were able to pull it off. Unfortunately, now I can't even look at the movie because all I see are the flaws.

TELL ME A LITTLE BIT ABOUT THE CASTING PROCESS.
It was a very traditional casting process with the exception that two of the roles were written for friends of mine. The character Worth was written for David Hewlett, who is a friend I have known since high school. He has been in every movie I have done and will be in every movie I will ever make. Andrew Miller, who is also a friend, played the role of the savant. The other roles were cast from the local talent pool. It was great because I got all of

my first choices. They may not be names that people are familiar with but they are all very experienced actors who have worked extensively, particularly in television. This was helpful to us because we were shooting on less than a television schedule, so they were terrific and would never flub their lines. I rarely had to do a retake because of an actor's mistake. This was very important and I think that that was one of the reasons we were able to get the film done. One of the nice things about how the Feature Film Project structured the program was that it was really a professional shoot. Even though we didn't have much money, the Feature Film Project had agreements with the unions so we were able to use a mixture of union and nonunion crew. We were also able to use Canadian unionized actors as well. We got the best young talent that was out there. Virtually everyone who worked on the film was in their twenties, and for most people it was their first time doing a feature.

WHERE DID YOU FIND YOUR CINEMATOGRAPHER?

My cinematographer was Derrick Rogers, who was someone that I met while I was at the Film Center. A producer who did one of my workshop projects introduced him to me. He shot *Elevated*, which was a perfect dress rehearsal for *Cube*, since we were dealing with many of the same elements. I was immediately taken by how cooperative he was, since most cinematographers that I had worked with before were difficult. I always felt that they were fighting me and fighting the process of getting the film completed, and it seemed like they were more concerned about how the film looked than how it would ultimately turn out when it was finished. Derrick was a very good cinematographer, but more importantly he understood the process of collaboration. He saw the big picture and understood what compromises were necessary in order for the film to be made for that kind of budget. He was very practical and the kind of person we needed to pull off a movie that was being shot on such a tight schedule.

DO YOU REMEMBER THE FIRST DAY OF SHOOTING *CUBE*?

It was one of the worst days of my life. It was just terrible. The set was completed and I had storyboarded the whole film. We were ready to go, but there was just one small problem with the set: the doors would not open. In the film there are six doors in each room, one on each wall. Throughout the movie the characters are opening and closing the doors and going through hatches. Unfortunately these were not typical doors that would just open and close. The door mechanism was a complex and rather tricky piece of engineering modeled after a van door. There hadn't been time to properly test these doors out, so on the first day we physically could not open them. It was devastating. So I had to throw out all my storyboards and improvise new shots to get around the fact that I couldn't show a door opening on camera. We started off on a bad note and by the evening we had a very serious meeting with the executive producer about whether the production should be shut down or not. Shutting down the production meant killing the whole movie because we didn't have enough money to just start over again. We made the decision to shoot the only sequence in the film where very few doors are opened or closed, which was dramatically the most intense scene. It was a testament to the professionalism of the actors that they were able to get through such intense dialogue considering they got a call at midnight telling them that they would be shooting scenes from the middle of the movie.

Cube started off on the wrong foot and things got worse from there. Every day there was some seemingly insurmountable crisis and the only thing that kept me going through the whole process was the thought that if I could finish the movie then maybe I would get a chance to make another one. I thought that if I didn't finish the film I was dead and my career would be over. I felt as if I was making the worst film of all time and it was very disappointing to me because I had carefully planned everything out and nothing was going according to plan. I thought that it would be so straightforward since everything was to take place in one environment. We weren't moving from one location to another and we didn't have to deal with weather, so it didn't seem like there would be any extenuating circumstances that would pop up. Of course, that was not the case. Every day I was throwing out half of my shots and every evening I was going over my shot list with Derrick deciding the simplest way to shoot each scene. Strangely enough this ultimately helped the film because it forced me to make certain editorial decisions that I may not have made in postproduction. I think that this was healthy for the film because it pushed me into being more efficient and concise in my direction. If I had had an unlimited budget, the film would have been much more baroque and maybe I would have been indulgent in ways that would have hurt the film. I was forced to be very economical. I believe that the strength of the film has always been its simplicity. We realized this when we were writing the script and it really became our mantra throughout production and right into postproduction. Ultimately we were able to use some of the budgetary limitations to our advantage. That being said, when I look at the movie now there are many things that I would have done differently if we had had more money.

HOW WAS THE POSTPRODUCTION PROCESS?

The postproduction process was great. I loved it. I like production, but it's always frustrating because I'm never able to get exactly what I want. Postproduction is different because I have the time to think and make decisions more carefully. I can also experiment and try different things. For *Cube* we actually had a fairly luxurious postproduction schedule, which was great. The shoot was twenty days but it took about six months to finish the film. During shooting I always feel like I'm giving up control, but in preproduction and postproduction you have absolute control. At least you do when you make a film through a film school. I'm sure if I was to make a movie with a studio I wouldn't have that control and then the postproduction process would also become very frustrating. I would suddenly have to answer to people who have a stake in how the film performs financially and who have the power to change the movie as they wish. In that regard *Cube* was an ideal experience because I had final cut.

WHAT WAS THE RELEASE STRATEGY?

We decided to premiere the film at the Toronto Film Festival. It has a great reputation internationally and has been consistently supportive of Canadian talent. At that point we had already secured a Canadian distributor and our strategy was to try to find an American distributor to pick it up. Ultimately, a company called Trimark bought it. This was great because I was not even expecting a U.S. theatrical release at all. It was a very limited release, but the amazing thing was that *Cube* found an audience around the world. It had a theatrical release in virtually every major territory. The more work I do and the more films I see my friends making, the more I realize how much luck plays into whether or not a film gets made as well as whether or not it is a success. *Cube* got the kind of response it did in part because it was in the right place at the right time. I was hoping that it would do the festival circuit, but I was skeptical since it is a science-fiction movie. I was afraid people were going to take a snobbish attitude and not program it. Actually the opposite happened because it was the type of independent film that doesn't get made very often. It was exciting for people to program the film in their festivals because it was so different. The film also went through the plethora of science-fiction, fantasy, and horror festivals that exist throughout the world.

HOW WAS THE RECEPTION?

Overall the reception was very good, but the first review we got was the worst review I have ever read for any movie. They called it "overstylized sci-fi dung." We got our worst reviews in Toronto for some reason, but ultimately the reception at the festivals was really positive and we picked up an award for best first feature film. That felt great. I had never won an award for a film before so it was very exciting and I feel that it really legitimized the film. A lot of people had a hard time understanding what the movie was supposed to be because it was not the kind of movie that gets made in

Canada very often. I think the Canadian distributor was uncomfortable with it and I think that even the Film Center was uncomfortable with it. Once we got that award and found some acceptance, then they really started to support it.

Making *Cube* had an enormous effect on my confidence level, because it was so difficult to get that opportunity. I got to shoot the movie that I wanted to make, and I didn't have to do some cheesy horror film sequel or something like that. I got to make a movie that was a little bit left of center that was my vision and mine alone. The thing that's been hard is getting a second project going that is equally original and personal and that can be made with that level of freedom.

HOW DID THE FILM PERFORM AT THE BOX OFFICE?
It did very poorly in the United States and even worse in Canada. But it did extremely well in France and in Japan, as well as in every other foreign territory for a variety of reasons. I think that foreign distributors understood the movie better, and they knew that this was a movie for sci-fi geeks like me. I don't think that the American distributor or the Canadian distributor understood who the core audience was. Even though this is a genre movie, it's a little bit difficult to categorize. It became difficult for the distributors to know what to do with it, and this is something I've learned about distributors: They really need a template for what the movie is in order to understand how to market it. They are not very good at taking movies, like this one, that are original but aren't art movies and finding a marketplace for them. This is still a problem for me. I have a number of projects now that I have been trying to make and it has been difficult to find support for them because they are similar to *Cube* in that they are science-fiction movies but they aren't easily comparable to existing films. In Europe there is more of a tradition for this type of science fiction. *Cube* is an escapist movie, but it has a certain cerebral content and it has a very dark ending. It's a little bit strange because you are never told when or where the movie is taking place and some of the questions are left unanswered. I think those aspects of the film are hard for an American distributor to digest. Europeans are used to ambiguity; in fact, they thrive on it. In France and in Japan there is a great tradition of serious adult science fiction in literature and in comic books. So I don't think it was difficult for those distributors to imagine the audience.

WHAT DO YOU THINK WAS THE GREATEST THING YOU LEARNED ON THIS FILM?
The power of simplicity. I think I learned that the film always got better the simpler we made it. Even after the script had been written and we had to eliminate a particular special effect or stunt because we couldn't afford it, we were forced to replace it with a character feat. That improved the script.

It was always a question of reducing the script rather than adding to it, and that always improved the movie. I think I learned to think on my feet more, which is something you have to do when you don't have a lot of money to work with. Even when you do have the money I believe that filmmaking is the art of compromise. It's about coming up with a compromise that doesn't feel like a compromise in order to get the film done.

HOW HAS THE FILM AFFECTED YOUR FUTURE CAREER?

I have an agent in Canada and in the United States. I've met a lot of people here in Los Angeles and in Canada thanks to *Cube*. Doing the film opened many many doors, but it's still a challenge. I think for anybody, no matter how experienced they are and no matter what kind of reputation they have, it is very difficult in this marketplace to make an original movie that is a little bit risky. My burden is to try to make another movie that is as original as the first one but with a little bit more money.

I go around now to meetings with potential producers all the time. In fact that's all I do. I find it very hard to find time to write because I spend just so much time meeting people. Unfortunately you have to do it because it is the only way. I enjoy meeting really interesting people, so I don't resent having to do that. There is one lesson that I have learned since I made *Cube* and that is that you should really have as many projects going on at once as is possible. I know that there is a great temptation when you are a first-time or second-time filmmaker to focus on just one thing because it is so hard to get a film made. But you have to invest yourself in a lot of different projects and you have to be flexible enough to jump from one thing to the other. That is the lesson I seem to have to learn over and over again. It is very hard for me because I don't like to do more than one thing at a time, but I don't think anyone can afford to do that. You really can't ever have enough material under your belt.

WHAT IS YOUR ADVICE TO PEOPLE WHO WANT TO BECOME FILMMAKERS? HOW CAN ONE GET STARTED?

I think that it is a very exciting time for new filmmakers because the technology has evolved in such a way that you can make a feature film now for virtually no cost. You could shoot a film on digital video, edit it on your computer, output it to videotape, and show that videotape to people. If I were starting again that's what I would do. I think you can do that or you can do two other things. If you are a good writer then you can write screenplays, and if someone is interested in your screenplay you can say that you are going to direct it. I think that that is a tried and true formula. The other way is to come to filmmaking from a side door. You can be a commercial director or you can get into television. There are many examples of commercial directors who have gone into feature filmmaking, although that approach never really appealed to me. I felt that the shortest distance between two points was a straight line and I was always inclined to make a movie that I wanted to make and use that as my calling card. You don't have to make a feature though; in fact, you could just make a short film. The point is that it is important to do something that represents you.

I know that there is a real temptation to make a movie that you think will please other people and that will fit into a category of film that is popular and would be accepted. Early in your career that's a dangerous thing to do. What people are really looking for in young filmmakers is originality. I think that they are more interested in that kind of creative energy than in technical polish. It's really about creating something that is totally mind-blowing and unique and that represents you. I'm a dinosaur quite frankly because there is a new generation of filmmakers out there that is growing up with digital cameras and Final Cut Pro software who are going to be so much more proficient than I am now just because they're able to practice. Things are more accessible to them, so I'm envious of this younger generation and I think it has a bright future. You might be able to distribute your films on the Net someday soon, and I suspect that the mystique that moviemaking has had for so long is going to begin to evaporate in light of this new technology.

There has been a tendency for the industry to make the filmmaking process mysterious and inaccessible. That has to end. Now anybody who has enough money to purchase or rent a digital camera and editing system is going to learn that making a movie is not so difficult. I think it is exciting for the people who are doing it and I think it is also exciting for the medium as a whole because it will allow people to be more expressive and more original than ever before.

HOW IMPORTANT ARE RELATIONSHIPS IN THE PROCESS OF FILMMAKING?
I think relationships are just about the most important thing. Film is by definition a collaborative medium because a film is never made by one person. It's always a very unique collaboration and that is what makes the process so much fun. It's not a lonely process, like writing a novel. It is an adventure that you get to share with others and you need friends and support around you to get through the rough times. I think one of the worst things that can happen to a young filmmaker is to be successful. It is so easy to lose yourself in the adulation that comes with making a successful first movie. One of the ways I think that can be avoided is by having a great group of friends who have known you for a long time and can help you keep your feet on the ground.

There's really no beating the film festival circuit. Festivals exist to a large extent to expose the world to new talent. They are also one of the rewards for making a film. The first time that you take your movie to a festival is one of the most exciting times of your life because you are getting to show your work to a real audience. Second of all, you will meet all kinds of people who are doing the same thing. You meet filmmakers and programmers and you are exposed to a lot of interesting films. That's the obvious route. In terms of getting exposed to the industry, you should try to get an agent because they can show your material to producers and distributors. They know all the people who might get you work. You can also be tenacious and just project your film on the street or send copies of it to famous directors. As the technology evolves you may be able to present your film on the web. That is already very possible, especially if you have a short film. You can show it on your own website or you can submit it to a web exhibitor. If they accept your film, then it is accessible to anyone who visits their site. One of the great things about the time we are living in is that the access to material is greater than it ever has been before.

Twenty years ago there really weren't a lot of independent films that were self-produced or self-financed. Now there are an infinite number of them. It is no longer special to have just made a movie; now you have to make a movie that's good or at least unique in order for it to be recognized. I don't believe that there are more talented people today than there were twenty years ago. Cream will always rise to the top. People who are truly devoted and disciplined in the process of making films will ultimately endure. That's really what it takes more than anything else. To be successful you must have the willingness to push endlessly until your work gets seen. I don't think people should be intimidated by the glut of independent films because the selection process is always going to be very competitive.

I think that "talent" is a strange word, especially when applied to filmmaking because a lot of what's required to be successful is just hard work. Obviously pure talent alone will not survive in this business because it is just too harsh. You need to be tough and you need to be able to push and push and be resilient enough to take a million rejections before you get one yes. I take comfort in that because who knows if I'm talented or not? What I do know is that I am tenacious and that I'm devoted to making movies. From this I'm guaranteed a certain level of success. I think that your talent will be recognized if you have that special ability or willingness to just trudge through the misery of getting your films made.

Buckaroo Banzai once said, "No matter where you go, there you are." One of the great lessons I have learned in this long and frustrating process of making movies is that you really have to appreciate every day that you have on the road to your destination. You have to enjoy the people around you and the process of constructing a movie. If you think too much about the endpoint, then you are setting yourself up for disappointment. Once you have made the film, the pleasure that you get from it is over because it is no longer yours and it has become its own entity. It is the process that is important, and that is what holds true for me. It is really about how you live your life rather than where it takes you. That's the secret to getting out of the *Cube*.

John Carpenter | DARK STAR

JOHN CARPENTER *was born in 1948 and grew up in Kentucky. He attended USC film school, where he made the short feature* Dark Star. *After five years of struggle, Carpenter found financing to complete the film and attained a theatrical release. His next film was* Assault on Precinct 13, *which he followed with the wildly successful* Halloween, *starring Jamie Lee Curtis. Regarded by many as the master of horror and science fiction, Carpenter's many renowned films include* Starman, Escape from New York, *and* They Live, *as well as* Ghosts of Mars, *starring Natasha Henstridge and Ice Cube.*

I was born in northern New York and I grew up in Bowling Green, Kentucky, where my father had a teaching position at the college. Growing up was very odd for me because I lived in a small Bible-belt town in the South during the Jim Crow days. It's a long way from there to Hollywood and the consensus was that I would never make it. That I'm here is against all odds.

I'm an only child. We didn't have a TV set, but my mom was a real movie hound. She would go to the movies every week and she would take me along, so that's how I got exposure to films. I just grew up watching them all the time. When I was eight years old, I took my dad's movie camera and started to make my own little films with my friends. It's kind of a familiar story to anyone who has gotten into movies. We usually all started by loving and watching them, and then making them ourselves when we were little. Some of us wanted to keep doing it forever, and some of us have.

I knew I wasn't gonna be a teacher. That was really the only other option for me, to be an English teacher or something like that. But I really just didn't have any interests other than movies, which I had always loved since I can remember. I was in a rock and roll band for a little while, but I wanted to pursue film and I figured I owed it to myself to at least give movies a try.

I applied to USC and UCLA, which were considered at the time to be two of the best film schools in the world. USC was the front-runner, and I also wanted to be in Los Angeles to see what it was like. Beyond my wildest dreams, USC accepted me.

So here it is 1968 and I'm in L.A. attending film school. Pretty quickly I realized that making films was what I had to do. I learned everything they could teach—directing, writing, everything. We had to learn how to operate the camera; we had to learn how to edit; we had to learn to work with sound. We had to project the films we shot during class; we had to work in the lab and take animation; we had to take acting courses. It was an unbelievable curriculum. USC had direct ties to Hollywood, so people like John Ford, Howard Hawks, Orson Welles, and countless others came down to lecture to us. Man, it couldn't have gotten any better than that. The big question everyone would ask most folks when they came down was, "How do I get an agent, how do I get in?" Oddly enough there was never an answer, and now I know why, having gone through it.

I started a student film at USC in 1970 and managed to scrape up enough money to finance about forty-five minutes of it. The film was called *Dark Star* and it was a science-fiction piece about a crew out in space and the things that happen to them. I wrote the script with Dan O'Bannon (who later went on to write *Alien)* based on an idea I had, and we got it down together. When the first forty-five minutes were finished, I took the film out and showed it to various distributors. Two years later, a man named Jack H. Harris decided he wanted to release the film as a feature. So he put in some finishing money and with that we completed the movie. It was released in 1975, five years after we had begun the project. Of course, when it was finished, I had the same expectations that many kids have, I thought, The movie's gonna be released, they're gonna be calling me right and left, their limo's gonna show up outside my apartment to take me to the next set, I'm ready to go. No, didn't happen. The movie was not successful at the box office, and no one seemed to care.

I never finished school. I left to work on the film, but I had to do other jobs to keep myself alive. I took editing jobs in Hollywood, I cut other people's work, and just did this and that to get by. Everybody has their own story of how they broke in. Mine is particular to me, but all of the stories have something to do with the combination of elements. First of all, it helps to have talent. It helps to have ability. It helps to have vision. It helps to have a lot of things. But what you can't buy is luck and timing. That's a whole big part of it, and I was lucky to be in the right place at the right time in a way because the one thing that *Dark Star* did get me was an agent, and this agent began encouraging me to write screenplays. That would ultimately be the way I'd get into the movie business, through writing. So I started writing and then, lo and behold, people began buying my scripts. I sold options to various people; I'd write freelance material for them, and I began to make a living as a writer. It wasn't what I wanted to do. I wanted to be a movie director; writing was not really my interest, but I could do it. And back in Hollywood, if you're good enough, you can make a pretty damn good living writing movies that nobody ever makes. At least in the old days this was true. I had options sold right and left. I was making pretty good money doing this.

Then an angel appeared. An angel with $100,000 came drifting down from the clouds and said, "I want to invest in a movie." It was 100 percent risk investment, meaning that I had no guarantee that he'd ever get his money back. But he didn't care. Well, that's the kind of luck that you need.

HOW DID HE FIND YOU?

Through a mutual friend. It's all about people you know really. You meet someone and they know someone and that's how it happens. So I made *Assault on Precinct 13* with that money. Of course, again we found a distributor, the movie was released, but it did no box office. But this time the movie was in the London Film Festival and to my shock drew terrific reviews. Because it was kind of a hit over there, word got back to the United States that I had released this movie that they had really loved in London, and I was some new talent or something. It was then that I met a financier named Moustaffa Akhad. He was Arabian, and he had directed a couple movies himself and wanted to keep making low-budget films. He saw my work at the London Film festival, took a meeting with me, and started talking with me about making films. This collaboration led to *Halloween*, and we made that in 1978 in a twenty-one–day shoot for $200,000. The rest is basically history, because my career was made from that; I didn't have to worry so much anymore.

HOW DID YOU COME ON THE IDEA OF MAKING *HALLOWEEN*?

You can look at a hundred books and find it, that kind of story has been told a hundred times. I was gonna make a slasher movie, a mass killer stalking baby-sitters; that's all it was. It was an idea that I just took and made my own film out of it. It was Moustaffa's suggestion to call it *Halloween*. Of course the film was a tremendous success. It really made me. But my luck came from having that first project to be able to show and at least get that agent, and having the luck and the will to make that first project. I think probably just the stamina to hang in there was what got me to *Halloween*. That's tough to do, to have that endurance, just to be able to say, "You know, it may not happen for ten years, it may not happen for fifteen years. I'm just gonna hang in there because this is my life." It's a commitment and it's tough. I don't know how else to frame it.

DID YOU EVER CONSIDER DOING ANYTHING ELSE?
Never. Not even when I was young. I think about it now all the time. I'm getting old in the business, it's gonna be time to get out soon. But regardless of that, thinking about getting started, you might talk to one hundred people, and you might hear one hundred different stories. A lot of how you get in is through people you know, but a lot of it is being in the right place at the right time. My father once told me, the opportunity will come for you; be ready for it when it's there. Be ready to do it when it comes. Be prepared. He told me that when I was a teenager, and it stuck with me. I have to tell you that my training at USC certainly helped me get ready for the business. I was set to go; I was set to direct. By the time *Halloween* came along I was ready to make it.

HOW DID YOU HANDLE THE TRANSITION FROM THE EARLIER FILMS TO THE LARGER FRAMEWORK OF *HALLOWEEN*?
All movies are essentially the same. You have a story to tell in 90 to 120 minutes and you have a certain budget to do that with. What you have to do is make sure the story matches up with the budget. In other words, if you have enough money to make a movie, then you're not being too ambitious for what you've got. The process is basically all the same. You have lots of difficulties, you have lots of easy stuff, but the process comes down to doing the same thing, over and over again. As you get more money you have larger problems, because now you have larger expectations. When you're dealing with a low budget there are really no expectations. You get what you get. But all that aside, the art and craft of directing is the same across all budgetary scales.

DO YOU THINK THAT THE INDUSTRY HAS CHANGED SINCE YOUR ENTRY INTO IT?
Massively. In some ways it's easier for you young guys to get into the business now. A lot of opportunities have opened up. When I was starting out there wasn't videocassette; there wasn't this digital revolution; there wasn't

cable television. You've got outlets to show your stuff. And the public is generally accepting of things like *The Blair Witch Project*, which was kind of an amateur movie, but they made it and it was a successful film and it's not bad. The chance of getting your stuff shown if you're tenacious enough and lucky enough is pretty damn good. What I see now with regards to the business of filmmaking is that all the big corporations kind of own everything, and there are very few. And the studio executives within those corporations viciously fight each other for territorial pull. But it isn't as pleasant and passionate as it once was, and people use words like "content" and "product" and all these weird geek computer buzzwords. They communicate certain ideas, but somehow some of the pure movie cinema stuff has gotten lost in the transition. I am, however, an old director now. If you talk to a young guy he'll definitely have a different story.

DO YOU THINK THAT IF YOU HAVE TALENT YOU WILL BE RECOGNIZED?
Not necessarily. The most talented directors that I knew in my class at school never got a chance. They were better than me, and they never got a shot at it. Why is that? I can't say for sure. Maybe they didn't push hard enough. Maybe they weren't lucky. Maybe life came along and spoiled their plans. There are a hundred reasons why people don't make it, but from what I saw they just didn't get a chance. Luck is definitely huge.

DOES THE ENORMOUS COMPETITION FOR DIRECTING JOBS TODAY INCREASE OR DECREASE ONE'S CHANCE OF MAKING IT?
Well, it's a very Darwinian process and only the fittest survive. There's a lot of natural selection going on. Those who are the most talented, the best equipped to do the job are going to make it. Competition forces that. It's extremely ruthless. But it always has been; a lot of people competing for not that many directing slots. With all the outlets today I think it's easier to push through though, and certainly writing is a good way to get in, because you don't have to make a movie to show. You can show people a script and maybe they'll buy it if you're a good enough writer. That's a good way.

WHAT DO YOU THINK IT IS, OTHER THAN THE SHEER TECHNICAL ABILITY, THAT DEFINES THE DIRECTOR AS TALENTED?
The director is a leader. What you're essentially doing is asking a crew of people, actors, editors, and set members to follow you and your vision, and you have to lead them. Make them rise to do their best. That can be done in numerous different ways. You can do it with kindness. It depends on how well people respond to it. It's that leadership quality. You have to be a natural leader. You have to be unnaturally motivated to do this and you have to believe in yourself. There's a narcissistic arrogance that goes along with it.

You have to believe. Ultimately you have to overcome that, but that's why a lot of young kids just strut around a lot when they're starting out, because they have to have that arrogance to keep going. And I understand that because I did it too.

I've had self-doubt forever; that never changed. But I listen to it too. If something is bothering me, well, what is it? Man's got to live with his own limitations. You have to know where you can't do it very well, and then don't go there.

I think of myself primarily as a director, although I have written during my career. Directing was my first love, and it's ultimately what I'm most passionate about. Although I have said I'm thinking of leaving the business, don't take it too seriously until it happens. I've said that on every movie I've made—I daydream about it. Because there is a downside to all this and it is that physical and emotional stress that is put upon you as a director over the period of your career; it is enormous and it takes a toll. And at some point you have to say to yourself, life should be fun as opposed to this. So I keep waiting for that day to arrive when I know that I cannot do this anymore. My personal life has been adversely affected by my career choice. There's no question about that. You could say that filmmaking is a kind of addiction.

You see, there's no mathematical analysis to this, it's against all odds. There's a skinny, shy kid from Kentucky; how could he become a film director? There's no way. The odds are huge. I didn't know anybody out here. I was never particularly interested in drama or directing actors. But I was drawn to making films, and ultimately it just happened.

I don't know if there's anything particularly unique about my vision; that's not for me to say. What I do know is that my parents gave me some enormous gifts. That's the one thing that I realized a lot of kids didn't have. My dad gave me the drive to create; he was a musician. And my mom gave me the gift of fantasy. A lot of other things I didn't get that I wish I had, but those two things were pretty big. I was always encouraged to create when I was younger. I had a really great childhood in that sense.

HOW RELEVANT IS AN UNDERSTANDING OF THE MECHANICS OF THE BUSINESS OF FILM?
It doesn't hurt. It's not crucial, but it doesn't hurt. You need to figure out at some point how the business works. But, you see, you're in a time now where you can make a movie with a digital camera if you want. It doesn't cost much. Get out there with a digital camera and a bunch of actors and a script you've written and do it and sell it and become rich and successful. That's it. It's easier now than it was. We had to always get cameras, movie cameras, process the film, and cut the negative. The only thing stopping you now is the script.

So find one. No one is gonna come to you really. They may. You may be lucky, but don't wait around for it. You gotta go out and make it happen for yourself. That's really the answer that every director who ever came to film school and lectured to my class gave. You have to make your breaks. You have to go out and do it. You have to show them one way or the other that you have what it takes. It may take you years to prove it, and you may indeed fail, but if you want it to happen you've got to try, you have to make your own breaks.

IS THE STRUGGLE WORTH THE REWARD?

In the beginning I had the same frustrations and empty voice and self-doubt that I think everybody has. Because it didn't come fast, it took a long time to happen. But when it started happening, I felt fabulous. I felt fantastic. I felt like the success gave me the courage that I needed to keep going. It was a great reward. I feel really lucky about what happened to me and my career, especially what *Halloween* did for me, simply because it established a career. You see it wasn't like I had a movie that was a hit and then I went off and did a love story that bombed. I got known for something, I got known for a certain style of film, and you can't buy that.

When you're young you may dream about this life, you may have all these fantasies about how it will be. I certainly did. But the reality is that what actually comes is vastly different, and there's no way to predict it. And that's both good and bad.

DO YOU FEEL ANY SENSE OF COMMUNITY WITH THE PEOPLE YOU WORK WITH?

Definitely. That's something that develops over the years as you work with people again and again; you develop relationships and friendships. Also, it's interesting that as I've gotten older, I've become more involved with the Directors' Guild. I am on the creative rights committee there now, and right at this moment we are responding to the new censorship pushes that are coming up and working on how to deal with that. I've become politically active in my guild, and that's a lot of fun. I have a certain camaraderie now with other directors, and that's something I've never had before. It's a great feeling.

Kris Isacsson | DOWN TO YOU

KRIS ISACSSON *was born in Syosset, Long Island, in 1972. His short film* Man About Town *won the Best Short Film prize at the 1998 Sundance Film Festival. Since then he has written two feature screenplays for Miramax and New Line Cinema. He recently completed his first feature-film,* Down to You, *starring Freddie Prinze, Jr., and Julia Stiles, which he wrote and directed for Miramax Films. Isacsson is single and lives in New York City.*

My father was the head of sales for CBS for a large part of his life. He was a major influence on me when I was growing up. Around 1978 he brought home a VCR and a library of films like *Star Wars, Jaws, Annie Hall,* and *High Anxiety.* We had a huge television so I was looking at films often. My mother was a painter and photographer and I have an older brother who works in security and is getting a degree in criminal justice.

Even though I watched movies all the time I thought I would be a rock star when I got older. I played the violin, trumpet, guitar, and piano. When I was about fifteen I decided I wanted to get into the movie business. It took a lot to convince my parents that I was serious about it, but I got a video camera when I was in high school. I loved shooting and editing. I found that it was a medium that suited me because it used my mechanical and creative talents. I had two VCRs and an edit controller setup in my room so I was able to make my own little movies. I had a great drive and I felt I was good at it.

WHAT KIND OF FILMMAKERS WERE YOU INTERESTED IN?

I didn't really have any favorite filmmakers growing up, although I did like Stanley Kubrick. In high school I did my own adaptation of *A Clockwork Orange.* I also did a comic version of *Hamlet.* At my school we sometimes had to do both an essay and a piece of creative work for an assignment; the other kids would write or paint and I would make a film. During high school I started doing documentary projects. I was fortunate enough to go to China with a choral group to film a documentary about them. I brought along video equipment and followed them around, putting together a film about their trip. That experience made me decide I wanted to go to film school in New York.

I graduated from high school in 1990 and I applied to NYU film school. Unfortunately I was not the best student in high school and I didn't get in. There was no other film school on the East Coast that interested me so I ended up going to Fordham University in Manhattan. I knew that there I could get a good liberal arts education. I did study film, but more from a critical theory perspective. I decided that I could also learn about the film business by working in it, so during my four years of college I held lots of internships and production assistant jobs. You name it, I did it, and by the time I graduated I had tons of experience. A few weeks before freshman year started, my father helped me get a job through a friend of his at Carolco Pictures. This was 1990 and I was seventeen. It was the time that Carolco was on top and they were making films like *L.A. Story, The Doors, Basic Instinct, T2,* and they had also done the *Rambo* movies. I got a job working there three full days a week from nine to five. I got paid $7.50 an hour to do everything from reviewing producers' expense reports to collecting Nielsen ratings. Even though this stuff was peripheral to filmmaking, the experience helped my knowledge of the business and helped me develop a work ethic.

HOW WAS YOUR OWN FILMMAKING PROGRESSING?

I continued making films with my Super-8 and video cameras, and by the end of my freshman year I thought I could make a real movie. So being as naive as I was, I plunged into making an hourlong 16mm epic. It was called *Sex Abuse,* and I wrote and filmed it and did everything on it. This was my first collaboration with Matt Gunn, a friend and actor whom I have worked with a lot. The film was a black comedy about a woman who finds out that her husband paid her high school boyfriend a lot of money to dump her. It was a sort of goofy Woody Allen–type thing. I bought a bunch of film and rented a CP16 movie camera and a Nagra sound recorder. My mother did the Nagra and I shot the movie myself and whoever wasn't in front of the camera would do the boom. I'm amazed that everything was in focus because we crossed the 180-degree line and we broke every filmmaking rule. Even though it didn't come out very well, making the film was a great experience. I spent one year on the project between earning the money to make the film, finishing it, and doing other things. I had learned about the technical process of filmmaking by reading books and by consulting with people who had done it before. When I was making the film I would go to whatever vendors I was working with and ask them for their help. When I was making the final print I learned so much from the guys at the lab, and I got to be good friends with the manager and the negative cutter.

HOW DID PEOPLE RESPOND TO THE FINISHED FILM?

The day I screened *Sex Abuse* was the day of the L.A. riots and that Friday everyone thought there would be rioting in New York as well. I had my screening at the theater at Fordham Law School and about thirty friends and family members came to see it. The film wasn't any good and I was only nineteen years old, but the whole process was a tremendous learning experience. After the screening and the lack of critical response I set out to do another film that was more serious and professional.

At this time I also got into a paid internship program at MTV where every few weeks someone like Tom Freston or Judy McGrath, who was the president of MTV, would speak. I worked as a production assistant on a couple of video documentaries where I got experience working with a director, shooting, and editing. Overall it was a great experience in filmmaking. Since I had no experience with actors or acting I got involved in theater at Fordham and I acted in some Sam Shepard plays. I did it to better understand how to relate to actors because the performances in my first short needed a lot of work.

I had always wanted to work for Robert DeNiro so I managed to get an interview with Jane Rosenthal, who was his producer and partner. She offered me an unpaid internship where I would be working forty hours a week, but of course I couldn't do it because of school. But before I left the Tribeca Film Center I gave my resume to the receptionist at Miramax, which was a few floors down. They had just released *sex, lies, & videotape*. A while later I got a call from Nancy Ashworth, who was the head of human resources at Miramax, and she offered me a position in the marketing department. I took the job and I worked there for the second semester of my sophomore year of college. Even though it was marketing and not filmmaking, it was fascinating and I learned a great deal from the experience. Miramax was so aggressive in the way that they marketed their art films and they cultivated their campaigns to be very user friendly. You wouldn't think that some of the films they were releasing would have a broad appeal, but they were managing to sell them well. They were pushing things like *Cinema Paradiso* and Peter Greenaway's films. The guys I was working with had been rock concert promoters and they were very talented at marketing. They saw a new wave in American cinema beginning and they saw a great opportunity to profit from it.

After I left Miramax I moved home for the first time in two years and got a job in a video store. This was something I had always wanted to do and it fulfilled my dream to be surrounded by movies. Needless to say, after a month and a half I sobered up and wanted out. My old boss at Miramax, David Dinnerstein, mentioned to me that his wife worked for Ridley Scott at his commercial production company and that she was looking for a paid intern. I went in and interviewed for the job and got it. It was an amazing experience from beginning to end.

Ridley and his brother, Tony Scott, had started making commercials in the 1960s and their company, RSA, had branched out from London to New York and L.A. They continued to make commercials and had protégés who had gone on to do feature films, like Danny Cannon, who did *Judge Dredd* and the sequel to *I Know What You Did Last Summer*. Here I was at Ridley Scott's company, where they had only four people working in an office and a studio filled with equipment like 35mm Mitchell cameras, Steenbecks, and a videotape library. I worked there as a full-time employee for my last two years of college and I ended up making decent money and getting a lot of free stuff for my next film. Since they weren't making a lot of commercials in New York, they were trying to sell their studio so I was put in charge of getting rid of the props and cleaning it out. Instead of throwing everything away I would have a garage sale and I made a ton of money. They would say, "Here, get rid of this," and before I knew it I was selling the contents of a refrigerator filled with film. I made two grand in one day selling film. Then I went to Fordham's theater department and made another grand selling lumber. The money was mine to keep.

Watching these guys shoot commercials was educational for me and it definitely influenced my aesthetic for a while. The biggest advantage of being there was that I was working in a film environment where I was learning stuff every day and at the same time gaining resources to work on my next 16mm project, a half-hour film called *The Brother and the Plumber*. It was a black-and-white 16mm short about a white kid living in suburban Long Island who wanted to be an inner-city black kid. I made this film in 1994 and I think that the theme of the film was a bit ahead of its time.

HOW DID THE SHORT TURN OUT?

Making the short was a great exercise, but it needed substantial editing and fine-tuning. The location was great and the actors were quite good. We had a crew of NYU grad students who were great, and we also used production assistants who worked on commercials for a living. I produced the film myself, which was a mistake, and I realized that no one should take on a film by himself. Producing, writing, editing, and directing was just too much and I lost sight of things. I didn't realize it at the time but the script needed a rewrite and the film was too long.

I learned that you have to collaborate in film. If you work in Hollywood, you will be shocked at how much collaboration there is in this business. I keep hearing stories about first-time directors who are eaten alive in Hollywood by producers, actors, and studios. A lot of studios hire first-time directors now because they know it's easy to manipulate them. They can tell them what to do and pay them very little money. Sometimes if a project is a star or producer vehicle, the director is just a gun for hire and not a real creative force at all.

I had a screening for *The Brother and the Plumber* that got mixed reviews. I felt that I had made a quantum leap since making my first film, but ultimately no one makes short films over a half-hour long that go anywhere and my film was thirty-five minutes long. Shorts are a strange medium and today film festivals rarely take shorts that are over fifteen minutes. At twenty-five minutes you are pushing it and at thirty-five minutes, forget it. I did manage to get my film into the Long Island Film Festival and it won a little award there. The experience I got making the film as well as the little bit of recognition I gained for it encouraged me to make another short film.

HOW DID YOU FEEL ABOUT BECOMING A DIRECTOR AT THIS POINT?

By this time I had realized that breaking into the movie business was hard and getting a great script to direct was damn near impossible. Ridley and Tony Scott, Alan Parker, Adrian Lyne, and all those guys started directing commercials first and then started directing features, so I thought that I would take that route. After I made the second short I started making public service announcements to build up a reel of work. I thought that if I could make some money and get my feet wet in the commercial world then I would be less anxious about making features.

By this time I had finished college and I needed a job. Since RSA was moving to L.A., that job ended. I felt then that I needed to work in development. After I did a brief stint at October Films, my friend Matt Gunn, who was by that time working at HBO, called me up and said, "You gotta come over here, it's a great place to work." So he got me into the temp program at HBO, where I worked with a lot of different executives. This was my first real job out of college. I ultimately ended up working as an assistant for Jack Lechner. At that time they were making films like *If These Walls Could Talk*. It wasn't my kind of material, but they had money and they were making original movies. In my job I was working with the BBC and Channel 4, and learning about relationships with the United Kingdom.

I shot a PSA with my friend Gabe Peterson, who was working at an advertising agency, and another guy that I knew named Paul Calangelo, who was a union assistant cameraman. I had written a short script about young heterosexual couples who didn't practice safe sex. At that time heterosexual HIV contraction was not an area of HIV awareness that was dealt with. Paul got access to a free camera and we shot the commercial for about $2,500.

HOW DID YOU FINANCE IT?

We shot it on spec, which means that you put up your own money and hope that someone will buy it when it's done. I did it because I felt that it was something I needed to have on the reel that I was putting together. I showed it to Colin Callender at HBO and he showed it to Harry Belafonte (who he happened to be meeting with), who loved it. Harry then showed it to Bob Cooper, the head of original movies at HBO. Bob showed it to Bridget Potter, a veteran at HBO, and she called me and said "Kris, I'll give you what you need to finish this," and she did. She provided some finishing funds and I got the piece done. It was a very arty, handheld black-and-white European-type thing, but I think it made its point effectively. Three months after it was finished another Washington, D.C., organization said, "We want to pay you everything you spent on that and put our name on it." Then they also found an organization called Cable Positive that was willing to put it on the air, so all of a sudden it was on everywhere; it played MTV for a month. This felt like real progress and I decided to keep making these until I had a collection of them on my reel.

Cable Positive then put up five grand for me to direct another PSA. So I did theirs for National AIDS day and made it in a completely different style. After that they wanted me to do another one and this time they had $10,000. Then finally another organization came along that had $80,000 and a $5,000 payday for me. From the time of the broadcast of the first PSA to the $80,000 PSA, one year went by. This seemed like a good accomplishment.

Also at this time I got an opportunity to be Barbra Streisand's assistant on *The Mirror Has Two Faces*, which was a big-budget Hollywood movie shooting in New York. Someone I knew from HBO had left to work for Barbra and called me to ask if I wanted to come work on the film. I'll say that outside of making my own film working for Barbra was the biggest learning experience I have ever had. She was very tough, which was understandable considering the enormous pressure she was under directing, producing, and starring in a major film that she didn't have enough prep time for. She was on camera 75 percent of the time and was constantly doing enormous costume changes. This was really hard on her and it made the production difficult for everybody.

I hadn't been a fan of hers before the film, but I didn't give a shit because an opportunity like that doesn't come along that often. Since she was directing, acting, and producing, I got to be everywhere. The only time she wanted me out of her way was when the head of TriStar was on set and they wanted me out of the room so they could fire someone. It was not, "Get me coffee or water"—she had another assistant for that. She basically gave me an arsenal of video equipment: a video steadicam, editing machines, two Hi-8 cameras, and said, "You are going to tape my rehearsals. You're going to edit location tapes for me and I want you to show the team what the shot is with the video camera."

HOW WAS WORKING WITH STREISAND?
Barbra was hard on me for the first month, but then we developed a nice rapport. She asked me my opinion, told me anecdotes and stories about Gordon Lewis, and of working with cinematographer Vittorio Storaro and things like that. The thing I could never get around was that this was one of the most famous women of the past thirty years and she really did live in her own world. I'd never been around that. We'd go to Planet Hollywood to look at the film's rushes and, by the time we got out, there would be hundreds of people outside trying to get a look at her.

I quit working for Barbra because they told me that the movie would finish shooting in January but it really finished much later. I was told it would be edited in L.A. in February and that I'd go to L.A. and be provided with an apartment and a car and be done in the spring. But production ran very behind because of massive snowstorms and other things and the movie was millions of dollars over budget. Suddenly my life was going to be moving to L.A. at the end of the spring and I would have no apartment and I would be editing all summer and living at Barbra's house, where her editing facility was. For me that was like being a prisoner and I had learned everything I wanted to learn so it was time to move on.

I went back to work for Jack Lechner at HBO in the beginning of 1996 when he was the head of HBO NYC. It was then that I said to myself, "I'm making a short film." I had just had this intense movie experience and I felt ready. I had turned twenty-three and my friend Matt Gunn and I went and hung out at a bar. He was going to quit drinking and it was the night that he had his last drink. He was really frustrated at this point because he was working at Cinemax doing programming, which was far from his dream of being an actor and a writer. We were talking and I said, "Why don't we make a film about the night you have your last drink? There are so many funny moments around it." He agreed and then he went home and wrote a four-page monologue about what happened; this became *Man About Town*. This was my first serious foray into filmmaking and I'm very proud of it.

To make the film Matt and I got everyone together who had worked on the PSAs with us. Gabe was our executive producer and he also put some money into the project. The film cost $40,000. Matt and I put in $15,000 each and we raised the rest from friends and family members. Matt and I put ten grand each on credit cards and another five was cash. It was financial suicide. I mean we weren't in college anymore. We were in the real world with real jobs and real rent to pay. Getting in the hole like that was insane. But, you know, we were blind with ambition. Our goal was really to become filmmakers and the short was part of a long-term plan as well as something we did just for art's sake. We loved it but I was reluctant to put as much into the short as I did. The PSA thing was going and I wanted to nurture that and not throw a lot of money at a short film. I was nervous about it. I had experience making films and Matt didn't, but he still said, "We have to put all the chips there, we have to go for broke on the film." So I knew that I had to do that too.

HOW WOULD YOU DESCRIBE THE AESTHETIC OF THE FILM?
I knew that I wanted to do something unusual. I wanted to make a black-and-white beatnik short with all voiceover and no dialogue. The film has a narrator although he sometimes speaks for other characters in the film and lip-synchs other character's words. Paul Calangelo, who shot all my PSAs, photographed the piece. We shot it on a 16mm camera that we rented and a third of it was shot on a Bolex camera with no sound. We shot a lot of film, executed a lot of dolly moves, and did a lot of camera setups. A third of the film we shot in March, a third in May, and then the final third in August all across New York and Long Island. We did tons of cutaways and pickup shots and things you insert into a film to get good editing flexibility and visual variety. The reason the production took so long was because no one could get off work for an extended period of time. It was frightening to go such a long span of time on the film and invest all the money, but I knew we'd done a good job as soon as we saw the footage; it was fantastic. I rented a Steenbeck machine and put it in my kitchen, where I cut the film. I was becoming more and more happy with it. We added music from a band called Future Dream, an ensemble of NYU music students that I found on the street. I brought them into a studio and they watched the film and improvised over it just like they made jazz scores in the 1960s; the music was phenomenal.

Jack Lechner was offered the job of being head of development at Miramax and he took me along with him in the summer of 1996. It was fascinating because I was able to read scripts for films like *Rushmore, 8mm,* and many others. I had been at Miramax for two months when I was offered $80,000 to do a PSA on mental illness, and at the same time I was trying to finish my own film to get it to Sundance. I quit Miramax because I thought I would go around with my PSA reel and maybe get a job. I met with commercial agencies and nobody was interested in me in the slightest. To compete, you need a company to say that they'll develop you and that they'll build your reel over time. This of course costs them a great deal of money, and no one wanted to take me on at a time when the market was saturated with up-and-coming people. To compete in that market you need to have at least $500,000 worth of productions on your reel and I only had about $100,000. The rejection felt terrible, but it made me realize that I was only doing the commercial stuff in the first place because I wanted to make movies. At a certain point I had to ask myself, What the hell am I doing? I finally thought, I've got this great short and life is good. I don't need to make commercials right now. Then I started looking on the bright side.

I gave up on the PSA stuff and began working on a script called "Down to You." I knew that if my short film garnered interest I would have to have a feature script ready. If you have a short, you've gotta have a script or you might as well not bother having a short at all. So I began writing my script around September 1996 from an idea that I had had in the back of my mind for a while. It's a romantic comedy about a guy who revisits his first love. I then got accepted into Sundance with *Man About Town,* so then all of a sudden it was, "Oh my God, we're going to Sundance."

WHAT WAS YOUR REACTION TO SUNDANCE?

The number of films that Sundance sees compared to the number it accepts is astronomical. It was a media event in 1997 when I went, and I am sure that it is much the same now. I stopped believing in Sundance after my experience there. Filmmakers who go to Sundance end up going to pitch meetings with people they meet there and they are told that a project will happen and it's going to be great. The reality is that those projects almost never happen. Sundance is about the studios, not the filmmakers. I went to eight other film festivals where I had more fun and a more genuine response to my film than I did at Sundance. Does an "independent" film really have to go to Sundance to be successful? My first feature is going into two thousand theaters and it is not going to Sundance. What matters if you want to make movies in America is that you have to make commercial films; at least that's my perception of it. Short film makers mean nothing to anyone, and Sundance is just another film festival unless you are a star or you win an award. Until we won an award no one cared about us in the slightest.

WHAT HAPPENED WHEN YOU WERE THERE?

At the opening-night banquet Matt Gunn was standing by the hors d'oeuvres double-dipping celery stalks when a man came over and said, "You were sensational in *Man About Town* and it was one of the best shorts I've ever seen." So Matt says, "Thank you. Who are you?" and the guy says, "Don Prucheso, film critic for the *New York Press.*" And then Prucheso said, "I shouldn't tell you this, but I'm a judge and I'm on the short film making committee." And then we met a film editor named Kate Williams who was also on the jury. And the response we got from them was an indication that we might win. And then awards night came and we did win. It was amazing. We won the award and it was, it was . . . What was great was that you spend all this money and all this time with all the people that you believe in and then you're all there celebrating and it's fantastic. We were really happy with the audience response.

WHAT HAPPENED AFTER SUNDANCE?

The month that followed Sundance consisted of, "We wanna meet with you, we wanna meet with you." I signed with a big talent agency and had tons of meetings with every development person and every junior executive at every company. It is their job to meet with the person who won at Sundance. You think it will feel great, but it's really just bullshit. It's like, "Yeah, you know! Fantastic!" They take you to lunch and dinner and you schmooze and nothing comes of it. I recognized the meaninglessness of it at the time because when I was working for Jack I would meet the same people. I remember the woman who won Sundance a few years earlier came to Miramax and met with Jack and I got her coffee. I would see filmmakers left and right when I was there and I know that usually nothing comes of it. The job of a development person is to meet with you, read your material, and then pass on it. The percentage of films that get made is so small. Unless you're Darren Aronofsky or you're the *Blair Witch* people, Sundance only really produces one star a year. Todd Solondz was a star, Ed Burns was a star, Steven Soderbergh was a star, Darren Aronofsky was a star. But everybody else, they just keep going at it, grinding it out.

WOULD YOU RECOMMEND THAT PEOPLE GO THE SUNDANCE ROUTE WITH A SHORT FILM?

I tell people not to think about Sundance if you are not gonna make the deadline. Don't rush because it's not worth it. Sundance is a huge part of selling certain feature movies so, as a producer, which I'm not, I don't know how important it is to premier at Sundance as opposed to Toronto. Often it doesn't even matter at all. *Swingers* didn't go to any festivals and it was one of the best acquisitions that Miramax made compared to all of their Sundance acquisitions. Miramax has had no major pickups at Sundance in the last few years that have done well.

WHAT WAS HAPPENING WITH YOUR SCRIPT AT THIS TIME?

I had finished it right before I went to Sundance. It was a first draft and it was loose, but the basic framework was there. I had some interest from three groups right away. I chose to work with Open City Films. At the time they were making a movie called *Three Seasons*, which just won all the prizes at Sundance this year. I said I wanted Joaquin Phoenix as the star. We managed to get him the script and he said he was interested. We did a budget and then we got a casting director. The week I finished Sundance, I went back to work at Miramax for my old boss Jack Lechner because I was broke. It was the only thing I could do. They had fired my replacement. "Sundance award winner back serving coffee at Miramax." And I did that for a year. Literally, the week after Sundance, I was back working. And you know, Meryl Poster, the head of production, watched my short and said, "Great work!" and some of the people there were very nice to me about winning and some people didn't give a shit at all.

That was awkward because I felt that certainly there were people there who might be jealous so there was no pat on the back at all. It was frustrating in that I was trapped because I had to work there because I had to make money. The upside was that I worked at Miramax and I just won a Sundance award, so things were okay. If you are any good at engineering your career you need to work at companies and manipulate them for your own use. That is what I did at HBO, RSA, and all the others. I figured that if I stayed around Miramax long enough that something good would come of it. But I expected that I would only work there for six months. By the end of the year, when I had been there for ten months, I was getting deeply depressed. I was turning twenty-five, my script was going nowhere, and my agents were encouraging me to try to get a studio directing assignment. Even if I could have gotten one, it probably would have been a sequel, like *Mouse Hunt 2*, so there was some danger to it.

HOW DID YOU ULTIMATELY GET TO MAKE *DOWN TO YOU*?

My producers from Open City were in Vietnam shooting *Three Seasons* and they had a guy working with them in Europe who was trying to raise money for my film. By now it was April and I had been working at Miramax for fourteen months. It had been fourteen months since the Sundance award, fourteen months of developing my script, fourteen months of work. I had managed to get a wonderful casting director named Doug Abel, who told me he'd work on the project for free until it got picked up. I was meeting with actors for character parts, but really we had nothing. By April of 1998 a company in the U.K. who had made *Shooting Fish* said that they would put up $3 million for the budget if we could close a deal with a distributor in North America who would commit one third of the budget after delivery costs. They would have worldwide distribution rights and whoever the other party was would take North America. It was a pretty good deal because we had Joaquin Phoenix interested and we thought with this commitment that it was time to go. Jack Lechner was a really big fan of the project and showed it to the acquisitions people at Miramax. Meanwhile we were meeting with Fox and Sony and over the course of a couple of weeks we managed to generate buzz on the project. It was all through bullshit, really. We said, "You know this person's interested, that person's interested," and I started to get really excited because it felt like progress. It really felt like something was going to happen. One Friday I had lunch with my dad and I told him everything that was going on and for once he actually had a shred of optimism, so I really felt like movement might be imminent. After lunch I went back to the Miramax office and I said, "Jack, I just found out that Bingham Ray is gonna read my script and so is Lindsay Law, head of Fox, and Michael Barker. You gotta give it to Harvey Weinstein because this is it." So Jack wrote a memo to Harvey explaining the project to him.

I think Harvey knew who I was because I won the award at Sundance and he had heard something about it, but the guy is so removed and untouchable that I had never really met him and I never had any interaction with him. He did get the memo and the script and it was very simple because it pointed out to him that all his competitors were reading the script. I started to clean out my desk because I felt that if a competitor were to take it then I would lose my job and I wasn't coming back anyway. The deal was that whoever called by noon on Monday got the project. At ten on Monday morning Harvey Weinstein called Jack and said, "I want this movie and I want full distribution rights." Jack and the lawyers call me and by one o'clock we were sitting at a table at the Tribeca Bakery with legal pads hammering out a deal. The next day I met with Harvey and he said, "We are making your movie." He also gave me a job doing some rewrites on another film. I suddenly had a job doing rewrites and a deal to direct my first feature. It was May 1998 and we were going to make the movie in the fall.

Within three months everything fell apart. Miramax was spending money getting our production ready while I was meeting with cinematographers and location scouts. Miramax still hadn't closed Joaquin's deal, and ultimately I think what happened was that they were making several movies at the same time and everyone was overextended. Harvey finally said to me, "We're gonna do it next year." He wasn't saying, "We're not going to make your movie," he was just saying that he was delaying it a year. What was I going to do? We didn't officially start production and we weren't pay or play (meaning that we would get paid whether the film was made or not) until we had officially started.

WHAT DID YOU DO?

For therapeutic reasons and because I had nothing else to do, I started working for my dad in his office. During the month I was doing that, my agent said, "There's buzz on you now, you've been in the trades, you've got a deal with Miramax, why don't you take some meetings?" I did, and I ended up taking some meetings with New Line Cinema. They thought that I'd be great to do a book adaptation for them, so they hired me to write a script. I met with Lynn Harris and Richard Brenner and I got a scriptwriting job. That was a great experience and it took me through to January of 1999. The script is an adaptation of a book called *Getting In* about a dysfunctional family traveling to colleges for the kids to visit.

By the time I turned in my New Line script the year was over. Miramax then called and said they wanted me to fly out to L.A. and meet with Freddie Prinze, Jr., who was interested in *Down to You*. I told them that I really liked Joaquin, but then I learned that he had already committed at that point to Ridley Scott's film *Gladiator*, for which he got paid a jillion dollars, so he was out. The only other person we were talking about was Casey Affleck. But Miramax and Harvey really believed in Freddie Prinze, Jr., so I flew out to L.A. and I met with him. He was wonderful and I loved him, and right then I said let's do it and we made a deal. As soon as his deal was closed the movie got a green light. It had been four months since my deal was killed and now it was on again. I had written the New Line script in between, so it really seemed like the blink of an eye. We started prepping in February and started shooting in May. I had a great cast that included Julia Stiles, Zach Ohr, Sean Hennessy, Rosario Dawson, and Henry Winkler.

TELL ME ABOUT THE PRODUCTION PROCESS.

The entire process was amazing. The script changed a bit because Freddie was the lead and we needed to accommodate some of his strengths. I think that Harvey really liked the project. He's a very smart man and he knew that at the time that he read the script the big in thing was the high-school movie renaissance. He read this movie and it was a little bit more sophisticated and it took place in college, so he probably thought that the next big thing was the college movie. The budget that we had with Joaquin was a lot lower, but with Freddie we had more money for the production. He was in a high-school movie called *She's All That*, and it was a huge success for Miramax. They were really excited about elevating him to be the next big thing and making a movie that would hopefully not fall into a trend and would be a little bit different and stand out in a good way. Freddie got us the green light. Once you have your star you are going. I always felt that the film would get made but the question was when. Would it be a year, two years? Everybody at Miramax was saying, "We'll go in the spring." I knew that the only thing that was going to make the film happen was getting the right cast. Luckily, we got the right cast very quickly.

We started shooting in May 1999 and we wrapped at the end of June. The budget was around $6 million and the crew was amazing. We were able to get a wonderful crew relatively cheap. I got a terrific cinematographer named Bob Yeoman, who shot *Drugstore Cowboy, Bottle Rocket, Rushmore,* and *Dogma.* He was a very talented and wonderful man and very fast, which is what we needed. Kevin Thompson was our production designer and he had done *Kids* and *Flirting with Disaster.* Those were the two core guys, and then the whole crew fell into place. We shot for thirty-seven days and we really moved. I feel that because I had an experienced crew and actors who really just showed up and worked without complaining, we lost no time. My editor kept asking how long did this or that take? Three days? I would say "No, one day," and he couldn't believe it. We would do at least twelve to fifteen setups a day and we had three days where we were shooting on Columbus Circle at night. It was very difficult to shoot a major dialogue scene on a Saturday night in New York City with crowds of people and flashbulbs going off everywhere. But we were able to pull it off.

WHAT DID THE EXPERIENCE TEACH YOU ABOUT WORKING WITH ACTORS?

I learned that what really helps everyone is when you can be as clear and concise as possible. If you give actors the trust and the respect that they need, then things will go well. Say you're working with an actor who isn't getting the performance right and you don't really have time to work on it. You really need to give the actor an adrenaline rush by telling them what they need to do and why they need to do it. At the same time, you need to create an environment where they can feel comfortable giving their performance. One time we were on a balcony shooting a major monologue by Zach Ohr. The sun was coming up and everybody was freaking out. The character had gone through a huge revelation, but Zach was still sticking to the earlier aspect of the character. What he needed to do was be a lot more open, but he just couldn't get there. We had done four takes and then we did the fifth take and I thought it was all right, but my sound guy told me we needed to go again because of a car horn. I let Zach go and instead of just redoing the one line the car horn was over, he did the whole monologue again. Since the pressure was off this time he relaxed and that was the good take.

HOW WAS WORKING WITH THE STUDIO DURING PRODUCTION?

This was my chance. They don't come that easily or that often and my chance was with Miramax with a script that I wrote, with a great cast, and with the right group of people. It wasn't a $30 million project, it was an under-ten project, so the backlash of a possible failure wasn't all that huge because, with that cast, it would basically make its money back no matter what. The film has my voice in it; it is my film in many ways. I definitely think that working with the studio and having it be my first time was not easy. But I was also working with a lot of talented people and with a studio that really does do things differently than all the others. Miramax was very tough on getting the script right, and with good reason. We had to cut about ten pages out because we just didn't have the time to shoot it; that of course affects the whole film. They didn't make that many editorial changes, but there were some very edgy things in the first draft that made it more of a hardcore R-rated film and they made it more of a soft R. But I think that that was a blessing in disguise. Harvey would say, "You know this guy says 'Fuck this, fuck that,' I mean, come on, Kris." That challenged me to write much better dialogue, so ultimately that was a good thing. I would say it's the same movie, but now shades of it are a little bit different. I really learned a lot about the process and I'm incredibly thankful for getting my chance. Having the attitude that "This is my movie, this is my vision, and I'm doing it my way" is not the right thing for anyone, because you can learn a lot from your collaborators.

TELL ME ABOUT THE POSTPRODUCTION PROCESS.

I first hired Jim Lyons (an editor who works with Todd Haynes a lot and cut *Velvet Goldmine,* which I thought was amazing editorially) to cut the film, but he got ill during the production and I had to replace him. We were in a real bind because in my opinion the only people that were available were really low-level or totally high-level. I managed to convince Miramax to go with a high-level person, Steven Rodder, a wonderfully talented man who started out as assistant editor on Arthur Penn's movies *Alice's Restaurant* and *Night Moves,* and then went on to cut with tons of great directors. He cut *The World According to Garp,* and he was one of the editors on *The Right Stuff, The Unbearable Lightness of Being, Rising Sun, Ishtar, My Blue Heaven, Dirty Rotten Scoundrels,* and many others. So not only has he worked with many people, but he's cut a wide range of great films. The man is in his fifties and he's seen everything, he's worked everywhere, he's met with every director, and he's the greatest guy. He wasn't patronizing at all. Sitting there with someone with that kind of experience, stories, and knowledge made it a real pleasure to go to work everyday. We would take a walk during lunch and he would tell me all about what it was like being in the editing room with Warren Beatty and Dustin Hoffman for eighteen months. He is a wonderful editor and it is good to be around people like this.

WAS IT A PROBLEM BEING SUCH A YOUNG PERSON IN A DIRECTORIAL POSITION?

It does feel a little weird to be so young, but all you really need to do to command the respect that you deserve is by respecting everybody else and treating them well. Some guys go in and treat their crew badly. They beat them to death because they think that that's how they'll get the best work out of them. That's one philosophy. My philosophy is the complete opposite. I feel that if the crew likes you and they feel that you're talented, then they're gonna want to work with you and they're gonna want to do their best. My crew was getting pushed around a little bit by the economics of the shoot. We had one of the top gaffers in New York and one of the top key grips. They were working on a relatively small movie with a first-time director. But all the issues like overtime and all that, they were all very gracious about. We had some hard nights and they really pushed themselves. There was one situation where we were shooting the last shot of the film, which is a sunrise shot overlooking Central Park where the characters are kissing and we pan up and see the sun rising. The sun rises from the east, which means that if you want to do that shot you've got to do it at sunrise. The production schedule was bad and they said, "You really should do this shot at dusk and play it for dawn." So we got there and I really thought that it wouldn't work, but I said we would do it. And we shot it as dusk and we cleared it out enough so that it sort of looked like it was dawn, but the sun wasn't shining properly and it didn't look picturesque at all. I mean, there was a helicopter flying around in the background. So we went through the night's work and we finished rather quickly. It was three-thirty in the morning so, technically, we could all have gone home, but I fought with the producers and I said, "We're staying and we're gonna shoot this at dawn." Of course they said, "No, no, no," but everyone on the crew backed me up. Nobody had a problem with it. And we just sat around in chairs eating bagels at Columbus Circle until it was time and then we did it. And that's the one we used and it looked a thousand times better. I mean this was the last shot of the movie and the last shot we were taking for the whole production. The credits were going to play over this shot. But it all worked out beautifully.

DID YOU HAVE MUCH SELF-DOUBT DURING THE PROCESS OF LAUNCHING YOUR PRODUCTION?

You know, in hindsight, I look back at connecting the dots and they're all connected pretty well without a lot of lag. But, going through it, there was a lot of lag and there was a lot of self-doubt. But I never let it stop me. People would pass on the script and the truth of the matter was that this was a film that no studio was going to make. It was one of those scripts that would take a long time to get off the ground. But I just never gave up on it even though I easily could have. And that goes the same with everything. People are going to say no because that's what this business is about; it's about "No." You hear it every day; you hear it a thousand times a day. I worked in an office where my job was to write letters that said no. The number of scripts that came through the office at Miramax was in the thousands. I wrote pass letters, day and night, constantly. Thousands of scripts came through, thousands. Scripts, scripts, scripts. Scripts with major talent attached. Pass, pass, pass. So, it's very easy to lose confidence in yourself. It's very easy. You've just gotta believe in yourself and push through as hard as you can. I feel that that's what has gotten me here, combined with the fact that the work stands on its own.

WHAT PART DOES LUCK PLAY IN THE SCHEME OF THINGS?

Getting into Sundance and winning at Sundance was not all luck, but part of it was. Getting Harvey Weinstein to green-light my movie was really hard to do and even getting him to read it was amazing. Getting an actor to commit, given all of the elements that get in the way, is very hard. You have to have a lot of tenacity, a lot of balls, and a lot of self-confidence. If you don't have the self-confidence, you'd better pretend that you do and just push through. For some people it happens when they're twenty-five, for some it's thirty-five or forty-five.

WHAT ARE YOUR GOALS NOW?

I do not want to be a filmmaker who's hugely popular now; I just want to make movies. I don't want to be written about as the next big thing because I do not want that kind of pressure. I look at the careers of great filmmakers and their real popularity hits them after they've been making movies for fifteen years. That's when they continue to make movies for the rest of their life. That's what I want for my career.

Abel Ferrara | THE DRILLER KILLER

ABEL FERRARA *was born in the Bronx, New York, in 1950. He grew up in Peekskill and studied film at the State University of New York, at Purchase. Beginning in exploitation cinema, Ferrara created the real-life horror shockers* The Driller Killer *and* Ms. 45, *the latter of which garnered critical acclaim. The success of* Ms. 45 *leveraged Ferrara into directing his next feature,* Fear City, *starring Melanie Griffith and Tom Berenger. Since then he has directed many classic films with an ensemble cast that explore the "dark side" of man's appetites, including* King of New York, *starring Christopher Walken;* Bad Lieutenant, *starring Harvey Keitel;* Dangerous Game, *starring Madonna;* New Rose Hotel, *starring Christopher Walken, Asia Argento, and Willem Dafoe, and* R Xmas *with Drea de Matteo. Ferrara is married, has two daughters, and lives in New York.*

I was born in the Bronx and grew up in a very Italian neighborhood. Everyone in my area was named Abel Ferrara. I thought my name was John Smith until I moved out of the neighborhood, and then I never heard Abel again. It was quite a funny situation. It was basically *Raging Bull*, Jake LaMotta, the Belt Parkway, and the Bronx Zoo. It was a very ideal childhood; I grew up in the Bronx of the imagination. It was wonderful.

During my teen years, my family moved to Peekskill, New York. It was a tough period in my life, you know, growing up and being an adolescent, so I would go back and spend my summers in the Bronx for a change of pace. I was back and forth between both places for a while, but then finally it was just Peekskill. That was a major change. I remember the first day I went to school, the teacher went around the class and asked everyone what they ate for dinner the night before, and I said pasta fazoule. I had to hear that for the next ten years. I graduated high school with that. "Hey, Abe Ferrara, can we have some pasta fazoule for Thanksgiving? What did he stuff his turkey with, pasta fazoule?"

My mother was Irish and my father was Italian. That's a very serious combination. My father's father had come to this country in 1900, when he was eighteen years old. At that time, Italians were basically slave laborers, building the railroads at the turn of the century. I don't know how he did it, but he somehow smuggled a boxcar full of grapes from California to New York, and when the New York guineas saw those grapes, they went wild for them. He made quite a bit of money doing that, but then he went broke in the Depression. But that moneymaking groove was something that my father had also, and I think that it's also there in me.

WAS YOUR FAMILY SUPPORTIVE OF YOUR INTEREST IN FILM?
My family was always very supportive, although filmmaking was not exactly my father's preferred career choice for me. As I grew up and tried to raise money for films, he would always get very upset, because he would want to shield me from people who ended up nine times out of ten never coming through. My father was from a world where if you said you were gonna do something, you did it. That's not very common in the film business, and I think it was hard for him to watch me go through a lot of the early disappointment and frustration.

Growing up I was always involved in something, whether it was a rock band, or making movies, or whatever it was, I was always out there. And in this country-bumpkin river town there were a few interesting people, and when I was fifteen years old I met a guy named Nicky St. John, who became first my best friend, and later my writer for many of my films. And then the two of us teamed up with a guy named Mac, who became our technical associate, and we started trying to make films.

This was before the days of Super-8, and we were shooting with single-eight cameras that we begged, borrowed, or stole to get. I remember the first time I shot something. I took it down to the Caldor to be developed, and when I got it back I looked at the first inch of it and just threw it out because it was so terrible. But I learned that it had to get better, and we kept practicing.

WHAT WERE YOUR THOUGHTS ABOUT GOING TO COLLEGE?

By the time I was about eighteen, the Vietnam War was really going on, and if you didn't go to school you were basically dead. All my friends were coming home in a bag. It was a serious trip. So I went off to college at SUNY-Purchase and started trying to study film. I immersed myself in filmmaking and creative thinking. The great advantage of school was that, unlike in high school, we could get access to real equipment to go out and make movies.

When I was in college, there were a lot of great retrospective theaters in New York that would show these important art films that we were all drawing our inspiration from. So those were great places to see classics like Federico Fellini's *Satyricon, The Seventh Seal*, and Jean Vigo films. Andy Warhol movies were playing. It was a great time; it was the Golden Age of cinema.

I made college last forever. I kept working out schemes so that I knew everyone who was my junior so that even after I graduated, I could keep getting access to the equipment. Because after you graduated, you were fucked. The equipment you got at school was top of the line: Arriflex BLs, Steenbeck editing systems, high-end lighting packages, and sound rigs. All of that stuff is extremely expensive to rent, and if I didn't keep the connections alive with the students still at school, I would have had no way to get access to the equipment I needed to keep shooting.

WHAT DID YOU DO FOR MONEY AFTER SCHOOL?

After I graduated college I was basically living off of friends. At first I bugged my mom for money, but then I sort of naturally shifted over to younger women that I was dating. I was adamant about not taking a regular job. You sort of get to a point in your life where you decide what you are going to do and then that's what you do. I had decided to be a filmmaker; so to take some other kind of job seemed like a step backward or a foreign notion. I was a filmmaker, and if that meant I had to starve for a while, then that's what it meant.

I continued making short films for a while, showing them anywhere I could, on a wall, at somebody's house, wherever. I wasn't savvy yet at that point, it wasn't like me and my friends were going down to these trendy venues in New York like the Millennium and hanging out with the hip artists—we'd come to New York and get ripped off by the guys from the Millennium, they'd sell us oregano for weed, and our girlfriends would run off with cool-looking blues singers. That was the state of our development.

I was still trying to figure out what I was doing, and I kept shooting films whenever I could. I would find people who were film students and who wanted to be cinematographers and get them to shoot something for me so I could get access to their equipment. I remember one time I was working with a kid named John Rosen, who was a brilliant still photographer who wanted to make films. And I get him over to my girlfriend's apartment to film. I was living with this gorgeous girl at the time, and the scene was basically her and another girl fucking each other under the guise of a story. So we're gonna do the sex, and we were all set up to shoot. My girlfriend pulls down her jeans (and she was a real piece of ass), and Rosen just froze up. But then he got it back together and started filming. And he was a good cameraman. Then later he had to show those dailies to his class because it was a requirement that you screen your work. I remember getting a telephone call from him a few weeks later screaming at me that the school was so upset with the dailies that they had actually called his mother. This was my effect on people kind enough to help me.

WHEN DID YOU START THINKING SERIOUSLY ABOUT MAKING A FEATURE?
I kept making short films for a while, but knew that it was time to focus my attention on getting a feature together. It was about 1975 at this time, and I was twenty-five years old. I was looking for an angle, a way to get into the business, and then *The Texas Chainsaw Massacre* hit. That film was an incredible success because it was made for some ridiculously low amount of money like $30,000 and grossed some absurdly high amount of money like $30 million. It was the *Blair Witch Project* of its day. I remember I bought *Variety* magazine one day and there was a sheet of the fifty top-grossing films of all time and *Texas Chainsaw Massacre* was on it. I thought to myself, if I can't make a film that's at least that good then I should just quit the business. I knew I could do something at that level. So that was how I came up with the concept for what would become my first feature, *Driller Killer*.

Nicky had started to write the script a while before, but it was sort of different vignettes that we were piecing together slowly. We had already started shooting a little documentary on winos in New York, and we tried to come up with a way to incorporate that into a story so that we could make a feature out of some of what we already had. We knew that the story had to be accessible to a broad audience, because that would be the only way we would convince anyone to give us money. I wasn't the John Waters type; I figured that I could hustle up a *Driller Killer* much more easily than I could a *Pink Flamingos*. Because the people I would go to for money could identify with the *Texas Chainsaw Massacre*. Even though what I really wanted to make and I think ultimately did make was a twisted art movie, I had to sell it to people as a kind of exploitation film to raise the financing. I mean, the guys who would put up the money understood *Deep Throat*; they understood *Night of the Living Dead*. They didn't understand a film like *Desperate Living*.

The film cost $70,000 in total. We had started with the wino documentary footage, and we put together a twenty-minute clip of scenes from what would become the film, and went around to try and raise money from all different sorts of independent financiers. I came upon a guy who was making a lot of money doing porno films, specifically *Debbie Does Dallas*. He was a Jewish man named Arthur Weisberg, and he had made a killing on *Debbie*; he put up very little cash and reaped an enormous return. And he took a chance on me and gave me the money to make *Driller Killer*.

Driller Killer was an odd story about a painter who is losing his mind and turns into a homicidal maniac who kills people with a drill gun. He lived with these two chicks, and he was painting a giant buffalo for a museum in Washington. He was from Los Angeles and had a real problem with bums. He hated them because they were dirty. So he would go around with a drill gun and drill them to death, hence, the *Driller Killer*.

We started shooting during December of 1977. Nicky and I put the clips together, raised the money during the winter, and finished the film the next summer. We shot it initially like a student film, but once we got the money we finished it quickly, like a regular movie. We shot at clubs around New York including Max's Kansas City, where we developed a lot of the punk-rock aspect of the film, with the live band footage. The cinematographer came from NYU. We put a sign up on the wall that said we were looking for someone with equipment who could work long hours, and that they could shoot the film, so we got a call from a guy named Polson, who worked with us very well. He had just come back from Vietnam, and he was a bit of a mess, but he had access to cameras and trucks, and he knew how to work with them, so it was a match made in heaven. We're still tight to this day.

WHAT HAPPENED WHEN THE FILM WAS RELEASED?

When we finally finished the film, it was a smash. It was one of my biggest hits and it had the biggest opening weekend of any of my films. I suppose it was beginner's luck. It opened in Kansas City in the summertime and it was the second biggest grossing film that week. At that time there was a market for violent films like this and there was a definite track for marketing them. This was a time when drive-in theaters were very popular and this film did well in those venues. The marketing track for films like *Texas Chainsaw Massacre* also included theaters on Forty-second Street in New York City that don't exist anymore. We put it out in theaters throughout New York. We ran promotions where we would put watermelons in the lobby of the theater and you could come and drill a hole in the watermelon. We did fantastic business with that film. I used the porno circuit to get distribution, and really played up the exploitation angle, even though it was really an art film where every once in a while we drilled somebody. People were looking for films like that at the time because they could exploit the sex and violence and could show the film in the wake of the *Texas Chainsaw Massacre*'s related success.

WHAT WAS IT LIKE HAVING A PROFITABLE FILM IN THE MOVIE THEATER?
It was a great feeling. I wasn't living off anyone. I wasn't borrowing money. I was making money making movies, making money on my own terms (as if *Driller Killer* was something on my own terms), but I actually had some measure of success. I hate the fact that I need those things to fucking justify something. It's really stupid, but it's the reality of our emotion. I was out there doing things. This is a very tough business and I really empathize with some first-time directors, especially those who work in television, or for a studio as simply a hand to get the job done. When I shot episodes of "Miami Vice," it took every fucking bit of my ability to be able to control the crew, to deal with the actors, and to tell a story in that incredibly compressed shooting period. If I had to do that every day, I'd probably commit suicide. It's an impossible situation. You have eight or nine days to make an hour-long film. But with a feature, you have far more control, time, and resources to get the job done. But you have to be able to do it on your own terms without a great deal of outside interference, and that's why *Driller Killer* was such a vindication. If things are out of your control then the actors and the crew and the producers will just eat you alive.

HOW DID YOU GO ABOUT GETTING YOUR NEXT FILM AFTER THE SUCCESS OF *DRILLER KILLER*?
After the first-weekend success of *Driller Killer* I went right back to the Arthur Weisberg with the idea for *Ms. 45*. The concept of the film was that a girl gets raped, goes home, and gets raped again. Then she begins a vengeance trip to exact her revenge on the rapists of the world. Weisberg loved the idea of a chick getting raped twice in the first ten minutes of the film. There was his hook.

The film's budget was the same scale as *Driller Killer*, around $100,000. That was about as cheap as you could make a film on 35mm, and this time we went all out with Panavision equipment. I guess I was out to prove something. *Driller Killer* was great, but technically I knew I had to do more. With *Ms. 45* I made an effort to improve the production value and make a film that looked and sounded like a typical Hollywood release. The theater owners really beat us up about the quality of the sound and image of *Driller Killer*, so that was another impetus to do better the second time around.

HOW DID YOU CAST *MS. 45*?

In order for the movie to work, I knew I had to cast the right woman for the part since she was in every frame of the film. You need a very special person to be able to carry that off. If you don't find the right person, then you don't make the film. I found Zoe Tamerlis. There aren't a lot of people like her that I've ever been able to work with; Harvey Keitel, Christopher Walken, Lili Taylor, there are few actors like that who can carry a whole film. But we found Zoe and it was clear that you could watch her for an hour and a half. I discovered her through a nationwide casting call that Robert Stigwood had financed for his next feature after he produced *Saturday Night Fever*. I knew the cats that were working on Stigwood's casting, so I just said, "Tell me who comes up second and third." And that was Zoe. So I was able to get a $50,000 casting call for a $100,000 movie. Zoe was incredible. She was seventeen years old with a beautiful, sweet voice. I think at the time she was living underground at Columbia University being part of some revolutionary hit squad or something.

DID YOU USE THE SAME CREW FROM *DRILLER KILLER*?

Since we were going for a more professional-looking film we used a New York crew consisting of union people who were working on their days off or who were in between gigs. The crew for *Driller Killer* was very much a pickup crew, and this time I went for a more organized, professional shoot.

Production went pretty well, but after the film was finished it was a great letdown. Weisberg really didn't know what to do with it and he couldn't market it very well. Fortunately, a year after we finished it, the director Billy Friedkin saw the film and because he liked it he went out of his way to help me. He got Warner Brothers to buy it for European distribution. Weisberg took the money we got from Europe to help promote American distribution (since Warner Brothers wanted nothing to do with it in the States), but he wasn't able to make a great success of it. This was my first real introduction to distribution. The plan was to release the film in forty-five theaters to start, but somehow we ended up with ninety theaters that wanted the film. There was a dearth of pictures to show at the time. These "mom and pop" theaters in the swamps of New Jersey just needed a film to play, and we'd show up with this print and they were just happy that they had something to put in their theaters. Unfortunately the film missed the chance of being the first female gun film because the John Cassavetes film *Gloria* had been released about six months before. It was marketed as an action film and everybody went to see it since Cassavetes was quite popular then. I think that by the time *Ms. 45* came out, people were burned out on female gun films and gun films in general. Also, the Pope had just been shot so perhaps it was a bit of bad timing.

HOW WAS THE FILM RECEIVED CRITICALLY?

Unbelievably well, in fact. We were very green; we didn't even know you were supposed to invite the critics to the opening. All of a sudden I started reading these beautiful reviews of the film in New York and L.A. I think it may have helped us that we didn't play up to the critics. I always get good reviews, but the response to *Ms. 45* was kind of shocking. Everyone was looking for the hot director of the moment, so I guess I was it at that time, and the critics like to be the one to discover the next big thing.

HOW DID YOU MAKE THE MOVE INTO LARGER BUDGET PRODUCTION?

After *Ms. 45*, I was running all around town. I went out to Los Angeles and basically beat on doors, trying to pitch whatever I could. I chanced into meeting some very wealthy Washington bankers (they were like the sons of Louis Mayer or something like that), and for some reason they got excited about a very old script I had developed even before I did the *Driller Killer* called *Fear City*. This was a classic slasher film, perhaps not that inspired and something that I really had no intention of ever making, but the financiers just thought it would work and said that they would put up $5 million for me to make the film. This was over twenty years ago and it was an outrageous amount of money considering it was not coming from a studio. The producer of the film had made two movies prior to this, including *Dreamscape* with Dennis Quaid, and he had made a lot of money doing that. After the initial meetings, we began casting and put together a crew of actors including Melanie Griffith, Tom Berenger, and Michael Gazzo. And with that we went out to make *Fear City*. We shot the whole thing in L.A. in sixty-three days. It was a total Hollywood scene.

WHY DO YOU THINK THE PRODUCERS TOOK A CHANCE ON YOU GIVEN THAT YOU HADN'T DONE A FILM OF ANYWHERE NEAR THAT SCOPE BEFORE?

I really can't tell you. The people who gave me the money really liked *Ms. 45*. I think that if you just keep pounding at it and pounding at it, eventually you may get somewhere. You can call it luck or hard work or whatever you want to call it, but sometimes things just happen. It's also about being ready to do something and being able to communicate what you want to do, but it doesn't happen overnight either. I hadn't made a film in three years when I got *Fear City*. I had a bunch of films that almost got off the ground but didn't. There were some tough times before that project finally happened.

HOW DID THE EXPERIENCE OF MAKING THAT FILM COMPARE TO *MS. 45* AND *DRILLER KILLER*?

Things didn't really change, because I was still out there with the actors. Once you are a director you have got to demand your space and when you are on the set you are in charge. In the end there really was not a lot of difference between the experiences of shooting the films since it is the same process, just with more money involved. You still have to perform the same functions as a director. You have to choose where to put the camera and how to talk to the actors, how to tell the story. That's it. It doesn't really matter how much money you have. At the same time, however, I was learning new things that I didn't know before. But every film has been a learning experience for me. You learn in the process of making the film; it can take a lifetime to learn how to make movies. I did learn that I was better off in New York. L.A. was just not my thing.

HOW INVOLVED WERE THE FINANCIERS WITH THE FILM?

The producer was a wild man and the fact that he hasn't done anything since this film speaks for itself. The bottom line is that if somebody puts up $5 million for one of your ideas, then you can't get too angry with them for throwing in their two cents. It would have been a better film without the producer being involved as much as he was, but I was still able to make the film and that was what was important in the end. We edited the film in L.A. with this guy Tony Redman, who was an old-time professional editor. After meeting him on this film he became the guy who cut my movies for the next ten years. I had problems with the producer at this point because halfway through the editing process he wanted to fire the editor and get someone in there who he liked but who I didn't like and didn't get along with. He thought if he did this then he would have more control over the film and get a position in the editing room, because the editor would be an antagonist to me. I don't know what the hell that logic is, but in the end I edited the movie and I made the decisions about this cut or that cut.

The release was disappointing to say the least. It did well and it made its money back in Europe, but in America it was barely shown. It was marketed mainly through a blaxploitation angle. I think that people put it up as *"Fear City* starring Billy Dee Williams." Billy Dee was in the film for about five minutes. It just didn't happen, and it was my introduction to the notion that seems to have borne out over my career: My films play well in Europe, but as for America, they've yet to catch on. Hopefully someday they will.

DO YOU HAVE ANY ADVICE FOR FILMMAKERS WHO ARE JUST STARTING OUT?

I believe that you have no choice but to do what you are driven to do, because if you got it, then you got it. I believe that everyone is born to do a certain thing. I really believe this to be true. For whatever reason it may be, certain people are driven in a clear direction by their talent, their background, and something inside them that tells them what to do. When you find this out about yourself you've gotta go for it 100 percent. As far as filmmaking goes, I wouldn't recommend this line of work to anyone since I'm not about giving advice, but at the same time maybe someone can be helped by me on some level from my experiences in this business. It's a tough one. The best thing I can recommend is, if you want to make movies then go out and do it. For $10 you can buy enough digital videotape to shoot a whole feature. This concept of starting as a production assistant to become a second assistant to become . . . I certainly never went that road and it was never even a thought. I was a director from the beginning, and that's what I had to do. It wasn't about making it big or whatever; it was just about making films because I knew that that was my thing. Find your own thing and do it.

Peter Farrelly | DUMB & DUMBER

PETER FARRELLY *was born on December 17, 1956, in Valley Forge, Pennsylvania, and grew up in Rhode Island. He went to college at the University of Massachusetts, where he studied to be an accountant. After graduating and working for a few years as a salesman, Farrelly began writing what would be his first published book,* Outside Providence, *and attended Columbia University's graduate writing program. An early collaboration with fellow student Bennet Yellin resulted in a comedic script, which through some almost unbelievable means received the interest of David Zucker and Eddie Murphy Productions, who both hired Farrelly to write scripts for them. After being joined by his brother, Bobby, as a cowriter and later as a director, Farrelly toiled for nine years as an unproduced screenwriter before finally making his own film,* Dumb & Dumber, *a box-office smash and critical success. Since then Farrelly and his brother have written and directed such hit films as* Kingpin, There's Something About Mary, *and* Me, Myself & Irene, *starring Jim Carrey and Renee Zellweger. Farrelly lives in Los Angeles.*

I grew up in Carpelin, Rhode Island, a town about twenty minutes outside of Providence and forty minutes from Boston. My father was in the Army when I was born and he was shipped around for a few years. Both my parents were from Rhode Island and they had moved back there before I was old enough to remember. Overall I had a pretty idyllic childhood. My father was a doctor and my mother was a nurse. My brother, Bobby, was born exactly a year and a half after me on June 17, 1958. I also have three sisters.

WHAT IS YOUR FIRST MEMORY OF MOVIES?

My mother had four kids in four years and a fifth two years later, so when I was young my mother would basically send us out to make our own fun. From the time I was four I remember we would eat breakfast and head outside to play for the entire day. We were real outdoor kids and we played at the baseball field, in the woods, and around the ponds. We were never really into movies; we weren't like those kids running around with Super-8 cameras making little films. We didn't even have a movie theater in our town. When I was in high school a theater opened, but it was really just a place to go party and talk. I do remember seeing movies on late-night television though. Some nights after our parents went to sleep we would sneak downstairs and flip on the TV. I remember movies with Frankie Avalon and Annette Funicello, movies like *Beach Party*. One film that did have a real impact on me was *Cat Ballou* with Lee Marvin and Jane Fonda. The humor in it just blew me away and it has influenced my work in many ways. The Jonathan Richmond troubadour character in *Something About Mary* was right out of that film in which Nat King Cole and Stubby Kaye were walking around narrating the story with music.

WHAT DID YOU THINK YOU WANTED TO DO WHEN YOU GREW UP?

I didn't know. When I was a kid my interests were girls and sports. We turned the pond next to our house into an ice rink every winter and we played a lot of hockey. I loved basketball and baseball and my dream was to play sports professionally. I wasn't a very good student and I wasn't very interested in school. By the time I started high school my father was asking me what I wanted to do with my life and I really had no idea. My father had known that he wanted to be a doctor when he was six years old and he became one. I had absolutely no calling until after college. When I enrolled I didn't have a clue about what to study, but I had high math boards and there was a need for accountants in the world. So on the first day of school, I met with my advisor and he suggested that I become an accounting major. I stuck with it for four years even though I hated it. It wasn't until I was twenty-three or twenty-four years old that I would have something that I would consider a "calling," and that was when I got interested in writing.

TELL ME ABOUT YOUR COLLEGE DAYS.

I went to Providence College and I had a great time there, but that was due to the "party" aspect of it more than anything else. I was in college when the movie *Animal House* came out in 1979. For me college was just a big beer fest. We drank a lot and chased women and I squeezed by with a C or D average. It wasn't until I was in graduate school years later that I actually became interested in school. When I became interested, I began to do well.

HOW DID YOU DEVELOP YOUR INTEREST IN WRITING?

When I got out of college, I realized that I couldn't really become an accountant because I hadn't paid attention during my accounting classes and there was no way that I could have passed the CPA test. The only option that I saw then was to become a salesman, and I got a job in Boston working for a shipping line. I was making $18,000 right out of school, which was huge money back then since most people were getting $13,000 to $15,000 a year. I was doing pretty well and I was having a lot of fun and I enjoyed the guys I was working with, some of whom were old college buddies. Living in Boston was pretty good, but I wasn't really satisfied with what I was doing for work. I remember that when I went out at night I would meet people and I was never proud to say that I was a salesman. My job also required me to take long drives all over New England to western Massachusetts and Maine. During these drives I would run stories through my head and I often thought about being a writer; it was really just a fantasy because I hadn't ever written anything in my life. I didn't write one paper in college; being a writer just seemed like a pipe dream. After about a year and a half of this conflicted feeling I thought that I might as well go for it and at least try to be a writer. I quit my job and began writing.

WHAT DID YOU DO?

When I first quit my job I didn't have the nerve to tell anybody that I was quitting to become a writer because it was such a ludicrous idea. I thought they would look at me like I just lost my marbles since I had never written and I really wasn't even a reader and hadn't read many books. Nevertheless, I had this notion that I had to write. I told everybody that I wasn't satisfied with my job and that I was trying to find another shipping line job. At this time I had a friend from childhood who was living in Las Vegas working as a dealer in a casino. I went out to Vegas and I stayed with him for about three months. During that time I just wrote furiously. I was putting down ten pages a day. I was really looking back at my life and just scribbling away because I had to get something done. In the meantime my parents and friends thought that I had gone to Vegas to look for a job. After about three months I had written almost 350 pages of what turned out to be my first book, *Outside Providence*. It was a mess, but it was *something* and it gave me the nerve to go home and tell my parents that I was going to try to write. I left Las Vegas and returned home.

WHY DID YOU LEAVE?

One night I went out with a friend to a bunch of clubs and had a great time. We walked out of a bar at about eight in the morning. I was totally wasted and was having trouble standing, and it suddenly hit me that this was not the life for me. I shouldn't be stumbling drunk out of a Vegas bar at eight o'clock on a Sunday morning. I was feeling a little lost, and I suddenly had this intense desire to go to church. I wouldn't consider myself a religious person, but I am definitely spiritual. I'm a big believer in God and I was raised Catholic, but I'm not into organized religion. Nevertheless, I felt this need to go to church, and I walked up the strip to a little Catholic church there and I went in looking for some kind of solace or something. Before I knew it, the priest started asking for donations. He said he would take anything in the collection plate, chips, whatever you could give. I remember being put off by this and I walked out. There I was standing on the steps of the church in downtown Vegas with the sun burning down on me. I looked down at the ground at that moment and there on the steps of the church was a used condom. I remember thinking that that was a sign that I had better get the hell out of Vegas as soon as possible. I went home and slept until five o'clock that evening. When I woke up I got into my car and I drove all night to Denver. A friend of mine lived there and I stayed for a day or two and then I drove by myself for thirty-eight hours nonstop from Denver to Rhode Island. When you stay awake for thirty hours you get a little nutty to say the least and even more so when you are driving. I had white-line fever (where the lines of the road seem to blur together), which made me sort of high, and I passed the point of intense fatigue into a state of delirium. At that point I stopped to call my parents. I was all excited and I told them that I was coming home that night and I wanted to sit down and have a talk with them when I arrived because I had something important that I wanted to tell them. After I arrived home we went out to dinner and I confessed to them that I wanted to become a writer. To my surprise they were relieved. In retrospect I think that they thought I was coming out of the closet or something like that. I was afraid to tell them that I wanted to be a writer because I thought that they would be critical of the idea, but after I told them they were happy to find that I actually did have some ambition. They were thrilled that I was back and that I had finally come clean.

SO NOW THAT YOU HAD MADE THIS DECISION, WHAT DID YOU DO ABOUT IT?

My parents basically said that they were happy I found something that I really wanted to do but they weren't going to support me since I was twenty-four and I had already been out on my own. They still had kids in graduate school and college, and in my family when you went to college you had student loans; my father wasn't giving anything away. Education was really big in my family, but there weren't any trust funds to pay for it. It was my decision to become a writer and I was out the door without a job. I moved to Cape Cod and got a job as a waiter so I could continue writing. I didn't really have a plan and I didn't know how to go about becoming a writer except to write. One night I happened to wait on a guy who was a creative writing teacher at the University of Massachusetts. I didn't even know you could study creative writing in graduate school. I told him that I could never get into a school like that because my grades in college were so poor. He told me that acceptance wasn't based on grades but on what you had written, so he encouraged me to send in thirty or forty pages of my material. I did what he told me to do and to my surprise I was accepted into the graduate creative writing program at the University of Massachusetts at Amherst. I attended for a year and a half, but I terminated my studies because I felt that I wasn't getting that much out of the program, not to mention the fact that I was bitter that I had been passed over for a job as a teaching assistant and I really needed the dough in order to live. I decided to find another writing program and I applied to Columbia and was accepted. Suddenly I was in New York and everything worked out from there.

TELL ME ABOUT YOUR EXPERIENCE AT COLUMBIA.
Columbia was the best school experience of my life. Suddenly I was surrounded by exceptional students and everybody was into writing and becoming a writer. The school was very social and at parties the talk would be about writing and that fascinated me. I hadn't been a big reader before that time, but at Columbia I started reading everything I could get my hands on. For a while I lived a kind of hermit's existence. I was alone in New York and all I had to do was to go to school. The first day of class at UMass, we went around the room and the professor asked everybody what their favorite novel was and somebody mentioned *The Great Gatsby*. I had heard of it, but for some reason I thought it was the name of a ship. Somehow I let this slip out and I was utterly humiliated. After that I was determined never to let something like that happen again. While at UMass I had become good friends with a guy named Bennet Yellin, who ended up writing *Dumb & Dumber* along with my brother and me. I asked him to tell me the names of fifteen or twenty of the greatest books ever written and he gave me a list and I just started reading them. By the time I got to Columbia I was at least a little bit more "cultured."

I worked as a bartender at the Grand Hyatt and I worked at Columbia in the painting and sculpture department. The job was really easy because I just sat at the desk not really doing anything, but they paid me five bucks an hour. For a while I was also a runner for a small literary magazine in New York. Because I was working so much and always running around, I would consistently show up late to class and I would have to leave early. One day I came in late and my professor called me in and asked me what was going on that would make me so late all the time. I told her that I had three jobs. She walked me up to the dean's office and sat me down with him and said, "Listen, this guy has three jobs and he's working too hard, so you must give him some money to help him out with his tuition." To my surprise, the dean cut me a check for two grand on the spot. That amount seemed like a million dollars to me. The dean said, "Quit two of your jobs but keep one. Take the $2,000 with no interest and pay us back in the summer." That's what my whole experience at Columbia was like. They were exceptionally kind and worked very hard to make sure that I got the most out of the program. It was the first time I was surrounded by really incredible teachers like Richard Price, John Irving, Elizabeth Hardwick, and Norman Mailer. It was really an eye-opener for me.

HOW WAS YOUR WRITING DEVELOPING?

My writing came along with time. Many people in the program were writing short stories or novels. I was not a good short story writer because of the style of writing. I believe that most people were aiming for that *"New Yorker* style," like the work of Gordon Lish. Gordon Lish was the big writing guru of the day and basically his style was about the words and not about the story. I would tell stories. My stories would have a beginning, middle, and end, which had more of an O'Henry type of feel. In any case, my book *Outside Providence* got a nice response from the students and the teachers, and I was encouraged by that and felt that I was learning a lot. The students in my course were exceptional and they included people like Rick Moody, Tama Janowitz, Helen Schulman, and Chris Bain. Virtually everyone became a very acclaimed writer. I could never say that I was the best writer in the program, but I learned a hell of a lot and I was very grateful for the experience.

DID YOU HAVE ANY INTEREST IN FILM AT THIS POINT?

Writing for films didn't occur to me until my third year at graduate school. I had kept in touch with Bennet Yellin, who was still at UMass. I had been working on my book for four or five years and my goal at the time was to get it published. I thought that I might then get a job teaching at a college so that I could continue to write novels. While I was thinking about my writing, I realized that my strength really lay in the dialogue and storytelling ability, and it seemed to me that this would shine much brighter in a screenplay than it would in a novel. I bought a book called *Screenplay*, by Syd Field, and looked at the format of a screenplay. I had discussed all of this with Bennet and we got together for two weeks and wrote a screenplay called *Dust to Dust,* which was a comedy about a down-and-out funeral parlor (this was essentially the seed for *Dumb & Dumber).* After we finished it we sent it out to people and got some interest. Nobody bought it, but that screenplay opened doors for us. Among the first two people who read it were Eddie Murphy and the Zucker brothers. They were looking for writers for other projects and they were the hottest comedy guys going at the time. They invited us to come out to L.A. and offered us a development deal.

HOW DID YOU GET YOUR WORK TO MURPHY AND THE ZUCKERS?
Neither one of us had an agent, so that was pretty much out. Bennet's sister lived in L.A. and she was in a Hebrew dance class with David Zucker on Thursday nights. Since we were in awe of the Zuckers we gave the script to Bennet's sister to give to him. She did and he read it. It was a similar thing with Eddie Murphy. I was on a first date with a girl in New York, and she mentioned that Eddie Murphy had just moved in next door to her parents in Alpine, New Jersey. She was looking for an excuse to meet Eddie Murphy, so she offered to deliver the script to him. I gave her the script and she called me the next day to tell me that she was out jogging and that she gave him the script when he came outside to get his newspaper. By this time, we had already heard from the Zuckers saying that they were interested, so things were good. Two weeks after this girl gave Eddie Murphy the script, I was watching David Letterman and Eddie Murphy was the guest. Dave says, "Hey, what's this I hear about your neighbor giving you a script?" I was shocked and I realized that I hadn't written my number on the script or given any information about where I could be reached. The girl who had given him the script was out of town and he wasn't able to find out who had written it. The next morning I called Eddie Murphy Productions and told them my name, to which they responded, "Oh, Mr. Farrelly, we've been looking for you." Suddenly Bennet and I had two deals, but no agent. It wasn't hard to get one after that.

WHERE WAS YOUR BROTHER AT THIS TIME? WERE YOU GUYS WORKING TOGETHER AT ALL?
Bob had started a company called Sunspot with his friend Clemp Franek. They invented the world's first round beach towel. Their theory was that rather than move your towel as the sun moves across the sky, you could just move your body. It seemed like a great idea, but it turned out that people didn't mind getting up to move their towels since they like to stretch every now and then so nobody cared that it was a round towel. They actually patented it, got the rights, and they spent about five or six years trying to sell it, but they had minimal success with it. During the time Bob was trying to get that business going I was writing screenplays with Bennet. We wrote three or four screenplays and I would send everything to Bob, who

has an excellent sense of humor. He would read the scripts and we would spend a couple of hours going over them over the telephone. He'd say, "Look, this is good, this sucks, and you gotta change that." He always had great comments. His business wasn't doing well and I was making a fairly good living selling screenplays, even though they weren't getting made. Bob had been doing all this work for me for free, so I asked him to write a screenplay with Bennet and me, and it turned out to be the best one we did. Unfortunately it didn't get made, but people were offering us a lot of other projects and Bob decided to stay on board at that point.

CAN YOU DESCRIBE YOUR WRITING PROCESS?

When we write we work in the same room. One guy is at the keyboard and one guy would be sort of the through line. It wouldn't work if all three of us talked at the same time. I would take the bull by the horns and say, "He's coming to the store," and Bobby would say, "Well what if he's got this in the store?" I would kind of keep it going and the two of those guys would punch it up as we went along. They would make suggestions on ways to make things funny. If I was going off the wrong way, they would tell me so.

WHAT DID YOU DO FOR THE ZUCKERS AND FOR EDDIE MURPHY?

We wrote a screenplay for the Zuckers that was an untitled prison movie. The only thing that we had written at this point was *Dust to Dust* and David Zucker read it and had a couple of laughs. He said it was pretty good and he brought us in to write something else. He didn't trust us fully because we hadn't done anything before, so he hooked us up with a third writer who had written many screenplays. Working with this guy didn't help but instead he put the reins on us. The guy kind of turned out to be our boss, so what he said went and we were a little stifled by that system. As you can imagine the script didn't turn out to be so good. The Eddie Murphy project was called *The Young Robbers*. Eddie Murphy had a one-line idea about some young Robin Hood–types. We came in and pitched an idea that was accepted. We turned it in and people loved it. Eddie actually called me on a Sunday night after reading it and said that he thought it was fantastic and that he loved it so much that he wanted to direct it, not act in it. Unfortunately it didn't get made. The problem was that Eddie Murphy was the hottest guy in Hollywood at the time. He was on fire and the last thing that Paramount wanted him to do was direct a movie and certainly the last thing they wanted him to do was direct a movie that he wasn't in. They budgeted the film at $38 million (which would be like $100 million today). It was really a very small movie and they just wanted to discourage him and that they succeeded in doing. He went on and made his movies and we never heard from him again. That was it.

I go back to Columbia every couple years and talk to the graduate students about my experiences. I loved my life, even though it took me nine years to get a movie actually made. From 1985 to 1994 I was always employed and I was writing screenplays for studios and making a nice living. It was not a hell of a lot of work, so I could take a month or two off and it didn't matter. I would get back into it and write a screenplay in three or four weeks. I liked the hours because they allow you to sleep late; you come in when you want and you cut out early if you want or you play golf if you want. Basically, you run your own life. Tuesday night, if somebody wants to go out partying, the hell with it, let's go. You go out and you start later. It's a heck of a nice life. When I go to these grad schools this is what I tell these people that torture themselves. They are writing screenplays or books and I tell them that half the fun of being a writer is that you don't have to wait for success to have fun. Even before I was moderately successful I was selling screenplays that were a notch above some people who were writing. When I was at UMass and Columbia and I had nothing working out, I was happy because I loved the lifestyle and the freedom. It's a very brave choice to become a writer when the odds are that you are not gonna make it and you are reminded of that every day. If you are going to make that choice then you need to treat yourself well. I know some writers who still get up at six in the morning because they want to feel like they have a real job. Why torture yourself? If you have made the tough decision about becoming a writer and accepting the pain that comes with it you should at least enjoy the other side of it, and I did. I really did. For me it was like being in college for many, many years. Besides that, half the fun of being a writer is in the struggle. You enjoy that struggle and that sort of energy you get from the fear that you feel. You say to yourself, Oh my God, am I ever going to make it? That's your life. Don't think that that is the agony part of life and when you make it, that that's the enjoyable part. Now I'm happily married and I've got kids and things have worked out great, but I'm no happier now as a writer than I was before I ever sold a screenplay. I was happy being a writer from the moment I made that decision. I was proud of being a writer and I enjoyed everything that came with it. I encourage other people to do the same.

I also want to point out that my book, *Outside Providence,* came out in 1988, and its publication was very important for my self-confidence. Even though I was already writing screenplays, I felt that the book was my first real success. It was a big moment for me when it was released. It didn't sell any copies really, but it gave me confidence, and it was nice to see something out there.

When we were in school, Bennet Yellin turned me on to William Goldman. I read *The Temple of Gold*, which was his first novel, and I was smitten. After that I went out and read every book he had written. He has always been my idol because he is a novelist and a celebrated screenwriter. He wrote *Butch Cassidy and the Sundance Kid, Princess Bride, Marathon Man*, and *All the President's Men*. He is as good as they come, and I also liked the fact that he wrote in the style that I wanted to write in; he was comical, but yet he told a good story.

I must say that when I read *Portnoy's Complaint* it opened up my eyes to literature. I think that I was afraid to let myself go in my writing before reading it, but after that I realized what really good literature is. It is about being completely 100 percent honest, even if it is painful to you. I meet writers and they say, "I can't do this or that because my mother and my family may read it." I tell them that thinking that way is the kiss of death. You can't ever worry what somebody close to you will think. That is not what writing is about. Writing is about being as honest as you possibly can and sometimes that is painful. I look back at parts of *Outside Providence* now and I do squirm because it embarrasses me in certain ways. But in another way I'm proud that I was able to put those embarrassments on paper. I don't think that it is a perfect book by any means and there are a lot of flaws in it, but it was the first thing I did and it is good. It is good because it is honest.

HOW DID YOUR INTEREST IN DIRECTING FINALLY MANIFEST ITSELF?

Over the years my brother and I had been writing many screenplays and we had been selling them, but we could never get them made. To get a movie made you need two main elements: an actor and a director. A lot of times we had actors attached to our scripts. Goldie Hawn was attached to a couple of our projects and I had Eddie Murphy attached at another time to a different script, and various times we had directors attached, but we never could get both at the same time. By the time you have a director attached, the actor you had before is no longer available, and by the time the actor becomes available again the director is off on another picture. Things just never worked out.

We wrote *Dumb & Dumber* in 1990 and the studio didn't like it. It got stuck in development, but we loved the script and were determined that it be made into a movie. My agent Richard Lovett gave me fantastic advice; he said, "Make the movie." He said that I had to believe that from that point forth that I was making that movie and that if it came down to it I would make it with my own money. If you start by saying that you are making the movie, Richard said, then people will perk up, and sure enough they did. I sent the script around town, and actors who wouldn't have ordinarily read it did. They all turned us down, but the word on the street was that this movie was getting made. We were able to raise money from two guys in Washington, D.C., named the Pedas brothers, who had financed a couple of the Coen brothers movies. We said that we were making the movie and they agreed to put in a few bucks, and all of a sudden I had a couple hundred grand from them. We went to New Line and said, "Look, we're making the movie, we got a couple hundred grand from these guys," and New Line said that if we could get Jim Carrey to be in the movie then they would make it. All of a sudden the project just mushroomed and took on a life of its own.

One other thing that Richard told us was to tell people that we were directing the movie so that we wouldn't have to look for a director. That knocked off one element, so really all we needed now was an actor. I suppose we were under the impression that somebody was going to notice that we had never directed anything and question our ability. I actually had a backup plan just in case that happened. I called a friend of mine named Marc Steilen. He had a reel of work that he had made in film school and I borrowed it from him in case someone asked us what we had directed so that I could show the reel. In reality if that had happened, we probably would have backed down and said well, if you have another director for the project, we'll use him. But oddly enough, that never happened. Nobody ever questioned our ability to direct the movie.

We worked and worked, and we got Jim Carrey to agree to star in the film, and New Line gave the project a green light. The first day of shooting finally came, and all of a sudden I had a massive panic attack. We had gone out to Colorado to film, and I was curled up in a ball in my bed. My brother, Bobby, was sitting next to me saying, "Come on, get your shit together man, we've gotten this far." I said, "Bob, this is out of control. We are directing a major motion picture and I don't even know when to yell 'Action.' I have no clue about anything and I don't know the first thing about cameras." We called David Zucker and I said, "David we are in a real jam here. We are about to direct a motion picture and we have no idea how." David told me not to worry. He said that I didn't have to know anything, but that I shouldn't lie to anyone. He told me to tell the DP something, and I said "Who is the DP?" Then he told me that that was the director of photography, and he explained who the assistant director was, and he told me to be honest with them and tell them that we needed their help. But he also told me not to forget that Bobby and I had written the script and that we therefore had an understanding of how the story should be told. And we did, and it turned out okay. What we focused on mainly during *Dumb & Dumber* was directing the actors. We left the camera to our DP and AD. It was a tremendous learning experience.

WHERE DID THE CONCEPT FOR *DUMB & DUMBER* ORIGINATE?

Somebody came to us with the idea. Universal wanted to do a story about two dumb guys who drive cross-country and end up in Aspen, Colorado. They were looking at a lot of writers for the project and we came in and gave a pitch. They liked it and hired us, but didn't like what we produced. We got the script back in turnaround and then made it ourselves. Often you will sell a screenplay or make a development deal at a studio. If they don't want to make what you have written after you hand it in and they say, "This sucks. We're not making it," you can ask them to give it back to you in turnaround, meaning that you pay them back what they paid you or sometimes not that full amount, but a portion of that amount. Universal hadn't paid us a lot for developing the script, so the turnaround buyout cost wasn't that much. The studio is happy because they figure that the script sucks anyway, at least they are getting some of their money back, and that it will never get made, but in some cases they are wrong about that and this was one of them.

HOW DID YOU CAST THE FILM?

This was very simple because we took what we could get. We offered the roles to every single person in Hollywood before Jim Carrey came around. At that point I didn't know Jim Carrey from a hole in the wall. The first movie that he starred in, *Ace Ventura*, had not been released yet. Everyone was passing on our script. Somebody said Jim Carrey read it and was interested. I said, "Who is Jim Carrey?" They told me that he was the white guy on the television show "In Living Color." I would have made that thing with absolutely anybody if the studio would have made it. At that point it had been nine years in the process. I didn't care who was in it and I felt, no matter who acted, that the screenplay was good enough that we could make it work with anybody. But lo and behold we ended up with the most talented guy in comedy and that turned it into something really fantastic.

Once we got Jim Carrey, we had a movie, but then we had a battle about the costar. Bobby and I really wanted Jeff Daniels and I was a huge fan of the movie *Something Wild.* Although he wasn't considered a comedic actor at the time, he had done some comedy. He had been in a Woody Allen movie and I just loved him. He was my favorite actor, so we kind of went to the mat for him. The studio had other ideas for who should be the sidekick, but we were eventually able to convince the studio and Jim Carrey that Jeff Daniels was perfect for the part and we were able to get him. The first day of shooting was nerve-racking. The first scene we shot was when Jim and Jeff ride into Aspen on a minibike. We actually shot it in another town in Colorado. The studio had told me right off the bat that during the first two weeks of shooting I could be fired at any time. It was actually in my contract that after two weeks they couldn't fire me, but within the first two weeks they could, so those first two weeks were just nerve-racking. Every time the phone rang it was a gripe from the studio and I always thought that they were going to shit-can me, but ultimately they liked what they were seeing and they stayed with us.

People always ask me, "How could you just step in and direct a movie?" If you are Andy and Larry Wachowski or Joel and Ethan Coen and you make films like *The Matrix* or *Blood Simple*, that's another thing. Those movies are about the camera; the camera is like a character in those movies. Our movies aren't. We look at it like shooting a play. It really is not about the camera; in fact, our approach is that we don't want you to think about the camera, and so I always compare directing the way we do it to waiting on tables. I remember when I was in college I had a friend who said, "I wish I knew how to wait on tables, I could be a waiter and make some dough." And I said, "Well have you eaten in a restaurant? Then you know what to do. You go to the table, you hand out menus, you take the drink order, you tell them about the specials, you get the drinks, you take the order, you go in the kitchen (they have their own system in there), you bring the food." Well that's what directing is. It's the same thing. My whole life, whenever I would come out of a movie, I would have my opinions and I would walk out and say, "God, that could've been a lot better if they did this or that." It's common sense. The way we make movies, it's not about the technical aspects, it's about telling a good story. Also we followed David Zucker's advice and we were very honest with the crew. I think that being honest with them made them want to help us more. Also, it was an opportunity for all of the crew to have a voice and to have some impact on the film as a whole.

I remember that during the first week of filming on *Dumb & Dumber*, Bobby was sitting next to the guy who owns the honey wagon. The honey wagon on a movie set is the trailer full of toilets. Well, Bob thought that the honey wagon was the food truck, because to him it just sounded like it would be. So he sat next to the honey wagon guy and said, "Well, what do you do?" and the guy said, "I run the honey wagon." So Bob says, "Oh my God, this is fantastic. It's excellent. You do such a great job." And the guy says, "You're kidding me. You know, I've got to tell you I've been in this business twenty years and you are the first person who has ever complimented me." That's how we were. We didn't know what we were doing. We didn't pretend we did. So people really bent over backward and worked hard and felt like it was their movie too.

HOW DID THE DIRECTING WORK? WERE YOU THE DIRECTOR OR DID YOU AND BOBBY SHARE THE RESPONSIBILITY?

I was credited for directing *Dumb & Dumber*, but Bob and I have directed all the movies together. After we were finished directing the film, the Directors' Guild wrote us a letter saying that we couldn't codirect a movie without prior approval. Since we didn't know this we didn't have the prior approval, so one of us had to take credit and we flipped a coin and I won. We both directed the film in the same way that we did the other movies and we ended up getting approval as codirectors. The way we would do it was that Bobby would look at the video monitor of what we were shooting, and I would stand directly in front of the actors. We would both watch the scene from different vantage points, with me being in the thick of it, but Bobby being a bit more removed and perhaps objective. The actors like to have a director in front of them because it makes them feel that he is very attentive and is "there." So after each take, Bobby and I would meet halfway and would confer on the results of the shot. I'd say, "Was that too big?" and he'd say yes or no, or "Bring that down a notch," whatever. Ninety-nine percent of the time we saw the same thing and we were in agreement on what we needed to do. And when we weren't, we worked it out.

TELL ME ABOUT THE EDITING OF THE FILM.

Again it was a learning experience. We edited on tape and on film. Now everybody has a computerized system called AVID and it's a lot easier because you are just making changes in the computer; it saves you a lot of time. Back then, if you wanted to put in a different take, you had to unwind an entire reel of film and that takes time. But, of course, we didn't know a better way. Editing was fun though and it's actually my favorite part of making a movie. Once you've done the grunt work of shooting the thing and getting all the stuff that you need, you find yourself sitting in the editing room just putting the puzzle together. You are throwing music on it and you are seeing it come to life. The work then isn't as hard as getting the material. When you are shooting a movie you are up at five in the morning and you are working until ten at night. You don't have a life at all. But when you are editing you can have a semblance of a life, so it is nice and that's really gratifying.

HOW DID THE STUDIO REACT TO THE FILM WHEN YOU TURNED IT IN?

They weren't overjoyed when they first saw it. I think they didn't really know what it was. They were supportive, but they didn't quite get it. Bob Shea, one of the top executives, was a little concerned about it; in fact, he was so concerned that at one point the studio tried to stop it from being reviewed before its release. What that usually means is that the movie sucks and they don't want advance reviews to scare the public away, and indeed that is the message it sends reviewers. Even if reviewers did like the film, that strategy would cause them to question themselves. We vociferously opposed that and we got the studio to let the film be reviewed in advance. We knew we would get some bad reviews, but we also knew we would get some good ones. We stood by the movie because we liked it a lot. I don't think the studio knew what they had until the film came out and it just went through the roof.

WHAT WAS THE RECEPTION, BOTH CRITICALLY AND AT THE BOX OFFICE?
At the box office it went nuts. The film was number one for four weeks in a row. It ended up at $128 million domestically, it did about the same overseas, and then it was huge on video. The film only cost us $16 million to make, and it was one of the two or three biggest hits of that year and certainly the second or third most profitable. The reviews were like they are for most of our movies. You get some really bad ones and you get some really good ones. There were some people who flipped and loved it. And then you get the Rex Reeds of the world who spend pages saying extremely hurtful things about you, things like, "This person came from the loins of the devil," that kind of thing. Some people were really put off by the film. It was surprising to us because we were just trying to get people to laugh and have a good time. We have gotten some truly horrible reviews for our films and we've gotten a lot of grief about our movies and how offensive they are to certain groups of people. The funny thing is that except for the critics, I have never received a negative letter. When *There's Something About Mary* came out, some critics felt that the depiction of mental retardation was offensive. I think they were offended just because we had mentally retarded people in the movie. I stand by that depiction. In fact I run into a lot of people with mentally retarded brothers and sisters and they have no problem with it and we've never gotten one letter from any group complaining about it.

HOW DID THE SUCCESS OF THE MOVIE AFFECT YOUR FUTURE FILMMAKING PROSPECTS?
After the first movie people weren't exactly bending over backward to work with us again. The success was nice and it was a little easier to get a movie made, but not a lot easier. The perception was that *Dumb & Dumber* was a Jim Carrey movie and that was it. We were lucky to have him. At that point in time he was very hot since *Ace Ventura* had come out, as well as *The Mask*, which was followed by *Dumb & Dumber.* He had three hits in a row so it seemed like whatever he did was gonna be a hit. Although our stock rose, it wasn't like we were the hottest guys in town, and we still got turned

down by a lot of actors and studios for our next movie, which was *Kingpin*. It wasn't until after *Kingpin* came out that we started getting some considerable respect, which is ironic because *Kingpin* was not a box-office hit. It only made $25 million domestically, but people really liked that movie and part of the reason they liked it, I think, is because it wasn't a big hit. *Dumb & Dumber* was such a smash that it was hard for people to get on board and say, "Oh, God it's a masterpiece." It was too big for that. Because *Kingpin* didn't do well people felt like they kind of discovered it and we got some very nice reviews about it.

WHAT DO YOU THINK ACCOUNTS FOR YOUR SUCCESS AS A WRITER-DIRECTOR?
I try very hard. When I write a screenplay it is not good enough for it to be okay or funny. I really work at it. First and foremost, my brother and I are screenwriters and that is what we are good at. We are very average directors. We can put it up and make it look okay, but we are certainly not in the same league with a lot of other directors. However, I don't think that there are better comedic screenwriters around. It is not just that we are funnier than everybody else; it's that we really work at it. We study it and look at it and constantly ask ourselves, How can this be better? Is this familiar? Every ten minutes in a screenplay we ask ourselves, What does the audience expect next? and we try to give them something different than their expectations, but yet satisfy them with it. The advantage I have as a writer is that I have a lot of time. When we write we take as much time as we want. We can sit here for two weeks and try to figure out a twist and that way nobody sitting in the audience is gonna figure it out in the ten seconds that it takes to happen. We do take that time and that is our secret to writing a good screenplay. Our secret to making movies is that we have always kept the attitude that we had when we did *Dumb & Dumber*, which is that we are not anything special in the directing department, we need a lot of help, and we are not afraid to ask for it from our crew. We also keep a really loose set. We know that what we are doing here is making movies and not changing the world. This isn't about creating a vaccine for AIDS or something like that, we are just making movies, so we don't stress about it. Hopefully, we will be able to make a movie or two that is great, but sometimes things aren't great. Hopefully, we're gonna make some more movies that we really, really like. What I do is not the most important thing in my life and I try not to forget that when I am on the set. It is important to remember to have a good time. I don't want people to suffer for three months making a movie just so I can have a piece of "art." I want people to enjoy their lives for those three months and remember that time with fond memories.

If you have any money or any friends or family with money you can make a movie now for under $100,000. It is done all the time. It may not become a huge hit, but it will get you in the door. There has never been an easier time to break into the business because there are so many film festivals and, in most circles, independent films are more highly regarded than mainstream studio films. You can go out and raise some small amount of money, as much as you can, and you can get one of those digital cameras and go and make a movie. If they had that ten or fifteen years ago, I would have been doing that with many of my screenplays. I would have said, To hell with it. I don't care if no one else will make them. I would have gotten the camera and actors—and there are a lot of actors who aren't working who will work for nothing, and a lot of crew members who want to learn—and gone out and shot the movie. The world wants to be in movies now and that makes it easier to make your own.

That said, I would still stress that the easiest road into the movie business is to write and that a screenplay is the best calling card you can have. It is the starting point for any movie. You can have all the actors and directors in the world, but if you don't have a screenplay, you don't have a place to go. I tell people that if they are interested in directing then they should try writing because it is the easiest way in. It is something that you can send out. An actor can't go out and do a skit in front of people and say, "Look at me, I'm a good actor." They don't have anything to work with until they've been in a movie. But a screenwriter has something. If you've written a screenplay, you have something to show people, something with which to say, "Take a look at this, I have some talent." It's a starting point. That doesn't mean that everybody's a screenwriter. If you don't have the ability to write screenplays (and certainly not everyone does), then I would encourage you to find a screenwriter. There are millions of them out there with unsold screenplays and some of those screenplays are very, very good. If you can direct but not write, then start searching for screenwriters and read every unsold screenplay you can find. Eventually you may find one that's pretty damn good and then you can raise money and try to get the thing made.

I don't think that it's that hard to get screenplays read. There are a million producers out there who are all looking for material. They have people who read screenplays all day long. If I had a screenplay that I thought was pretty good, I would send it out to all of them. Of course it is important to copyright the material first so that you don't get ripped off.

WHY DO YOU MAKE FILMS?

The main reason I make films is because I like telling a good story and I like entertaining people. Before I got into this business, when I was a salesman or when I was in college or in high school, I always liked telling and hearing stories. I like writing screenplays because I start with nothing and I create something that is entertaining to people. Hopefully, you think that the story that I'm telling to you now is somehow entertaining or useful, and that's why I'm telling it.

Amy Heckerling | FAST TIMES AT RIDGEMONT HIGH

AMY HECKERLING *was born in the Bronx, New York, in the 1950s. She studied at NYU film school, and went on to make her short film* Getting It Over With *during her time at the American Film Institute. Her twenty-year career in the movies has produced such audience favorites as* Fast Times at Ridgemont High, Look Who's Talking, *and* Clueless, *starring Alicia Silverstone. Heckerling has one daughter and lives in Los Angeles and New York.*

I am what you would call a member of the baby-boom generation. I spent my early childhood in an apartment building in the Bronx where most of the other residents were survivors of the Holocaust. My grandparents had relatives who had been in concentration camps, and they brought them to the United States after the war. The parents of my two best friends were also survivors. Most of them had tattoos on their arms and for me there was a feeling that all of these people had a story to tell. These were interesting formative experiences.

Both of my parents are accountants, but when I was young my father was still studying and hadn't yet taken the CPA exam. My mother was practically a teenager when I was born and had my younger brother two years later. After having children, my mother went back to work, so I shuffled back and forth between her apartment and my grandmother's home in Brooklyn. Brooklyn was a much more fun place than the Bronx and it was close to Coney Island, which was always a fun destination. Once my parents were doing better financially, we all moved to Queens. I felt I didn't really fit in there and I didn't want to go to school with kids from the neighborhood, so when I was fourteen, I decided to go to high school in Manhattan. I enrolled at the High School of Art and Design. I was interested in art and I felt that that was the best place for me. It was at that time that I joined the Museum of Modern Art and I spent almost every weekend there watching movies. I have been doing pretty much the same thing ever since.

TELL ME ABOUT YOUR EARLY INTEREST IN MOVIES.
I can't remember a time when I was not interested in movies because they were always a part of my life. It just didn't occur to me that they were things that were made by people and that there was an industry behind them. I approached them simply as a viewer. I loved watching them. I spent a lot of time watching black-and-white television movies, and I was a great fan of James Cagney. I watched mostly cartoons and movies on television. I really liked gangster movies, musicals, and comedies. My parents could never find a baby-sitter when I was young, so I was a latchkey kid at home alone until my parents got home or I was in Brooklyn with my grandmother. When I stayed with her we would stay up watching films all night long.

WHEN YOU WERE IN SCHOOL, DID YOU HAVE ANY IDEA WHAT YOU WANTED TO DO FOR A CAREER?
When I was young I wanted to be a writer or artist for *MAD* magazine. I loved *MAD* as a kid and I'm still reading it now; in fact, I have a collection. When I look back, I realize what I really loved were movie satires. When I first saw *Blazing Saddles* it was a revelation to me because it was like a *MAD* magazine article come alive. I remember that on the first day of high school we had to write compositions detailing what we wanted to do in life. We were seated alphabetically, and I sat next to this guy who always was copying from my papers. I wrote that I loved musical comedies and I wanted to be a writer/artist for *MAD*. The guy sitting next to me wrote that he wanted to be a director. I was really annoyed because I thought that if an idiot like that guy could say he wanted to be a director, then so could I, and certainly I should be a director more than he should. It had never occurred to me that that was a job possibility. He put the thought in my head because until then I would never have thought of saying that I wanted to do that; it didn't seem to be one of the jobs in the world that could be open to me.

I was fourteen at the time and I decided that would be my goal. I ended up focusing on photography in high school. I was pretty much just doing homework and going to the movies at the museum on the weekends. I was focused on my goal to become a film director and I was determined to get into NYU film school. I knew that it was way expensive and out of my league, but I was determined nonetheless to get there. Eventually, I did get in, but that began my long financial struggle that continued throughout my twenties.

HOW DID YOU FEEL ABOUT NYU?

The first day I was sure that they would discover that I wasn't worthy of being there and kick me out right away. I was always angry about money and I couldn't get a break anywhere. My father made just enough money for me to not get any scholarship funds, so I had to take out a student loan. Aside from my financial worries, I liked making movies at NYU and I had a great time. I met some people that I am still close with including Martin Brest, who remains a friend, and Rob Hann, a director of photography who shot my last movie. I had some great professors at NYU who really encouraged and nurtured me. Marty Brest was ahead of me in school, and it became apparent that he was very talented and whatever he was doing was the thing to do. He was going to go to the American Film Institute, so I wanted to follow his path and go there too.

WHAT KIND OF FILMS WERE YOU MAKING WHILE AT NYU?

I was making musicals. I was the only one doing them and they were weird. It was the mid-1970s and it was a bizarre combination of long hair and bell-bottoms, the tail end of the hippie movement at its schlumpiest. With this I sort of infused a 1930s idiotic grace that didn't go with the post-Watergate mentality that was prevalent at the time. They were very weird films, but they got me into AFI.

I noticed that people were not going directly from NYU to movie directing. New York also didn't seem to offer the opportunities for breaking into film that L.A. did. At the time there was no market like there is now. There were no videos, no MTV, and there were only thirteen television channels, a couple of television networks, and a couple of movie studios. There was no Internet and the vast market structure that there is today.

YOU WANTED TO MAKE HOLLYWOOD FILMS?

Absolutely. But it was not an easy climb because for one thing, there were really no women making Hollywood films then. So I came out to Los Angeles to attend AFI and it was a horrible shock because I didn't drive and I had no money. I was in a relationship with Marty Brest at the time, and he took me in and helped me so much. But I was really miserable in L.A. because I couldn't get around at all. From the time I was thirteen I was able to go from Queens to Manhattan, to bounce all around the city and do whatever I wanted to do, and suddenly I felt like a child who needed a mommy to take her to soccer practice; it was just horrible. I tried to learn to drive, but I failed the driving test five times. I thought that somehow I was gonna have to get over this hump and become rich because then I would have a driver. I just couldn't see myself ever learning to drive. Finally, Rob Hann, my other friend from NYU, who is the most patient guy in the world, was able to calm me down and teach me how to drive. The problem was when Marty would try and teach me I'd just freeze up and then he'd freak out because we'd be in traffic, so it never happened. Once I learned to drive my life changed and my career moved forward. Before that I couldn't even get myself to meetings.

HOW WAS THE AFI?

At the time it seemed to be pretty elitist. It was a big mansion on the hill and they made a big thing over how the students were hand selected and blah, blah, blah, how special we were to be there, and so on. When I was at NYU it was very hands-on and sloppy and nonprofessional; we were making films with little wind-up cameras. At AFI it was like, "No you'll start on video and then you'll do this and that and then submit something for a grant." NYU was like bricks and sloppy cheese with broken-down equipment and late-night emergencies to try to find a replacement camera and all that nonsense. AFI was much different and I felt like a little rat there.

At the AFI, you make a film in your second year, which is really like your thesis film. I made a movie called *Getting It Over With*. It was about a girl who wanted to lose her virginity before her twentieth birthday and her adventures that take place between her psychology final and midnight of her birthday. There were a lot of personal things going on in my life at the time that had a great impact on me as well. Marty and I eventually broke up but remained friends. He was a big influence on me then and he still is. He's a great guy and a great filmmaker. I don't think I would have known what to do if I hadn't had him to look up to, to say, "Well, what's the next step after NYU?" There were a lot of us who were working in the industry and Marty was always there for us to go to and ask about what was happening and how to get things done.

I continued to work on my film after the completion of my second year, so I was still at the AFI finishing it, although I wasn't paying tuition anymore. I had started working at Warner Brothers, during the day, and at night I would edit my film. I had gone to Warner Brothers because I had run out of money and couldn't pay the lab costs on my film to finish it. Another AFI student who was a bit older than me was working for a producer named Fred Weinstein on the Warner lot. They were doing a movie based on *That's Entertainment*, but theirs focused on animal footage. Through these guys, I got hired as an apprentice editor on the film, but really ended up as an assistant editor, synching-up dailies. I would have to lip-synch the animals. When I went to the interview they said, "Okay, have you ever worked with 35mm film before?" and I said, "Yeah, of course." In reality, I had never even seen 35mm film before.

I was in one of those little cottages on the lot where all the editing rooms were from the thirties. I had to be very discreet and hide a lot because I wasn't in the union and the studio couldn't let anyone know that. I was very fortunate to get that job because I really had no experience at all. The hardest part of this job was the Flipper stuff because Flipper only made one sound: "Aahhh." If you play Flipper backward and forward as you do when you're synching stuff up, it sounds just the same backward and forward. There was no reference point so that you could find the beginning of a sentence. I had hours and hours of this footage, but the only reference was splashing. It drove me nuts, but I finally made enough money to finish editing my movie. Eventually my movie came out and it had a screening that elicited a very positive response. All these people came and saw it and said, "Amy, you are gonna work." That was one of the best days of my life.

HOW DID YOU PROCEED TO FIND AN AGENT?

That was a problem because I couldn't get any agents to come to the screening. That's part of the Hollywood bullshit that I had to deal with. I had friends working in the business, but nobody I knew was an agent and, of course, that's who needed to see the film. Somebody told me to go see Tom Mount, who was at that time the head of Universal. He actually called me in because someone he knew had seen my film and told him about me. I met with him and I remember that he was really young. He was not even thirty and he was running the studio. This was during the post–*American Graffiti* days: Sean Daniels, Tom Mount and Bruce Berman were the ones in charge. The oldest guys were twenty-eight or twenty-nine and Tom was the boss. He said, "You've got to get an agent because we want to work with you." So he told me to show my film to Mark Rosenberg, who was at a new up-and-coming agency. Everyone kept telling me that Mark Rosenberg was a great agent. So I sent my film out to him. There was only one problem; I only had one print of my film. This was before the days of video, and making prints was very expensive and quite beyond my means. So what that meant was that if I sent my print out to one person, and they kept it, I was screwed. That was that. I was still synching animals at this point, but I knew that if someone would watch my film, they would recognize my talent and my career could then start. So of course Mark Rosenberg kept my film for a very long time. Every week I would call his office and ask if he had seen it. This went on for weeks, if not months. I was going insane until finally he saw it and called me in for a meeting. By this time I was doing another editing job for ABC television.

So I finally get in to meet Mark Rosenberg, and he tells me that they really didn't start off with people like me, but that they would represent me *after* I had done a feature. I was furious and I couldn't believe it. After all of that time that I waited to see this guy who had the one print of my film, he basically told me adios. Frustration is the one thing that you know about when you are twenty; that's when you are most anxious to do things because you have so many ideas, so much confidence and excitement. People just keep pushing you down and wasting your time and you want to kill them for it. Add to this the fact that I had no money. This also happened around that time that I got into a car accident.

My friend and I were driving back from seeing *Mean Streets* and *A Clockwork Orange* at an art house theater at the beach when I was hit by a drunk driver. I had just joined the editors union, but I didn't yet have insurance coverage, so I wound up in the hospital with a collapsed lung, bruised kidney, and amnesia. Not amnesia like, "I don't know who I am," but amnesia like, "I don't know where the footage of the icebergs is." I couldn't remember anything and I wasn't able to do my job as an assistant editor, so I got fired. Marty Brest and my friend Stuart from AFI just stayed with me all the time during my recovery. The doctors kept doing X rays and fucking them up and then sending me back for more X rays. I kept saying, "I hate this, I wanna leave." But they wouldn't let me go because I had a collapsed lung. All of this happened during the time that Mark Rosenberg had my film. It was not a great time in my life.

I remember sitting in my little apartment in Hollywood with no money and no car trying to figure out how I was going to get to my physical therapy that day. I was trying to figure out what bus to take when the telephone rang. It was Tom Mount calling to tell me that Universal really wanted to do something with me, but that I still needed to get an agent. That's a pretty backward scenario because usually people go around looking for agents and then they get work. Here I've been through all this shit and suddenly, when I least expected it, I get the call. I had no car, no way to get to my therapy, no money; if I had been an alcoholic this would have been rock bottom. Then out of the blue, the president of Universal was calling and asking me to do a feature.

WHY DID YOU THINK HE WAS CALLING?
Well when he first met me and saw my film he said, "Well, what do you wanna do hotshot?" I wanted to do movies like *Mean Streets* and *A Clock-*

work Orange, so that's what I told him. He actually had this idea that after I got representation, then he would have me work on some TV show and I'd observe for a couple weeks and learn how it was done. Then I would get to play with the cameras and maybe do an episode myself. He was going to have his own mini–studio system training program for me. He would send me home with a bunch of scripts to read and make notes on; this was his grand plan for me. I think that he ultimately called because he liked my film and I seemed like a good match with the kind of stuff he wanted to do. My style was in keeping with the kind of place they were making Universal into.

One of the students that I knew at the AFI gave me a couple of names of agents to talk to, and told me that two good people were Peter Turner and David Gersh. David was with his father at the time, running the Gersh Agency. There weren't that many agencies back then since the number of players was much smaller. I managed to get in to see David Gersh and I showed him my film. He liked it a lot, and he really wanted to work with me, especially after I told him that Universal wanted to work with me. So suddenly I had an agent.

One of the first things Gersh did was to send me over to meet with the executives at Warner Brothers. They asked me what I wanted to do and I told them I was interested in making a female version of *Carnal Knowledge*. They really liked that idea and they hired me to write a script. So I went off and wrote it and they loved it. I kept rewriting, and finally I had done everything they wanted and was on my last rewrite when there was an executive shift at Warner Brothers. This is something that happens often in the movie business; executives change jobs with regularity. Just at the moment that I had something to show, all of the executives left and in came new ones. The new one that came was Mark Rosenberg. So again I'm waiting for Mark Rosenberg to read a script that I can't take anywhere else unless he either makes it or lets it go (because they owned it), and I'm in the same exact position that I was with him before when he held on to my short film. This goes on for weeks and weeks. Finally his office called me to schedule a lunch meeting with him. I go in with the assumption that he's read the script, and maybe he'll have more notes or tell me that this is the last draft. So I get into his office, and he makes a big production of ordering lunch and this and that, and then while we are eating he tells me that he hasn't yet read the script. After hearing that I was ready to jump out the window. They had a project in the works called *Going in Style* with Martin Brest, and the only reason he wanted to talk to me was to ask me stuff about Marty. Weeks and weeks go by. Finally Rosenberg reads the script, and I have another meeting with him. This time I went in and told him that I wanted to do the female *Carnal Knowledge* revolving around the sex lives of two women in three different time periods of their lives. At our long-awaited meeting he says, "Why do the two women stay friends? I mean they're not like men." Now how do you talk to somebody like that? Do I just jump out the window or, what the hell, should I just kill this guy? I couldn't believe it. So the project died at Warner Brothers, and it went around to some other places, including Universal, but Tom Mount couldn't get his bosses to approve it. At that time there were not that many movies that featured women and they couldn't figure out how to sell them. There was only one woman making profitable movies in Hollywood, and that was Barbra Streisand.

Gersh continued to try to help me, and he showed me other scripts, and he also showed my short to Art Linson at Universal, who was a producer and friend of his. Art had just done *Car Wash*, which was typical of what Universal wanted to do at that point in time, something that was cool and had a great sound track. They were really glad that the black community was responding to the film, and it was something that was making a big profit for them since they had spent very little money on it. At this time it was coolness, music, and irreverence that were making money instead of the typical Warner Brothers thing which was, "Hey, we have Goldie and Clint and we make big movies." Universal wanted to be the place for a younger generation. At that time studios were really trying to create personalities, to kind of make a brand. Universal was where you could go if you were young and hip. Now you can go any place if you're young. Back then it was the only really accepting place for young people and new ideas.

Art Linson really liked my short and we quickly became buds. He was the oldest person I knew at that time in my life, and he was probably only forty. But he was just so cool; he had that Frank Sinatra, Bruce Willis, "Fuck 'em if they don't get it" kind of attitude, and he was nurturing of young talent. He would give me scripts and ask me what I thought of them and I would give him notes. We went back and forth like that. Then one day he showed me a script for a movie called *Fast Times at Ridgemont High* that was written by Cameron Crowe. What was great about that script was that it had such a reality to it. You totally get into these kids' lives. Art gave me the book on which the script was based. The book blew me away. In reading it I felt like I had entered this other world and there was no question about the validity of everything in it. It made you really care about the characters and their experiences. I loved it but I felt that much more needed to be mined from the book than whatever development process the script had been through. There was a lot more depth to the story than what was in the original script.

I also really felt like there was a change coming. The hippie thing was over and it was the era of disco and punk. If I had to be labeled as something then I was a punk. I identified with that stuff. But it also seemed like the importance of a work ethic was coming back at that time. There was something really nice about that book that captured a little bit of that ethic in one of the characters, and I thought, Let's get much more of that work ethic for all the young people in the film. This is the new thing.

I felt that it was important to condense everything into one location and that the location had to be a mall, as they were representative of the times. These characters were not just sitting around drinking sodas like Richie and Fonzie, they were working. Everybody had a job and they all had different uniforms. Once they were working you didn't feel so bad about them having sex, using drugs, and dealing with grown-up problems. It seemed okay because you expect somebody who works hard all day to have a girlfriend, to have sex, and to need a drink after work. It was not a scenario of people who went to school and smoked pot and asked their parents for money. The interesting thing was that these characters were too young for all the adult stresses in their lives. Their childhood had come and gone too fast. The point was that the times were going too fast for a period of life when adolescence should be extended. These characters were already worried about getting people pregnant, dealing with a job and the politics of the workplace, and all of that stuff. What did it mean for these kids to be faced with adulthood so early? Universal liked what I had to say and quickly said yes to the project. Then Cameron Crowe and I sat down and talked about our own childhood experiences and teen years and figured out how to work certain characteristics into the story.

HOW INVOLVED DID YOU GET IN THE ACTUAL WRITING?
I worked closely with Cameron, who is so brilliant. It was really fun for us to be going through all this material together. We went through his book and picked out wonderful stuff and tried to figure out how to fit it into the script. Working with him was one of my favorite experiences.

LET'S TALK ABOUT THE CASTING PROCESS FOR *FAST TIMES*.
Casting this film was fun. There were a lot of really amazing actors out there at the time. Ralph Macchio came in to read for the part of Marc Ratner. He was about nineteen and he was really good. But even though it was before *The Karate Kid*, we still couldn't afford him. We had a certain amount of money and that was it. The movie was made for $5.5 million and we shot it in thirty-five days. I really liked Scott Baio. This was right after he did the Jodie Foster film with Sally Kellerman about a bunch of teenagers. This was before he was Chachi, but he was a big star at this point and Art said, "You know, we don't want to get into that whole 'one person's a star and the others aren't' thing. It's too dangerous for the rest of the cast." But I was still okay with it. I had also heard about this kid Sean Penn and I

saw a scene from a movie that he was in called *Taps* that was just being edited, so I watched it in the cutting room. They showed me this stuff that was mostly over Tim Hutton's shoulder and that was all they could show me at the time. We asked him to come in and I remember that he came in at the wrong time when I wasn't there. Art and Cameron met him and they liked him a lot. They asked him to come back so I could meet him.

I was on my way into the casting room, and because of the layout you had to pass all of the actors waiting in the outer office. Sean was sitting on the floor as I passed, and he looked up at me and he was the most intense human being that I had ever seen. I don't know if you've ever experienced love at first sight, and it wasn't that, but it was something closely related. I just thought, Oh, my God. That person is amazing. It was the intensity of him. In that look there was just so much coming out of him. He came in and he read, and even though he was not the best Spicoli we had seen, we had to go with him. He blew me away and it was a matter of faith because I just knew he had something incredible. He was definitely more the type that becomes the character than somebody who has a bag of tricks at a reading. Sean is someone who came in not fully developed; it was a thing that evolved over time.

I was having a lot of trouble finding the girls. Ally Sheedy came in and read. She was adorable, but I felt that physically the female lead character shouldn't be a grown-up–sized person. I wanted somebody who was a little bit vulnerable and waiflike. I felt that if the character was more childlike, then her pregnancy and the complications of her life would be more shocking to the audience; her mistreatment would be more pronounced. Art Linson then ran into Phoebe Cates at a juice bar in New York and thought she was the hottest thing, so he told her to come in to read. She was just gorgeous and we decided to go with her. We couldn't find a good Mark Ratner in L.A., so we went to New York to cast for a short time. Brian Backer had just won a Tony award and every New York critics award for his part in *The Floating Lightbulb*, where he played a young Woody Allen. He read for us and was amazing. We had our Ratner.

WHAT WAS THE FIRST SHOT OF THE FILM?
For my first shot I had to film a car driving by a street in the Valley. I had no idea what I was doing. I didn't know what size it should be, how far down the block it should be, what lens I should be using, if I should stay with the car or let it pass out of the frame, or what. Once that shot was over I felt a lot better. It's a bit overwhelming when it seems like everything you can do with a car driving on a street means something and is so significant, but then you step back and realize you can't focus so heavily on all the minutiae. Everything is not as complicated as it may seem.

HOW DID YOU FIND YOUR CINEMATOGRAPHER?

The studio and Art Linson helped a lot with pulling a crew together because I didn't know anybody. I watched all the films of the people they suggested and once again that was harder because there was no video. I would have to set up a screening of all of these things. For the cinematographer we went with Matt Leonetti, who had done *Poltergeist*. He was great because he was very protective. Cameron and I and almost everybody in the cast were all in our twenties so he was the professional on the set. His kid brother, John, who was also our age, was his assistant, so we had a member of his family in our gang. It was a great time.

HOW DID YOU GET ALONG WITH THE STUDIO DURING PRODUCTION?

Well, before we started the actual filming, Tom Mount's boss, Ned Tanen, called me in for a meeting. He showed me a letter that he had received from a stockholder in the company who asked why the studio was doing the movie with an unknown director. Why take that risk? Then Tanen asked me to explain to him why we should make *Fast Times*. I gave him all the reasons that I thought it was going to be a good movie and why I thought it was something worthwhile. It was quite strange because I thought to myself, What are they gonna do, shut us down because a stockholder was unhappy? I guess my answers were impassioned enough to make him see that we were doing something worthwhile, because after that it was smooth sailing.

The only real hitch during production was the football stuff that appears in the film. I hate football and all sports. To me the whole football subplot was not really important, so I shot as much stuff as I could in one night and it ended up not being enough for the scene that the studio wanted. Normally you would say go back and get some more, but I couldn't deal with it. I just thought, Football? Who cares! While we were shooting other scenes, they sent Art Linson to get some extra shots to complete the scene. These were close-ups of Forest Whitaker screaming. I used them in the film but I always felt kind of weird about it. Not weird that I didn't shoot it, but weird that there's a scene in a film that I directed with a black guy getting really angry and yelling. It's just not me.

WHEN THE FILM WAS FINISHED, HOW WAS THE EDITING PROCESS?

I was fighting with my husband all the time, so the main thing was getting the phone out of the editing room because he kept calling and harassing me, and then he'd come stomping in unannounced and yell at me. There was also a problem with Irving Azoff and the soundtrack he was putting together for the film. I didn't like the fact that he wanted to use all his acts. Basically the Eagles had split up and he wanted to use them all in their various capacities. Here's Don Henley, here's this one, and so forth. They may be terrific guys, but the music didn't suit the film. It was like, "Where are you putting your Joe Walsh song?" I guess a lot of people like that stuff, but being as young as I was at the time, I really wanted a new edgy eighties music soundtrack. I wanted Fear, Oingo Boingo, the Go-Go's, the Talking Heads, and the Dead Kennedys. I was one of those obnoxious teenagers who thought that the music I liked was great and everything else sucked. Getting that Oingo Boingo song in the film was a big fight. But I had to make some compromises and put in some songs that I didn't like at all. Ultimately I used them as a kind of low background room tone in the film. But then they ended up on the soundtrack album and I had a big issue with the studio about that.

WHAT WAS THE STUDIO'S APPROACH TO MARKETING THE FILM?
The studio initially wasn't gonna release it widely. They didn't think a broad audience would want to see it, so they were just going to open in a couple hundred theaters on the West Coast. They didn't really even advertise. But once the film opened, it was a success, so they quickly opened it around the country, but with no fanfare whatsoever. That was their support for the film. I was clueless; I didn't know what a marketing budget should be or what "opening wide" meant. I didn't know anything. Art Linson tried to explain things to me, but you know, you don't really learn in film school how to market a movie. I mean, who knows about that? At one point they had a meeting where they presented a poster for the ad campaign for the film. It had a bunch of girls in a french fry box, like the girls were french fries that spelled out *Fast Times*. That was really disturbing.

HOW DID THE SUCCESS OF THE FILM AFFECT YOUR FUTURE PROSPECTS?
For a couple of weeks after the film was released, I was the flavor-of-the-month director. But I had no experience in how to exploit that moment. My life pretty much stayed the same. I still didn't get into any cool clubs. The only thing that changed was that I got many more scripts to read. Mostly they were about girls losing their virginity. So it didn't seem like my life had vastly improved, aside from the fact that I did succeed in doing a movie by the time I turned thirty.

The reviews of the film were generally very positive. Reading them was intense because it was like getting your report card published in the *New York Times*. Pauline Kael gave it a great review, which was an amazing and wonderful thing. One television reviewer gave the film a ten on a one-to-ten scale. All of this was great because it meant that I would work again and that is really all I ever wanted.

You know it's all so different now. I'm a different person, the market is different because of the outlets that exist, and the audience is different because of the world we live in today. It's all different. It is hard to glean any wisdom since everything has changed so drastically.

I will say that the hardest times were when things weren't working according to plan. When I was standing there watching a scene, and it wasn't funny or entertaining, I would say to myself, What do I do now? How can this be better? If something was off and you have all these people working, all these lights burning all this film, it is money going, "Bye, bye." You have to tell yourself, Now I have to think of something good right now, or else. That is a hard thing to deal with. How did I deal with it? That's the big question. Can you dig something out of yourself at that moment? Hopefully you can and, if you can't, can you let everybody know what the problem is and listen to others? Can you allow yourself to look for a solution from someone else? Sometimes people forget that option even though they say it is a collaborative process. The thing is, an idea that's good from anywhere is still an idea that's good.

I won't say that I had as much self-doubt as I did a sense of unbearable frustration, depression, and anger. I experienced all of those things. Self-doubt comes later in your life. When you are in your twenties self-doubt is not really an option because of the almost absurd determination and belief in yourself that you must have to succeed. Making *Fast Times* was like walking a tightrope. There was no reason to think that I would make it across, but I really couldn't stop and think about the possibility that I wouldn't. I couldn't do that. I just had to press on.

WHAT ADVICE CAN YOU GIVE TO SOMEONE WHO IS STARTING OUT AND WANTS TO BECOME A FILMMAKER?

The first question is, Who do you go to for help? Would you go to a writer/director? Would you go to a producer? Would you go to a studio head? First you need to make sure that you are going to see someone who is already looking for something. If there is a director who writes their own material and stays inside and never leaves, this is not a person you want to see.

If you have material, you need to get it out there. A short film, a music video—you need to have something to show to people. But is your work the kind of work where people say, "Yeah, that's nice," or do they say, "Wow, amazing"? There is a difference. You may have an idea and want to go the whole independent route. That is a whole other thing that I know nothing about, but it certainly didn't hurt the *Blair Witch* people. You know the industry will take people from anywhere they can, and they love to think that they have found something better than the next guy. The advertising industry is a place they didn't think of looking at at first. It's a no-brainer to throw a bunch of money at a director who's already done films, but to find a young director out of nowhere and to create a hit with him, that's something they'll pat themselves on the back for.

If you have a good short film, which is theoretically what I had, and if you can get yourself in to see some studios that have stuff that they want to make, they might show it to you if they really liked your film and feel it reflects the style that they're looking for. Often they'll say, "Here's a bunch of stuff that we wanna make, why don't you tell us if you have any ideas, or if any of it interests you, and then if we think that you're the right match with one of these projects, we'll explore that further."

You have to just continue to push yourself out there. Comics send me demo tapes because I have a TV department. I might be doing absolutely nothing relating to a comic at one point. But then it's always possible that I'll be working on something about a working-class black guy who finds himself in comedic situations, and you happen to walk in and be the next rising black comic; then that might click and suddenly we're working on something together. But also it's that you're out there pushing, pushing, pushing. It's like in *Fast Times* when Mike Demone is saying, "You have gotta give the attitude to these girls. You give it to five hundred girls and one of them is bound to happen." When I was starting out my scripts would go out and my agent would say, "You only need one yes, that's all you need. You can hear three nos or you can hear five hundred nos but all you need is one yes."

There is a problem related to getting your work seen. Reading a script is a commitment of a lot of time and that's hard to get people to do. Everyone comes to me and tries to get me to read scripts. People constantly want me to look at their material, and this becomes an ongoing problem in your life. Some people get into legal disputes over scripts. This is why people don't read what is called "unsolicited material," meaning that it did not come through an agency. Even some agents won't read unsolicited material, so it is always a challenge to get the work in front of them. But if your work is good, and you push hard enough, you will find an agent.

One thing you should remember is that you are in Hollywood. They talk about a "Hollywood ending" when they talk about a Hollywood story. That means something. It doesn't mean the area east of West Hollywood. You know I'm the world's biggest *Mean Streets* fan, but because I did *Look Who's Talking*, I have this house and my daughters go to a good school. Hollywood is Hollywood. They've been making these movies for over one hundred years now. People look to Hollywood for a certain kind of satisfaction, even if it's an Adam Sandler kind of satisfaction. You want to see problems go away and to see the happy ending. I can't tell you how many times I've heard of movies where they have a test screening with the cards and people don't like the ending. They are thinking, "We want them to be happy, so we want this and this to happen. We paid our money. We sat through the bad times, and now we want to know that there is something good at the end." There will always be the critics who say, "But no, that's not real life." Well, fuck life because we're all living life and movies are supposed to be better. Most people have shitty jobs, most people fall in love, and then after a while it gets boring. I don't know, but that is what I see when I go outside. This isn't great shit. It looks like people have a lot of fun in their twenties, or at least pretend to, and then they settle into stuff that they know that they have to do. They have little peaks of joy like the birth of their child, and hopefully not too much crap like the lingering illness of a loved one. But that stuff happens, it is unavoidable. So most people's expectation for a movie is that it is supposed to be about the two cute people overcoming obstacles and finding a love that's greater than any we could ever know about. If you want to do movies here with the two thousand theaters, that's the kind you'll have to make.

But there is always hope for a fresh vision. I saw a film recently that I really liked called *Requiem for a Dream*. This film is far from that Hollywood vision of a happy ending, and I know it's not making much money, but based on the style of it and its excellence, the director, Darren Aronofsky, has been hired to make the next Batman sequel. Maybe he'll breathe some life into it. There's always hope.

James Toback | FINGERS

JAMES TOBACK *was born in 1944 in New York City. He attended Harvard University, where he experimented with LSD and went on an eight-day acid trip. After returning from what he terms "the dark side," Toback knew his life's work was to be an artist and share his vision with the world. After teaching and writing for several years, Toback penned the script to the critically acclaimed film* The Gambler, *which was directed by Karel Reisz. He then went on to write and direct his first feature,* Fingers, *starring Harvey Keitel. Since then he has written and directed many films including* The Pick Up Artist, Two Girls and a Guy, *and* Black and White. *Toback was nominated for an Academy Award for Best Original Screenplay for his script* Bugsy. *He lives in New York City.*

I grew up on Seventy-second Street and Central Park West. I went to the School of Ethical Culture and the Olsen School and after graduation I went to Harvard College. My father was a stockbroker at Dreyfus and Company and for years my mother was the president of the League of Women Voters. I grew up as an only child. My family was fairly affluent and they were active in New York politics and society, so from the time I was very young I was in an environment of literature, politics, and culture. Everyone was very encouraging of my intellectual pursuits. Even when I went off on my own tangents, I was supported when I did anything that was intellectually ambitious and productive.

WHAT IS YOUR RECOLLECTION OF THE MOVIES FROM YOUR CHILDHOOD?

I can remember images from musicals with Doris Day and Donald O'Connor. I remember when I was four years old I saw Gene Kelly at Grossinger's. I was fond of Westerns like *Hopalong Cassidy* with Jimmy Stewart and I really liked Anthony Mann pictures. Musicals and Westerns are what I remember more than anything else. I had a mad crush on Doris Day and I idolized Tom Mix, Donald O'Connor, and Gene Kelly. The film that most deeply affected me was *Moulin Rouge.* I saw it with my mother in Atlantic City and it had a profoundly unsettling effect on me. It was the first time a film consciously affected me that deeply. I think if any movie influenced me to make the kind of movies I make it was probably that one. It wasn't so much that I liked it (in fact, my reaction at the time was probably anything but enthusiastic), but that the impact was so powerful. I was very much aware of an experience that was different from anything else up to that point and I had a sense that I was clearly in new cinematic terrain. This feeling lingered with me for a long time and it was pervasive, powerful, and even a bit frightening. It evoked despair, humiliation, and loneliness, and the sense that life was somehow never going to be right, that it was just gonna get worse and that doom was right around the corner. The outlook on life that is depicted in that film was something I think I had within myself already, but it was cinematically visceral. I have often wondered whether my own proclivity for making movies that generate that unsettling feeling didn't begin on some subliminal level that afternoon in Atlantic City.

DURING YOUR CHILDHOOD, WHAT DID YOU ENVISION YOURSELF DOING AS AN ADULT?

Until the time I was eleven or twelve I hadn't decided whether I was gonna be playing in the NBA, playing tennis on the American Davis Cup Team and winning Wimbledon, or playing major league baseball. I was quite serious in all three ambitions and it was not an entirely unrealistic hope until I became a teenager. I was an extremely good tennis player and I beat a lot of players my age who later became known. I was a really good basketball player and I was determined to do that until I was about thirteen. Then my aspirations became more intellectually based; I began to think I might be a conductor or a novelist. Film never entered into the equation until much later, and I never even thought about it as a possible career choice. Instead I focused on writing poetry, stories, essays, and letters. I wanted to go to Harvard or Oxford for college because that was where my educational path was leading me and I somehow felt that that was where I belonged. Ultimately I enrolled in Harvard.

TELL ME ABOUT YOUR TIME AT HARVARD.
I found the academic part of college to be interesting and remarkably easy, and I finished college in three years. I graduated Phi Beta Kappa and magna cum laude with a major in comparative literature. My freshman year at school, I started experimenting with drugs, and I flipped out on LSD for eight days. That experience turned out to be the seminal event in my life. In fact, it is the substance of my movie *Harvard Man*. I got a sense of my life changing permanently during that experience. I escaped it only through the miracle of finding a doctor who was able to get me back from the brink of madness. I had eight days on the other side, uncertain if it would ever end. That experience was a turning point in my life and after that I knew I would never do another drug again. I also knew that that experience had taught me about identity, self, and madness, which became the theme of my further work. At the psychological core of my films are questions of self; how does one project himself to the world? I would not have been a film-maker had it not been for this experience. The essence of what my films are about wouldn't have developed because I wouldn't have been someone who had experienced the essence of these questions. And even if I did know about these questions I would never have developed the obsessive passion to make movie after movie exploring them. I had to experience that ride to uncover my passion. It was six or seven years later that it occurred to me with great certainty that film was the medium for me to expound on these themes.

TOWARD THE END OF YOUR HARVARD DAYS, WHAT WERE YOUR CAREER ASPIRATIONS?
I didn't yet know what outlet I would choose, but I did know that I had to find a way of expressing my experience and I thought that I might do it as a novelist or a poet. Teaching was a temporary alternative but never really one that I felt could become an artistic outlet. I had to be a creative artist; I had to make works of art that would be taught and discussed, as opposed to being someone who found and discussed them. It occurred to me that it might be useful to be a critic, journalist, writer, or teacher along the way to my goal of finding the avenue to my means of expression.

After I graduated I taught writing and comparative literature for two years at the City College of New York. I also married a woman who was the granddaughter of the Duke of Marlboro and I lived an elaborate social life. During this time I wrote a considerable amount and some of my work was published in academic journals. I knew that I had to be an artist, but I had not yet found my medium and I was still searching for it. What I did know about myself was that I had to impulsively follow my instinct wherever it led. I felt that the more freewheeling, more adventuresome, and less inhibited I was, the better. I somehow thought that the more risks I took the more likely it would be that I would find my artistic outlet. At a certain point it became hard for me because when you reach a certain age and you are still saying, "I'm an artist" or "I'm going to be an artist," and you don't yet know what your art is, it becomes hard for other people to take you seriously. Even though I was teaching, I considered myself an artist and I continued to do so for six or seven years after college. I was the only person who still believed that it was going to happen.

WHEN DID IT START TO CRYSTALLIZE FURTHER?

By the time I was twenty-seven, I was divorced and moved out to the Hollywood Hills with my friend football player and actor Jim Brown. We had an array of very wild personal experiences that I was able to draw upon for my writing. I knew that it was time for me to start writing a novel and I was also spending time with Jim on movie sets, which was something new to me. I had been doing some writing for magazines and I wrote about Norman Mailer's movie *Maidstone* for *Esquire*. I had spent time on the set of the film and part of what I wrote is the introduction to the published script to the movie. I rethought the themes that I had dealt with in that article and I started writing about them in a script. It was then that I wrote the script for the *The Gambler*, which took me about two weeks. I had already been thinking about the story as a novel, so it sort of wrote itself. The only prior experience I had with screenwriting was when I got together with Jacob Brackman and Arthur Penn and we started working on a script called *The Shade Below*. We never finished it, but elements of the story evolved into what eventually became the first feature I directed, *Fingers*.

I had acquired a literary agent through publishing my magazine pieces. When I finished the script for *The Gambler*, my agent gave it to Mike Medavoy who was at Margaret Josephs and Associates, which was then the movie agent for International Creative Management. He read it, immediately liked it, and became determined to make it into a film. He asked me who I wanted for the director, but I really had no idea. He suggested Karel Reisz, who was one of his clients who was looking to make a movie in America. Reisz was one of the top three directors in England at that time and had a big following around the world. He was very sought after during that period. Karel Reisz liked the script and was interested in making it. I went to England to meet with him and we immediately hit it off. We talked about the script and he was able to give me a new insight into the story. We then spent six months revising it.

HOW DID THE CONCEPT OF THE SCRIPT ORIGINATE?

The script was a combination of my life and my imagination, which is where most of my work has been derived from; I know the world of gambling all too well. More importantly, I know the psychology of the character. I have been inclined almost exclusively to make movies about characters and worlds that I really know. I think that in the majority of films that are out there, the script is not written from a personal experience or knowledge of the world that is depicted. Most everything is researched and seen from an outside perspective of what the writer imagines that world to be like. It seemed to me from the beginning that that was a kind of moviemaking that would have no interest to me. My aspiration was not just to call myself a director and stand around and say "action," nor was it to be a glorified journalist and do research on a subject I didn't know and present it. For me the goal was to dramatically engage characters I felt I knew, and connect them in situations that would enable me to explore the themes that interested me. The subject matter, writing, and directing inevitably became one process for me. With *The Gambler*, I realized that I was not thinking or feeling things as one does in a novel, but that I was watching and listening to things as a film playing in my mind.

Karel Reisz and I worked for six months preparing the script, and during that time I introduced him to the world within the movie, since he knew nothing about gambling. I spent the entire shoot watching, advising, and learning from him. I really believe that my confidence as a director came from the experience of being with Karel Reisz during that shoot. Even though it was my script and my world, I didn't have a clue how to direct it, and I would have been lost had I tried to do it myself. By the time shooting ended I knew that I was ready to do it on my own. I thought Karel's work was phenomenal and he gave me the confidence to know that I could direct. He had an extremely clear and interesting way of doing things, some of which I borrowed for my own style of filmmaking. Karel was a sympathetic and artistically inclined director and I learned immensely from watching him work. I consider that shoot to be my cinematic education. I was involved in everything except the editing of the film. And it wasn't until much later, after I directed a few of my own films, that I realized how important it is. In fact, I now look at editing as my last draft of the script.

HOW WAS *THE GAMBLER* RECEIVED?

The film got terrific reviews, but it didn't make money. It was a rather dark and powerfully intense movie and it didn't find an audience so it was dumped by Paramount. Unfortunately, Fran Blonds, who had been in charge of the film, was 100 percent behind it, but was fired before the film opened. The studio backed off, as they usually do when they have a movie that somebody else has been championing. Ultimately, there was a limit to how big an audience the film was going to reach, but it did get tremendous acclaim and I was immediately at the center of the map and considered someone to watch. Suddenly there was a buzz about me that allowed me to do pretty much what I wanted to do for a while.

WHAT DO YOU THINK ACCOUNTED FOR YOUR FLUENCY WITH THE PRINCIPLES OF DRAMATIC STRUCTURE?

I believe that came from the fact that I read a great deal and that I had been writing poems, stories, novels, and essays for quite a while. I certainly had a good sense of dramatic structure. I had a sense of how to create a voice and a point of view and I was able to apply that to the film. After *The Gambler*, everyone wanted to hire me as a screenwriter. If Hollywood does one thing well, it takes a cue and follows. In the next year I was offered about forty scripts. Most of them were original screenplays from an idea or a book, but nothing really interested me. What I wanted to do was direct something I wrote, but since I hadn't written anything since *The Gambler*, I was open to possibilities. I was about twenty-eight by this time.

George Barry, who ran Fabergé (the world-class jewelery and perfume company), asked me to write a script about the life of Victoria Woodhull. She was a great spiritualist, feminist, and generally wild person who was the first woman to run for president and who led a spectacularly fascinating life. Fabergé was getting into the film business at the time and wanted to make interesting pictures. The appealing thing about this movie, which was called *Vicki*, was that I was writing about a great character. I had Faye Dunaway in mind for the part and she loved the script and agreed to do it. The next question was for us to find a director, and I suggested George Cukor, and George Barry liked the idea. I worked on the script with Cukor every day for six months in his house in Los Angeles. It was fascinating and a great deal of fun, but we didn't get a hell of a lot done because Cukor had terrible back pain and was taking a lot of Percodan, which unfortunately had an effect on his powers of concentration. We finished the script, but by the time we were ready to shoot *Vicki*, Cukor's film *The Bluebird* had opened and it was a disaster. It didn't perform at the box office and it got terrible reviews. It was the first American movie shot in Russia and it starred Elizabeth Taylor, Ava Gardner, and Cicely Tyson. This was a devastating blow to Cukor, who was in his mid- to late seventies at the time. Because of the failure of this film, George Barry lost hope in Cukor and basically said he would not finance the film with such a big budget, which was about $6 million. I went berserk after having spent that amount of time on the script and getting that close to finishing it. Faye was deeply upset and depressed that the film wasn't going to be made. It was a great shock and we were all fucked up from it. But George Barry liked me and said that if I could come up with a movie for less than $1 million, then I could direct it and he would finance it. This offer temporarily took some of the fuel out of my rage about the Cukor project and over the next four days I made myself write a script that I could direct called *Fingers*. The idea for the film came mainly from my experiences at the time. My friend Jim Brown was a great influence on me during this period. I also worked gambling into the script as well as my musical ambitions.

George Barry agreed to do the film and we got a cast, which included Harvey Keitel, Tisa Farrow (who is Mia Farrow's younger sister), Danny Aiello, Michael Gazzo, Michael Chapman, and Jim Brown. We had a budget of $1 million and everything was ready to go. Here I was with a budget and a film that was ready to be made and out of the blue George Barry announced to me through his production manager that he had decided not to make the movie but instead was going to pay all of us off. I went totally berserk. I think he really wanted to get out of it because he was listening to a lot of people around him who said, "Toback doesn't know what he's doing; he's never made a movie before. You can't make this movie for $1 million, it's gonna be chaotic. He's not a director, and look at the behavior in this movie; look at what these people are doing. You're gonna give a first-time director who has never even made a short free rein to do this? We're Fabergé, this is a perfume company, what the hell are you thinking?" I don't want to say that George was intimidated because he was not a guy who was intimidated easily. I think he just listened to so much shit over a three- or four-week period that he had to get out of it.

When I went to confront George, Cary Grant, who was a very good friend of George's and who was on the board of Fabergé, was in the room. I loved Cary Grant and I had never met him before so I said, "I have to tell you that I am so overwhelmed to meet you. I don't think I've ever felt this way meeting someone before." He shook my hand and said, "I want to thank you for saying that because I do not hear it all the time." After a few minutes of small talk, I found myself in the position of justifying my movie to George Barry, hoping he would change his mind, while Cary Grant was waiting for George Steinbrenner to pick him up to go to a Yankee game. Grant heard our whole conversation. At a certain point, George Barry turned to Cary Grant and said, "What do you think Cary, should I do this?" Grant said, "Sure, why not?" So to this day I think that Cary Grant was at least partially responsible for *Fingers* getting made. If he had said, "Don't ask me, George," I think that might have been the kiss of death for the film. But he was very encouraging and George Barry put the film back on. This entire up-and-down episode happened one week before shooting was to start.

Jack Clayton, who was a friend of Karel Reisz, introduced me to Harvey Keitel in the Beverly Hills Hotel. I told him that I had written a script and I said, "Harvey I want you to commit to this movie without reading the script." He said, "Why?" and I said, "Because you should just say yes, you should feel lucky that we're gonna be working together." He said, "Well, I hope I feel the same way, but why don't I read it first?" I just wanted him to make a leap of faith in me, an irrational leap of faith. But he was a little more realistic and wouldn't commit right away, so I let him read the script first. He loved it, and he signed up for the project. I feel so fortunate to have worked with Harvey on my first film because he brought so much more to the table than most actors. He came to the film with a vast reservoir of skills of which I was the beneficiary.

Jim Brown's part came out of my friendship with him. It was quite bold of him to accept that role because it involved cracking two girls' heads together in what went from a sexually seductive scene to a violent scene. Jim was a rising football star at this time and it was very brave of him to take on a role like that. Jim felt that since we were friends he would accommodate me and he agreed to go to that dark side of himself for the film. The result was a frightening, unsettling, and stunning scene, which has caused not only a great deal of talk but has also generated an inordinately large amount of analytical writing. The response was very similar to the response to the Mike Tyson scene in *Black and White*. The danger in having a scene that loaded in any movie is that it is taken out of context and it is impossible, at least in a first viewing, to see the movie as a whole when one scene has such a powerful impact. It crosses the line between role and role-player into what is real and what is cinematic. In my films I have always tried to create a sense that there is no dividing line between film and life, and that film is coming out of life dramatically. This has always seemed to be a natural corollary of writing and directing movies based on my own experiences.

When I first met Tisa Farrow she was driving a taxi in Los Angeles. She was also a bartender at Barney's Beanery. She had a mischievously luminous personality and I thought she would be right for the film. I convinced her to quit her jobs and do the movie. I think Tisa had an unfortunate penchant for self-sabotage. After she did *Fingers*, François Truffaut pursued her relentlessly and begged her to come to France to do a film for him. Robert Altman was also interested in her for a film, but she never showed up for her auditions. She didn't care enough about it and wasn't ambitious enough to pursue these things. It's a shame because I think she was a terrific actress and could have had a long career.

DO YOU REMEMBER THE FIRST SHOT YOU TOOK DURING FILMING?

Absolutely. The first shot was the easiest, from a technical point of view. It was a tracking shot near the Fifty-ninth Street bridge of a homeless woman in a doorway. This was a precursor of things to come in the city since homelessness wasn't really an issue at that time. There were homeless people on the streets, but no one acknowledged it or talked about it. We shot the woman in the doorway and Harvey coming up to her and telling her that she had nice eyes. That afternoon we shot the second scene, with the little girl doing cartwheels while Harvey is being arrested. It was a complex scene because several things were going on at the same time. What Harvey Keitel did in relation to the girl's subliminal presence is probably the essence of the scene, which is often the case, I think, when one is open to it. That is when you discover what a scene is really about, when you film something that doesn't necessarily have anything to do with what is being depicted in terms of the narrative, but carries a strong subtext related to the theme.

DID GEORGE BARRY LET YOU MAKE THE MOVIE WITHOUT INTERFERENCE?

George Barry didn't interfere with the film and he let us do what we had planned. He did ask me to put his girlfriend and later wife, Georgette, in the film. I gave her the part of Michael Gazzo's girlfriend. She later became the wife of Robert Mosbacher, who was George Bush's treasury secretary. She was one of the richest and most socially notable women in America for a period of time. I was fortunate that I was able to do pretty much all I wanted to do with the film. I think it is grotesque that there is a system in place in which marketing strategists determine what is going to be in a movie during endless manipulative committee discussions. That is the way of the studio.

I attribute a lot of my personal survival in this business to the fact that I have been able to make movies the way that I want to make them. They are financed independently and then a studio buys them for distribution. From the standpoint of Fabergé, as long as I could stick to the budget and they could sell the film, then I could pretty much do what I wanted. Since they were not investing a great deal of money they really couldn't have much say in how the film was made. Most movies are controlled by a defensive investment-based approach, which most directors willingly go along with; instead of allowing the movie to have its own logic and style those directors are basically carrying out a predetermined marketing plan. But everybody wants a hit and everybody believes in the indestructibility of market research so the process becomes one of making a "product," as it is referred to without any sense of irony. The goal of the product is for a large number of people to buy it. Unfortunately, the numerical fact is that if you want most people to come see the film, then you have to aim at the most people. So the way to avoid making a film that has to appeal to the least common denominator is to do what I started doing early on with *Fingers*, to make a movie that doesn't have to appeal to a broad customer base because the investment to produce it is small.

To work with a small budget, you have to know what you want because there is less leeway to improvise. Now that is not to say that I don't use improvisation; in fact, I use it a lot. But as a director you have to recognize what you want when you see it and you have to have an instinct for what you're looking for. This is important because you will not waste time with indecision and uncertainty. You can be chaotic, instinctive, intuitive, radical, wild, and unfettered, but still fast and ready to see what you want and what you don't want. It is about controlled experimentation.

This is much more practical than having a small committee of studio people debate every time you start to vary even slightly from the original plan. In most movies there is an elaborate original plan and anytime something is veering slightly out of the plan, there is a discussion and an analysis of the situation where people express their opinions. There are arguments, debates, and numerous telephone calls, and managers and agents come into play and things become very complicated. If you want to make a movie fast you have got to be able to determine with confidence what will work and what will not work. This must come from a director in a nondictatorial kind of way. A director has to know his actors and they have to trust him. You can't afford to use actors who are going to lose faith in you so you have to know that they really believe in you and think you know what you're doing. You have to convince yourself that you think you know what you're doing and you must believe that.

I am convinced that any director who fakes his confidence will be detected immediately and have a miserable time in the process. This happens to many directors and once you lose the respect of the cameraman, the actors, or the crew, everyone will start operating in a far less effective way. Everything starts with a director's sense of himself and his ability to express confidence and have other people believe in him. I saw that in Karel Reisz and it was one of the most important lessons I drew from being on the set of *The Gambler*. I have seen over the years how unusual it is to have a director like that who is that sure of himself and articulate in expressing his understanding of what he wants from the people around him. *The Gambler* could not have possibly worked the way it did if Reisz hadn't had that ability to deal with a totally diverse group of people, adjusting a bit each time he explained something. He could talk to people and he knew how they needed to be spoken to. Half the battle is won when you understand this. You must have it and you must feel it. You cannot fake it.

TELL ME ABOUT THE PRODUCTION, EDITING, AND RELEASE OF THE FILM.
We had a really rapid-fire ferocious shoot that weirdly enough went quite
smoothly. We just did what we had to do every day and we shot the whole
movie in twenty days. Bob Lawrence, a famous Hollywood editor who was
very smart and very sharp, edited the film. He edited *Spartacus* as well as
films for Anthony Mann and Nick Ray. In the beginning he had been opposed to the movie along with the others at Fabergé, but by the time he
started seeing the footage he got very excited and wanted to become involved. We became good friends and he really taught me a tremendous
amount about editing. Because of him the postproduction process on *Fingers*
went according to schedule. There was nearly a finished cut of the film the
day we finished shooting and there was a finished cut of the film nine days
later. Usually there is a three- to five-month postproduction period and we
were way ahead of schedule from the start. We did the minimum looping
for the music in one week. I will admit it is not one of the great mixes or
sound jobs in the history of movies by a long shot, but the music was all
source music so I knew exactly where it was going to be and we placed it
fast.

Unfortunately, as we were getting ready for our release, George Barry
had a series of setbacks with some movies that had come out and his distribution deals with Fox and Warner Brothers were not renewed. George hired
Maury Lefko, an old-timer from MGM, to handle the distribution of the
film. Maury was a funny guy who was always smoking a cigar about as big
as his body. *Fingers* was not his cup of tea and he told me that he put that
Michelangelo "Antonioni piece of shit over," and that he could put my piece
of shit over too. The Antonioni piece of shit in question was *Blow Up*. So he
was not interested in my idea of marketing the movie as a kind of art film.
It wasn't marketed effectively and they labeled it an exploitation movie and
basically threw it out. *Fingers* opened over most of the country in exploitation or closet exploitation houses. Roger Ebert stumbled into it by accident
in a black neighborhood in Chicago where it was playing as a double bill
with *Drum*. On the marquee it read, "Jim Brown is *Fingers*, Ken Norton is
Drum." That was the level of distribution savvy that it was getting. I actually saw the movie at the New Amsterdam theater in New York on Forty-
second and Broadway with an all black, largely Jamaican audience who
went crazy for the scenes that Jim Brown was in. During the head-banging
scene black audiences were cheering and screaming with glee. It was a politically incorrect perception, but it was a real one and it was a nerve that
Maury Lefko probably felt he could tap into since he didn't quite know what
else to do with the film. There was no money put into advertising the film.
This was because George Barry was in a very rough position at the time
with the board of directors of Fabergé saying, "We are a perfume company,

what are you doing with these movies?" Although he ran the show he was getting a lot of pressure to cut his spending so for us everything went well until the release of the film, at which time it was basically dropped.

My friend Maureen, who was a photographer, came up with a poster for the film which was a stark shot of Harvey on the streets of Soho wearing a leather jacket holding his boom box. George paid a substantial amount of money to an ad agency and they made a horrendous poster that made the film look like a horror film. I told George that the poster was terrible and that they couldn't use it, and I showed him the poster that my friend had done for free. No one at Fabergé wanted to feel that they had wasted $50,000 on something that they could have gotten for free, so my poster was vetoed. Harvey and I went to the Loews Tower East cinema in Manhattan, where the film was playing. Over a period of three shows we asked 415 people which poster would make them want to see the film. I held up one poster and Harvey held up the other. Harvey wasn't well known at this time so he wasn't in any danger of being recognized even though he was on the poster. Maureen's poster received an overwhelming response. Over three hundred people chose Maureen's poster. I called George and I told him what we had done. I was all excited and I thought he'd be thrilled to hear it. He said that what we did was not a scientific way to take a survey. He said, "I have my own surveys so don't argue with me about it anymore." This was the first time I ever heard him take that tone and he hung up on me. I felt bad because if they had taken a shot with the other poster it might have paid off. The release was fucked up over a poster and a marketing campaign. George and I really had an unfortunate temporary conclusion to our relationship over that. I am glad that he financed *Fingers*, but it turned into a mess at the end. To this day I believe that if a few things had been done differently, something could have been done with the film. The film didn't do well at the time it was released but has actually made money over the years because it only cost $1 million to make.

It is very interesting what happens to a movie after it is finished. The idea of ownership changes completely. Maybe a director still has some control over it, but usually not. Suddenly the director becomes a necessary evil or tolerated advisor, but in fact very few distribution and marketing people want directors around for their advice. My experience with *Fingers* was a precursor of things to come.

DID *FINGERS'* LACK OF COMMERCIAL SUCCESS AFFECT YOUR FUTURE PROSPECTS?
There was a great undercurrent of serious critical excitement for the film. Pauline Kael gave it a great review and in England David Thompson basically called the film a masterpiece. Tom Miln, who was one of the top critics

in the world at the time, referred to me as the "American Buñuel." Gene Siskel and Roger Ebert both loved the film, but unfortunately there was an enraged response from a few American critics like Janet Maslin and Vincent Canby, who hated the movie and wrote scathing reviews. They had immense power because they were reviewers for the *New York Times*. But some people liked it very much, and Sue Mengers, who was one of the top theatrical agents at the time, saw the movie and said it was a calling card for actors. She said that any actor who saw the movie who was even vaguely ambitious about the art of acting was going to want to work with me. That turned out to be true and a lot of major actors called and wanted to work with me after that.

WHO HAS INFLUENCED YOUR VISUAL STYLE?

Orson Welles is the only guy who ever influenced me dramatically. I learned everything from watching his films. Welles's work was a kind of stylistic bible for me, with his use of wide-angle lenses, deep focus, movement of the camera, sudden hard cutting, juxtaposition of very radical wide shots, and angular perspectives with very tight shots of faces. He clearly and permanently altered my whole cinematic sensibility. I was influenced by all of his films but if I had to pick three that had the most impact I would say that they were *F for Fake*, *Touch of Evil*, and *Citizen Kane*. There is a vast array of other directors who are interesting to me and I appreciate their work, but Welles was the most influential.

WHAT DO YOU THINK IT IS THAT MAKES ACTORS RESPOND TO A PROJECT?

I don't think actors necessarily respond to good material alone. I think they respond to a combination of things. First of all it depends on the actor but I think that most of them respond to the combination of the script, who is directing it, and what that person has directed before. A first-time director doesn't have the luxury of having material to represent him. I was fortunate to have met Harvey Keitel and we hit it off right away. I think he got a sense of me and knew that we would be able to do something interesting together. He was able to respond to me almost solely on a personal level, so I don't think that the script mattered as much to him, although it was clearly important. With some actors the script is definitely the biggest selling point.

I don't think that as a first-time director you should ever approach actors through their agents. Some agents are useless and they are not gonna do anything because they don't want to be in the risky position of losing a client who says to them, "Why the fuck are you recommending this schmuck who no one has ever heard of?" I would even go as far as to say that you shouldn't even say you know somebody who knows the actor. Knowing somebody can help, but I personally would not do that. I think that the kinds of actors who are going to be most interesting are those who are available and open to a more direct approach. If you go up to them like a nut and they think you are crazy that's another story. It is a question of doing it right. It may be easier with some actors than with others since some people are much more visible and accessible. Some actors are around and you can find them, while others surround themselves with bodyguards and are just not reachable. If you have a known actor who is interested in a project this will help immensely. The advantage of getting a name actor involved is that he may send it to his manager or agent, who will know where to take it for funding. Any other way to get a first feature made would be purely by a lucky accident or if you approach filmmaking with a short film or a bunch of music videos under your belt. I'm not talking about coming in cold without anything to show for yourself. Having something to show does work. If you write, direct, and shoot a commercial or video that looks really slick and sharp, people will take notice. That shouldn't be as much of a criteria as it has become, but it helps because if the work is really good then it is almost as if you have made a movie before rather than being a first-time director.

WHAT DO YOU THINK ABOUT GETTING INTO DIRECTING THROUGH MUSIC VIDEOS AND COMMERCIALS?
Brett Ratner, who was in *Black and White,* is a friend of mine and he did it that way. He was very shrewd about it and it was always his intention to go from videos to features. Anyone who is going to consider financing you will look at you differently than someone who comes in cold because you have work done and they are able to judge you as a director. There are a lot of people who do it this way.

HOW BIG OF A ROLE DO YOU THINK LUCK PLAYS IN THIS BUSINESS?
Luck plays a tremendous role. If I hadn't met George Barry, who knows if I ever would have gotten my first movie made. I like to think I would have, but who really knows? *Fingers* would never have been written had it not been for George Barry. There were not a lot of people who would have said, "Okay, I will finance anything you wanna do for $1 million, but get it to me right away." Thankfully for me *Fingers* came into my head. It is really a kind of hit-and-miss fate-oriented proposition and I've never felt that anything happens without a dose of luck or accident. Almost everything happens because you make a left turn instead of a right turn and the right person happens to be there when you least expect it.

DO YOU THINK THAT IF YOU HAVE TALENT YOU WILL BE RECOGNIZED?

I don't think this is necessarily true, unfortunately. I think that there are a lot of very untalented and stupid people who are quite successful and a lot of very talented people who never get a break. They just don't know how to use their personalities to advance themselves. Half the movies that are made just suck and they are made by totally untalented people. This doesn't stop them from working and from being successful. Can you have a huge hit and be very untalented? The answer is yes. Can you be tremendously talented and have a movie that is a commercial disaster? Yes. Talent is not a direct link to commercial success. It is only a direct link to doing something interesting. Talented people are brushed aside and defeated and discouraged all the time and untalented people with a relentless determination and a certain shrewdness advance all the time. A stupid untalented person could never write a successful good novel, but a pretty untalented director could make a successful and even pretty good movie if he is working with the right people. If the director starts to really fuck it up, people will straighten him out so it will be okay in spite of him. That is what makes this a weird profession. Some directors are totally into controlling every aspect of a movie that they are making for better or worse and other directors are just kind of going through the motions.

WHAT IS YOUR ADVICE TO SOMEONE WHO WANTS TO BECOME A FILMMAKER?

It is important to start with as much strength as you can muster. First, you should have a script, either one you have written yourself or something you own the rights to. Whatever you have, you need to own it. Second, you should have at least one name actor who you want for the part who wants to do it. In order to achieve this you need to be aggressive. Script and personality are essential. Actors are people and they will often respond to a personal approach. It has always been important, but today it is even more important that you have a name actor involved in a project. I'm not saying that there aren't movies that get made without name actors because there are. But your chances of getting a project financed are exponentially higher if you have an actor attached; actors are helpful in terms of foreign and domestic sales and distribution. Even though a lot of movies that don't have big names in them do well at the box office, we live in a star-oriented culture and by far the most reliable way of moving ahead is to have someone attached who is known. The first question everybody asks when you talk about a movie is, "Who's in it?" That is just a fact of cinematic life and that is also the first question asked by the people who are financing these movies.

I would advise filmmaking as a career only if you are obsessed with it because I think that the chances of it working out are slim, given all the things that have to be in place in order for you to be successful. Do it if you feel that you have to do it and you can't see yourself doing anything else. You have to really feel that there will be some kind of unfulfilled aspect to your life if you don't do it. That will also motivate you and you will be better at getting it done because your energy level will be higher and your determination will be greater. For me filmmaking is rewarding, exciting, and interesting, but I am never really satisfied. The minute something works there is always something else to do, so I can't sit back and feel truly content. Ultimately, I am always vaguely dissatisfied, and my mantra over the years has always seemed to be, "What now?"

Tamra Davis | GUNCRAZY

TAMRA DAVIS *was born in Los Angeles, California, in the 1960s. After a brief internship for Francis Ford Coppola she attended Los Angeles Community College film school and became engrossed in the L.A. art scene, hanging out with and interviewing luminaries like Jean-Michel Basquiat. After directing a low-budget music video, she was discovered by EMI, which hired her to direct videos for them. Davis then began a successful career making many music videos, including those for such artists as NWA and Eazy-E. After making several short film and documentary projects, she directed her first feature,* Guncrazy, *starring Drew Barrymore and James LeGros. She has directed several successful features including* CB4, Billy Madison, *and* Skipped Parts, *starring Jennifer Jason Leigh. She lives with her husband, Michael Diamond, in New York and Los Angeles.*

I grew up in Los Angeles, right in Studio City, so I was around the Hollywood studios all my life. I grew up with my parents. This was during the seventies, so it was all about chaos, breakup of the family, that kind of stuff. But we were all surrounded by Hollywood. When I was about fifteen, I moved in with my grandparents, who lived right above Sunset Strip. They were in the movie business, slightly, as my grandfather had been a comedy writer. We lived right near Universal Studios, and when we were kids, my brother and I would sneak in and ride on the rides, go crazy, stuff like that.

My father was a management consultant, a headhunter. If you were an IBM president and you needed to switch to Xerox, then he would place you there. He had really good communication skills. My mom was a mom, but this was during the whole women's lib movement, so she worked at a place called I Am Woman. I have one brother and two sisters. I have an older sister, one younger sister, and one younger brother.

ARE THEY IN THE MOVIE BUSINESS?

My little sister is a casting agent, and she's really good. I've worked with her three times, and she did my last two films. She also does Spike Jonze's videos and did his movie, *Being John Malkovich*. She also works with Drew Barrymore—which is how Drew came to be in *Guncrazy*—and did *Charlie's Angels* and *Never Been Kissed*, and she's just awesome. She is my little sister, but she's my closest friend also. When she was little, you know how you always make your little sister do everything for you, I would be like, "go up to that girl and ask her if she wants to be in a music video, do this, do that," you know, just to make sure that she had no fear about approaching people. "Go up to that cute boy and find out if he wants to do a movie." I think she kind of bought into that.

WHAT IS YOUR FIRST MEMORY OF THE CINEMA?

This is scary, but my first memory was when we went to go see *Snow White*. I was three or four years old and I remember it because it was a traumatic event. I forgot to wear underwear, and my mom found out and was very upset with me. I remember that I was wearing a dress, and she pulled me out of the theater when she realized. So that's my first memory of going to a movie theater. As far as movies at home, we would constantly watch old movies; I think that that was basically my baby-sitter through every weekend. My mom would sit us in front of the television, and we would just watch old movies all weekend. I totally loved it. I think because the actresses were really good role models. Katharine Hepburn, Bette Davis, and Joan Crawford, you know, all those great old movie stars. They were great, fun people to watch.

WHEN DID YOU START GETTING INTO MOVIES IN A SERIOUS WAY?

At first, I thought I would be an actress. That's what you do when you're a girl, I thought, so I started going out on auditions and studying. I was about twelve years old when I first got into it. Then in my teens, I was going out all the time. Growing up around that world, I was going to parties at Hugh Hefner's house and Bob Evans's house when I was like fifteen years old. People were very protective of me, but in that way of "Stay away from her, she's underage." I was hanging out at these places, I think, because it occurred to me, Oh, if you want to be an actress, that's how you meet people, by going to these places. Of course, that's never how it works ultimately, but I didn't know that then. But once I got into all those places and around those people, and I think this is a typical thing that happens with anybody in their mid to late teens, I started to believe that I was as smart as everybody else, if not smarter. And, as a young girl, I observed all these men, and the power I had over them sexually, having something they wanted. I felt that having that I was able to get into their innermost places, and then once I was in, I was just as intelligent as they were, so I would be able to handle myself.

When I was about seventeen, I met an agent who took me to Italy to be an actress. It was at that point that I went to movie sets and fell in love with the making of films. I was lucky enough to be able to watch a lot of people direct: Federico Fellini, Peter Bogdanovich, Michelangelo Antonioni, even Francis Ford Coppola. I hear often that it's hard to be a female director. Of course, that's true, but when you're starting out, it can be to your advantage. I mean, what guy wouldn't mind having some young girl sitting there by his side watching him? But of course, they didn't realize that I was paying attention.

I was there about six months and did a little bit of acting during that time. But the guy who brought me there was also working with Nastassja Kinski (he ended up marrying her), and I was always going places with them, thinking, she is the movie star, I'm not the movie star, and as that became more apparent to me, I got much more into watching people than being the center of attention.

I never really thought of ever doing anything else other than working in the movies. I mean I worked in restaurants and health-food stores and clothing stores when I was going to school, but I never really thought of having any career other than being an actress, and then once I went and saw Fellini direct, I was like, "Whoa, that's it. It's so much better to direct." You have so much more power and control. And I think one other thing is that as an actor you have control over your talent, but no control over being hired. As a director you have much more power.

SO AFTER YOU CAME BACK FROM EUROPE, YOU WERE SOLD ON BEING A DIRECTOR?
Definitely. When I came back I did a few more auditions, but basically that was it. And you know, the way I looked at the time, they sent me out on all these silly auditions for a young blond girl and the dialogue was just terrible.

Then, around this time, I had met Coppola in Europe and had developed a friendship with him. He was doing this thing called the High School Assistants Program and was making the film *One From the Heart* at that time. So I got into the program and became a trainee on that film. It was fascinating, because he would let me sit in his trailer and just watch everything, learn everything. Of course, that was a crazy film because he was trying to shoot the whole thing in sequence, but it was still an amazing experience to watch.

Francis is a great teacher, and he loves talking to people, especially young people. So he was always pointing things out, explaining his moves. He was really into technology at the time, and it was one of the first films where video assist was used. So I was watching and learning from him, and then he asked me, Tamra, what do you want to do? And I said that I wanted to direct. He told me that I would never be a director if I worked as an assistant, you know, working my way up from PA or whatever. He said that if I really wanted to be a director, then I should go to film school and find out if I had any talent, and that that was the only way I was ever gonna know.

I thought for a long time about what he said. My family didn't have a ton of money, and the choices that I thought were available to me were just USC and UCLA, which would both still require a lot of cash. Then there was a new program, at L.A. City College (LACC), where the tuition was like $50, and it was totally awesome. So I went and checked it out and then I signed up.

HOW LONG WAS THE PROGRAM?
It was two to three years, and I went on and off for about three and a half. So by the time I got out I was twenty-three years old. During this time, it was the heyday of Coppola, George Lucas, Steven Spielberg, and guys like that. The LACC program was great. Before that, I had taken some extension courses at UCLA. Everybody there was so pretentious, they acted like they were already filmmakers. And I had no idea what I wanted to do or how to do it at the time, I was still learning. So LACC was great because the people who went there were Iranians, Mexicans, and blacks, you know, young people, and housewives too, just people who wanted to learn. I liked it because when I would show my films, I wasn't showing them to a group of intellectual film students, but a real audience, real people. Having that training was very helpful to me. It taught me who the audience was and how to reach them.

I still have all the projects I did in school. Probably the most ambitious one was where we were given an assignment to remake a famous Hollywood movie. So I chose *Sunset Boulevard,* and did a fifteen-minute remake on Super-8. It was really fun to go back to the original Billy Wilder script. I just loved the material. I shot it at Rudy Vallee's house, this big mansion, and I used his wife in the film. The first sound film I made was called *Mary in the Water*. I used this woman Mary Waranoff, who was in a bunch of Andy Warhol movies. It's a film of her swimming and talking about swimming. It has an interesting look.

While I was at school I had a few jobs. I worked for this crazy guy who had an enormous house that he would rent out for movies and photo shoots. But mainly I worked for the Aretha Kampers art gallery. This was the early eighties, and the whole downtown L.A. art scene was really happening right then. I became friends with Jean-Michel Basquiat, and we started hanging out a lot. He was really into filmmaking and we worked on a few projects together. Also, I met my first husband at that time, a painter from the gallery. He had lived in Germany and France, and he really introduced me to European cinema in a way I wasn't exposed to before.

WHAT WAS YOUR APPROACH TO A CAREER TOWARD THE END OF YOUR TIME AT FILM SCHOOL?

When you go to film school, you're totally prepared by the time you get out to make a movie. You're basically ready to make a feature. So that's how I felt when I got out. I thought okay, I've got this idea I wanna make; I'll do it. I began to put together all the bands I wanted in the soundtrack, and started preparing the whole thing. I was twenty-three years old, and I started going to meetings trying to get the film made. It was really kind of a sad thing, because I realized that people were literally laughing at me. Nobody thought I could make a movie. They kind of giggled when I told them. It was really shocking for me. I mean, it seemed like any guy out of film school would have been at least taken seriously, at least had a chance. But to be a young girl at that time, there was just no way. I had grown up with a strong mother, women's lib and all, and the idea that you can do anything you want. But then it was like, "Welcome to Hollywood. No you can't."

At this point, I realized things were gonna be harder. And this is one of the things that stays with me, and I think still drives me, is having all these people telling you that you can't, and then standing up and proving them wrong. Another thing is the idea of changing the way the system works. Even today when there are a lot of girls making films, there's still almost none compared to guys. It's pretty bad out there. I think that girls have a really amazing voice in this world and it's a shame that there's not too many of them out there using it. There are probably only five women making films for studios.

What happened to me was quite strange. When I was putting together the
feature, I had figured out which bands I wanted on my sound track. One of
the bands was brand-new, unsigned at that time, and they had this great
song, but no music video for it. This was in the early days of music videos,
and I decided to go out and make one for them. I shot it on Super-8, filming
them on a stage, at concerts, backstage, etcetera, and I put together a kind of
homemade music video from this footage. Then the band got signed to
EMI, and I got a call from the president of EMI, who said he wanted me to
come to his office right away. I was totally afraid that I had done something
wrong, messed with their image, that I had done something I didn't have
the permission to do or whatever.

I went into the guy's office, and then he sat down and played the video.
All of a sudden he was saying, I want to know how you did this, I want to
know how you did that. I was so embarrassed. I said, "I shot it on Super-8,
this was a film school thing, you know, nothing special." And he said it was
fabulous, he'd never seen anything like this before. Then he told me that he
had another band that he wanted to break into the same market, and if he
gave me $50,000 to do the same thing would I? I couldn't believe what he
was saying. Then he said, "I'm gonna call Jeff Ehrenoff over at Warner
Brothers. I want you to go meet him and he's gonna give you some work too.
We've never seen anything like this." And I just thought, Oh my God.

I don't think it had to do with being a girl or anything like that. It was
just that I was doing something that nobody had seen before, and MTV
needed something new, because at that time it was all about "Uptown Girl,"
those big bad eighties videos.

The first band I did a video for was called the Trooper Loopers, and then
I did the Delroids, and Hüsker Dü. I loved these videos. For me it was the
best of both worlds because I got to work with bands that I was a huge fan
of, and I was working as a director, making money at the same time. This
was right out of film school, and straightaway I was making friends with
people I really liked. I would go to England and do videos for Depeche
Mode, and The Smiths, all my favorite bands.

CAN YOU TALK A BIT ABOUT YOUR AESTHETIC FOR THESE VIDEOS?
I actually still have it, I don't know what it is but somehow I don't always
have the money or resources that I want, so I approach the project with the
materials that I have. You realize how to turn the lack of things that you
have into things that actually work better. You have to create with what you
have, so your creations are more from inside, more about what you can do,

not what the money can. When I did the first video, I had Super-8, and I was down in the middle of the mosh pit filming. That's why the camera was shaking, because I was right down there. Then that shakiness became a style.

WHO ARE YOUR INFLUENCES IN TERMS OF FILMMAKERS AND STYLE?

I had a lot of influences then and I still do. I'm constantly looking for inspiration. In the early days, I really appreciated the American film directors, like Billy Wilder, Preston Sturges, and John Huston, and later, Bogdanovich. Then I got into European filmmakers also. But sometimes, you get your influences from the people you work with and from younger people coming up around you. You see something that someone else tried and you think, "Wow, that person went someplace new!" I get just as influenced by seeing *Buffalo 66* or *Laws of Gravity* as I do from the old classics.

SO WAS THERE A PERIOD OF SELF-DOUBT FOR YOU AFTER NOT GETTING THE FEATURE OFF THE GROUND?

I've never had a true moment of self-doubt. I think that to be a director you can't have self-doubt, and even if you do, you can't let anybody ever know. One thing that a director needs is an ability to lead and an ability to lead fearlessly. The moment you show self-doubt you show weakness, and whether your crew, the studio, or your actors see that weakness, it's the thing that will destroy you if you don't watch out. So I think that I always thought that I could do anything, and that the films that I've done, nobody else could do the way I've done them. I don't think that Spielberg could have done anything that I've done (and the times that I've done it with the very limited money).

DID YOU HAVE ANY MENTORS WHO WERE HELPING YOU ON THE TECHNICAL SIDE, IN TERMS OF THE PROCESS OF MANAGING THE CREW AND LEARNING, OR DID YOU HAVE TO LEARN BY YOURSELF?

Mainly I had to learn everything alone. I have excellent producers. I worked with Sharon Nakor and David Mailer, so I was surrounded by people who were really talented, and they put me with crew people and postproduction people who were really talented as well. I also think that at that time I was doing new things, I wasn't trying to do what somebody else had done, so nobody really knew the "right" way to do it. I was shooting with a Bolex. Nobody else was running Bolexes then. And I was experimenting with video colorists late at night, so my work had a unique feel. It wasn't like I had to go in and do something somebody else had done, and get it to look perfect like that. I was just doing my own thing. There was a time that our film came back from the lab, and there was an enormous scratch through it.

Everybody in the room was all freaked out. So instead of going crazy, I took some sandpaper and scratched up the rest of the negative to match. I just thought that it looked really cool.

In terms of a feeling of arrival, I think that with music videos or anything in your career really, the moment that you think that you've made it, or that you're the one who's great, then somebody's gonna come right up and steal your seat. I never really felt that, that sense of, Wow, I finally made it. I think that you have your accomplishments and you feel happy about them, but I don't feel like I ever got to a place where I felt the wow. I think it's always a sense of knowing that you took the steps to get you where you wanted to go, that you did something that brought you the next job, and so on, but never have I felt that I've reached some final goal. What I like most is that you get to work with people who you really like a lot. That's the accomplishment that I still enjoy—to work with my favorite bands, work with my favorite cameraman—those are the real accomplishments when you feel good about yourself, that you've made it enough to hire who you wanna hire and do the projects you wanna do.

HOW LONG WERE YOU DOING VIDEOS BEFORE YOU STARTED TO SERIOUSLY THINK ABOUT FEATURE PROJECTS?

I was always thinking of feature projects. I still had the scripts of the movies I wanted to make. I was making good money shooting videos, so what I would do was save up my money and every year I would make a short film. I have about ten short films and documentaries that I made during my video career. Usually I kept the budget to around $1,000 a minute for the finished film. So if I made a twenty-minute piece then I spent around $20,000 on it.

One thing that I found interesting was that a lot of people that I used to make videos with always talked to me about how they wanted to make features. It was always, "Oh, I really want to make movies . . ." But in the end, they didn't. I mean, I can understand in a way, because the world of videos and commercials is very seductive. You're working, you're the director, it's easy to get stuck doing something and years will go by where you don't make a film. So I realized that what I had to do was stop working. I had to say to myself, for the months of November and December, no matter what, I'm not gonna take any work, I'm gonna make a short film. That's a hard thing to do. And even now I have to do that. You have to remember not to let the seduction of work, of just working, distract you from a project that you really want to do, no matter what that project is. What's important is that that project means something to you.

I always felt that there were a lot of people who were just using music videos and commercials as a stepping-stone to features, and I was quite upset at that. For me that's totally dishonest. It's like saying, "I'm only dating this girl until the right one comes along." If I'm going to do something then my heart has to be in it. I can't just make a video to make a video. I have to become the biggest fan of whomever I do the video for. I really have to believe in the band and get into their music. You have to be that way. Otherwise the work suffers. And I think that attitude is why I can still really like the videos I've done and continue to have a good relationship with the bands and record companies that I made them for.

So I was always thinking about feature projects, always trying to get my film made throughout the time I was making music videos. To that end, I had a philosophy. I would go to any lunch and take any meeting that came up related to my film. That way, if the film didn't happen, you could never say that it was because I didn't take a meeting or didn't believe in the project. And another thing that I was starting to learn was that you really don't know where the financing will come from or how a film is going to get made. Some of the films that get made are strange films with strange reasons behind them. You really never know. So I kept myself active, doing the legwork, going to all the meetings. At the same time I knew that the videos I was doing, the success that I would have with them, would help me, that they would at least open the door and establish that I had some talent. I knew that I needed to prove my narrative skills, and I was doing the shorts in part for that, but I did feel like, okay, I've done the most successful music videos on MTV for the last eight months, that should count for something.

HOW DID THE WORK AFFECT YOUR PERSONAL LIFE?
I had married a painter named Roget, and he was a bit older than me. Our marriage had deteriorated and I think that in the end he started to resent my fascination with a lot of the bands I was working with. I told you that I have to become a really big fan of who I'm working for, so I would really get into the bands, and I would say, "Oh, Depeche Mode are the greatest, this guy's so cute, this guy's great," and I think he had a certain amount of jealousy over that. I also felt that I was growing in a different direction than him. When I met him I was nineteen, and at this point I was about twenty-five, and things were just different. Also at that time I was starting to see Mike Diamond, and we were becoming best friends. We loved joking about everybody, all the bands and the people; we could relate to each other. I was doing a lot of rap videos at that time and because of the Beastie Boys he really knew that whole world. So I was separating from Roget and finally Mike and I moved closer to each other.

Professionally, I had really moved into these rap videos. It was strange at first. I had done the Tone Loc "Wild Thing" video and "Funky Cold Medina," different hits for Delicious Vinyl. That was a company that was run by friends of mine I knew through the club scene in L.A. And when I was doing those videos it was no problem because they were crossover videos, a combination of black and white people together. Then I started working with NWA and Eazy-E, and Eazy was really into a whole different world, the world of gangsta rap.

I think what was interesting about my relationship with Eazy was that I was the one woman he totally respected. He understood that I was a powerful director and that I had the ability to break bands into different markets, the ability to make a number-one video. Once I had his support behind me, then I had total power on a set. If someone acted silly or offensive, or anything, Eazy would step in and handle it. It was the same experience when I worked with Chris Rock. Eazy was just like, whatever Tamra says, goes. And when you have the support of those guys behind you, it makes everything okay.

I was working on other things while I was doing the videos. I created a show called "Pump It Up" for Fox, which was a rap TV show that starred Dee Barnes, and then I did an episode of "America's Most Wanted." In total it was about six years of doing various projects before I could convince anyone to give me the money to make a feature. And the feature that I finally went out with was *Guncrazy*, the same feature that I had tried to make out of film school. Matthew Bright, who was a childhood friend, had written it. One thing that's worth noting is that when I was first out of film school and was taking this script around, some people I showed it to called Bright and optioned it directly. So they had cut me out of the process and it took about six years before I got the rights to it back. Many people had tried to make it, but nobody had seen the film the way I'd seen it, and nobody had been able to get it off the ground.

So I got the script back and I met with this slightly nutty guy named Zane Levitt. He's a producer to this day, and he was the one that finally got me the financing. I had convinced him that I could make my first feature for $400,000, and I was just so determined to make the film that I had convinced myself it was possible also. So he believed in me, and he started looking around for the money. Then he met this wonderful young, cool girl named Dianne Firestone. She was one of the heirs to the automotive fortune and Zane had gotten her to come on board as the financer. Although substantial, $400,000 wasn't that much money for her. And once we had the money, we started casting. What was great about Zane was that that was the way he thought about making films; you just start making them. So we started casting and all the pieces finally fell into place. We got Michael Ironside to play the role of the father and from that we were able to pre-sell Japan for $400,000. So now I had a total of $800,000 to make the film! I also knew Ione Skye and got her involved.

My sister knew Drew Barrymore through being a casting agent, and she had told me that I had to meet her. She had done a few films, something called *Motorama,* and *Poison Ivy* had just wrapped shooting, but nobody would let me see it. At first I was like, "No way. I saw her dancing on a table at a club last week. I'm really not interested." She had a terrible reputation at that time. But then Drew called me on the phone. She had read the script and she kept on me until I agreed to meet her. I thought that it was cool that she called me because I wanted an actress to have the same kind of passion for the film that I did. So I met with her, and then I just immediately fell in love. I really believed in her. At that time, she was out to prove Hollywood wrong. She thought, [the perception was] any guy who does drugs and then cleans up always becomes a hero, but a girl, forget it. And she wanted to challenge that. I believed in her and I said, Let's do the film together. And then we became best friends. We had sort of a mother-daughter thing, which became a wonderful working relationship.

So once I had the cast, we started going. And we shot with $800,000 in twenty-three days. When I look back at everything, I think that music videos really taught me a lot. They taught me how to work with crews; they taught me how to structure my day; they taught me how to deal with clients, the studio, the producers, and how to deal with talent. The one thing I didn't know was whether or not I would be able to keep a pace up, shooting for twenty-three days. It's almost like being in the army, being at war; it's really hard work. But I knew that I would be able to handle things, and music videos had taught me how to do that. In a weird sense, I think that if I had been able to direct that feature right out of school, I might not have made the same movie. I might have made something a little more amateurish or not made it as confidently as I did with what I had learned in those six years. So, as much as I was kicking my feet, asking why won't people believe in me, I actually got my skills together and learned a ton of stuff in the meantime.

I think that anytime you approach something, even if you did something yesterday, and you come back and revisit it today, it's always going to be different. If you shot a scene today and they tell you that you have to reshoot it, come back tomorrow and it will be different. Anytime you do something, it's going to have a different effect. I definitely feel that I was a different person when I directed *Guncrazy* at twenty-nine than the person I was at twenty-three. I think that I had matured. I traveled a lot and I learned a lot. I think that in life you can always be receptive to things; you can always learn things. Even if you're just watching tons of movies or reading books, you're still learning. If you are just mad at the world because you weren't given the opportunity to make something, then that's going to degrade your creativity, not nurture it. So I believe that even if you're not able to make a film right at this moment, you'll be able to benefit from doing something in your life that you know is going to be watering your garden, and making yourself grow.

You know, there are old people now who have been making films for the last twenty years who have no more life experiences; they are living in Hollywood in their Beverly Hills mansions. Where are they getting their experience? And their films are lame because of it. They are not getting out and getting life experiences, so they have nothing to say. It's important to live. If you're going to tell stories about people, then you have to know people and go out and experience what people are like.

LET'S TALK ABOUT THE PROCESS OF MAKING *GUNCRAZY*. WHAT WAS THAT EXPERIENCE LIKE?
Wonderful. Absolutely wonderful. But it was also really, really hard work. I was working with Lisa Rensler, with whom I'd made a lot of music videos as my cinematographer. We had done a lot of preparation for the film and created a look that we wanted to execute. We were very pressed for shooting time, so we had to be specific about our shots, about preplanning them. I looked at a lot of Orson Welles films, because he was really good with conservative shots. He knew how to move the actors instead of moving the camera so that, within a single shot, you would have multiple different kinds of shots. The actors would be far away and it would be a wide, then they would step into a two shot, then someone would turn and it would be over-the-shoulder. There are scenes in *Guncrazy* where I'm totally inspired by that, where I'm doing eight different shots within one setup. Also, that's something you learn doing music videos, that the moment you call "cut" and start to move the camera, it's an hour or two of downtime. So you really have to be specific in figuring out what you want and planning in advance to get what you need to edit the film together later. That's an important thing.

It was crazy the amount of camera setups I had to do each day, it seemed almost impossible. But you just figure out a way to do it, you stay focused, and you realize what you need to make it happen. You know, I storyboard, and even though I'm really bad at drawing, it still helps. You just do as much preparation as you can, pretending over and over again that you're making the movie, and when that day finally comes and it's a reality, you're ready.

Working with actors was interesting. I had just come from the video world where everybody was dancing, and now I had to make a film with a narrative, with performance. But I had been making shorts also, so I had some experience working with actors. Right before I made *Guncrazy* I made a short film called *To the Curb,* with Adam Horowitz, Ione Skye, and Max Burlich. And it was good, it worked, I had it in film festivals, and it made sense. You could see that it had a narrative quality and a sense of style. But it really benefited me in that I knew how to work with actors and had experience doing it. And the more experience you have, the more you realize that each actor is different, each actor has a different way of working, a different technique. Drew Barrymore has a specific way of acting that's just completely different than her costar for that film, James LeGros. Working with them was interesting, seeing how they each came from a very different place and yet were both correct in their methods; they both gave great performances. And also you learn how to give direction differently to each actor, to see what he or she needs from you.

After the film was finished and during the rough-cut stage, I showed it to a bunch of friends and asked them to fill out questionnaires, things like that. Kevin Tent, my editor, was really helpful in making the film. He kept telling me about transition shots, which was something I knew nothing about. And he showed me how to use them, how to create a kind of flow to your film, which is a really nice thing. When you show a film to people, there are certain things you find out that you would have never thought of even if you had read the script a billion times. You always wish that you had had that foresight before making the film, because you think, God, what a waste of time it was to spend half a day shooting that scene. You could have shot it in one look, the audience already knew what you wanted. So you have to be very creative in your editing, and listen to suggestions that you receive.

It's very important to keep your own perspective on a film. When I read the script initially, I saw *Guncrazy* as a love story. I think that the reason the film was never made before was because everyone who read the script saw it as a film about two kids who go out and kill a bunch of people. I learned that the tone that a director brings to a film is very important. You can have a great script, but the way the film's made is equally as important to the final product. And your perspective, the tone that you end up with, is something that you could have never read on the page.

After we finished a cut that we liked, the first place we showed it was at the Cannes film market. Right after the screening, my producers, god love 'em, immediately got an offer of $2 million to premiere the film on Showtime, and they took it. I was quite upset at that. I wanted the release to be a theatrical release. In the meantime, though, the film got accepted to the Toronto Film Festival, the Chicago festival, and many others, so I started going around to the festivals and showing the film, getting responses. I was also happy because it did premiere on Showtime, but then it went back out and had a theatrical release. That was totally awesome. I think it only made it to about sixteen theaters. But it got excellent press, really good reviews, and people seemed to enjoy it.

By that time, though, I had started doing preproduction on *CB4*, so I barely had any time to focus on any of that stuff. I had always had this fantasy that I would take my film around to all the festivals like Jim Jarmusch does, and travel around the world, but it didn't end up that way. I was already on another film.

HOW DID THE *CB4* PICTURE COME ABOUT?

It was actually very natural. I had known Chris Rock because I had done a music video for him, a comedy video called, "Your Momma's Got a Big Head." Chris and I just got along really well, and Nelson George, who wrote the film, was a close friend of mine. He knew my husband, Mike, and we were all just friends. I was just finishing *Guncrazy*, doing the sound mix at the time, and I got a call to go over to Universal for a meeting about *CB4*. So I went over and met with Sean Daniels, Brian Grazier, and Ron Howard, and Chris and Nelson, and we started talking about the film, how we would do it, and it went really well. The next day I got a call and they said, "Let's do it."

I think that I was offered the film mainly on the strengths of my music videos, and my relationship with Chris and Nelson. No one had yet seen *Guncrazy*. I think that even without that film I would have received the *CB4* offer, but it also didn't hurt that I had finished a feature. I think that one of the things they liked, and that they might have seen from the Tone Loc videos, was that I had a sense of humor, I could direct black actors, and I could find the humor in that world. Also, there weren't that many other directors at the time who could have done that film. Perhaps the Hudlin brothers, but I was a good candidate.

Once I started making *CB4*, it was a wonderful experience. What I really liked about that film was that it was a style of comedy that hadn't really been done so much yet, a style where anything goes, you can do anything for a joke. If the joke's under the table, then you put a camera under the table, you just go for it. Chris and I had a ball making the film together; we just laughed all the time.

It was a bit weird making the film under a studio system, because now my budget was $6 million, and this was a much bigger film for me, obviously. But at the same time, even though it was a Universal film, the budget was low for them, and we got to make it outside of the studio, sort of like an independent production with studio money. So I really never saw anyone from Universal until the film was done.

WHAT DO YOU THINK IT IS, ULTIMATELY, THAT GETS FEATURE FILMS MADE?

Definitely I think that producers are central. I work with producers; I'm even titled an executive producer on my latest film. You really need that effort, that undying spirit that no matter what we will keep the flame going that a producer brings to a project. Producers help you a great deal. So that's one thing. Another thing is, I think, that I had many projects going at the same time. You have to keep a couple plates spinning and hold on to that determination that you're going to get a film made, that you will make it no matter what. As a young filmmaker these days, you have so many opportunities to go out and make a film. Digital video is the most unbelievable thing—you don't need anything technical anymore. All you really need are friends to help you. If you have a story, you can make a movie. You can edit it on your computer. I think that that's an important way to look at things, to think to yourself, Someday somebody will give me millions of dollars to make a film, but if they don't, that's not gonna stop me from being a filmmaker in the meantime. I'm gonna go out and make films. Recently I made a film on digital video. I went to Africa with the United Nations and made a documentary, I didn't have a crew, I just did it myself. So I think that's an important thing, just going out there and doing it by yourself.

And then once you do that, you show your work. Usually the film you make last sets you up for your next film. People don't just go, oh, okay, I made a film, I'm done. It's about making that next film. So even if you want to make *Star Wars*, but you don't have the things you need, then you make *THX1138*, so when you show it to somebody, then they can have the confidence in you to help you get to the next level.

I work a lot with young filmmakers and I always try to help young people make films. If you want to make films, take a good look at what you've done up to now and what you're currently working on. Try to ask yourself, What is it that interests you? Where are you as a filmmaker? The most important thing, I think, is that you need to be incredibly determined. You have to believe more than anything that your film will get made, no matter what it takes. Even with *Skipped Parts*, my most recent film, I drew the whole thing out before anybody gave me any money to make it. You do everything you can to prepare. I think that sometimes I push myself even more than others, partly because I never wanted to be that girl who comes onto the set and five macho crew dudes sit around saying, "She's a girl; she has no idea what she's doing."

It's also important to hit every avenue, because ultimately you have no idea where the money's going to come from. You don't know whose lives you'll intertwine with, who you'll have relationships with, and which ones will last. If you are really in this business, then the people you work with now, the ones who are really pushing themselves, those are the people you'll be in business with ten years from now. So remember to respect the people you work with, because if you respect them, then they'll remember it when you need their help—and you will need their help. You don't just make a feature by yourself; you really need a lot of people who care to get a film made.

People get work two ways in this town: by being ambitious or by being talented. To be talented *and* ambitious is a wonderful thing. Not everybody is. I know a lot of talented people who are not at all ambitious, and I know a lot of ambitious people, who do indeed work all the time, who are really nontalented. So, if you are ambitious enough, you'll get work. You have to finish the things that you start, and you have to be pushy and get your work out there where people will see it, but if you keep pushing, you will get work.

Talent is something you have to invest in. You need to try and figure out what you're talented in, and nurture that. Are you talented in writing, are you talented in directing, or are you a talented producer? There are not that many talented directors. To be a talented director, you really have to come up with something that nobody else has seen before or a way of illustrating things that is new to people. There are a lot of people who are working now, and who want to work, who are more talented than you or I, so that you can't control. But at least you can control your ambition. Also, things can never be a question of budget or a question of money. If you feel you don't have enough to make a film now, you won't have enough later. I made Tone Loc's "Wild Thing" for $398, and it was one of the most successful videos in MTV's history. It's never about the budget, it's about having a style, an energy to your work that shines through.

The music video and commercial industry today is more competitive than it's ever been. In part it's because MTV has changed, they no longer play anywhere near as many videos, they mainly play other programming, so in a sense there are no more $30,000 or $40,000 videos. The videos are all $250,000 and up. So for someone new going out there today, you're competing with me, with Spike Jonze, with Mark Romanek. I pitch myself now. I just wrote up two concepts and I know Spike is writing too, so you have to work hard to get the jobs, even when you're established, because of the competition of the field. Unless you show something that we can't do, a vision that we're not working on, then it's hard to break in. There are other avenues to pursue than big-budget videos, though. It's always possible to try to find record companies who need a small video, something maybe $5,000 for the Internet, or something like that. I would discourage people using all their money to make a spec reel, as unless you have a career where you're making a lot of money and can afford to spend it, then you'll just become desperate. And desperation is one thing that's very hard to sell.

Finally, remember that you have to be able to make people money, that that's what this is ultimately all about. I can make something that Universal wants. I know what a fourteen- to twenty-five-year-old boy wants. I can make films for that market because I understand it. That's a marketable ability; I can make people money.

LOOKING BACK AT YOUR CAREER, WHAT WAS ULTIMATELY THE DRIVING MOTIVATION FOR MAKING FILMS?

There were a few different factors. I think that I always wanted to make movies and be involved in the film industry—that came from my youth. Then, once you start to do it, it's very intoxicating; you really get into the lifestyle of doing it. I'm really honest about this, because I believe in it, I believe in the myth, but you come to feel that you're working with people that you've always been a fan of, that suddenly rock stars are your best friends and you get to direct actors you really care for. I love that kind of stuff. So you're working with people you love, and that pushes you to keep going. Also, I feel that I give something back to those people, that I provide something that helps them. And then it starts to feel a bit like a community, that everyone's friends, and you can all make it through this crazy world together. There's something nice about that, to feel some kind of safety and support in a crazy world.

There's something else. At this point, I can retire. I mean financially I don't have to work again, I'm married, and I have a very happy life. But I think that maybe there's a girl growing up somewhere in Oklahoma who is incredibly talented but who doesn't have an image that she can be something, that she can do things with her life. If there's a small chance that she sees a picture of me somewhere or hears about what I've done, then perhaps that can give her some hope that she can be something, that she can do something with her life instead of ending up some smoking, desperate girl who gets tattoos and has bad boyfriends. You can create something out of your life, and if you don't have an image of that to guide you then it can be hard to do. Helping to provide that image is important to me.

John McNaughton | HENRY: PORTRAIT OF A SERIAL KILLER

JOHN MCNAUGHTON *was born in 1949 and grew up on Chicago's South Side. In search of some adventure, McNaughton spent his youth traveling the country and worked in the circus, as a boat builder, as a silversmith, and as a bartender. A chance meeting in a bar led to his affiliation with early videotape distributors who would give him the money to make his independent film* Henry: Portrait of a Serial Killer, *starring Michael Rooker.* Henry's *critical success led McNaughton on to make films including* Sex, Drugs, Rock & Roll; Mad Dog and Glory; Wild Things; *and* Speaking of Sex, *starring James Spader, Bill Murray, and Lara Flynn Boyle. He is single and lives in Los Angeles and Chicago.*

I grew up on the South Side of Chicago and lived there during the fifties and part of the sixties. When I moved to the North Side of Chicago, it was like I was moving to Moscow, and I felt as if I had betrayed the South Side. My father was raised in a community called Pullman, which was a planned community on the South Side of Chicago designed by George Pullman, who manufactured the Pullman car, which in its day was a first-rate passenger car for railroad trains. When my father left school he went to work for the Pullman Company and then he later worked in another factory for International Harvester, which was a manufacturer of farm machinery. My grandfather had worked there and my mother and my aunts worked there during the war. My uncle worked there for his entire life and I also worked there at one point in time. I grew up as an only child. My mother was a housewife and an extremely gifted seamstress. She made almost all of her own clothes and my clothes until I was six and she also did upholstery work like slipcovers, curtains, and draperies. I grew up in an area called Roseland.

WHAT ROLE DID MOVIES PLAY IN YOUR CHILDHOOD?

When I was three my mother took me downtown during the Christmas holidays for the premiere of *Peter Pan*. The film blew me away and I think I wound up seeing it eleven times. That was a big experience in my very young life. In the 1950s Alfred Hitchcock was still working, John Ford was still working, and Howard Hawks was still working. A lot of great American directors were making films in that postwar period. This was before people were thinking of film as an art form; you would go and see *Psycho* or *North by Northwest* or *The Man Who Shot Liberty Valance* and they were just the movies that were playing. At the time I was born, my father owned a bar, and he bought a television to put in his bar. It was the first one in the neighborhood and it did well for business because people came in to watch television. Shortly after that experience, my dad bought a television for our home. Being an only child, I lived in front of the television for a good deal of my youth.

WHEN DID YOU KNOW THAT MOVIES WERE IMPORTANT TO YOU?

When I was in high school from 1963 to 1967, films from people like Federico Fellini, Ingmar Bergman, Akira Kurosawa, François Truffaut, and Jean-Luc Godard were coming to the United States. I remember seeing a full-page ad for *La Dolce Vita* in the Chicago paper. I was very much interested in the arts from the time I was a little kid and I loved to draw and paint and I loved music. The sixties were an incredibly fertile time for the arts in general. I went to art school at the University of Illinois in Champaign, but in 1969 I had an epiphany that the most influential form of communication in my life indeed had been television. I decided to abandon art school to attend Columbia College in Chicago, which was a small communications college. Columbia was a really interesting place at the time with great facilities. Those were the sixties and the faculty was very liberal. There I majored in film and television with a minor in photography. I had convinced myself that film was dead and an electronic medium was going to take over. I thought that the means of production would be disseminated to the people and that there would be a revolution in communications. Columbia was a completely left-wing school and all the teachers were working professionals. In the television department there were people who worked in television and most of the film department people worked in the commercial film business. The photography department was probably the finest in Chicago and one of the best in the country. Columbia College was set up in such a way that you really had great access to practical equipment where you could go out and make a film or a photograph instead of sitting around and talking about it. I didn't make any films while I was there because I concentrated on still photography. The city was a very textured place and it was just a wonderful time to be a kid and hang out on the streets. I loved street photography and I took pictures of people and places in and around Chicago. I spent more time doing still photography because I was still coming out of art and images and it took me a little while to make the next step into filmmaking.

WHAT DID YOU DO AFTER GRADUATION?

I graduated in 1972 during a period of economic recession and I wound up working at the International Harvester factory. Every weekend I would read the employment pages in the newspaper and there would always be a "sucker ad" with things like "Assistant to famous producer," and I would rush over to that employment agency. There would be my entire graduating class sitting around looking for the same job. But the only real television jobs in Chicago were in the in-house video departments of major companies like Sears and Standard Oil or the local affiliates like WGN and Channel 32. They did the news and some public affairs stuff, but the actual programs on television were coming from Los Angeles. There was very little production in Chicago so there wasn't that much film or television work at all.

I went to work on an assembly line in a factory on the South Side of Chicago and I became a United AutoWorker. I worked there for the longest continuous employment that I've ever held, which was nineteen months, and it just really was awful. I got married after college and my wife worked for an advertising agency. Someone she worked with in the audiovisual department was leaving, so I zipped in there and got a job working for a man named Jack Mirabelli. We did all the audiovisual work for that agency, including still photography, motion photography, and projections for meetings. I lasted ten months there and I really hated the advertising business, but Jack was an incredible man who was very skilled and taught me a great deal. I would say that in the ten months I worked there I learned more than I learned in four years of college.

So here I was, a child of the sixties, someone who always thought he would lead an artistic life of adventure, and I was married and living in Pullman in a little row house, commuting downtown everyday to a job at an ad agency. This was the absolute antithesis of the spirit of the sixties. My marriage started to fray and my wife and I split up. I had sort of a rough period where I lived with an old friend of mine in a converted garage in Calumet City, Illinois. If you know anything about the Blues Brothers, they supposedly came from Cal City, which is this scummy place in the South suburban region of Chicago where all the mills used to be. It was famous in the fifties and sixties because it was where all the strip clubs were and the steelworkers went to drink and beat the shit out of one another. It used to have the highest prostitution rate in the United States. I lived there for a while and then I lived with my aunt for a while, but I really wanted to travel and I wanted adventure. I was doing street photography and actually did some work I'm pretty proud of during this time of my life. My friend Dave knew some people who traveled with the Royal American Show, which was the largest traveling carnival in North America. I was at rock bottom and had run out of places to stay when Dave said he was going to join the carnival and asked me to come along. I packed up what little I had in life at that point, which was basically myself, and I went to join the traveling carnival and see the world a little bit. I spent the next year traveling throughout Canada and the United States with the carnival.

WHAT WERE YOU DOING THERE?
I remember we showed up in Dave's 1964 Studebaker station wagon in Davenport, Iowa, and the carnival had its own train and seven hundred people working for it. I worked for a man named Frank Russell who was from Chicago originally. Frank was a huge 260-pound man who chain-smoked Pall Malls. Dave knew Frank and he introduced us, and Frank hired both of us on the spot. Ten seconds later I was unloading a truckload of boxes and at once I became a "carny." It was a pretty intense experience and I made it through one season. Fortunately, I was able to photograph my experiences. After I finished my carnival tour I wound up in Texas and stayed with a couple of friends for a while. Then I bought a 1950 Plymouth coupe and drove to New Orleans. I was gonna stay in New Orleans for a couple of weeks with one of my very best friends from Chicago, Jim Cole, who was working as a deep-sea oil diver. From there the plan was to take my photographs to New York because I had a lot of friends who were working in publishing.

I ended up staying in New Orleans for two years and I had some of the best times of my life there. This was in November of 1975 and I arrived in New Orleans with my Plymouth, a few dollars saved from my Carnival days, and a batch of photographs. There was something about New Orleans that was pretty wonderful especially in those days when it was a time of economic prosperity. The oil business was booming so the city was safe and you could pretty much go anywhere and hang out with anybody in any neighborhood and the people were cool. I happened to be looking at the want ads in the New Orleans newspaper, the *Times-Picayune*, and they had all the various categories of employment. I came across one ad under the miscellaneous section where all the unusual jobs were listed. It said, "Wanted: Silversmith's apprentice." I thought, Hmm, that sounds interesting, and I decided to check it out. The next day I borrowed a suit from Jim (even though he was a deep-sea diver he had had a fancy suit made in London) and went to this little place on Bourbon Street that was kind of a tourist silversmith joint. I went in to apply for a job and saw the man that I had to interview with. He was known in New Orleans as Uncle Bob. He weighed about 300 pounds, and he worked for a young man named Victor Duncan II, who had opened this great shop on Bourbon Street. Duncan and his young wife lived above the shop, and Uncle Bob lived above them. Victor Duncan was a very macho, strange guy, and he had left town to open a store in Boca Raton, putting the care of the silversmith shop in the hands of Uncle Bob.

Uncle Bob was a gay guy, and the true love of his life was a gangster in St. Louis named Buster Workman, who was I guess bisexual. Buster was long since dead and Uncle Bob, who had once been a very attractive young man, was now a huge man running a silversmith business. He was one of the nicest and most fun guys I've ever known in my life, but his whole deal was rough trade, and when Duncan left town, Bob took over the big apartment on the second floor and threw open the doors to have parties. He basically abandoned us and left us to run the shop. I worked learning a few things while Duncan was still in town, but once Duncan left I think we worked from four till midnight. I was getting along with some of the other guys, like Curt Reese, who worked with me, but then Uncle Bob began throwing these insane parties upstairs. I didn't really know anything about gay life, and these guys started walking in who would be missing teeth, tattooed, scarred, from prison, and the big thing with all of them was guns. Duncan was a gun collector, so there were some antique guns in cases in the shop as props, and these guys would always play with them at Uncle Bob's parties. I don't know exactly what went on in those parties upstairs and I don't want to know, but Uncle Bob always remained one of the most generous, big-hearted men I ever knew. He was also an amazing cook. He would just open the cash register and take money out and send the young woman who also worked with us down to the grocery store for supplies. Then he would make incredible meals for us every evening. It was a wonderful time and I got pretty good at making jewelry along the way.

WERE YOU THINKING ABOUT FILM?
I was thinking about it, but before I actually made films I wanted to have some adventure in my life. It was always in the back of my mind that eventually my adventuring days would be finished and then I could focus on making films. So I kept adventuring for a while.

It was at this time that Victor Duncan II's fortune took a turn for the worse. Uncle Bob was giving the store away and things weren't going well for Duncan in Florida. The business was about to fold.

My friend Curt and I decided to start our own silversmith business, which we got set up, but which quickly went bust. I then went to work for a man named Tommy Dravis, who made big racing sailboats. I spent one year building high-end racing sailboats in New Orleans. After that I started working in construction, renovating an old building in the French Quarter. One drunken night I got into a fistfight with my best friend over a particular young woman who we were both involved with. We were going at it, duking it out on the sidewalk, and I suddenly had another epiphany. I asked myself, What am I doing fighting with my best friend in the middle of the street at five in the morning? I was twenty-eight years old and I knew at that moment that it was time for me to decide what I really wanted to do with my life.

I packed up my belongings and I set out for Chicago, where my cousin Brock Lassin had an old-fashioned saloon, and he offered me a job tending bar there. I arrived at my parents' house with a truck full of odds and ends, a 1957 Jaguar, and ten dollars in change to my name. The next day I was working for my cousin tending bar. I worked there at night for about a year, and during the day I tried to get myself into the film business.

One day a man came into the bar and we started up a conversation. He told me that he worked for a company called MalJack, and gave me his business card. MalJack was a business started by two brothers, the Ali brothers from Jordan, who had set up their own shop distributing audiovisual equipment. At this time there was no videotape, and the Ali brothers were buying 1 hour loops of Super-8 film of public domain things like Charlie Chaplin and Buster Keaton, and projecting them into nostalgic themed restaurants like the Ground Round or Shakey's Pizza. I went in to meet with them and they offered me a job bicycling from Ground Round to Shakey's Pizza, rotating out film cassettes to change the content. So I began doing that days and working nights in the bar. The Ali thing wasn't leading anywhere, and I eventually left them to work in construction again. Then one day I went back to visit my friends the Ali brothers, to sort of say hi and see what they were doing. While I was at their office, I met a man named Ray Atherton. Ray had been a film collector from the time he was a boy and was an expert on what was and was not in the public domain.

Since I had left the Ali brothers' employ, videotape had taken off, and they had started buying the rights for various movies for video distribution. Their operation eventually became one of the very large video distribution companies, and both of them are today extremely wealthy men. They were starting to have some success at the time, so they agreed to distribute a documentary I planned to make called *Dealers in Death*, a history of gangsters in America. Ray and I started working together, and we got a bunch of old photographs, and film clips of people like Dillinger, Capone, and Bonnie and Clyde. I managed to raise $40,000 from a lawyer I knew in Chicago, and Ray and I made two documentaries that the Ali brothers distributed on videocassette.

By now I was in business with Ray Aferton and the Ali brothers. The Ali brothers were making a lot of money from the video distribution business and they were thinking about producing. Ray was getting them all this stuff that was public domain and duplicating it and they had a distribution network selling it and making a great deal of money. I was quite confused about what I was going to do at this point. I was around the Ali brothers, who were starting to have some good success, but to support myself I was working nights in construction remodeling Burger Kings. I wondered how I was ever going to become a film director. I met with Waleed Ali and told him that I wanted to make something for him. He said that he would give me $100,000 to make a horror film for him and he didn't care what it was about. That was the basis of our agreement, and I was pretty shocked that Waleed was going to take a chance with me and let me make a film for him. But I was pretty elated, and as I was leaving the building I ran into a friend of mine who worked there, Gus Cavoures. Gus and I had been friends since I was very young, and I told him that Waleed had just offered me money to make a horror film. He pulled out a videotape that he had of the show "20/20." It had a whole segment on Henry Lee Lucas and Otis Elwood Toole, who were serial killers who were believed to have killed over three hundred people. I had always been interested in true-crime stories and episodes of bizarre human behavior and had explored some of that in the earlier documentaries I had made for the Ali brothers. But I had never heard the term "serial killer" before, and I was immediately fascinated.

I now had $100,000 and an idea, but I needed a writer to help me put the film together. I took the "20/20" cassette to my friend Steve Jones, who worked in the advertising business and was well connected in Chicago's film production community. He had done some video work with a group in Chicago called the Organic Theater. During the late sixties and seventies there was a renaissance of theater in Chicago, and Organic was part of that. Through the group I met Richard Fire, who wrote the script with me for what would become *Henry: Portrait of a Serial Killer*.

Henry was basically an art film that happened to borrow from the horror genre, but it was a character study before it was a horror film. I knew that making that film was a shot for me to get noticed and if I got noticed that I would have a career. Over the years there have been certain pictures that push the envelope of their genre. In that tradition I wanted to make a film that was so shocking that it would supercede anything that had come before it. We wrote *Henry* in a couple of months. Waleed gave us a check for $25,000 and told us to get started making the film. We used my loft in Chicago as the production office and Steve Jones provided contacts to help us start casting. We were of course trying to cast the central role of Henry and that was the toughest part. We initially found a guy who was a really good actor, but who wasn't really that sexual, and we were getting ready to offer him the part, even though we were concerned about how he would affect the love story. Our makeup artist told us that he knew an interesting actor who grew up in Alabama that he thought we should meet. That actor was Michael Rooker. He showed up at Richard's apartment to meet us, and he was wearing the clothes that he ended up wearing in the film. When I first saw him and he said something, I said a little prayer inside my head. I said, Please God, let him be a great actor because physically this guy is exactly what we need for the film. He was.

Michael grew up in a welfare family in Jasper, Alabama, and moved to Chicago with his father when he was a kid. He had lived in a rotten place and had a very difficult childhood. Somehow he got himself to drama school, graduated, and worked in theater in Chicago. He was completely raw and so unlike most of the kids that go into theater and the arts. After he read for us we offered him a lead role and he accepted. Then we got Tommy Towles, who was a member of the Organic Theater Company to play Otis and we also hired Tracey Arnold to play Becky.

HOW WAS THE PRODUCTION PROCESS?

We shot for twenty-eight days without a break with a crew of three and ten lights. We were able to get a very experienced production designer named Rick Paul who traveled a lot but made his home in Chicago, and a costume designer named Patricia Hart who worked in theater in Chicago as well. They each took a fee of $700 for the entire production. I believe we paid the actors two grand apiece. The day players we paid $100. We were fortunate that there was an incredible theater community in Chicago where we could find people who were willing to work with us on the project for little or no money.

Having spent a great deal of time doing a lot of other things besides making movies, I had always felt that I had a pretty good feel for people and class, and how people behave in certain situations. I felt that I understood how the working class behaves as opposed to how the professional class behaves. I think that my understanding of people gave me the ability to get naturalistic performances out of them. We did rehearse for this film and I spent a lot of time with the actors before we made it so that they could become familiar with the characters and, in a way, become the characters.

I learned that if the director is smart, then he will defer to those who know more than he does. I had professional actors who knew what they were doing because they had all worked in theater, so I was going to learn from them. I wasn't necessarily going to teach them what to do. I think that the mistake that many make when they first start out is that they act like a supreme dictator. A lot of bad films get made that way. I studied still photography, so I knew about lenses and optics, but I had never worked with a cinematographer before, and a person who has spent a lifetime doing that will likely know more than I do about how to move a camera. It's important to try to listen to develop good instincts for picking the right people for a job, but then giving them the space that they need to work. If someone gives me their best I am not going to come in and limit them. I will shape that person, but at the same time I will give him the space that he needs to achieve maximum creativity.

WHAT HAPPENED AFTER THE FILM WAS FINISHED?

Since we were very inexperienced our first cut was two and a half hours. The lesson you never completely learn is that you can't fall in love with every frame. When the Ali brothers, who funded the movie, wanted to see it, we had no money left for a video transfer, so we used the actual camera that Henry uses in the film and taped the image from the flatbed editing machine into the video camera. It was highly degraded, and the sound was terrible since the video camera was basically picking up the sound from the editing machine, which was an unfinished scratch track to begin with. It couldn't have looked worse. I took it over to show it to the Ali brothers. They were appalled and our relationship was never the same from that day forward. They had hoped for horror exploitation, and they felt that the film was terribly made, and worse yet, it was an art film. The important lesson that I learned from this is that you should not show your film to anyone until it is presentable. Even if you show it to someone and tell them to disregard the state it's in, they will always have a problem with it. The money people will tell you that they have seen films in this stage and that they understand, but that is not true and it doesn't work that way. The Ali brothers basically took *Henry* and put it on the shelf and said no one would want to see it.

Ultimately we got the film out by making tapes of it and sending it to people. The Chicago Film Festival wanted to show the film, but we only had a good-quality videocassette, not a film print. They had no video projection, so Michael Rooker and I rented a video projector and brought it to the theater for the first public screening of the film. It was well received. The film was also shown at a festival in New York by the artist Joe Coleman, who would eventually make the poster art for us.

To promote the film I made a series of one thousand handbills. I got a can of red spray paint and I squirted a glob of red paint on each one and let it drip like drops of blood. The headline was "Yeah, I killed my Momma." There is nothing more riveting than matricide, and it worked to draw attention. A friend and I went down by the *Chicago Tribune* and posted them everywhere. I hand-delivered cassettes to people like Siskel and Ebert, Michael Medved, and Jeffrey Lyons. They were all reviewers on television shows, and I made sure that they and everyone else in the press got a cassette. We started to get noticed and Elliot Stein of *The Village Voice* wrote that it was the best film of the year and a must-see. But even though we started to attract attention, we still did not have a distribution company that could buy it and market it. A company called Vestron became interested and offered to buy the film, but some complicated legal issues arose. They held on to the film for seven months before they decided not to release it. It was then taken by Atlantic Releasing, a company that had seen a tape of it and become interested. They sent it to the Motion Picture Association of America for approval and got back an X rating. It was the "moral tone" of the film that earned the rating, and we were told that there was nothing we could do to cut it that would change that as far as the MPAA was concerned. Since they couldn't get an R rating for the film, Atlantic dropped it.

The film was finished in 1986, but it was not released to the public until 1990. I was unemployed after I finished the film, and I spent eighteen months without a job living at my cousin's house for free. But during that time we were still sending out tapes to people, and on the strength of the film I managed to get signed for representation by the Gersh Agency in New York. I began being sent scripts for horror and science-fiction films, but even though I was broke they were so bad that I couldn't bring myself to make any of them. Eventually I broke down and made a sci-fi film called *The Borrower*. I liked the concept but it was a nightmare experience.

HOW DID YOU MOVE INTO MAKING LARGER-BUDGET FILMS?
Marty Scorsese gave me my first studio job, which was amazing, because I am a huge Scorsese fan.

After I completed *Henry* I heard through my agent that Scorsese had *The Grifters* under option with his production company. I had read the book and loved it, so I asked my agent to send a cassette of *Henry* to Marty Scorsese. His assistant watched the movie and just hated it so she never gave it to him. A couple of years later a woman named Melanie Frieson, who was working for Scorsese, saw *Henry,* was impressed, and showed it to Marty, who loved it. I remember that one day I was sitting in my old loft in

Chicago and the phone rang and it was Melanie Frieson. She said that Marty liked the film and wanted to talk to me. I thought it was someone making a prank call. Fifteen minutes later Martin Scorsese called me to tell me that he liked my film, was developing some projects, and asked me if I had anything to show him. I sent him a few film ideas that I had, but he didn't like any of them. Then he told me that he wanted me to read a script called *Mad Dog and Glory*. I read it, and I liked it, and he hired me to direct it. That was my first studio film.

WHAT IS IT THAT ACCOUNTS FOR YOUR SUCCESS AS A DIRECTOR?

As I grow older I think of the role of fate as a force in the universe. I spent many lonely nights remodeling Burger Kings. I remember one particular night when it was twenty degrees below zero outside and nobody was on the streets. I was alone in an empty Burger King in the middle of a bleak industrial neighborhood cleaning up after a construction job. I remember thinking that I knew that one day I would be a movie director even though at that point I didn't know how I would get there. All I knew was that I had to become a movie director. I determined that that was what I was going to be and the only thing that would stop me from achieving that goal would be my death.

HOW WOULD YOU ADVISE SOMEONE WHO WANTS TO BECOME A FILM DIRECTOR?

Make films even if they are only five minutes long. If you try to work your way up in this business it is unlikely that you will become a director. Being an assistant director doesn't teach you to be a director. If you become an assistant director then you are much more likely to end up producing, because you learn different skills. I think that today with digital cameras you can make a film very cheaply and that film festivals are starting to show a lot more digital video films. Shooting on digital video is one way to learn and to make work that you can get seen. You can make a feature-length picture if you are willing to run up your credit cards and work at some other job for however long it takes or are fortunate enough to have relatives or know someone who will give you a little bit of money to make a film. If you can come up with a story that you think is good, then write a screenplay and scrape up the resources to shoot it on digital video. If you are affiliated with a university you can access to computer editing systems for free.

Thomas Edison said that genius is 1 percent inspiration and 99 percent perspiration. I think that you just have to be relentless in the pursuit of your goal. I have seen a lot of people who wanted to be directors who ended up working in production and becoming comfortable making a bit of money but not having that creative role. It's easy to get used to living a certain way, and then it becomes much harder to make the sacrifice of going without income, which is often what you need to do to make an independent film that will get you noticed.

It doesn't get any easier as the years go by and this is a very uncertain way to make a living. I thought I knew what my next project was going to be a few months ago and now it is going up in smoke. If I wanted to make a lot of money, maybe I could by making more broadly commercial films, but I try to make films that I believe in and feel that I should be making. That's a trade-off. But I believe that once you make your first feature film, no matter what the budget, you are spoiled for honest work for the rest of your life. I can't think of anything else that I would want to be doing more than making films. There are some wonderful people in this business, some of the most interesting people you could ever hope to meet in your lifetime. If you're lucky like I've been, then you'll get paid a reasonable amount of money to work with them to manufacture a fantasy from a blueprint in the script. It is an interesting way to spend your days.

Neil LaBute | IN THE COMPANY OF MEN

NEIL LABUTE was born in Detroit, Michigan, in 1961. He attended Brigham Young University and received his M.F.A. from Kansas State University. He then went on to both study and teach at New York University's dramatic writing program and returned to BYU to take a teaching position. LaBute attended the Sundance Playwriting lab and developed a relationship with Good Machine, which asked him to write a script and introduced LaBute to the process of trying to sell a film to Hollywood. Frustrated by this seemingly endless pursuit, LaBute decided to make his own film, In the Company of Men, *which he financed privately for $25,000. The film won the filmmaker trophy at the Sundance Film Festival and went on to garner both box-office success and critical acclaim.*

I grew up in Spokane, Washington, about ten miles from the Canadian border. My father was a truck driver and my mother was a hospital receptionist. My father was a long-haul trucker, so he was gone a lot, sometimes for weeks at a time. I have one brother who is five years older than I am who works at a digital company. I worked on a farm much of my life. My brother still does. I was not exactly an indentured servant, but I was certainly dragged along into most of the family's farming escapades. Farming was not my passion or interest at all, but it was something I spent a lot of time do-

ing. I think I had a traditional American upbringing and I was always looking for someone to take me to the movies.

WHAT IS YOUR FIRST MEMORY OF THE MOVIES?

My most vivid early memory is of when I went to see the rerelease of *Gone
With the Wind* with my mother at the Dishman Theatre in Spokane. I remember falling asleep and waking up at the moment when Rhett Butler
carries Scarlett O'Hara up the stairs. I vividly recall the convergence of the
red stairs, the overblown soundtrack, and the romantic interlude. It was
quite overpowering, and it is still a vivid recollection. My mother was a
great movie fan and we watched a lot of movies on television and went to
the cinema quite often.

I was always interested in the arts and theater was my first passion. My
interest came about through acting because that was really the only artistic
activity that was available to people my age. I acted in plays during high
school, and I really enjoyed it. I think that it helped me develop what would
later become my writing style. After high school, I took a year off and traveled for a while. Then I applied to Brigham Young University in Utah, got a
scholarship, and decided to attend. While I was there I studied theater and
English, and it was a great pleasure to study what I was interested in and to
stay out late and do all those things that I tended not to do before college.
My mom was always very supportive of me in my artistic pursuits and continued to be as long as they made me happy. My father, I think by virtue of
him not being in love with his own career, never actually pushed me toward
anything. His advice was that I should make sure that I always made money
and had a job that was solid. He had always wanted to do something else
himself so he was pretty good about letting me do what I wanted to do.

DID YOU SEE A LOT OF MOVIES WHEN YOU WERE IN COLLEGE?

Before going to college I worked in a theater, which was very close to going
to the movies almost every night of the week. I saw a wide range of films
during that time. I saw all the mainstream movies, but I also managed to
see a lot of international films as well. This was before videotape existed, so
it was rare to get access to noncommercial films. When I got to college, I
was really into theater, but BYU had a great international cinema program.
Every weekend throughout the year they would show classic films from all
over the world and I saw a lot of them. The film that made the most impact
on me was *Slave of Love* by Michael Cove. That was a fantastic film and it is
still one of my favorites. I also liked Federico Fellini's *La Dolce Vita*, which
also remains a favorite. It was very much a "Cinema 101" situation where I
was getting more of a cross section of films that were out in the world.

During college, I began to develop my writing and concentrated on it heavily, thinking that I might become a writer or a teacher when I finished school. I looked at graduate and doctoral programs for teaching, and it was something that I always considered very seriously. I was writing a lot of short plays and a lot of sketches similar to "Saturday Night Live" things. Pieces like that were easy to write and didn't require the same investment as a screenplay or a novel. After I graduated, I thought that I would go on to graduate school, but I wanted to take a year off first, so I moved to New York and began working full-time for a Utah-based computer company at their New York branch office. I was writing the text that went with educational software programs. I went to the theater a lot and enjoyed being in the city where so many artistic things were going on. I was doing a lot of writing while I was in New York and I was all over the place writing about an assortment of themes. I was basically trying to find a voice and to find something that interested me and that I was good at writing about. Most of what I was doing was just for my own development, but at one point I did get Lorne Michaels's telephone number. I called him, thinking that he might like to see my writing, and he listened for a second and said, "Don't ever call me again." That's the kind of thing you do when you are first starting out and you think, Yeah, I'll just give him a call and see how it works. I don't know that that's the best approach. I think that you have to develop a bit more organically.

After one year in New York I went to study theater history and playwriting at the University of Kansas. By this time I was married and moving to Kansas turned out to be a very good experience. I was doing very environmental theater. I staged outdoor shows, and I was forever evaluating every space I walked into to see if I could stage a play there. I did a show under the steps of the natural history museum and I emptied out a basement storage room in a dormitory and put on a play in there. I was mostly directing other people's work and occasionally testing some of my own material.

DURING THE TWO AND A HALF YEARS YOU WERE AT THE UNIVERSITY OF KANSAS, DID YOU EVER CONSIDER BEING A FILM DIRECTOR?
I did have thoughts about it, but practically it didn't make much sense since writing was what I understood and could do best. Also writing was just easier to accomplish. It always seemed like the thing that you needed the least amount of stuff to create it with. You didn't have to audition or cast or produce or light, you just had to write. I could write a show and send it to a theater and never even have to leave my house.

WHAT IS YOUR WRITING PROCESS?
I don't have one of those mandates that I must write a certain number of pages each day because I've spent too many days staring at a screen trying to

fill pages that way. I remember years ago reading something about Oliver Stone. It said that he would write five pages a day even if he threw the pages out. I can't work that way. I don't have a regimen where I'm up at six and done by noon or anything like that. I tend to think about things a lot. Sometimes I write myself into a corner, but usually what comes out of it is more interesting. Sometimes I throw what I have written away and I have a drawer full of that stuff. I think that most of the things that I have written are interesting because they have a quality of uncertainty to them that reflects my uncertainty in writing them. You are not sure what is going to happen next.

After I finished my M.F.A. program I made a decision that I was not going to go for my doctorate because I felt that I had sucked the place dry in terms of faculty and facilities. I thought I might take a different road, and I was accepted into the dramatic writing program at New York University. I was able to teach there with my M.F.A. and that setup suited me better than continuing on for a doctorate. I received a full scholarship and moved to Westchester with my wife and young child. While I was commuting to school, I was also working as a technician at a psychiatric hospital in Westchester where my wife was working as a therapist. I found the work fascinating because as a writer, you examine psychology and try to justify people's actions. Here I was experiencing severe psychological issues firsthand. It was great work and it paid very well also.

I spent two years at NYU developing my writing. I received mixed reviews from my peers, but it continues to be the same now. Some people liked my writing and some people thought it was putrid. There were a number of professors who didn't think much of my work at all. Fortunately I am quite thick-skinned about that type of criticism. I continue to read every review I can of my work. I like getting some sense of how an audience reacts to what I'm doing. It forces me to continue working and to strive to make my work better.

After NYU, I was still pursuing teaching, so I moved back to BYU and began working on a Ph.D. I was happy to be back there because I always thought that BYU had fantastic facilities and a great talent pool. That was the year that I met Erin Eckhard, who later played the lead in my first film, and we worked together on theater projects as much as we could. The faculty was happy to have me back at BYU, but as the years went on I think they became less interested in my presence there. We had different philosophies about entertainment and art—the Mormon church believes that the purpose of art is to glorify rather than to examine the way people should live. They are less interested in using theater or film to show the bad as well as the good. I always thought that showing everything was a more powerful approach. Even though I may disagree with certain positions of the church,

I became a Mormon when I was at BYU and have remained with the church for fifteen years.

HOW DID YOU ULTIMATELY MAKE THE TRANSITION FROM PLAYWRITING TO FEATURE-FILM DIRECTING?

I had written a play called *Rounder* while I was at NYU, and sent it to the Sundance Playwriting Lab, where it was accepted and I was invited to attend. I went there in 1991 and had a great experience at the lab, and it was there that I met Stacy Edwards, who would later star along with Erin Eckhard in my first film, *In the Company of Men*. The people who run a production company in New York called Good Machine saw a staging that I did of *Rounder* and asked if I could write a screenplay based upon it. *Rounder* was a piece that offered a tough look at white teenagers and dealt with infanticide and some difficult issues like that. It kind of predated *Kids* in a way. Good Machine asked me to write a script on spec—which means that you aren't paid for it up-front, but rather hope to sell it outright after completion—and they ultimately took an option on the script with the hope that they would get it made. From this I was quickly introduced to the long trail of independent film financing. I was so accustomed to working in theater and mounting productions quickly that I couldn't believe how long the waiting periods were that were associated with filmmaking. I had always been a film buff, but I was never one who was avidly seeking a career in filmmaking. I suppose that in retrospect *Rounder* was a tough sell because of its difficult subject matter, and it was very hard to get anyone to commit financing to it. The project never really went anywhere.

At the time this was going on, the Sundance Film Festival erupted. *Reservoir Dogs* was an enormous hit. Every year there seemed to be some new story of someone making a film for $20,000 and having unbounded success in taking it to the big screen. I knew that those stories were ultimately fairy tales. They were very romantic to tell and worked great for the press, but at the end of the day, no one took a film to the movie theater for twenty grand. *Brothers McMullen* may have cost $20,000 to shoot, but it took a couple hundred thousand more to finish through postproduction and printing. Somehow though, perhaps because of the frustration of *Rounder*, or my desire to just make a film, I decided to make my own $20,000 movie, regardless of how impossible that task might have been. I think that perhaps my unfamiliarity with the process was what ultimately served me the most. I was pushed toward a "do it yourself" style of filmmaking—had I known about cameras and lights and cinematographers and grip trucks maybe I would have been put off from the idea of going out and making my own film. But I had heard of all the stories of Robert Townsend or Kevin Smith, who had done projects for small amounts of money that had become very successful, and I just thought, What the hell? I'll give it a try. I had written a script called *In the Company of Men* a few years earlier, and I set about rustling up money from whatever sources I could find to get the funds to shoot it.

HOW DID THE SCRIPT DEVELOP?

I was interested in making something that was familiar, but hadn't been seen before. I wanted to do a new take on the standard love triangle. I was intimately familiar with office settings from my experiences working at the computer company after college, and I felt like I knew something about that world. I rode the bus and the subway with the workforce, and I was aware in a general sense of the mechanics of business. For the theme, I brought together ideas about betrayal that seem to run consistently throughout my work. I was interested in the idea of a person playing with someone romantically just for the fun of it; I wanted the story to be an ironic examination of office politics.

GIVEN THAT YOU ARE A PRACTICING MORMON, WHY DO YOU THINK YOUR FILMS DEAL WITH WHAT COULD BE TERMED THE DARK SIDE OF MAN'S APPETITES, THE HORRORS THAT PEOPLE CAN PERPETRATE ON ONE ANOTHER?

I suppose I don't really think about my films in those terms. I don't think of myself as a Mormon writer or filmmaker any more than a male filmmaker or a Midwestern writer, or whatever political animal I perceive myself to be. I'm sure my beliefs have influenced me, but I've only been a Mormon for a certain length of time; I didn't grow up in it. I grew up in a community church, so I've always been influenced by the churchgoing experience, but I don't consciously think of my work as being shaped by that.

I will say that I like that friction that comes from formalism, and I enjoy creating a certain severity of frame and composition, sending characters to wild places and forcing them to deal with difficult issues. I like that juxtaposition of formalism and romanticism. The kind of passion that comes from characters fraught with really emotionally charged ideas in a very austere environment has always fascinated me as a filmgoer, and I've tried to deal with those issues as a creator of film.

AFTER YOU HAD COMPLETED YOUR SCRIPT, HOW DID YOU PROCEED IN MAKING YOUR FILM?

I next looked for every possible place from which I could find money to make the film. The first to get hit were of course the friends and family members. I was looking for that $25,000 investment and, at that minimal level, I think that people were suspicious that I was not really making a film. Understandably, they were wary of the idea that someone could actually make a movie for so little money, so it was difficult to find anybody to put up money at all. I guess people suspected that I might just take that money and go on vacation with a video camera.

I knew that any investment at all was a risk, because even if we had a good script and a decent production, the film might not get bought or get into the right festivals. There are many things that can affect the success or failure of a movie that are often outside of your control; the cultural climate, other films that are released around the time you are trying for, and so on. So it was hard to ask people for money, but I believed that we had a shot at making a good film that would get distributed. I had heard that some former students of mine had been injured in a car crash and had received a fairly healthy insurance settlement as a result of this accident. I called them up and asked them if they wanted to invest any money into a film that I was making, and they said that they would. They put up $10,000 each, and Matt Malloy (who plays Howard in the film) who was a friend got one of his brothers to put up $5,000. So we had the $25,000 that we thought we needed and we set off to make the film.

I cast Stacy Edwards, who I had met at the Sundance Lab, as the female lead, and I invited my old friend Erin Eckhard out to play opposite her along with Matt Malloy. I hit my brother up for frequent-flyer miles so we could fly Stacy out to Indiana to join us. Matt drove up from California and Erin hitched a ride with a trucker coming out from New York. He literally got off at a truck stop in Indiana, where I picked him up. It was that kind of communal spirit with lots of passionate people that got the film made. I had a lot of students and people in the community who felt that what I was doing was a unique thing. They liked film and they believed in me. Ultimately that is the way that you get low-budget pictures made. In a way it is like strip mining because people are so seduced by the idea of a movie being made in their town that they help you out in remarkable ways, by giving you free locations or equipment or labor or props. You don't get those kind of breaks in Los Angeles because out there everyone's savvy and knows to the nickel what it should cost to shoot in a restaurant in Santa Monica at 4 P.M. on Tuesday. *In the Company of Men* was very much a community project and it was that support that made shooting the film on our ultra-low budget possible.

GIVEN THAT YOU HAD NEVER BEFORE EVEN MADE A SHORT FILM, HOW DID YOU WORK THROUGH THE PRODUCTION PROCESS?
It was a definite learning experience. I hired a local cinematographer and line producer who were experienced and had done things before. Ultimately the line producer stayed on with the project throughout postproduction and became a full producer, going out and raising money for the lab completion

costs that finally surfaced. I had of course by this time watched a tremendous number of films, so I had a certain sense of how you constructed shots. I guess I had a kind of aesthetic that I was trying to realize: I really liked the idea of a very still camera with long takes. I liked imposing a certain theatrical element to filmmaking. I was comfortable with the frame being a kind of stage box. The film wasn't about the movement of the camera, it was about the movement of the characters and their placement within the space of the frame. The films of Eric Rohmer were a great inspiration to me. I appreciate the quiet and calm of his movies and the intellectual dialogue and the kinds of questions it raises.

DID YOU HAVE A LEVEL OF COMFORT WORKING WITH ACTORS, GIVEN YOUR THEATER BACKGROUND?

Well that certainly helped, but I was also comfortable with the actors because I knew them before we started working together. Unfortunately there wasn't as much rehearsal time as I would have liked. The thing that I like about theater over film is that you can rehearse many times before you do something. Film is always a kind of mad dash. I'm very comfortable working with actors though because I like what they do and I understand it even though I'm not able to do it well myself. I'm an admirer of the process and I think that the actors pick up on that. I don't see them as pawns or objects for me to move around a board or make stand still while my camera circles around them. I'm very interested in what they do and I think that they are an integral part of movies as a whole. Working with the actors was a pleasure. It remains a pleasure; it is my favorite part of the process after writing.

HOW DID YOU APPROACH EDITING THE FILM?

There wasn't much to edit. We had to be extremely conservative with our film stock since we were shooting in 35mm for such a ridiculously low budget, so we pretty much put everything we shot into the final cut. I edited the film in the basement of a local church on two videotape machines. I had no AVID, just an old-school video-to-video system that moved very slowly. One of the big frustrations of cutting on "on-line" videotape is that you can't go back and change something once it's done without starting over from the beginning again. You have to build the film from start to finish straight through; you can't do any insert edits.

After we finished our rough cut, we sent it to Sundance and it was accepted. We didn't have enough money to even get it out of the lab, so my friend Joel Ploch started to work on producing the film and canvassed the New York financial community, which he knew, to raise the finishing funds. He even went to his parents and he was able to whip up a certain amount of money for us to get it to the screen. When we found out that we were going to Sundance, it was like there was an enormous ticking clock reminding us that we had a limited amount of time left to find the money to finish the film. It was one thing to get accepted to Sundance, but the other thing was the horrible possibility that we wouldn't be able to go for financial reasons. But ultimately we finished the film in time.

HOW DID THE SUNDANCE ACCEPTANCE AFFECT YOUR FINAL EDIT OF THE FILM?
You certainly can't help but think about an audience. For me there is a point when you are looking at the film wondering, Does this thing have any bite? Does it have any humor? I work in a vacuum, but it is very important for an audience to react to the film, and you need to see how it plays in order to make your final adjustments. The Sundance audience played that role for me.

The experience was fantastic. I don't know how it couldn't be, because really no matter what happens monetarily or award-wise it is a wonderful experience just to go there and to have your film shown. There were many people who wanted to see the film before Sundance, but I refused to show it. Today you write a script and you want to show it to one actor, and then whatever agency represents that actor practically publishes the thing and you could read the book by the weekend. It just gets around town really fast. That was what I wanted to avoid, and since we had made the film independently I was able to do so. The first screening was for a room of five hundred people. It was great to feel the energy of people watching something fresh, and the audience responded as well as I could have hoped.

WHAT HAPPENED DISTRIBUTION-WISE?
Buzz about the film built through the week, and we were awarded the film-maker trophy for it. We sold the international rights and the sales rights to a company called Alliance early on and with that we made back our entire production and postproduction budget. We flirted with a couple of different companies for the U.S. rights, but we didn't make a domestic distribution deal at Sundance. Overall we walked away a bit stunned about that, and we were wondering what we did wrong. In fact, we did everything just right.

After Sundance, we were accepted into the New Directors Festival in New York. Right before the screening Sony Classics came forward and said, "Yeah, we want the movie," and they grabbed it. It got into the Cannes Film Festival and Sony took it under their wing. It played festivals in the spring and was released by summer. The distribution strategy was par for the course for the way Sony tests "platform" movies. They put us on the road to talk to journalists early on, and they released it in two theaters in New York and Los Angeles. Then as positive word of mouth built, they increased the screens. By the end of the release, the film was playing on over a hundred screens around the country.

The box-office gross was around $3 million, and it was critically very well received. It was the second-highest grossing film of the year in terms of cost-gross ratio. It didn't make a huge amount of money, but it was a great success. My future prospects were greatly enhanced by the film. It made people aware that I was out in the world doing things. After Sundance, someone who worked for the actor Jason Patric approached me about making another film. By the time *In the Company of Men* was released, I was in preproduction for *Your Friends and Neighbors*.

LOOKING BACK AT THE EXPERIENCE OF BOTH MAKING THE FILM AND ESTABLISHING YOURSELF AS A DIRECTOR, WHAT DO YOU THINK WERE THE CRUCIAL STEPS TO MAKING THAT HAPPEN?

I think that everyone I came into contact with was crucial in one way or another, but the bottom line is that it was perseverance and hard work that made a difference. It was hearing someone say no and not really believing that answer. For me the answer was, "No, but . . ." I had to believe that that person just didn't finish their sentence. You just keep going like a little toy car that runs into a wall and bounces back and goes the other way. It is about not giving in and saying, "Well, you know this isn't working out so I better study law and then I'll have at least some sort of career and money coming in." I had a lot of friends who were very talented actors and technicians who just sort of gave up on a career in theater or film. It was just too hard and it was just too long for them to wait for things to happen. I always felt that it was a matter of when it would happen and not if it would happen, so I had to be ready to seize the opportunity when I saw it before me. This happened when I felt that I had the right script and could make a movie that people would watch for the amount of money that I had. It wasn't about having a large budget or well-known actors; it was about being able to look at the film and say, "I shot it that way because I wanted to, not because I had to." Another thing to note is that while making the film I did my best to be prepared. Lack of preparation can kill. When you have an eleven-day shoot you have no margin of error and you can't be ruined by a couple days of rain. In that scenario you have to be a little bit lucky, but completely prepared for every contingency that you can think of. I can't stress that enough.

WHAT ADVICE CAN YOU GIVE TO ASPIRING DIRECTORS?

It is really about making your own fun. When I was doing theater I would work with what I had, but I would never let that become a boundary of what I could do. I was often either creating my own theater groups or taking over space outside the theater for my production. I was always looking for new ways to do things within an established system. I was doing plays under stairwells, in open areas, and at the natural history museum. One time I cleaned out a storage room in the basement of a dormitory to stage a play. I just wouldn't let convention get in my way. I think the same thing applies to student films. Use what is available to you but be inventive and get whatever advantages you can through whatever means you can. If I were making *In the Company of Men* today, I would shoot it on digital video. Today technology is cheaper and more available, and many young filmmakers are using that to their advantage.

The script is the basis of film, and you should work on developing yours if you can. I'm in love with the things that characters say, and I feel most clever and creative in developing them. I think you should rely most on whatever talents you think you have, and for me I think that writing is my best talent. But I've studied other things as well, like acting and directing. Studying acting has given me a practical knowledge that I can use to communicate with actors that I couldn't have gotten just by studying camera techniques alone.

Make a film. Go out on weekends for the next four months. Edit it on a computer and show it to people. They may say that you should throw it away, but they may also give you money to finish it or tell you it's a great idea and give you money to reshoot the whole thing on film. It is often hard for people to visualize an idea; sometimes people need that visual representation of what you are talking about in order to understand the merits of your project. With the advent of video people are subverting the idea that the costs and complexities of film production cannot be overcome without "professional" backing and are doing it on their own. They are able to shoot quicker and more compactly with less light. They are able to move quickly from location to location so that they can shoot more setups in a day. The ability to take what is in your head and put it on the screen has grown exponentially in the last couple of years.

FOR EVERY INDEPENDENT FILM THAT ACTUALLY GETS A THEATRICAL RELEASE, THERE ARE PROBABLY ABOUT A HUNDRED THAT DON'T. WHAT DO YOU SEE AS THE DEFINING FACTOR OF A FILM'S ABILITY TO GET A COMMERCIAL RELEASE? There is certainly an element of luck; there are many factors that work in favor of or against a film being a success. But what is success? Is your film successful if it makes $2 million? Is it successful if it gets screened at a festival? You have to qualify what success means to you. When I was making *In the Company of Men,* my success criterion was a distant fantasy that the film might someday play at Sundance, since that was where I had heard all the guys who made independent films and became filmmakers showed their films. There are hundreds of festivals and many of them are quite good, but Sundance was the one I read about and that was what I aspired to. I wanted to get the film into Sundance, but that didn't mean that that would translate into sales and fame and all those things some people fantasize about. It was just the place where they showed movies that I liked and where people could get their work seen. That was success to me. There was probably no higher high than when I was told I was accepted into Sundance.

But if you talk about making a film, getting it released, and getting a chance to make more films and have a career, I have absolutely no idea what makes that happen. In my case it was as much luck as it was anything else. But I combined the best elements I could to give myself the greatest probability of success. I wrote the script and I made sure I thought it was good; I cast actors who I thought would be right for the part; and I worked as hard on the film as I could. The rest was out of my hands.

Tom Dicillo | JOHNNY SUEDE

TOM DICILLO *was born in North Carolina in 1953. After college, he received his M.A. in directing at NYU film school. While there he began his collaboration with fellow student Jim Jarmusch and photographed the films* Permanent Vacation *and* Stranger Than Paradise. *After a ten-year struggle, DiCillo raised the financing to write and direct his first feature,* Johnny Suede, *starring Brad Pitt. Subsequently he made the films* Living in Oblivion, Box of Moonlight; The Real Blonde, *starring Catherine Keener and Matthew Modine; and* Double Whammy, *starring Steve Buscemi and Denis Leary. DiCillo is married and lives in New York.*

I was a military brat, so I grew up all over the place. My father was a colonel in the Marine Corps and we never lived in any one place for more than two years. I attended college in Norfolk, Virginia, at a small school called Old Dominion University and after that I moved to New York to attend graduate school at NYU. I have one brother and one sister.

WHAT IS YOUR FIRST MEMORY OF MOVIES?
My first memory of the movies is of going to see *Fantasia* when I was about five years old. As a kid I remember that film being the most erotic thing I had ever seen, and I could have sworn that the dancing nymphs in one of

those sequences were topless. The next thing I really remember seeing was *Rebel Without a Cause* when I was about ten years old. I distinctly identified with the film not because of any of the cool James Dean stuff, but because I understood the story. The film is about a guy who's on the outside who comes to a new school where the other kids immediately look at him like he's a freak. I felt like that every two years whenever I moved to a new school. That was the first film I'd seen with a drama that I identified with personally. It really made a distinct impression on me. It was a little bit more than the story of a guy getting shot, or falling in love, or ending up in some silly high jinks.

I saw a lot of movies as a kid, mostly because of my father. He was a strict disciplinarian and he refused to let us have a television in the house. Up until the time I was seventeen, the only time I watched television was when I would sneak over to a friend's house. I was addicted to the screen and I couldn't take my eyes off it. My father didn't seem to have any problems with me going to the movies though, so every Saturday my sister, brother, and I would head on down to the local theater to see whatever was playing. We would catch a double feature every weekend. Surprisingly enough my parents never even asked what we were seeing. It was the early 1960s and I was about ten. We were seeing at least eight movies a month, which is pretty intense for a little kid. I remember films like *Davy Crockett* and *Old Yeller*. That was an intense movie and I distinctly remember the scene when the dog dies. When I was very young it never once crossed my mind that I would have a career in film. Since I knew nothing about it, and I had no concept of how films were made, it seemed to me that they must have been made by people who were infinitely smarter than I was.

When I was a teenager I thought about being a writer. I have to thank my dad for that since not having a television in the house prompted me to read from a very young age. I read many things that a lot of kids my age weren't interested in. I had read everything by Mark Twain by the time I was twelve. I wrote some short stories in high school. I had developed a skill at being able to put words together and to describe things vividly, so when I went to college I decided that I was going to become a writer. By the time I got halfway through college my aesthetic was quite defined. I was deeply influenced by Joyce, Hemingway, Twain, and Kafka. Those were the guys.

DID YOU ENCOUNTER ANY RESISTANCE TO THE WRITER LIFESTYLE IN LIGHT OF YOUR FATHER'S MILITARY CAREER?

Not at all. However, when I was fourteen he made a halfhearted attempt to convince me to join the military, and later on he tried to get my brother and me to go into law or medicine. But he didn't really push us into that. I find it interesting that, given the rigidity of the military lifestyle (where you literally have to obey the person above you no matter what they tell you), my father was able to instill in me the ability to remain open-minded. I'm not sure how he did it, but he did. At one point before he joined the military he wanted to be a writer himself. He was constantly saying, "Don't sit around on your ass and let your brain turn into mush." Some of the things he tried to tell me I didn't agree with, but that had a deep influence on me. He gave me an inquisitive mind that is open to many things.

But I think my lifestyle completely freaks my father out because he has no concept of it. He is always saying, "You don't know where your next check is coming from, you don't have health insurance, and you don't know what your next job will be?" Sometimes he has a really difficult time with it. My career has basically been an enormous struggle right from the beginning and it wasn't until about a year and a half ago that I didn't have to freak out at the first of the month when my rent was due. My father has witnessed the fact that it has taken me three years to finance my current movie. Every time I call and tell him that I lost the money, all it does is reemphasize his belief that this business is built upon quicksand.

WHAT DID YOU THINK YOU WOULD DO AFTER COLLEGE?

As Joyce would say, I had an epiphany. When I was in college one of my professors invited me to a film class where they showed movies every Monday night. The first movie they showed was *La Strada*, and I was blown away by the experience of watching it. I had been taking black-and-white pictures on my own before the movie, so I already had an impulse to work with visual images somehow. But the photography in *La Strada* was like nothing I had seen before. It was the first film where I saw the kind of story I wanted to tell that looked at the human condition but was also entertaining. That is important because a lot of people think some of the films like this are art films and that they are not enjoyable on an entertainment level. To me they're very entertaining because they stimulate you emotionally and intellectually. Before *La Strada* I had never seen a story in which the lead character was a kind of a brute who ends up making a decision about his life where he rejects the only woman who loves him and he ultimately ends up alone. This really affected me, and I began to go to every one of the film appreciation screenings. It was there that I saw my first Ingmar Bergman film, there that I saw François Truffaut's *Shoot the Piano Player,* and there that I got my first introduction to Jean-Luc Godard. For an American kid who didn't live in a big city, it was fairly rare to have access to these films and I didn't know anybody else who had seen them. There wasn't much on videotape and the whole idea of repertory theaters didn't exist as it does now. At that point a lot of these films were only being shown on college campuses. The first time I saw John Waters's *Pink Flamingos* it was projected on a sheet outside my dorm room. It was the experience of seeing those films that made me take a look at my writing and see that if I had a camera I could tell a story using all the visual elements that I was interested in exploring.

My impulse to get into the film business was from purely an artistic aesthetic. There was never any sense that any of these films I had seen had generated huge amounts of money and I hardly even knew who the directors were, so it wasn't about celebrity or fame. I had no idea how to pursue this until someone suggested that I go to film school. Since I was on the East Coast, I applied to NYU. I sent in my photographs and some writing, and to my utter amazement I was accepted into the master's program in film. It was a three-year program and my parents paid for the first year. To pay for the rest I took out a loan and worked. My brother and I moved to New York and started a painting business with a friend. I would literally run from class to throw on my paint clothes to go do a job. I also had a job as a teaching assistant while I was there.

Jim Jarmusch (who went on to direct many films) was at NYU at the same time I was. We became friends almost instantly. I really respected his sensibility and his great sense of comic irony. I think he and I are the only ones from our class who are actually making films today.

Film school was hard, and I didn't like it because it was different from what I expected. There were a lot of guys walking around with full beards and hats who thought they were going to be the next Martin Scorsese. What NYU tried to teach had no relation whatsoever with the reality of what making a film is like. You cannot teach someone aesthetics. What you can do is say, "If you were in this situation and this is the kind of story you wanted to tell, here are a couple of ways you could try to make things work." But they didn't really do that. I did my three years there, and I have said at times that besides my childhood, going to NYU was the single most destructive experience of my life. It took me eight years to recover. For me, the whole idea of a learning institution is to create an environment where people are encouraged to try and fail. They used "fail" in the most general sense of the term because what the fuck is failure? Failure is that if you try something and it doesn't work, you learn something about how you are going to try again. This is more productive and useful than any sort of success. Unfortunately, the entire school was based upon condemnation for failure. The message there was that you shouldn't try anything, because if you did try something that didn't work then you would fail and be lambasted by the faculty.

I distinctly remember a screening of the Godard film *Vivre Sa Vie*. Jim and I were sitting on opposite sides of the room. Jim and I really enjoyed the film, so I said what I liked about it, and then he said what he liked about it, and the entire class was in an uproar. They all thought the film was a piece of shit. This was the heyday of George Lucas and Michael Cimino; I was kind of an anarchist. I was furious most of the time I was there. NYU was going to screen *The Deer Hunter* and they pasted announcements throughout the school. I had seen it and I thought it was the biggest bunch of shit, so I put a fake notice up on the board that said that the deer would be there after the screening to answer any questions. I guess I was angry that I wasn't in the learning environment that I expected to be in. There was also an intense aura of pessimism and negativity from the faculty.

TELL ME ABOUT SOME OF YOUR NYU FILM PROJECTS.
I wrote and directed all of my own films, and my ideas reflected some aspect of what I was doing in New York at the time. I didn't work as a cinematographer for anybody until my second year of school, when one of my instructors was handing out assignments for a project and she randomly chose Jim to direct it and me to shoot it. That is how I started working with Jim Jarmusch. I had never shot anything before and this collaboration was exciting because I didn't approach it from the technical aspect that many "cinematographers" at the school did, and he appreciated that. I had a strong visual sense, and I would bend the rules to create interesting shots. I was very interested in taking the camera and finding out what it took in order to design a shot so that it would cut easily into another shot in the editing room. There is a lot of thought that goes into that process. You have to ask yourself, What does it take to build a scene? What is a shot? The film I did with Jim was a student exercise about a murder, and he fragmented the entire story so that it was just a series of shots. By the time the film was over, you had to add them up to determine what had happened. We had fun doing it together. He gave me great freedom as a cinematographer and he knew that I was not going to tell him he couldn't do something. After this collaboration, Jim asked me to shoot his thesis film, *Permanent Vacation*.

HOW WAS THE EXPERIENCE OF CINEMATOGRAPHY COMPARED TO DIRECTING?
On a certain level I found it liberating because I could focus purely on the visual choreography. When I say choreography I mean it. When I would think about a shot for Jim, I would start with what was going on in the script, and then try to figure out how to use the camera to pull out whatever was happening to make it better and more interesting. I do this with my own films now. It is a means not only to complement the action that is taking place, but also to embellish it. It is not like you are sugarcoating anything, it is more like, What can I do with the camera to make this scene spring into life? Sometimes it may only be a static shot that could make this happen, but I enjoyed finding creative ways to use the camera. One time

when I was tired of having to deal with the technicalities of the dolly, I put the camera on a rope and suspended it from the ceiling so I could easily move it around. I was never into doing things in a traditional way. I never thought, Oh no, I must have this key light here and the actress has to sit right there and not move. That kind of thinking is absurd.

When I was working with Jim as a cinematographer, I never felt like I was just a cameraman. I felt like our work was a combination of our mutual sensibilities. There is no question that these were his films, but if working on them had been a more traditional kind of shooting situation I probably would have just done one film with him and that would have been that. What excited me was that I was allowed the freedom to think as a director in the capacity of a cinematographer.

Permanent Vacation did the festival circuit and started to win awards. The whole independent movement in filmmaking had not really begun yet, so Jim's impulse to make a feature out of his thesis film was very brave and smart. He started to work on *Stranger Than Paradise* while I was still thinking in terms of half-hour ideas. I had no idea how to get someone to give you money to put together a feature-length film.

My thesis film at NYU was a disaster. I don't want to go into it in too much detail, but I tried some things, and they didn't work. That experience illustrated a brilliant example of everything that I didn't know about directing, performance, shooting, and story. All I can say is that I was grateful for the learning experience. I got out of school a little shaky and I knew I never wanted to go through that nightmare experience again.

It was 1979 when I finished film school. I was twenty-three and I had no money, so I was still painting apartments with my brother to support myself. I went out looking for film work and I made the rounds at all of the film production houses in New York with my NYU master's degree and my little resume. I can't tell you the number of doors that were quickly slammed in my face or the number of people who scoffed at my degree and literally told me I could sweep their floor. It was so depressing. My first paying job out of NYU was sweeping the floor in a Crazy Eddie commercial. Remember Crazy Eddie? After about a year of searching for a job this way I realized that this was not the way to go. It was quite frightening because I thought, Christ, why did I go to school all this time to get a worthless degree? That is how naive I was.

DID YOU HAVE TROUBLE GETTING PEOPLE TO LOOK AT YOUR WORK?
I didn't have trouble getting people to look at my work, but unfortunately people could not quite make any sense out of *Permanent Vacation*, since it was not a wildly accessible movie. Even if someone were interested, it wouldn't get me a job. I was getting tired of painting apartments, so I did

try to concentrate on getting work as a cinematographer because I knew I could make money that way, and it was at least work in film. At this time I was also studying acting with Frank Corsaro, who was a well-known acting teacher in New York. I was always interested in acting and I really started studying to understand the craft from a directing point of view. One day during a class Frank said to me, Tom, why don't you get up and act in a scene? I did one scene and it changed forever the way I work with actors. Now I knew what it was like to be in front of people, somehow trying to convince them what I was saying and doing was truthful. I developed a tremendous respect for the craft, and I realized that if you respect good actors then you will really get something great from them. I ended up studying acting for eight years. I took a leave of absence when Jim asked me to shoot his next film, *Stranger Than Paradise*.

Stranger Than Paradise was the most significant project to come along up to that point. At the time, I had shot a few music videos and a documentary. Music videos were just starting to become a big thing, but it was something I was just never able to break into. I had also shot some ultra-low-budget movies like *Underground USA*, but I was trying to stay away from that scene. I never considered myself to be a cinematographer, and it was a reputation I didn't want. My collaboration with Jarmusch was different. I am really proud of our work together and Jim and I had a great time doing it.

I will never forget that day when I looked down and saw the Arts & Leisure section of *The New York Times* with a headline that *Stranger Than Paradise* had won the Golden Camera at the Cannes Film Festival. I remember I was at work painting at the time. I said to myself, Tom, what the fuck are you doing? You came to this city eight years ago to become a director and here you are with a master's degree in film from NYU, and you are painting an apartment. That is when I made up my mind to make my first film.

In my acting class I had written a series of monologues that I would perform based on a character I created called Johnny Suede. They were very successful with my fellow students, so I put them together into a one-man show and I found a theater that gave me five nights to perform it. The response was so strong that I realized I could make it into a feature and I started to write my first screenplay.

TELL ME A LITTLE BIT ABOUT WHAT INTERESTED YOU IN THE CHARACTER AND THE WORLD OF *JOHNNY SUEDE*.

I've always been fascinated with the reality that lies behind a glittering surface. A lot of people spend enormous amounts of time creating an image. Most of the time what is under the surface is considerably different than what you expect. The whole East Village scene was in full bloom at that time and I saw so many fascinating phonies. I began thinking about a guy who had these aspirations that were real, but underneath he was lost. I do believe a lot of people are in their own ways very lost, confused, and frightened. I think it is only when you address that fact that you find out what you are capable of doing and what you really are. I love the comedy of a guy who could say, "Oh yeah, I play the guitar," and then he goes home and you see that he can barely play a chord. Or the guy who brags that he is great with women, but when he is with a woman he doesn't even know the first thing about what to do. I took this idea and constructed an image that was so exaggerated that the character didn't know that he looked like a fool. The strangest criticism I ever got for *Johnny Suede* was that it was "an exercise in cool," when in fact it was a movie about the utter idiocy of a character who is contemplating what it is to be cool. I learned at an early stage to take things that really happened to me, and to exaggerate and twist them to find their essence while putting them in a context that would relate to other people. *Johnny Suede* isn't just about me, although it related a lot to me. Johnny Suede is an outsider. He is a guy who doesn't fit in, and he's walking through a world where everybody just seems like they are crazy. That mirrored a lot of my own experience.

Finishing that first draft of my first feature-length script was such an enormous accomplishment that I will never forget it. It took me about six months. The problem was that since it had been based on a theatrical performance, not all of the scenes in the play would work visually. Every other one of my films had been conceived as a visual idea and written from a visual standpoint. There is a big difference between the two. My challenge was to visualize the film and make it cinematic. I think I succeeded in doing that to a certain degree, but I also think that there are still long passages that are purely verbal and that could have been handled much better by the camera.

I showed the script to Jim and he liked it and was very supportive. At this point I didn't even know what a budget was, let alone how to put one together. I didn't even have a producer. Jim gave me a couple of names and he told me to go down to the grant library on Fifth Avenue and write down all the places where I could get grants. I spent three days writing out all the grants and I began writing proposals to the New York State Council of the Arts and the National Endowment for the Arts. He gave me the name of a German company called ZDF that he had had some success with for both *Permanent Vacation* and *Stranger than Paradise*. I contacted them and, to my utter amazement, they called me back after a couple of months and said they wanted to give me $80,000. They already knew who I was because ZDF had paid for some of *Stranger Than Paradise*, and the film was huge in Germany.

Then when I got $25,000 from the National Endowment for the Arts, I could not believe it. Even to this day I can't believe it and I don't know how it happened. I had never won anything in my life, so this was all like winning the lottery. It didn't have anything to do with my sense of whether I deserved it or not, but it did give me a little more faith in the project.

I needed a producer, so someone from ZDF gave me the name of Yoram Mandel, who had produced *Parting Glances*. I called him and he agreed to be my producer. Then things got kind of complicated. We tried to come up with a budget, and I wanted to shoot 35mm. We came up with a budget of $400,000 for a New York shoot with a nonunion crew on 35mm. We had only a quarter of the money that we needed, so we began trying to get the rest of it.

Somehow we got hooked up with a South African guy who had a company called Distant Horizons, and he said he would give us the rest of the money. I was elated and we signed a deal, even though there were a couple of things that I felt very nervous about, including the fact that he had the right to fire me from my own film. He also had final say over the casting and the final cut of the film. But he was giving us over $300,000 so we agreed to do it. We began to do the casting and then he told me that he wanted me to cast Timothy Hutton as Johnny Suede. It didn't go over too well when I said no to Timothy Hutton.

I had been looking for the actor to play Johnny Suede for months and had met Brad Pitt when he came in for an audition. At that point it felt as if I had seen every single actor in New York City. We had an open call, but nobody could do the part. They were all coming in and doing these horrible imitations of Fonzie from "Happy Days." When Brad came in he was very young and had only done a few things for Canadian TV. He had shot one feature, *Thelma and Louise*, but it hadn't been released yet. I knew immediately that he was the guy; he gave a tremendous audition and he worked well with Catherine Keener, who was auditioning at the same time. I told the producer that I wanted to cast Brad, and he said no because he wanted a name in the role. At this point I knew I had to get out of this deal that we had made. I wasn't being arrogant; it just wasn't working. Legally the financier's option had expired, but once we told him we wanted out, he threw in all of these "expenses" that he had into a termination fee. So I had to pay this guy $60,000. That happened on a Friday, but by Sunday I was already in another deal with a Swiss woman I had met through a friend. Her name was Ruth Waldburger and she had produced for Godard. She loved the script and she agreed to do it giving me total control over everything. In just a couple of days I went from one of the worst deals that you could imagine into one of the best possible. Ruth was a great producer and she put up $300,000 of her own money. We figured that pre-sales in five countries would make her that money back. This was based on the script I guess, because it was certainly not due to my nonexistent reputation. Our original producer, Yoram Mandel, was still involved in the project. He was the hands-on producer and she was the money producer. I cast Brad as Johnny Suede and we started to make the film with a budget of $400,000.

Originally I was going to shoot the film in the East Village, because that was where the story had originated. But by that point the East Village was no longer the East Village that I had known. It was now Starbucks, the Gap, and Banana Republic, so I had to come up with a fictionalized version of it in Williamsburg, Brooklyn. That is where we shot the entire movie.

THE FILM HAS A SORT OF "OTHER WORLD" QUALITY TO IT.
The film was a fable. I tried to make it so that it wasn't a glorification of that East Village bohemian lifestyle. It was a strange kind of cartoon about a guy caught up in a world he didn't really understand, and his struggle to try to find himself in it and define what was real and what was fake. There is some pretty weird shit that happens in there. If you go back and look at *La Strada,* you will see that it touches on many of those same things.

TELL ME ABOUT THE PRODUCTION OF THE FILM.
It was an utter nightmare from beginning to end. On the very first day of filming we shot some simple exteriors in Williamsburg and had a lot of fun with Brad in costume walking down the street. On the second day everything came crashing down like a tidal wave, and every day after that there was a crisis. I bear almost all the responsibility myself, but there was a miscommunication between Brad and myself as to what the performance of the character should be. I never imagined Johnny as somebody with a frontal lobotomy. I gave Brad the idea that he was kind of like a child in the sense that the child's attention will be here and there and all over the place, but I didn't mean to suggest that Johnny had the intellect of a child. I didn't have that much experience directing actors and it was too late to do anything, so unfortunately this lethargic rhythm was bred into every scene and it would later dictate how I had to edit the film.

I ended up with a director of photography who later admitted to me that he was intentionally sabotaging my film. This guy was doing shots that were out of focus with action out of frame. I'm not lying to you; this is true. It makes you realize that 99 percent of the people who get drawn into this business are psychotic and are in it for all the wrong reasons. The danger is that you never know it until it is too late. If you find someone who you work with who is not insane, you should do your best to keep them. Finally, the cinematographer's attitude got worse and worse, and I had to fire him. When I was editing the film and I needed a shot, I started thinking about what this guy had done. I was still baffled as to his motivation, so I called him from the editing room and I asked him why he had done what he did. He broke down in tears and told me that he was so jealous that I was directing my first film that he had intentionally screwed up the shots. I was stunned and I can't tell you what profound effect this had on me. Another thing that happened was that all the wardrobe was stolen while we were shooting. Brad's costumes were actually my own clothes that I had accumulated over twenty years of going to different thrift stores around the country. Two weeks into shooting somebody left the wardrobe van unattended and everything was stolen.

Every single day of the shoot something went wrong. I would walk onto the set and tell myself, Tom, listen man, your attitude dictates the attitude of the production. If you come in with a bad mood everyone is going to pick up on it. So every single morning I would come in and try to make things as positive as I could.

WAS SOME OF THIS STUFF THE INSPIRATION FOR YOUR LATER FILM,
LIVING IN OBLIVION?

Completely. It was stunning to me how utterly devastating it can be for a low-budget movie once things start to go wrong. You don't have the time or money to go back and fix things. Much of the final product is dependent on the luck of getting it right the first time because if you don't, you'll never get it. I believe that's why a lot of first-time directors are so crazy, especially on independent films, is because the pressure is so intense.

Brad was very brave and creative. His work in *Johnny Suede* is some of the most courageous work I've seen him do. He is very funny and I really enjoyed working with him. He was very open and at times he came up with ideas that were very helpful. There was a scene where Johnny walks around in his underwear. I wanted the underwear to look a little grungy so we had them treated and ripped. He looked at them and said, "No, that's not right," so he took them and just ripped them some more. I remember reading a quote from him a couple of years later when somebody asked him what it was like to work with me. He said, "It was intense, man. It was like being in an acting class." This was true because in an acting class what you are doing is trying many different things. I was forcing him to be focused and inventive so he didn't get locked into one mechanical thing.

Working with Nick Cave was great too, even though there were nightmares there as well. I idolized him, so when he said that he wanted to act in the film, I was really amazed. My concept was to create a sort of Albino Elvis, so we hired a wig expert to create his look. On Nick's first day on the set I arrived at 8 A.M. to meet with him. By 10 o'clock there was still no sign of him. I went to the makeup trailer and there I found Nick Cave sitting in this chair with a look on his face like he was ready to pick up an ax and kill somebody. He had a wig on his head and this "wig expert" was poking wads of flesh-colored putty on his forehead with a fork trying to make it blend in. He looked like something out of *Planet of the Apes*. The woman was nervous and sweating and she looked at me and said, "I don't know how to do this wig." Then Nick says, "I should never have taken this fucking movie." You may think that being a director is great and exciting, but at that moment it was not glamorous at all. Here was a guy that I idolized who had agreed to be in my movie, and he looked me right in the eye and said, "I'm off this fucking movie," and he walked out. One part of me agreed with him, but another part of me wanted to wring his fucking neck. I had to find him and convince him to give me one more chance. We found another person to do the wigs, and six hours later the wig was on his head and we shot that scene.

There was yet another disaster that we had to deal with as well. We had been shooting in an abandoned building and had established all of the wide shots of Johnny's apartment. When we showed up the next day to finish filming, there was caution tape around the entire building. Apparently during the night the building had settled and the walls had separated from the floor by two feet. We had to sneak into the building to get our equipment out, and overnight we had to find another apartment and redress it to look like the first one. I can't say that this was one of those beautiful, amazing, first experiences where everything was so perfect. It was trial by fire.

CAN YOU TELL ME A LITTLE BIT ABOUT THE POSTPRODUCTION PROCESS?
My first cut of the movie was two and a half hours long. I took an hour out but it still played slow. My challenge was to keep the film moving but not make it look like it had been surgically altered. I saw all the shooting mistakes that I had made and realized where I had been distracted. I came to a point when I knew that I had no way out of some of the problems. I worked out a lot, but some were just unsolvable, and as a result there are editing problems in the film. I did enjoy the process though. I liked being able to fine-tune the material that I had to tell the story as best I could. I agree with John Sayles who said, "You write a film three times: once when you write it, once when you shoot it, and once when you edit it." Ultimately that is what editing is.

WHAT WAS THE RELEASE STRATEGY AND HOW WAS THE FILM RECEIVED?
Despite the shooting problems, the film had great potential. My first festival was the Locarno Film Festival in Switzerland. The whole experience was like a dream and I still remember it vividly. My wife and I flew to Zurich and immediately got on this train that would take us to the festival. Since

Locarno is near the border of Italy the train went through the Alps all the way down to the south of Switzerland. Looking out the train's enormous window, completely jet-lagged, and seeing vistas of snow-covered Alps drifting by was like watching this unbelievable film unfolding before me.

Before I knew it people started telling me that they thought the film would win an award at the festival. I remember the first public screening of the film and the moment that "Written and Directed by Tom DiCillo" appeared on the screen. It was an amazing experience. I remember my first interview with some kid with a tape recorder who wanted to interview me for his college newspaper. It was all very new in a strange and dreamlike way. Ultimately, the film won best picture at the festival. Someone from Miramax had seen the film and reported back to Harvey Weinstein. *Thelma and Louise* had just been released and Harvey Weinstein sensed that Brad Pitt was the next big thing, so he bought *Johnny Suede* without even seeing the film. This was huge because Miramax was just starting out and they paid $750,000, which was considered an enormous amount of money in 1990. I was in disbelief. Not only had I made the film, but it won at a film festival and it had one of the best U.S. distributors.

I was sitting back waiting for the thing to take off when I heard that Miramax wanted to delay the release of the film until Brad became a bigger star. *Thelma and Louise* was a big hit, but it wasn't huge, so Harvey decided to wait for *Cool World* and *A River Runs Through It* to be released. Meanwhile, Harvey had a test screening of *Johnny Suede* and, verbally and vocally, the audience was responsive to the film even before the cards were filled out. This had been my first test screening and I got a phone call the next morning from Miramax asking me to come down to the office. Apparently in the cards the "really recommend" section was less than what they expected, so they told me I had to cut the movie. We had a big fight and Harvey insisted I put a voiceover on it. We won best picture without a voiceover so why did we have to have a voiceover now? They said that they were trying to help me but that if I didn't want to help them then they really couldn't do their jobs as distributors, which I took as a not-so-veiled threat they were going to dump the film. So I did the voiceover, although I really think it hurt the film. By now one year had passed since the film won at Locarno. They finally set a release date for July in New York City. At midnight the night before the film opened I got a phone call from Harvey Weinstein and I knew it wasn't going to be good news. He said, "Tom, let me read you Vincent Canby's review of your film." This is condensed, but Canby basically said, "There is something going on in this movie and if anyone can tell me what it is, please do." Harvey's last words to me were, "I'm sorry Tom, you know what this means."

Why did that one review determine the fate of my film? Why do critics have that much power? Was Weinstein lying to me, was he using the review as an excuse? The film only played for two weeks in New York and L.A. as well as a few other cities and that was it. They didn't pull it, but they put no publicity behind it. It was excruciatingly painful. It felt like a roulette wheel had turned and that was my fate. It was unbelievably difficult to accept that after all those years of work that my hopes and dreams were gone in two weeks.

As a result my next script, *Box of Moonlight*, was extremely difficult to get off the ground. I ended up making *Living in Oblivion* instead, just to keep myself from going insane. The actors put in the money and I was able to make the film very quickly. Its eventual success was quite a relief.

DO YOU FEEL CONFIDENT IN YOUR ABILITIES AS A FILMMAKER?
In the actual aspects of making the films—the writing, the directing, the editing—I feel extremely confident and I'm still learning with each film. The other aspects of being a filmmaker today are a little more troublesome for me. Raising the money, dealing with the idiots who make the decisions that affect the next three years of your life, dealing with critics—these are hard. The most important thing I learned from the *Johnny Suede* experience is that this business is not fun and games. It is life or death and it takes a certain resilience in order to get through it. No matter how difficult, the actual filmmaking is easy compared to this other stuff.

I had to survive and I did. I knew I was going to. I just had to figure out how I was going to survive and how I was going to be able to make my movies and not sell out and make Hollywood movies that didn't mean anything to me. In my film *Double Whammy* there are two twenty-something screenwriters working on their first screenplay. Before they even finish writing it they are talking about who will walk up on stage when they win best picture at Cannes. I fell victim to that fantasy myself. The truth about success in filmmaking is that it is mainly attributable to hard work.

IT SEEMS THAT PEOPLE RECOGNIZE YOU FOR *LIVING IN OBLIVION* MUCH MORE THAN THEY RECOGNIZE YOU FOR *JOHNNY SUEDE*.
Probably a lot of that is due to the fact that no one even knows that I made *Johnny Suede*. A lot of people think that *Living in Oblivion* was my first film. But I will say that there is something in *Living in Oblivion* that is not in *Johnny Suede*. There is a kind of vitality, a kind of crazy energy that drives that film. *Johnny Suede* is a much more contemplative film. *Living in Oblivion* came, in a way, out of the disappointment that I experienced. The experience of making *Johnny Suede* provided every ounce of inspiration for *Living in Oblivion*. It was incredibly cathartic for me to make a movie about somehow being victorious over aspects of the business that had thwarted me

for so long. It also gave me a clear sense of what was real. I guess it shouldn't be so amazing to me that serious filmmakers and critics responded most negatively to the film. The film was about putting a little pinprick in the fucking stupid balloon of glamour and mystique that surrounds the independent filmmaker.

When I started out I had a lot of the arrogance and Hollywood dreams that many people in the business had and still have. But after the whole experience of *Johnny Suede* I said, Whoa, man, I want to make the movies that really inspire me, like *Midnight Cowboy* and *La Strada. Midnight Cowboy* is one of the most amazing films of this past century. It's about being out in the world exposing your emotions and being open and vulnerable to the most horrible bullshit. It's really a terrific film and my first feature experience focused me on making things that were important, no matter what it took.

WHAT ADVICE CAN YOU GIVE SOMEONE WHO IS INTERESTED IN BEING A FILMMAKER?

It seems to me that the basic question every filmmaker asks is, How do I get to where I want to go with basically no car, no gas, no shoes, no nothing? I can assure you that almost everybody in this business has experienced that sensation and it is absolutely terrifying. The first thing you should try to do is be as clear as possible about the kind of filmmaker you think you want to be. If you want to be the next Quentin Tarantino or the next Michelangelo Antonioni, then figure that out and start working toward it. Do what is truthful to you. You still may not know how to get there, but at least you know you're moving in some kind of direction.

Know that it's difficult. Ask yourself what you're willing to sacrifice. Try to differentiate between the myth of *Premiere* magazine and *Entertainment Weekly*'s assessment of success and what it really is. That's one of the most destructive things in the business—comparing yourself to people who you read are more successful than yourself. *Entertainment Weekly* actually has a list of winners and losers. It's very easy to buy into that.

Every single person you ask for money is going to say, Did you make a movie before? What did it gross? How did it do? What are the numbers? You can't fight that. That's what it's about. But the only arsenal you can have is to find a way to understand that part of the business and to keep working on your projects. I can guarantee you this: The more personal, the more passionate you feel about a project, the more difficult it will be to make. It's a strange dichotomy. If you really believe in something, that means that it's activating something in you; it means that it's really moving you. Most stuff that really moves people never gets made. Instead it gets homogenized.

I often think that it was very hard for me to get to where I am. But then

I compare my journey to that of other filmmakers I know who have never even had a film released. I'm extremely fortunate that all my films have been released. They haven't been great releases, but at least they were released. So you have to recognize your successes and really be thankful for the luck that you do have. But it never feels like things have been easy. It feels like throughout every inch of this road I've been down, I have left a pint of blood behind.

WHAT DO YOU THINK WAS THE BIGGEST ELEMENT THAT FINALLY LED YOU TO MAKING YOUR FIRST FILM?
Absolute conviction that I was going to make it. I was not going to give up. I looked ahead and I saw a giant waterfall, and I just started swimming as hard as I could over the top. It was blind faith, really. I believed in my idea, I really did. I still believe that the essence of what *Johnny Suede* was about was a really worthy idea. The achievement of that idea could have been better, but I still believe that the idea had merit. It was a story that I believed in.

Luck is very relevant. Since the release of my last film, I have spent three years trying to raise money for my current project. A month ago I was all set to go, a company was giving me all the money. We were a week from starting preproduction. Suddenly my phone rings and this company says to me, "We're not making your film. Good-bye." That was it, no warning, no nothing. I was cast, I had locations, I had crew, everything. My state of mind after that call was suicidal. I was going to give up. So I left everything alone for two days, until finally I started making a few calls. Denis Leary was starring, and he called his agent for me. His agent called someone he had met three years earlier after finding his number in an old phonebook. One thing led to another, and in two weeks I was completely refinanced. There's got to be luck in there. A terrifying kind of luck. I don't think it's all just luck. If it was just luck then your efforts and hard work and determination would be meaningless, and that's certainly not the case. So ultimately it's a balance.

One thing that's disturbing is that quality is usually not the bottom line. There are so many incredible movies that come and go, so many meaningful films that are overlooked. The business today is about what's *immediately* going to grab the audience's attention. The distributors think that if they are putting up money that they have to grab people immediately to recoup their investment. But I've often been drawn to films that are a bit more complex, films that don't necessarily have an immediate hook. But it seems that immediate gratification is often what drives the business and that astounds me. This business is more and more about glamour and celebrity.

I managed to luck out of that by working with smaller sums of money and with people who really care about the films I'm making. I feel extremely fortunate that I haven't had to direct a piece of shit movie just to pay the rent. As difficult as making films is, I have never felt more energized and more alive, more utterly at peace with myself than when I am involved in the making of a movie. When things go right, and even when they go wrong, there is a sense of urgency and excitement that is better than any drug I've ever taken. It is an utterly exhilarating feeling and that is why I do it. If it were only the agony, then nobody would last. Sometimes I wish it was easier, but I don't regret a second.

John Dahl | KILL ME AGAIN

JOHN DAHL *was born in Montana in 1952. After attending Montana State University film school, Dahl made his way to the American Film Institute, making connections that would lead him to his career as a storyboard artist and music video director. After forming a partnership with a fellow writer, Dahl directed his first feature,* Kill Me Again, *starring Val Kilmer, from a script he and his partner had written for MGM. His critically acclaimed and stylish noir work includes such films as* Red Rock West, The Last Seduction, *and* Rounders, *starring Matt Damon, Edward Norton, and John Malkovich; and* Joy Ride, *with Leelee Sobieski. He lives in Los Angeles with his family.*

I grew up in Montana, the second oldest of four children. My parents are married to this day. My brother is also now in the film business; he's a writer and we work together. I also have two sisters who are in other industries.

I spent my entire youth in Montana. Growing up, I remember that in the summertime there used to be deals where you could go to see a lot of movies for not that much money. The first time I really became aware of movies was through my father. He had been raised in Sydney, Montana, grew up very poor, and at one point had a job where he would deliver pamphlet advertisements for films; he'd go around and give out handbills. So my dad saw virtually every movie that came to Sydney for years. He's like an encyclopedia of old movies. He really loved them, and he would take me to films with him at drive-in theaters. I remember distinctly seeing specific movies, like *Dr. Zhivago*, at a drive-in wearing my pajamas, or early Clint Eastwood films like *For a Few Dollars More*, which I saw on my twelfth birthday. My dad said that at the age of twelve you were considered an adult, and he insisted on paying the adult price for me. I said, "Dad you could have gotten me in cheaper, I could have been eleven," but he insisted on paying adult price. I have many memories like that. Movies were a big part of growing up, and then ultimately, on weekends, when I was a kid, I would sit around and watch movies on television with my dad. Films that I loved to watch were old musicals, and old Fred Astaire movies were among my favorites. This was in the sixties, and it's important to remember that you didn't have the same access to movies as you do now. There were no video stores and there was no DVD, so when movies started playing on television, that was a big deal. They had just started "Saturday Night at the Movies," I think, and every now and then they'd have to have filler. So they would show these little documentaries about making movies. The memories I have are of watching the making of *Jeremiah Johnson*, and that's the first time I saw dolly tracks, and figured out how they moved the camera.

In high school I made a couple of films with some friends, but still the idea of being a film director was pretty absurd.

WHY ABSURD?

Well, I either wanted to be an artist or a rock star, and so I played in bands, did a lot of artwork (mostly commercial), and film just seemed like something that was great to watch, but the idea of becoming a film director just wasn't in my universe. Where I grew up it was like, if you were an artist, maybe you would become an art teacher or if you liked music, maybe you'd become a band teacher. There wasn't really an outlet. The idea of making money, or making a living being an artist or a musician, it didn't exist. My mother was raised on a homesteaded farm; my father grew up dirt poor. He went to serve in World War II, got out of the military, got a college education and went into business, and was in the insurance business for years thereafter. So the idea of making a living at art was just quite foreign.

AND YET YOU GREW UP IN A MIDDLE-CLASS HOME.

My parents have done very well. They're very successful, and they're both pretty ambitious, so I would say it was a middle-class upbringing. But it was one of a conventional sort. It was more likely that I would have gone into some kind of business. My sister's a very successful accountant and my younger sister is a very good engineer, so that was more traditionally expected. I mean in Manhattan, you can turn around and see people who make a living just decorating windows for stores. Nobody gets paid to do that in Billings, Montana. The salespeople do it in between. If someone is looking around trying to find out how to be a film director, being able to talk to film directors is helpful, because all of a sudden you see the similarities between you and them, and you may get some ideas for things you can do to further your career. If you don't have access to that, it's suddenly very unattainable. The people who made livings as artists in my town were art teachers and watercolorists, and they really didn't make much.

HAD YOU BEEN READING AT ALL ABOUT FILMMAKERS?

Not so much at that time, I was really just playing in rock bands and working on my artwork. But I remember I was a senior in high school and I took a girl to the drive-in to see the movie *Clockwork Orange*, and I didn't really see much of the movie because I was busy with the girl, but the next night I came back and watched the entire film by myself and I was really blown away. It was a pivotal moment for me because it combined a lot of the things that I really liked. It had classical music. Also, I was a huge fan of cartoons. I loved cartoons, and in a way, my drawing background, when I first decided to go to film school, was more oriented toward a possible animation job than one in film directing. *Clockwork Orange* had very stylized sets, it had very stylized wardrobe and very stylized artwork, and this completely fueled my imagination. Something clicked, and I thought that somewhere, somehow, somebody had to make that stuff, make all that artwork and dress the sets and build all that stuff. Somebody was responsible for that. It was the first time that I thought to myself, People actually *make* movies, they don't just crank them out somewhere. Being that I was from this small town in Montana, having never had any kind of exposure to the business at all, *Clockwork Orange* was a movie that opened a huge door for me in terms of the realization that there were people behind these films. So from that point on film started becoming more of something that I was conscientious about. I still hadn't really read anything about film or even thought about it much other than that, but at least the seed was there.

I went off to the University of Montana in Missoula where I was a fine art major for two years and watched movies, but that was about it. My interests remained focused in fine art. I had always wanted to go to school in California, so I had applied to the Pasadena School of Design, but my artwork just wasn't up to snuff to get it admitted to commercial school. I wasn't really happy at Missoula, and I felt like I was in the wrong place at the wrong time, so I quit school and went back to Billings. I played in rock bands with my friends, and I got a job designing billboards (which is one of the few art jobs you can get paid for in Billings), but after doing all that for a year, I became really fed up with it. I had heard that there was a good film school in Bozeman, Montana, at Montana State University and I thought, well, maybe I would go to film school and see what that was like. I was twenty-one at that point, and I initially went in thinking that I would get into animation, and perhaps if I was good at film and liked it that I might end up at UCLA after a while.

HOW DID YOUR PARENTS FEEL ABOUT YOUR DECISION?
By this point they knew that I wasn't gonna become an accountant, so they figured I'd get some kind of college education and then I'd figure something out. I started school in Bozeman, and the film program wasn't bad. It was quite small, but they had lots of equipment, and they'd let you use it pretty freely. I met several people that I still work with there. I think that's the one thing, if anything, that film students fail to realize, that the greatest assets that they gain in going to film school are the people who are in class with them. Everybody gets out of film school and thinks they've got to beat down the door and convince people to hire them, but the reality is that if you look around the film business, most people establish these friendships with people in the early years and those working relationships pretty much continue throughout their career. I went to school with Scott Chestnut, who has edited two movies for me, and Lori Eschler, who now is composing for me. Carl Biker has won several Writers' Guild awards doing documentaries. There were five people who helped do my senior film: One I married, and the other two live here in Hollywood, and both have careers. So four of us ultimately came to Hollywood and have careers in the movie business. That's just five people going to school at Montana State University. It was the same when I went to the American Film Institute; a lot of the people that I still work with now went to school at the AFI.

TELL ME A BIT ABOUT YOUR EXPERIENCE AT MSU.
I took all the film classes I had to take, as well as a lot of writing classes. I think I realized early on that if you're going to be a filmmaker then you've got to be a writer. I took a lot of theater courses, and I also tried to branch out and not just take film classes. I studied mythology; I read Joseph Campbell; I tried to broaden my interest. It was very interesting to try to learn this new technical language of film. Everyone wanted to be a cameraman at our school; nobody wanted to be a director. Almost by default I ended up directing a couple of projects, and I guess also, weirdly enough, the fact that I always liked cartoons or comic books led me in this natural progression to start drawing storyboards. It was a great concept that you could draw a picture and then turn it into a movie; that just completely thrilled me. It's still mind-boggling to me.

Only what I was seeing in film school. Again this was Bozeman, Montana, in the seventies, there wasn't a Blockbuster and there wasn't a rerun house. But a student organization would bring in films, so I saw a lot of foreign films that way. You have to be a little subversive, because ultimately schools are very pedantic. One time the school got Federico Fellini's 8½ in, and we just stole the print and the projectors one weekend and took them down into our living room and watched the film, but brought it back Monday morning before anybody caught us. We were forever doing stuff like that. Because if you just played by the rules that they created for you, you'd never get anywhere. I think most film schools can only do so much, and they are almost in a way this strange sort of bureaucracy that doesn't necessarily help you that much, other than that you learn some of the basics of filmmaking. You've got a camera, you move it around a little bit, you can take pictures from certain angles and you cut them together, but that's pretty much it. The hard part is, what's the idea, what's the story? I remember I went to a summer program that they had in Germany. We were studying with a guy in Munich, and I bullied him and begged him to let me take a camera one weekend and some film and get on train and take it down to the center of town to shoot something. And he said, "Well, what are you gonna shoot?" I had no idea what I was gonna shoot, I just wanted to do it, and so he let me go. It was incredibly valuable, because I remember getting to the center of Munich, standing there with an ARRI M and two rolls of 16mm film, just feeling like a complete idiot. I had no idea what to do. So ultimately I shot some pictures of downtown Munich and went back to put it together, but there was nothing there really. I think it was probably at that moment that I realized the huge value of the script. And then later when I was at the AFI, Tony Vellani, head of the American Film Institute, said the best thing that anyone ever said to me, which was, "Look, making movies is hard. If you have something to say, say it, but if you don't have anything to say, don't say anything." It sounds remarkably simple, but that's what it is. Directing is way too difficult to waste time shooting nothing, because ultimately it's just as hard to make a bad movie as it is to make a good one. It takes the same amount of work and the same desires, ambitions, and perseverance, and pain. All that goes into making a bad movie too.

SO, WHEN YOU WERE COMING TO THE END OF YOUR TIME AT MSU, WHAT WERE YOUR PLANS FOR THE FUTURE?

I don't know whether I was arrogant or what, but I remember at one of the last classes of the year, my professor said to me, "So, what are you gonna do when you get out of school?" And I said, "Well, I'm gonna go to Hollywood and direct a movie before I'm thirty." I was twenty-four at that time. So he basically said, "Good luck, that'll never happen." But that's what I wanted to do. I didn't know how I was gonna do it, but I thought I would give myself about seven years to try. I figured it would take some time.

After I got out of school, I worked several jobs. For a while I directed some local television commercials in Montana for $200 a pop. After that I worked on a made-for-TV movie as a wardrobe assistant. Then my friend Dave Warfield got me a job in Washington, D.C., doing some grip work, but I really hated it and knew I wanted something more. So I managed to convince the producer that I could assistant direct (because I knew what a breakdown board was from school, and other things) and got a chance to do that ultimately. I assistant directed six half-hour episodes of a dramatic television show for children called "Powerhouse." When the show was over, the cameraman who had shot it, a guy named Tom Richmond, left to go out to a place called the American Film Institute. My friend Scott Chestnut had gone there also and so had a bunch of other people working around the business that I had heard of. So I thought, well, maybe that would be something for me to do, that that might be the way I could become a film director. Because I needed experience—I was just a kid from Billings, Montana, in Washington, D.C., and that seemed like the wrong place to be because how the hell are you gonna make a movie in D.C.? I was low on cash, so I moved back to Montana with my parents, and I made a deal with them that I would apply to both the AFI and the University of Montana Law School, and whichever one I got accepted to was the one I would go to. Fortunately, in 1982 I got accepted to the AFI.

TELL ME ABOUT THE AFI EXPERIENCE.
It was fantastic. What they assumed about you when you got there was that you already knew how to make a movie. They didn't talk to you about editing; they didn't talk to you about cameras; they didn't talk to you about any of the technical aspects of filmmaking—they just talked about story and acting. For me, that was fantastic. Basically, I'd go to school at nine in the morning and leave at eleven-thirty at night, and it was solid movies. You'd be watching movies, talking about movies, directing actors, just always working. It was just an incredible experience. I got a tremendous amount out of it. Tony Bellani, head of the school at the time, has passed away since, but he was really fabulous.

They taught everything on videotape, and for each project they would give you three days to shoot and five days to edit, at the end of which you'd have to show it to the class. And you would get up and sit in front of the class on a bench. You couldn't say anything, you just had to sit there and listen to the criticism. You couldn't defend your work in any way. It was very intimidating for most people. But the whole point of the exercise, as Tony would say, was, "Look, everything you had to say, you already said it up there on the screen. The fact that the grip truck showed up late or the actor you wanted you couldn't get, we don't care. If you didn't finish the show, that's your tough luck." That was really important to me. I think what happens with a lot of filmmakers when they get into the movie business or when they start film school is that they find themselves unprepared to deal with critics. They become very defensive, angry, and upset, and that's foolish, because it gets you nowhere. Nobody knows when they're eighteen or nineteen years old how to make a good movie. I mean I'd love to see Steven Spielberg's early movies. I'm sure they're brilliant, but I'm sure *Saving Private Ryan* is a little better. So many things that they never teach you in film school are management skills. They never talk to you about financing; they never talk to you about how do you get an actor out of his trailer when he doesn't want to come. All of these things, you're just not prepared to deal with at that point in your life. And the fact that it was such a struggle to become a filmmaker was actually very beneficial, because I had to become a human being first.

When I was in film school, virtually the only people who got to direct a movie out of film school were people who directed a second-year film at the AFI, and occasionally one out of one hundred of them would direct a real movie for a studio. But most of us got out of school and started floundering like everybody else. Film festivals hadn't become that popular, and when I got out of film school, I thought, well, maybe I could direct a movie for Roger Corman, you know, some kind of low-budget movie or something like that. Even that was impossible at that point, and it was very frustrating, but fortunately I lucked into the help of a lot of people who I met at school, mainly Dave Warfield, and got to direct a $5,000 music video for a real-estate salesman from Las Vegas who had a band. It had break-dancing in it.

DID YOU MAKE A THESIS FILM AT THE AFI?
No. I was asked to submit a thesis film, and Dave and I spent the summer writing scripts, but they were a little bit too obnoxious. One we did was called *Meathouse Man*, which was about prostitution and the future. But if they don't invite you back to make a thesis film, then that's it. And they didn't like any of them, so I was out on the street. I worked around the industry for a while, doing art department stuff through friends, working on videos and films, driving trucks, being a production assistant, and getting paid fifty dollars a day. Ultimately I ended up working for a woman named Rosemary Brandenburg. She gave me a job in the art department on a low-budget movie and so I drove around a truck for her. It was terrible. But she knew I could draw, and she asked me if I could do a few sketches for her. In the back of my mind I had been thinking that I should be doing story-boards, because it would be a better way to make some money and keep

writing scripts than doing a lot of other jobs I had been doing. But also I thought that if I could convince people I could do storyboards, then maybe I could direct something, because they would see that I could visualize things. So she paid me seventy-five dollars a day to stay home and draw, and then I went from there, starting to work on some storyboards for low-budget music videos. After a while I was getting regular calls to storyboard through a lot of my friends from the AFI. I had gone to school with Greg Gould, who was one of the founding directors of Propaganda, and through him I met the filmmakers Steve Dolan and Yanni Sevatni, as well as Dominic Sena. This was in 1983, when MTV was just getting started. After a while I finally got to direct a music video, my first real video, with a young singer who had a deal with a Japanese record company and had $30,000 to do two spots. So Dave Warfield did one and I did the other. Not much happened with it, but Steve and Yanni were smart guys, and they realized that we should all be doing videos instead of trying to chase down low-budget movies.

Making that first video was great fun, but it was really hard also. I cut the thing myself on a half-inch video system, and after it was done, I got to do another one. At the same time I was still doing storyboards and it was then that I finally got a break. I did the storyboards for David Lee Roth on "Just a Gigolo," and the people really liked me, so they asked me if I would do the storyboards for a feature film that David Lee Roth was going to do on his own. I ended up working on that movie for six months. It was really grueling, but it was fun to hang out with David and his crew. Ultimately they never made the film, but I saved all the money I made while working and met a lot of people. I kept working, made another video for Kool and the Gang, and continued storyboarding work. I was getting pretty big after that. I did the boards for *Robocop*, and then for Jonathan Demme on *Married to the Mob* and *Something Wild*. Directors liked me because I could talk about movies with them; I wasn't just a graphic artist.

At the same time as I was storyboarding, I was also working on writing scripts with Dave Warfield. We had written a horror movie that almost got made, called *Silent Night*, about an insane Santa Claus that killed everybody on Christmas Eve. Then someone else put out a film called *Silent Night, Deadly Night* basically about the same thing and that just put the kibosh on the whole project. But we were thinking of other films, and maybe even other titles for our Santa Claus film, and Dave finally stumbled across the title *Kill Me Again*. How do you get someone to say "Kill me again," in a movie; that's what started the idea for what would become my first film.

In art school, I had really been attracted to all those pulp fiction covers, things like *I Wake Up Screaming*, and *D.O.A.*, those kinds of shocking titles, so when we stumbled across *Kill Me Again*, it seemed like a great noir hook. So we went around and began to pitch this script to different people. We had been through the pitching process before—this was our seventh script—so we knew a little bit about that.

HOW LONG DID IT TAKE YOU TO WRITE THE SCRIPT?

About six to eight weeks. After I come up with the idea, I usually write about ten pages a day and then go back and rewrite a little bit. Once we had the story down, we went out and started pitching it, but nobody was very interested. We were talking to our lawyer at that point, and he said, "Guys, if you want to write you've just got to write. Don't waste time trying to get someone to pay you to write this, just do it." So we just sat down and wrote it.

When we actually had the script, people liked it, which was a new experience for us. I had an agent at the time who was representing us for comedic work. Most of the scripts that I wrote were comedies, so he didn't really like *Kill Me Again*, but we said, "Well, screw it, we'll go get a different agent. We like this script, we think it's really good, so let's go for it." We made a deal with ourselves that if we could sell it for $300,000, which then and even today is a lot of money, then we would sell it outright, but if we couldn't sell it for that much money, then we would make it together, and he would produce and I would direct. We got an agent at William Morris and he went to work.

HOW DID THE AGENT COME ABOUT?

If you have something that people want, then it's pretty easy to find an agent. You just have to have something to sell. Agents are in the business of discovering new talent. That's their job. So we got an agent and he shopped it around, but the most he could get for it was $250,000, and since we had made this deal with ourselves we knew we would just have to make the film. Steve and Yanni hadn't yet started Propaganda officially, but they were on their way to doing that, and they had a deal with Polygram at that point, so they brought it to Polygram. Michael Koone was the executive in charge and he said okay, go make your movie, and he let me direct it because I had written the script. It didn't hurt that I had also worked with Polygram before, writing a script for a film that was never produced. So I had a bit of a reputation, albeit a small one, and I was seen as somewhat dependable.

MGM was really interested in the movie, so we were able to kind of cofinance it. I don't know exactly how they did it, but MGM was the distributor of the movie. Polygram owned the foreign side of it and MGM did the domestic side. Basically MGM said, well, if you can get Val Kilmer to be in the movie, then we'll make the film. They gave us a list of actors and the one who was most realistic at that point was Val Kilmer. He had just made *Willow*, so he was big at the time, and we had to pay him twice as much as he got for that movie to do *Kill Me Again*. It wasn't exactly a labor of love for him. The budget was around $5 million and we started in shooting in 1989. I was thirty at the time.

WHAT DO YOU THINK IT WAS THAT LED TO THE FINANCING OF THE FILM?
Pretty much the script. I had directed about twenty-five music videos by that time, but when I was doing the film, a lot of music video directors had tried to make movies and failed; their movies had nice cinematography, but the story was unintelligible. They were almost unwatchable. So I didn't tell anybody that I was this video director—I just kind of downplayed that completely. I just said, Look, I've written the script, I went to the AFI as a directing fellow, and now I'm making this movie. That was really the pitch.

LET'S TALK ABOUT THE PRODUCTION PROCESS.
Probably one of the most difficult things about making that movie was that Val's not an easy guy to work with. He wasn't then and he isn't now, so it was pretty hard having a guy like him in your first movie. I think that he's a really talented guy, but that maybe he's frustrated with the process of the work, so he is very aggressive about it. I just wish that he would give himself over to the process a little more because he really is a fine actor. It's very hard to put yourself in the hands of a director and say, "Okay, tell me what to do." Maybe that's a difficult thing for him. But there was no bond between us. Basically what it amounted to was him saying, "Why should I listen to anything you have to say, who the hell are you?" He was very intimidating. He'd show up an hour late every day, he'd want to change lines—it was hard. Even though his wife was in the movie, he didn't seem to care.

Oddly enough, we liked Joanne Whalley for the female lead before Val was involved. We had seen her in a couple of movies and thought that she would be great for the part. When we had cast Val and we were talking to him about who he wanted to work with, we mentioned Joanne Whalley, and he said, "Oh, that's interesting because I'm actually married to her." We had no idea. We had been wanting to meet with her, but she had always been in England. So she agreed to do the movie and after that we got Michael Madsen. The thing about Michael is that he doesn't really act, he just is. Michael Madsen is Michael Madsen, that's the only role he really plays. After we were cast, we started going. It was about nine months from the completion of the script to the time we were on set shooting.

I had directed music videos, so I sort of had an idea of what to do with the camera, but working with the actors was always a big challenge. I remember that before we started shooting I had a panic attack. I thought, Everybody loves this script, what if I totally screw the movie up? I'll be the scapegoat. But then I thought, You know what, I've been working my ass off for the last six years, I deserve the opportunity to screw up. So from that moment on I relaxed. Everything seems really precious at first, like, Oh, this is that scene that I've slaved over for hours at the typewriter, but all of a sudden you get on the set and you think, He's gotta walk through the door. We gotta get this thing, we gotta do it before lunch, and it becomes kind of like factory work. And of course, the better prepared you are, the faster it moves. I was fairly well prepared, although I was working on a film where everybody working on the set had more experience than I did, so I was constantly being told that I didn't know what I was doing, or I did this or that wrong, or whatever. One person who was very supportive was my cinematographer, Jacques Steyn, who I had hired because he had shot features before; he wasn't some music video cameraman with no experience. We worked very well together.

Being a first-time director is really an ugly, terrible experience. Not very many people are that supportive. Most people assume you don't know anything, and in reality you don't, and you just sort of stumble your way through it. I remember the first time I was ever at a mixing stage was when I was mixing that movie. I had no idea what to do. I had mixed a movie in college, but there were only twelve tracks in that film. To get a TODD AO with sixty-four channels was kind of mind numbing, a totally wild ride. I was actually in Montana recently and showed the film to a group of students. I hadn't watched the movie in about ten years. Looking at it again, I felt that I was so lucky to ever get another directing job, because it's really not that good a film. But of course you are always most critical of yourself and that's hard to see through.

WHAT HAPPENED WHEN THE FILM WAS FINISHED?
Basically, not much. MGM really wasn't crazy about it, and they didn't really believe in it or support it. So they put it out into two hundred theaters with basically no promotion. Back then they had a particular deal where they could sell product as part of an overall content package for a predetermined price as long as it met certain qualifications. The film had to have been released theatrically and that had to demonstrate they spent some money on prints and advertising. But really they only made the film to get paid for it in this nontheatrical package; they never believed in it or tried to push it into domestic theaters. Also Val didn't like it very much, so it wasn't exactly like he was going to go out and support it and do press for it. So it kind of went out there and nobody saw it. But then we started getting these reviews back, and they were all really great. The problem was that the only major market that MGM released it in was San Francisco. So we went to MGM and said could we please release it in Los Angeles in one theater, at

least so our friends could see it and it could get local reviews, and have some impact in Hollywood. They told us that nobody would go to see it in L.A. But we pushed them and finally they agreed that they would screen it for the *L.A. Times*, but they promised us the *Times* would hate it. So they managed to put it in one theater in Westwood, right next to UCLA, and the review came out in the *L.A. Times*. It wasn't a glowing review, but it was a B plus, and that generated some local interest. It ended up playing at that theater for about eight weeks. But MGM just wouldn't get behind it because they didn't think they could make enough money with it to justify the effort, and that was that. So it was kind of disappointing, but it was a great learning experience. My next film after that, *Red Rock West*, was a totally different production experience, where I had an ideal shoot and worked with terrific and supportive actors like Nicholas Cage and Dennis Hopper. So it does get better over time.

SO WHAT DO YOU RECOMMEND TO SOMEBODY WHO WANTS TO MAKE FILMS TODAY?

All the clichés that you've heard since you were a kid are probably true. You have to work hard; you have to do all the obvious things. Probably the most important thing is that you have something to say. What is it that you have to say that is unique? People go to a movie theater to have somebody tell them a story. Why should you be the one telling them a story? What's unique about the way you're gonna tell it?

When you're making a movie, it is always a grueling journey. You're always tired. No matter how much preparation you've done, you can basically throw it all out the window. The crew is always grumpy and tired and couldn't care less about your precious little vision. They're just there working; they just want to go home. When I was in New York doing *Rounders*, everyone would always say that Sidney Lumet was a great New York director. Why, I would ask them? "Because he works about eight hours a day." That's where they're coming from. You go to film school and you think won't it be great if we do this and that, but the crew doesn't necessarily share your passion or enthusiasm—nor do they share much in your rewards. So it's very disheartening at first to realize that many people don't care about your movie. The only person who cares about a movie is the director, and to some degree the writer. Of course that's a broad generalization, but when people are standing around for fourteen hours a day, they get bored. So you have to be charismatic and you have to persevere; you have to have a personality that shines through and makes people keep going. That's very important too.

There's a lot of luck involved. I'm extremely fortunate; I've been very lucky. I've had my movies *Red Rock* and *Last Seduction* sort of rescued from the ashcan. If it wasn't for a few breaks I'd probably be a storyboard artist right now. I'm keenly aware of that. But then again my films did appeal to audiences; people really liked them. I think that right now the best thing for somebody to do in terms of becoming a director is to really study and understand film, but focus on script and story, really understand and know what a story is. The easiest way into directing right now is to write a script. If you can put down your thoughts on paper and convey them in 120 pages in a precise, clear manner, then all you've heard is true. People are starved for a good story, contrary to whatever you've heard, and Hollywood will open its arms to a talented young writer. The only way to find out if you can do it is to do it. And don't give up, keep trying. We wrote seven scripts before we sold one, so keep doing it until you can't do it anymore. The great thing about writing is that you don't need any money to do it. You don't need a camera, you don't even need a computer. You can write it out longhand and have somebody type it. You just have to have the time and the desire to do it. And how do you become a writer? There are dozens of great books out there. The one that I studied the most as a young film student was *The Art of Dramatic Writing* by Lajos Egri. That is the only book that they used as a textbook at the AFI while I was there. There are some great books out there like that. Read twelve of them. Read fifteen of them. Try to find out or figure out what your voice is. What is that you have to say that is unique and why is it that you want to say it?

IT'S INSPIRING TO HEAR THAT YOU WROTE SEVEN SCRIPTS BEFORE YOU SOLD ONE.

Unfortunately, we are a culture that celebrates youth and instant success. I remember hearing years ago that the Japanese's favorite baseball player was not Babe Ruth, but it was Pete Rose. In other words, they favored the guy that was there, consistently trying hard. As a culture they respect that, whereas American culture loves the guy that can party all weekend, walk in on Monday morning, and ace the test. It's as if somehow we think success should be easy, whereas the Japanese as a culture embrace that work ethic. I've been in the movie business almost twenty years now, and I've seen people who have made one film or written one script and all of a sudden they have this huge success. Then what do they do next? They haven't really had a chance to grow as a person and yet there's this enormous pressure on them to perform.

I've probably written twenty scripts. One thing I know is that I can write a script. I don't know if it will be any good, but I know that I can get through it. There is, given my track record, about a fifty-fifty chance that if I do write a script, then I'll be able to sell it to somebody or be able to make it into a movie. My directing ability has improved too, because I don't waste my time on things that aren't important to me anymore. I like to focus my attention on what the priorities are.

As a result of the expansion of film festivals, music videos, and film schools a new trend has developed in the movie business where studios will hire somebody to direct an $80 million picture who's only maybe directed a couple of commercials. What that's really about is being able to get some young director and tell him how they want the thing done. They are not really interested in his opinion in that scenario; they just want him to make it look good. The actors will do the acting, the editor will edit, just move the people around. It's almost like turning that director into a TV director. They want somebody to do it, but they don't want some seasoned veteran like John Frankenheimer who's gonna kick em' off the set and tell them to go fuck themselves when they've got a stupid idea. They want to retain control. And I think that's unfortunate for that young director because you have to wonder whether or not he's really had a chance to develop his abilities and his ideas.

Try things that you wouldn't normally try. Experimentation is great. There is so much to be said for experience, for experiencing things other than those in the film business. Unfortunately, once you're in the film business you become this parasite because your entire world revolves around movies and all you're doing is sucking off the blood of another movie. That's why movies have become so uninteresting, because they're so derivative. The worst kinds of movies are the ones that just imitate movies the writer has seen. The film director should have a unique voice and a unique story to tell. Unfortunately, the thing that speaks the loudest in Hollywood is money. Critical success only goes so far, but money is forever. And that's why sometimes movies are so similar. Filmmaking is not a science, and Hollywood doesn't know what to bank on, so it makes sense to the studio executives to go with what worked before. But then you're just recycling something, and how interesting can that really be?

I think one of the biggest wastes of time is to spend your own money making a movie. That's generally a disaster. Every now and then there is somebody that does it and is successful at it, but ultimately most people end up spending money they could've used to buy a house to make a movie that then sits on a shelf somewhere. Yes, they had the experience of making a movie and that may be satisfying to them, but if you can't get somebody excited enough about buying your script, then its probably not worth making the movie anyway. You need to have people enthusiastic about your scripts all the way down the line for the thing to work. You're gonna need to get actors excited about the material. You're gonna need to get investors excited about the material. If you're not really attracting the kind of heavyweight money that it takes to make a movie, then you should probably write another script. If all you can dig up to make a movie is $100,000 of your own money, then take the $100,000, buy some stocks, and sit around and write another script. That would be a much better use of your time. But of course there are exceptions to every rule.

Working on other people's material is great, if you can get it, but the problem when you're starting out is finding good material. The reason you can make it into the business by writing is because good material is scarce. I never really wanted to be a writer. I just kind of ended up doing it by default because I couldn't find a script that I liked. Once I got clicked into movies, I just wanted to be a film director. I didn't really want to write any more scripts. But you always end up writing in one way or another. You may as well do it from the start.

Brett Ratner | MONEY TALKS

BRETT RATNER *was born in Miami Beach, Florida, in 1970. After graduating from NYU film school at the age of twenty, he went on to direct his first music video for Public Enemy when he was twenty-two. He began his own production company and made some of the most successful music videos in America for the next four years. His first feature was* Money Talks, *starring Chris Tucker and Charlie Sheen. Since then he has directed the box-office smash* Rush Hour, *and* Rush Hour 2 *with Jackie Chan and Chris Tucker, and* The Family Man, *with Nicholas Cage and Teá Leoni. Ratner is single and lives in Los Angeles.*

I grew up in Miami Beach, and the only filming that was going on in Miami back in the day was "Miami Vice." So when I was a kid, I used to watch them shoot all the episodes. I saw Michael Mann, Abel Ferrara, all these great directors shooting episodes of the show. And I would watch them film, and then I would go home and get a video camera and a bunch of my friends, skip school, and go make mock "Miami Vice" episodes. My friend Joey would be a drug dealer, and another girl would be a prostitute, and then someone else would play a cop. It was 1980 and I was about ten years old at the time.

I grew up alone with my mother in Miami. She raised me by herself; I had no brothers or sisters. Ever since I can remember, I wanted to make movies. I was always telling stories, and for me, shooting films was a way to express myself.

By the time I was fourteen or so I started watching a lot of films. I was really into Martin Scorsese at the time, and I asked myself, How did Martin Scorsese become a director? Well, I found out that he went to NYU film school, so I said, I'm going to go to NYU film school. I started skipping grades from a young age, because I knew I wanted to get out of there. I was sixteen years old when I graduated from high school. I applied to NYU, and back then admissions was really based on academics more than it is today. Today academics are important, but if you have a great short film or a great script then it's easier to get in. But back then they really cared about grades. I had lousy grades and the worst SAT scores ever, but I had excellent recommendations from my teachers. So I thought, you know what, I'm gonna go for an interview, and hopefully I'll get a female interviewer and I'll charm her and she'll let me in. So I take the plane up from Miami, and I go off to my interviewer. Sure enough, I get a female interviewer, except she's a complete bull dyke and she hates me. She tells me, "You're not getting into this school. Go to Dade Community College in Miami, and if you get straight As for two years then maybe you can transfer in." I was so upset when I left that I was almost crying as I walked down the street.

Then I just thought, fuck this, I'm gonna go to the dean's office. So off I went and the first thing they told me was that I needed an appointment and that I had to make it three months in advance. So I said, "No, you don't understand, my plane is leaving in two hours." Finally, the woman was cool, and she said that I had two minutes in between the dean's meetings. So I walk in and I say, "Dean, I came all the way from Miami for an interview, my interviewer told me to go to another school, and this is the only college I've applied to. I've dreamed my whole life about being a director. If you don't let me in, then I'll be living on my mother's couch for the rest of my life. I'll be making films, but it'll be in the back yard with my friends. You've gotta let me into this school." So he says, "Get this young man's file on my desk!" And two weeks later I got a letter of acceptance. That moment showed me that nothing is impossible. I just said fuck it, fuck the lady, I'm going to the dean. And by not giving up and not taking no for an answer, I learned that I could do anything.

WHAT WAS IT THAT ATTRACTED YOU TO FILMMAKING?
I think it was about storytelling. I was always asking people, how did you do this, how did you do that? And I was also always telling people stories. My imagination would run crazy. But that question is sort of like, why are there maestro piano players? What makes them gravitate toward that? I think it was just always there my entire life.

The interesting thing about NYU is that they teach you how to make films, but they don't teach anything about how to get a job. Apparently now they invite Hollywood executives to come to screenings a bit more. Back then, I can tell you, Hollywood wasn't coming to my screenings.

While I was at school I made a short film called *Whatever Happened to Mason Reese*. You can watch it on the DVD for *Rush Hour*. It stars Mason Reese, and it's about a child star who thinks he's still super-famous. He travels around in a stretch limousine with six models.

After I completed the film, I decided to send a letter out to forty of the biggest people in the film industry. I attached a clip of the short, and I said that I was in postproduction and that I needed money to finish it. I actually didn't need any more money; I just wanted the relationship with the people I sent the letters to. No one in my family was in the movie business; I didn't know anyone in Hollywood, so I figured I'll send out this letter, and maybe I'll have some kind of a rapport with Jon Peters, Peter Guber, George Lucas, or somebody like that.

People often don't realize that the people who are on top are accessible. You can just call them up and get them on the phone. You just have to have something to say. That's important to remember. So one day I get a call from the dean's office to come have a meeting. Mason Reese had broken his leg during shooting and I had heard that he was suing NYU for a million or something. I thought that I was in trouble and about to get kicked out. So I walk into the dean's office, and he says, "Steven Spielberg called here looking for you." Of course I'm like, "Bullshit. One of my friends called pretending he was Spielberg. This is insane." So the dean gives me a number that was left and told me to call it. I left, and then I rang up the number. And they answer the phone, "Steven Spielberg's office." And I say, "Is Mr. Spielberg in?" "Who's calling?" "Brett Ratner." And then the woman says, "Oh, hang on a minute, he's expecting your call."

So I'm waiting on the phone, freaking out, and finally they come back and say, "He's in a production meeting right now, but we'll call you back later tonight." So of course I don't sleep all fucking night. I'm losing my mind, thinking, Oh my God, Steven Spielberg called me. This is insane. I'm thinking he'll call in the middle of the night when I'm asleep, because L.A. is three hours earlier, or something crazy like that. Finally, the next morning around eleven, I get a call from some woman named Kathleen Kennedy (who at the time was not known, but is now a big producer). And she tells me, "Steven saw your clip, and he was very impressed, but we don't finance short films. We give all our money to USC. So good luck in the future, and send us the film when you finish it." And I said "No, you don't understand, I'm gonna be bigger than Spielberg, you've gotta believe in me . . ." I don't know what the hell I said. But a few weeks went by and then one day I went to get the mail. Inside was a check for $3,000 from Steven Spielberg. I fucking went crazy. I blew up the check the size of the wall and put it in my dorm room. I didn't cash it; I framed it. I would show it to girls in the hallway, and be like, "Yo, Steven Spielberg sent me a check." I was ready to put, "Steven Spielberg presents a Brett Ratner film" at the head of *Mason Reese*.

After I got out of school, I was hanging out for a while and learning my craft. I would hustle for work. Someone went to Ecuador to film a documentary on the oldest people in the world. They shot hundreds of hours of footage. So I hired a narrator, went through the footage cataloguing it, and spent about a month in the editing room working on it, honing my skills. I created a beginning, middle, and end to the piece. I also made another short film that I got someone to pay for called *The Good Life*. I graduated school when I was twenty, and I didn't make a video until I was twenty-two, but I was learning how to do things along the way, really practicing making films.

I had finished *Mason Reese,* and I entered it in a bunch of festivals and ended up winning a lot of prizes. My best friend at the time was a guy named Russel Simmons, and back then he was just starting up his company, Def Jam Records. So he said, "Why don't I have a screening of your film at the Tribeca Film Center," which had just opened that week. So we showed the film there, and Russel invited all his friends, who at the time were all his artists, different rappers. Those were the only people he knew. So all these rappers came to film, including Chuck D from Public Enemy. About a month later, I was in Miami at the Public Enemy concert with Russel. Chuck D came over and said, "Russel, we want Brett to do our next video." I was standing right next to Russel, and he said, "Brett Who?" And Chuck D says, "Little Brett, white boy Brett, your Brett right here." Russel was so happy. He was just overwhelmed because Def Jam's whole philosophy was about the artists making their own music, their own videos. So he was happy because his artist had wanted me to do the video, and this was my first video, and it was an important thing. So he gave me a budget of about $30,000 to make the thing, and I traveled around with Public Enemy while they were on tour with U2, all the while filming the video. I used the Arri 16S to photograph it because that was the camera I had used in school, and the only one I really knew how to work with at this point. I spent about a month editing the video, and when I finished it, it was released to MTV. The first day it aired was the first day they started putting director's credits on videos.

You have to understand: When I was at film school, nobody wanted to be a music video director. There weren't guys like David Fincher or Michael Bay who had crossed over to making features. Music videos really sucked at the time. They were horrible. So nobody really wanted to be a video director. And when I was in school, the guys I admired, the directors I looked up to, were Hal Ashby, Martin Scorsese, the Coen brothers, you know? But Hollywood was not going to music video directors for features. They weren't going to the film schools either, actually. Mostly they found directors like Spike Lee, or the Coens, guys who had gone out and made movies with their credit cards. Once they had completed a feature film, then the studios were like, "Oh, We know these guys can make a feature film, because they already did."

But when MTV put the director's credit on videos, that's when Hollywood started recognizing video directors, and people crossed over into making features. Now music videos were opening up many more avenues for people to get into making films. Before the director credit, you might see a good video, but you had no idea who had made it. And I think that's why the work was so bad. Once people had their name out there, it was much more like, oh, now we better do a good job.

CAN YOU TELL ME A BIT ABOUT YOUR EXPERIENCE MAKING VIDEOS?
It was completely amazing. For me, music videos were another film school. But this time, I was getting paid to learn. In film school, you have a tripod, and you have wheelchairs for dollies, and you get a camera with three lenses. So that's what you learn with. But now, I was getting to learn many more toys. And the bigger budgets I got, the more toys I got. First I tried a steadicam. Then I learned what the steadicam did, and I said, you know what, instead of a steadicam I'll try a dolly. And then after the dolly I said let's get a luma crane. And I was learning how all that stuff worked. By the time I made a feature film I had made seventy-five music videos, so I really knew what everything was. When I said to my cinematographer or my gaffer, "This is the shot I want," I knew how to communicate that to them, and I knew how to achieve what I wanted.

As a filmmaker, I consider myself a storyteller above all else. And so I tried to bring a kind of narrative style to the videos I was making. And I think that shows in the work. My work didn't look like music videos; my music videos looked like movies. That's why I kept getting hired. People would say, "Oh, we're gonna do a movie video, hire Brett Ratner."

I think that it was very important for me to develop my own style, because I believe that the directors who have the most longevity are the ones who have a real style, a definitive style that you can see in their work, and when you see it, you know it's theirs. I wasn't ready to make a film until I found that, even on my twentieth video. I think that I could have done it if I had had a really important story to tell. I think that if a film has an important story, then it can lack in the technical department. But I really wanted to develop myself. For instance, I recently did two videos, one for

Madonna called, "Beautiful Stranger," and another for Mariah Carey. They're two completely opposite videos, with completely disparate artists, but when you watch them, you know that they're both Brett Ratner videos. It's not one particular shot, not one thing, but more of a feeling and a tone and a look.

WHERE DID YOUR AESTHETIC FOR THE VIDEOS COME FROM?

It always came from movies. Most music videos at the time were pretty much the same: three different locations intercut with each other. They were essentially abstract; shoot the singer against a white wall, then shoot him on the beach, then back to the wall again. You'd cut to like, four different locations, and there was no plot really. It didn't matter why you cut from here to there. What I always try to do with a video is create a beginning, middle, and end, where you follow something throughout. One video I did was D'Angelo's first clip, "Brown Sugar." It was simple: D'Angelo gets in an elevator, goes up to a club, gets up on stage, and starts playing. The record company told me to cut to him in another part of the club. I said, "How could he be in another part of the club? He's on stage." The point being, how can he get from here to there unless we show him walking over? Unless it can be justified, it just doesn't make sense in this context. And that video was nominated for best R&B video of the year. It was a career-making video. You felt like you were there with D'Angelo in that room. So instead of just shooting a one-dimensional crosscut video, I would do insert shots, I would shoot reaction shots of the crowd, coverage to get D'Angelo to the point where his hands touch the keyboard. It was done in a narrative style.

One thing that's important to note technically: When I started out in school, I never thought to learn things. I mean, I didn't care about how to work the lights or hold the boom pole. I thought, I'm a director; I'll hire someone good to do that. But that's a mistake. Until I started to learn how to do those things myself, making the videos, I couldn't really command the respect of the crew. Because if I don't know what each crew member's job is, then how can I have their respect, how can I evaluate their performance? I have to feel that at any moment, I could do that job myself if I had to, I could replace that crew member. That way, if I don't like the lighting, or I don't like the way something is being done, then I can articulate that better.

WHAT WAS THE RESPONSE TO THE PUBLIC ENEMY VIDEO?

Once I did the Public Enemy video, then everyone started calling. The director's credit was really phenomenal, because now everybody saw that and said, "Let's get Brett to do our video." That's how a lot of people became successful at the time. I mean, the video played thirty times a week, so everybody saw it. And I realized, you do a good video, you get five more jobs. You do a bad one; maybe things will slow down for a while. But you keep going. Really that video broke me. Overnight, my production company did $1 million in business, in the first year.

I worked on videos for many years before I made my first feature. What happened was, Heavy D had asked me to do a video for him, the video for "I Got Nothin' but Love for Ya, Baby." This was the first video where I put models in (now there's models all over videos.) My girlfriend, Rebecca Gayheart, was in it, along with every beautiful model in town. And it was the first time that rap artists really used beautiful models. Before, we used "round the way" girls with big asses and fucked-up hair, but now it was time for models.

I also asked this comedian I had seen do standup to be in the video. His name was Chris Tucker. I paid him $500 and put him in the video. After that, Chris went on to do "Def Comedy Jam," and then he made the films *Friday, Dead Presidents*, and was about to star in a film for New Line Cinema called *Money Talks*. The head of New Line, then and now, was a guy named Mike DeLuca, a very young, cool guy who was into making films. And New Line had fired the director of *Money Talks*, a week before going into production. So DeLuca was looking around for somebody pretty quickly, and Chris mentioned my name to him, because he remembered me from doing the Heavy D video long ago. He told DeLuca, "I know this white boy, Brett Ratner. I worked with him before. He's cool." DeLuca was very hip to what videos were hot and who the hot directors were. So he told Chris that he loved my work and that they should get me in there for a meeting. And I went in and met with them. A week later they hired me.

HOW DID IT FEEL TO DO THAT FIRST FILM?

I didn't even realize I was making a movie until I saw it. When I saw the film then the realization was there, it was like, oh my God, I made a movie. It is different from making videos in that it's a much longer and more involved process, but the work is the same. You use the same crew and the same equipment. It's just more.

For *Money Talks*, I had one week of preparation. Since they were already in preproduction by the time I came on, DeLuca said I could change anything about the film except the location. And I did. I changed the script; I changed the scenes. I made it my own. But it was really jumping into the middle of something, so I couldn't even stop to think about what I was doing. I just had to do it. It worked.

DeLuca is a great fan of movies, and he is in total support of a filmmaker. It was a pleasure to work with him. I feel that my video experience really prepared me in terms of dealing with people, dealing with problems that may come up. I remember when I was shooting a Jodeci video, it was the middle of the night, and a performer told me, "I ain't doin' that, I'm not gettin' on top of that building. No way. I'm scared of heights." So here it is midnight, and we've just spent four hours pulling equipment up on to the roof. Those are the kind of problems that come up. But what you've got to do is think fast and come up with ideas. So fine, we don't shoot on the building. We'll shoot a driving scene instead; put the cameras on the car. You know what I mean? You just make things work. And that's one of the reasons I think I'm good at what I do is because if something doesn't work, then I can come up with an idea very fast.

I never took an acting class and I don't know anything about it. But what I do know is what's real. If I'm watching a scene with Chris Tucker and his girl, and he's trying to get laid and what's coming out of his mouth is not believable to me, and she's actually supposed to be digging it, then I'm gonna know something's wrong. If he's not working it right then she's not gonna be digging it, and then I can't believe it, I know something's wrong. So for me it's really about human behavior. If I believe that what he's saying to her is gonna get him laid, and she's really responding to it, then that scene is working. You also have to remember that I need to not only shoot the person delivering the line, but also shoot the reaction. And the reactions can always ruin things. If the reactions are wrong, then the scene just won't work. If you watch me on set, I'll do tons of fucking takes because I'm just trying to get every moment to be real. I want it to be like you're there with the people as this is happening. That's a movie, when you can create a reality on the screen.

WHAT HAPPENED WHEN THE FILM WAS RELEASED?
Before, I would do a video and then I'd see it play on television, and it was a great feeling. But it's a big difference with films, because films are an international thing where there's a great deal of acclaim and publicity connected to them. I try to not let that faze me though, to let the fame go to my head, and I think I do okay. But I will never forget one moment, when I was sitting in the audience watching my film, and people laughed when I wanted them to laugh, said "Oh shit," when I wanted them to be nervous—it just worked. I was sitting in the audience looking back at people's faces in the light and I was like, oh my God, I made a movie. My dream came true.

What I think is really important is perseverance. It's really about not being afraid to fail, because if you're afraid to fail, then you won't be driven, and you won't take risks. I thought to myself, So what if I fail? My mom's still gonna love me, I'm still gonna be who I am. I won't be as wealthy, I won't be famous, but I'll still be Brett. So it's really about not being afraid, going out there and not accepting no. And if you do fail, do it again. I'm not any more talented than the next guy, but I'm absolutely as driven or more driven than anybody who's become successful.

People don't understand, someone with 10 percent talent and 90 percent drive is gonna be as or more successful than somebody with 90 percent talent and 10 percent drive. There were kids in my film class who made me feel like I was never going to be able to direct. They were so fucking brilliant. And those guys are working in a video store right now. When I was at school, I watched their films and I thought, I could never do that. So brilliant. But they didn't have any communication skills; they didn't know how to go out and make a film. They didn't know how to get money. They didn't know how to talk to people. It was some art shit. And that's okay, but they just weren't driven. They were 99 percent talent and 1 percent drive. They would have probably rather have smoked pot and just got high and hung out.

Another thing that's huge: You've gotta create your own opportunities. Nobody's gonna call you and say, "Hey, I want you to direct a movie." That is never gonna happen. That's what people don't understand. You have to wake up in the morning and say, "I'm gonna go and get recognized." When it comes to movies, you can be the best bullshitter in the world, but if you can't deliver once you get on the set, then you can't command the respect from not only the crew, but from the actors. Then you're worthless. You know, I knew everybody in New York City, every socialite, every person. It was like, wow, Brett's really connected. But what if I see Steven Spielberg at a party and I say, "Hey Steven, oh my God, I'm a director," and he goes, "Oh great, send me one of your films," and all I have is girls' panties and party invitations? If I don't have any film to show him, it's worthless. You gotta have the film. That's the thing, you've gotta do the work.

If I was doing this now, if I was a kid who wanted to be a filmmaker, then I would take a video camera and film. Brilliant ideas and a video camera, that's what it takes. Because it's all about storytelling. If you have a story to tell, then it doesn't matter what medium it's in. You don't even have to know about lighting anymore. Look at *The Blair Witch Project*. When I was in film school there were very few ways to become a feature-film director. Now some fat girl in Wichita, Kansas, can take a video camera and become a major filmmaker. If you have a story to tell, take a fucking video camera, get some actors (and there are a million starving actors who want to be recognized), and go and shoot a fucking movie. That's the way to do it. It's so easy now to do what I'm doing.

Making music videos is definitely a way in, if you are able to do it. But what really matters is honing your skills. If you don't have a story to tell, or a movie you really want to make, go do music videos, go do infomercials, go into other areas. But you have to be ready when it's time to make a film. That's one way, but if you have a movie then go for it. Before it was really expensive, it was $10,000 or more. Now with twenty bucks you can become a movie director.

HOW DO YOU FEEL ABOUT YOUR ABILITY TO MAKE FILMS NOW?

I feel like I'm only getting better, because I've learned so much along the way. Every day I learn something new. And the other thing I've learned is not to be afraid to ask people things. Don't act like you know everything. Those are the people that I can't stand being around, the people who act like they have the answers to everything. A lot of directors act that way because they are afraid to look bad. But you get more respect by hearing people out. If a PA on the set, if a garbage man walks by and says, "That shot sucks," I'm gonna stop and say, "Why does this guy say this shot sucks? Maybe he's right." My assistant says shit to me all the time. I don't always listen to it, but he does give suggestions. He's not afraid to write something down and say, "What about this?" You have to create that environment. And it's in your interest anyway, because at the end of the film, the credit says "A Brett Ratner Film." So I get all the credit anyway, what's wrong with listening to people's opinions? The important part is having taste and knowing if something fits or not, if something works, if something makes sense. And anyway then you have a better set. Everyone on the set is working hard and busting their ass because the environment makes people feel like they're a part of the process.

I would say that the biggest challenge to me so far has been a constant striving for perfection. Of course, I'll never achieve it, so the thing to learn is that you have to pick and choose your battles and your choices. Otherwise you can bury yourself in the details and forget what the big picture is. And it's important to remember that directing is not about your age or your experience but about your point of view. When you're a director, you have to have a point of view. If you don't, then people will look at you sideways; they'll start doubting you. They'll say, "He doesn't know what he wants; he's unsure." And it's okay to be unsure sometimes, but you always have to keep the big picture in mind.

HOW ARE YOU DIFFERENT FROM THE GUY WHO MADE *MASON REESE* TEN YEARS AGO?

I'm the exact same guy. I mean look at me. I feel like I have an understanding of what someone like Nicholas Cage or Chris Tucker likes about me; I'm my own person, I'm something of a personality. Abel Ferrara's a personality. Why do they love Ferrara? Ferrara's a fucking nut case, but he is who he is, and people love me because I am who I am. I'm not trying to be anybody else. I don't pretend to be an actor's friend, I tell them, "This is who I am, and this is what I want for the picture to play. I want you to fucking stand there and say your fucking line because it will make this story work." And also I think that I'm a positive, fun person and that my movies are a reflection of that. We have fun making them. We really do.

ARE THERE ANY SPECIFIC LONG-TERM GOALS THAT YOU WANT TO ACHIEVE WITH YOUR WORK?

I made *Money Talks* and *Rush Hour* because they were a reflection of the movies I grew up watching. I grew up watching *Midnight Run, Beverly Hills Cop,* and *48 Hours. Rush Hour* is to ten-year-old kids now what *Beverly Hills Cop* was to me when I was ten. What I want to think when I read a script is, Here's an opportunity for me to make a movie that's gonna say something and that's gonna affect people and that's going to make people think. And it's still gonna be entertaining, you know. Totally commercial, but award-winning-type stuff because it's gonna change the way people feel and think. People are going to walk out of the theater and they are going to say, "I'm gonna call that girl, I'm gonna take that job." They are going to be inspired and make choices and that's what movies ultimately are supposed to do. I feel that's the type of movie I'm doing now, the type of movie that can last for many generations, just like *It's a Wonderful Life.* It's very dated, but it still affects you now. I cry every time I see that movie.

James Foley | RECKLESS

JAMES FOLEY *was born in 1953 in Bay Ridge, Brooklyn. After finishing Catholic school Foley attended several colleges, ultimately settling on designs for a medical career. When he attended a brief seminar at NYU film school, he finally found his calling: making films. He attended USC film school and began his career with the feature film* Reckless, *starring Aidan Quinn and Daryl Hannah. Foley's twenty-year career in the cinema has produced such classic films as* At Close Range, After Dark, My Sweet, *and his critically praised, cinematic tour de-force* Glengarry Glen Ross. *He also directed* The Corruptor, *starring Mark Wahlberg and Chow Yun-Fat. Foley lives in Los Angeles.*

I was born on December 28, 1953. My family moved to Staten Island when I was very young and that is where I spent my childhood. I attended Catholic schools throughout my early education. I come from a very Catholic family; two of my father's brothers are priests. My father was a lawyer for an insurance company and my mother raised us. I have an older brother and sister and a younger brother and sister so I am exactly in the middle. My parents are no longer living, but my siblings all live in New York and I see them often. It is a bit disorienting when I'm with them be-cause growing up as a middle child I was the most quiet of all my siblings. I remember my maternal grandmother telling my mother, "He doesn't talk, he doesn't talk!" Now people who know me find this hard to believe because I have made up for it in my adult life. My siblings all remained in New York; I was the different one who moved away from the East Coast and went the Hollywood route.

WHAT WAS YOUR FIRST EXPERIENCE WITH CINEMA?

The first film that I ever saw was a horror film. I don't remember much about it except that it had witches and evil people in it. I recall it being a bit like Polanski's *Macbeth*. I was terrified and quite disturbed after seeing it, and to this day I'm incredibly squeamish about horror films, especially anything that involves knives. I can watch *Scarface* or *The Godfather* because seeing people being riddled with bullets doesn't bother me a bit; it is only when somebody pulls out a penknife that I am under the seat closing my eyes. As a child I wasn't really into going to films and it wasn't something that was big in my life. I didn't become interested in it, really, until my last year of college.

WHERE DID YOU STUDY?

I attended three different colleges in three years and finished after my third year. I was interested in psychology and thought about being a psychologist or a social worker. During my senior year of high school I looked in a college guidebook to find the school that was furthest away from Staten Island that I could afford. I ended up at San Francisco State University, which was $89 a semester or something like that. After one year there, I felt alienated and decided to return home to be closer to people I knew.

For my second year of college I enrolled at the State University of New York at New Paltz. I chose that school because it was definitely affordable, since it was a state university, and I also liked the way the campus looked in the brochure. It was known as a stoner college, which was appealing to me at that point in my life. It was during that year that I decided that I wanted to be a psychiatrist and I needed to take pre-med classes that weren't available to me, so for my third year of college I transferred to a college in Buffalo, New York. It was there that my relationship with film changed.

Buffalo had a very vibrant film studies program, and there was at that time a very experimental film movement developing through people such as Stan Brackage and others like him who were screening films and giving lectures on the subject. This was 1974, a time that I now refer to as the renaissance or golden age of American cinema. At this time the critical study of these experimental or "independent" films (as they were then considered) went hand in hand with Hollywood movies. There wasn't the differentiation between the two that exists today. I preferred the critically acclaimed Hollywood movies like *The Godfather, Dog Day Afternoon*, and *Last Tango in Paris;* I didn't really get into the experimental stuff.

After Buffalo, I decided to take some time off before starting medical school and to explore this blossoming interest I had in film. I enrolled in a twelve-week film course at New York University. That experience completely changed my life and, of course, I didn't end up going to medical school as I had planned.

I can tell you about that single moment where I knew that this was what I wanted to do with my life. At NYU I was in a class where I was given 100 feet of black-and-white film and a small camera. The assignment was to go out and shoot for half the day and edit for half the day. I went to Washington Square Park and shot a bunch of kids in a sandbox, since I really had no idea what I was doing. While I was shooting the children in the sandbox, the father of one of the kids saw me and decided he didn't want his child in the film so he pulled the child out of the frame while I was filming. Into the frame come the feet and legs of the man as he picks up the child and takes him away. I cut the film together randomly with shots from the sandbox that end with the man coming in and taking the child away. The other kids who were left playing look up with odd expressions on their faces as this happens. Most of the films that were screened by the other students were really all about nothing but somehow, quite by accident, my one-minute film elicited great attention from my classmates. Somehow it gave the impression of some weird kind of child exploitation happening, and in the screening room it brought quite an audible response. The class went "Oooh . . ." I remember to this day the physical reaction I had to this experience of creating something that had a communal effect like that. This was something that I had never before experienced and I thought of it as literally discovering a sixth sense. After the screening everyone in the class (there were twenty-five or thirty of us) was standing out in the street talking about my film. I was the hero that afternoon and I liked that feeling so much that I decided then and there that I had found my calling and I would not go to medical school.

WHAT KIND OF FILMS WERE YOU WATCHING AT THIS TIME?
During the twelve weeks I was at NYU, I had become more and more obsessed with films and I was seeing one or two of them a day. I was still living in Staten Island and the quickest route into the city to get to Fifty-ninth and Third became engraved in my head so I could get to Cinema 1 and Cinema 2 because that was where all the first-run big Hollywood films would open. I was taken by the work of François Truffaut and Roman Polanski. Films I particularly liked included *400 Blows, Rosemary's Baby, The Godfather,* and *Last Tango in Paris.* These films had a great impact on me and

they made me think about the types of films that I wanted to make. It was trendy to be involved with film at the time and when I enrolled at NYU I would have never expected it to inspire me to forgo my career as a doctor. I feel that I was very fortunate to have had that experience with that first one-minute film and to have been visited by pure inspiration, which drove me unambiguously toward something so meaningful. After I made that decision to give up medical school I was so single-minded in my approach to this career path that it didn't occur to me that it would be a difficult thing to do and to do well. I realize now that I was incredibly naive and perhaps a bit delusional, but at the time it made sense. It never occurred to me that it was a difficult thing. If I had to do it now I would never have succeeded because I know what the odds are and how complicated it is. I was naive and dumb and that helped a great deal.

WHAT DID YOU DO AFTER NYU?
Since my goal was to make Hollywood movies I decided the best route would be to go to film school for real. I chose USC over NYU not only because of its location, but because USC was the birthplace of George Lucas and John Milius, who were filmmakers that I admired. USC was not a place like NYU where people were making 16mm art films for the Film Forum; people were making real movies. I was fortunate enough to actually be accepted into graduate school at USC and I spent three years there. I felt so much at home there and it was a connection I had never really felt during my undergraduate years. When I got to USC I felt like this was where I was meant to be and it was quite literally there that I had found my psychic home. I had an extremely prosperous three years there and I was successful in achieving my goals in this incredibly competitive program.

The course was set up so that everyone made Super-8 films for the first year and then, in the second year, a five-minute black-and-white film. For the third year a twenty-minute, half-hour color film with synch sound was assigned. Not everybody could direct their own film this final year and only one out of five were chosen. In order to get to be the director you had to pitch your script to a board of faculty and senior students to explain why they should let you make your film. It helped if you had your own script and if you could sell them on it. Fortunately, I had written my own script, and I had people lined up to be my editors and other crew members. Most of this was political, since I also had to convince my classmates that they should not direct their own film but rather help me make mine. Now when I think back on this experience I realize that it was a perfect entrée to what Hollywood is really like. When I left school what I had to do to get a job was very similar and I felt like school had been practice so I had confidence about yapping to people. In fact, just yesterday I went to a pitch meeting and I had to explain to "the board" why they should give me $40 million to make a movie.

Understanding the politics is very important in this business. For me the whole thing is an innate ability to deal with situations and people where communication skills are so important on so many levels. Dealing with actors, writers, producers, or anyone for that matter, requires great communication skills. This is an incredibly competitive and difficult business. Out of the seventy-five people who graduated from USC with me, I'm only aware of one other person who is currently working as a director. While I don't think I was the most talented director that went to USC, I do think that there were definitely people with much more talent who did not have those communication skills. They were not comfortable having to seduce people into something, which is basically what you have to do in this business. You really need to have the ability to recognize that it is not only talent that can make you successful. It is so much more complex than that. I have often thought about why films aren't better. Is it that the cream doesn't necessarily rise to the top? Getting a film made is a combination of things, including a great project, but often times it really all boils down to who you know.

TELL ME ABOUT YOUR FIRST SHORT FILM.
My first film was called *Silent Night* and it was about Christmas Eve in a hospital psychiatric ward. While I was in film school I worked at a psychiatric hospital from four to midnight. It was great for me because I had a flexible schedule, it was high paying, and most of the time things were quiet late at night and I could get my school reading done. We would take the patients on outings to the movies, do all sorts of things like that, and mainly just talk with them. For the most part it was interesting, but in the worst moments it was pretty bad, like when someone would freak, a new patient being admitted or someone in a psychotic episode. Part of being a psychiatric technician was to deal with psychotic and violent patients so it was my job to wrestle these patients down so that the nurses could zap them with Thorazine. Of course, the more they gave them the easier my job became and it was less likely that I would be beaten up.

I made a film about what I knew. In the film there is a young male technician as the protagonist. I didn't play the role in the film, even though I based the character on myself, but I almost wish that I had. It is painful to think of now since the acting in the film is so bad. It was so corny. There was a patient who was a saxophone player who is playing this music that was inspired by the score of *Last Tango in Paris*. He wants to play his music and the nurse wants to shut him up, and because he resists, the nurse wants the male technician to give this free spirit tranquilizing drugs, but the technician doesn't want to do it. It is all very symbolic and very ridiculous, but it is nice visually, and it is kind of slick. I get off on the editing. I was obsessed with Bernardo Bertolucci's stuff, *The Conformist* and *Last Tango in Paris* and I tried to emulate that in a way. Ultimately though, my short was quite dark and I really needed something more to help me cross the threshold and get noticed in the industry because the film wasn't getting me enough oomph. We had industry screenings for our films through USC, but the film just wasn't doing it. The best thing to do was to make another film.

So at the conclusion of my third year at USC, I managed to find an obscure proviso in the school's program where you would be able to continue for one more semester after the normal course and make a second film. You would essentially have more freedom, and you would work with one professor who would be your advisor. I had no money to make films at the time, and if you could get a film made at USC, then the school would give you your funding. So this extra semester afforded me the opportunity to make a second film.

My second film was called *November* and it was about a young, depressed Catholic schoolgirl who is living outside Dallas. The film takes place on the day President Kennedy is killed. The girl misses her bus to school and ends up hitching a ride with a James Dean–type who drives a cherry-red Chevy. The film was influenced a lot by Terrence Malick's *Badlands;* there are direct shots from it. The driver is on his way into Dallas to see Kennedy and tells the girl that he can drop her off at school on the way. So along the way of course they fall in love and she decides to go into Dallas with him. At the height of their excitement the news comes in on the radio that the president had been shot. It breaks their romance and they experience a loss of innocence and it's all sad. He drops the girl off and she goes home.

DID YOU FEEL THAT BY MAKING THESE SHORTS YOU DEVELOPED MORE OF A MASTERY OF THE TECHNIQUE?

Absolutely. I definitely feel that that is true, especially after the second film. But more important than the mastery of process was that I developed confidence. I learned so much each time around and I developed an incredible confidence in myself that allowed me to become successful. In retrospect I see that it was probably the beginning of my being corrupted by Hollywood. In making that film I was driven not by the intrinsic value of the film but by the desire I had to get noticed. I did what I thought would be most useful to me to get Hollywood to let me direct a feature film. It worked.

Looking back on it, of course, it is always in the back of your mind that there is an audience that you need to please, and it becomes an interesting thing that you deal with every day when you are trying to become sensitive to why are you making certain decisions. There is always that struggle with the audience that on the one hand, you need to give them what they want, but on the other you need to go with your own beliefs about how something should be done. What makes sense to me? What moves me? These are questions you need to really answer for yourself if you want to do anything good. I am sure that the reason why I have not had larger commercial successes is because I am not responding necessarily to the mass audience's demands or tastes. And that comes in the choice of material that you develop. Sometimes you think maybe you should develop more mainstream material because that way more people will see it and hopefully you can get something across to them that has value. I made that decision once on a film that I did called *Who's That Girl?*, starring Madonna. I went with what I thought an audience wanted, and it felt different than anything I had ever done or have done since. I was totally disconnected from it, so I was mechanically shooting scenes and it ended up a film without any kind of sensibility or point of view. I learned a valuable lesson from that experience. Now I am much more aware of the difference between being influenced by a desire for approval and success and what makes sense in terms of communicating what you want to an audience rather than pandering to their expectations. I wanted to do the former and not the latter. What makes test screenings so terrific is that I am interested in the cards because it is like a line sample, because it is anonymous, people are just checking off boxes, you know, which scenes do you hate the most, stuff like that. That is interesting to me. What is not interesting to me at all is a focus group where people are saying, "I don't understand this," and suddenly you are being asked to essentially remake the film in their vision of what it should be. Of course if you ask somebody that question they are happy to tell you how it would be if they did it, but then they would be making a different movie than you are, wouldn't they? Focus groups are a sadistically corrupt and meaningless process.

AFTER MAKING *NOVEMBER*, HOW DID YOU GET "DISCOVERED" BY HOLLYWOOD?
It is important to point out that while I did have the product in hand that I felt they were looking for, it was also essential to have connections and I was quite fortunate in that regard. It is this combination of having the actual goods, a film that you can show somebody, and a manner of presentation through which you come into the consciousness of other people. I'll put it this way: A cassette in the mail from a film student at the University of West Texas does not get someone's attention because of the package it is in. Now if that same film comes from some established person in Hollywood and he says, "I want you to take a look at this guy's film, he's a bright new student at USC," the film is viewed in a whole different context. Now someone is interested in taking a look, even though the thing from Texas that they never opened could be a far better film. You get the idea.

Connections are essential in this business. A friend of mine from USC named Josh Donen was very much a part of the Hollywood scene and knew lots of famous people since his father was the director Stanley Donen and his mother was married to Robert Wagner. He was also a friend of Carrie Fisher's, so through them I just got to know people in Hollywood socially. Because of this friendship I was then in a position to have my film seen by people who actually worked in the industry who knew other important people and could tell them about me. Josh kept up his relationship with Robert Wagner because he was like a stepfather to him even after he and his mother divorced and Wagner married Natalie Wood for the second time. Josh spent a lot of time with him and Natalie and Robert considered their home Josh's home. During film school I lived in a house with Josh and his brother. We would often go over to hang out with RJ and Natalie and I actually got to know them very well.

The first job I had was very connected to Josh. It was toward the end of film school after I had finished my film *November* that we decided to have a party. Josh worked on the film with me and had invited an actress named Colleen Camp to the party. She had a bunch of roles a while ago in a Peter Bogdanovich film and also in *Apocalypse Now*, but never really succeeded as an actress, although she was well connected in Hollywood and still is; she is married to John Colin, who is the head of production at Paramount, and she has become a producer. She was with the Zoetrope people in those days and had met Josh through some mutual friends. She had a crush on Josh, so she came to the party.

Meanwhile, the director Hal Ashby had a big crush on Colleen and had been pursuing her for a while. She agreed to go out with him, but told him that they had to come to our party. So they arrived at our party just at the moment my film was going to be screened on the wall. I knew exactly who Ashby was the moment he walked in the room. So there was Hal Ashby at the top of his career in a room with a bunch of ravenous film students and me, the most ravenous of all. He sees the film and appears to like it, and he smokes a joint with us and I just glommed onto him. He was really at the height of his power back then. He and an English producer named Andy Brosberg who had worked with Roman Polanski were starting a company called Northstar and getting financed by Lorimar. He was looking to finance other people's films at that time, so he said to me, "Do you have an idea that you want to make into a movie?" I hadn't gotten to that point yet, and truth be told I hadn't even yet graduated from school, but I immediately said, "Yeah." I said it so quickly because I was so desperate to make it. He didn't even want to know what my idea was. He said that whatever it was he would give me some money to write it down and even though it was Lorimar's money he had the discretion to do with it what he wanted. So I wrote a script and they gave me $25,000. It was my first real job. I was working and by then I had graduated.

HAD YOU WRITTEN A SCRIPT BEFORE?

Up to this point I had only written the two short films. For this first feature-length script I wrote about gay street hustlers. In L.A. there were a lot of teenage boys who were gay hustlers on Santa Monica Boulevard, a section of L.A. that was quite sleazy. These young boys—some were gay, some were not—were mostly runaways and lived on the streets. They would make money by giving blow jobs and stuff like that. I went and talked to them and found out what they did and from that I wrote a script called *Cowboys of the American Night.* I wrote it exactly as I wanted to write it and by the time I finished it, Hal Ashby had gone bust. He'd made two movies at the same time, *Second-Hand Hearts* and *Lookin' to Get Out.* They were both disasters and don't figure very high in the Ashby canon. Lorimar was new to feature production and they had put in about $25 million into these films, which was a fortune at the time. The money was gone, so they decided they wanted to get the hell out of there, and of course now they were not interested in some student's film. It was one more thing that Hal was gonna vouch for, but now Hal had lost his credibility. Hal's company just sort of melted down, and that was the end of that.

But it was also around this time that I got to know Natalie Wood. Natalie and I got along well and we talked about a project to do together. She asked me to adapt a book into a script for her at Ray Stark's company. This relationship was important because I got my foot in the door by getting introductions from Natalie to her agent, Guy Meckerling, who had become head of production for Stark. Natalie's career wasn't so hot at that time, but Meckerling was her good friend and he financed this project for me to write a script from the book.

I had already written a script and most importantly, I had been employed by Hal Ashby and, despite his troubles, that did mean something. I came in a box that had the right labels on it, along with a film from USC film school, and the combination of those things was what mattered. All of the elements were coming together at the right moment. It's also important to note that the first deal I did with Hal Ashby I did without an agent. After that, I needed to get one, and through the actress Teri Garr, who I was friends with through Josh, I met Rick Nicita, one of the owners of CAA [Creative Artists' Agency], at a dinner one night. Because I met him socially through Josh and Teri, and he had heard good things about me, he wanted to see my film. Again, here I was packaged in the right way at a dinner party at Teri Garr's house with a script written for Hal Ashby under my belt. He watched my film, liked it, and signed me up.

So now I had an agent at CAA, but not much happened. I wrote the script for Natalie, but not much went on with that either, and neither one of them got made, so I didn't really know what to do. Then out of the blue one day, Rick Nicita calls to say that Michael Eisner and Jeffrey Katzenberg, who were running Paramount at the time, had seen my short films and particularly liked *Silent Night*, the one about the psychiatric hospital. They had a project called *I'm Dancing as Fast as I Can* that they wanted to make for very little money and they wanted to meet me. I remember Rick admitting to me that it was strange that they were contacting me, and he thought that there must be some hitch. So I went and had a meeting with them and they talked about their movie (which took place in a psychiatric hospital) and how much they liked my movie and they said that they wanted me to make this movie for them. I said, "Well, yeah, great, I'll do it." I remember walking out of Paramount and Rick Nicita telling me again that there had to be a hitch because this just didn't happen every day. Sure enough within forty-eight hours the hitch was revealed. It turned out that the film had a producer named Edgar Scherick who was a very big deal back then and still is now (he produces movies in partnership with Scott Rudin). Rick calls to tell me that Eisner and Katzenberg want me to talk to Edgar Scherick. Scherick had been in New York when I had the meeting at Paramount with Eisner and Katzenberg, so I called Edgar Scherick and introduced myself. Before I could finish talking, he exploded into a rage. If you knew Edgar then you would know that this is something you get used to. But of course I didn't know him, and he just started screaming at me saying, "I don't give a fuck who you are. You could be Steven Spielberg and David Lean and everybody else all wrapped into one. It doesn't matter because that studio is not going to hire a fucking director without my approval when I am out of town, and then announce to me that the film has a director!" I'm like, "What?" And then he said, "Good luck. Maybe we'll work together in the future." And that was the end of that.

A couple of months later I got a call that Scherick wanted to talk to me. I called, he yelled at me again, and then he offered me a script written by Chris Columbus called *Reckless*. The only reason this happened is because of what had happened before and the fact that he knew me through that episode. In between those calls I was offered two other movies that I actually turned down. They were both horror films and one was actually a sequel. It could have been *Friday the 13th* or *Halloween*, one of those where the original film had been successful and they wanted to make a low-budget sequel. I just couldn't do it. I didn't know how to do it. I thought it was all over for me and that I would never work. Then Scherick called about *Reckless*.

I remember reading the script for *Reckless* and not loving it. I had been out of school for about a year and I was running out of money. I really didn't have a choice but to do it and make the most of it. I thought the script was full of clichés, but I wanted to work, and I discovered a context in which I could get excited about the film. It was essentially the idea of making a "Last Tango in West Virginia," and I thought there was a radical sexuality that I wanted to do and then I got excited about the script again.

It all came back to those basic questions about motivations. I didn't love the script, but I wanted to work, and I realized it was an opportunity that I couldn't pass up. I asked myself, What are your motivations and how are you rationalizing them? I knew that I needed to find a way to make the film unique, to make it my own instead of a simple genre piece. So I decided that I would subvert the genre and exploit those sexual ideas that were there. This leads me to the one regret that I have. I must say I have no regrets about how any film I have done has been cut because it has been done exactly as I wanted. No one has ever changed anything except for *Reckless*. I did indeed succeed in making my "Last Tango in West Virginia" movie and it got an X-Rating, which meant that I was forced to cut out some pivotal moments in the film and that I deeply regret. One of these days I would love to go back and reconstitute it, if the footage still exists, because the whole heat of the movie that made it rise above its teen genre thing was this great scene when Aidan Quinn is fucking a waitress in the bathroom. That scene was cut in its entirety. There was an even better one on a bunch of old tires, and that was cut too.

CAN YOU TALK ABOUT THE EXPERIENCE OF MAKING THE FEATURE?

I suppose I have a kind of blissful naivete that has allowed me to feel comfortable in doing what I do. I have incredible anxiety in life about many things (like being attacked by a knife-wielding maniac), but I never had anxiety about making a movie. I always felt so lucky that I discovered what I wanted to do because you realize that your ability has no limits and that it can grow in certain situations. Every film I've ever done, including that first one minute film in Washington Square Park, has always seemed like the same experience to me. That includes the $50 million film *The Chamber*. It is never any different because it is always essentially you and the camera and the same Kodak film in that camera. No matter what the budget is or who is starring in the film, I've always looked at it from that perspective. I had this movie in my head and I never felt it was bigger than that even with the money I was given. Sometimes people would say, "Well you've done these small films, but can you handle a big budget?" Did they think that you had to physically carry the money in your hands? What does that mean, "Handle a big budget?" If that's the camera and you're the actor, and I'm talking to you, you are doing for free the same thing you could be doing for $20 million. It doesn't affect me; it affects the actor's bank account, and it is still the same situation, a camera filming a person. So that was never a problem for me with making films because I was never intimidated by making them.

Reckless was budgeted at $4.5 million, which was definitely low-budget at that time since the average was about $10 million, although compared to a student film budget $4.5 million was a lot of money. The casting process was taking longer than expected and while we were in the process of casting, MGM was having financial difficulties trying to get the money to do the film. It was during the recession in the early eighties and they were just about to go out of business. I remember getting very involved in the process because they really wanted to do the film and didn't give up trying to get that money. They were literally trying to find a way to borrow the $4.5 million because they thought the film would be very commercial and would help them stay in business. Because of the process, I became very aware of interest rates and loan rates and things like that because they were talking to banks for months. Everything seemed easy in the beginning, but then it dragged on. So while this dragged on they wanted to keep the project alive and continued to fund the casting process, which wasn't going very well either. When they did finally get the green light, we still didn't have actors. I really wanted to get Kevin Bacon for the role, but the studio needed to be convinced. We tested a lot of people: Tom Cruise, Sean Penn, Emilio Estevez, Rob Lowe, and Kevin Bacon. I subsequently became friendly with Tom Cruise and it was always a joke between us that when you are casting you get a sheet with the actor's name and a space for comments. When Tom left the room I wrote "Kind of chubby, not very attractive." He also had a tooth blacked out because he was working on *The Outsiders,* and he had told his agent to be sure to tell us that he would be coming to the audition in character. Of course, the agent didn't mention that.

We decided to go with Kevin Bacon and that was fine with me since he was who I wanted. So he signed on for the role, and then I had a meeting with him when I was in New York, and he announced to me that he wouldn't do any nude scenes. He and his girlfriend or wife or whatever had made that decision. This was surprising to me because he had read the script, and the script was very explicit about everything and quite detailed about what would be required for the part. I remember even doing rewrites on the script and I specifically put in as much detail as possible about sexual stuff so that there would be no misunderstanding when it came time to do the film. There would be no room for the actors to say, "What do you mean?" But Bacon wouldn't do it and I remember leaving the restaurant after that meeting thinking that my career was over before it had started. What was I gonna do? I didn't know what to do since he had already been approved and I was the only one who knew that he had backed out. I had to call Edgar Scherick and Edgar started screaming at me. At least now I was used to the screaming. But this time it was focused on Bacon, and it was, "Who the fuck does he think he is? He's got a contract." I knew that it wasn't worth getting the lawyers involved, so I said I didn't want to use him. If he was uncomfortable with the nudity, then he was wrong for the role anyway. I asked the casting people if there was anyone else who could do the job. I had seen virtually everyone with a SAG card by that time and I was at a complete loss.

A tape came in from an actor in Chicago named Aidan Quinn. I saw it and immediately knew that this was the guy, but it was a fight to convince the others. He was very improvisational and mumbled in a James Dean way and I loved it. And I knew I could fix those simple problems. You can get people to pronounce things correctly, but what you can't get them to have is a soul and a heart. That's the rare part. I am not interested in any actor who when you already have seen their work needs to come in and read something to prove to you that they can do a part. If you know they can act, you hire them. When you meet that person you know then if they are right for the part or not. Reading for a part is a ridiculous process; it is so artificial. When you read something you haven't discussed or rehearsed it is pointless. People will come in really prepared, enunciate properly and I could care less about it. If someone is prepared like that it completely turns me off.

I knew Aidan was right for the part but it took some convincing to get everyone to agree to use him. We had a fight about it, but luckily it worked out. We had already cast Darryl Hannah for the female lead. She was not well known at this time and had only been in a few films in very minor roles. I knew her because she shared a house with Rachel Ward and I had met her through a producer who was a friend of Hal Ashby. I subsequently became involved with Rachel and knew Darryl through her. I think they met when they did a slasher movie together about a bunch of beautiful people who are in a camp and get all chopped up. So I saw a lot of people for the role, but I ultimately went back to Darryl in the end. That was a good choice because things worked out well.

When we went to make the movie, we had a remarkably trouble-free experience. This far into the mix, by the way, I dealt much more with Scott Rudin than I did with Edgar Scherick. Rudin worked with him and was really the guy who was around more and involved in the script rewrites and things like that. I really credit a great line producer named Bob Culsberry, who was a great help to me and helped make things run smoothly. That isn't a job that people really attribute a lot of credit to. The line producer plays the most important part in how you wrestle the machine into doing what you want it to do and I have always insisted that I must be involved in the selection of the line producer. I cannot make a film when I feel like I am somebody's employee. If you tell me it is going to be a $4.5 million film, then I will make it for that, but I have to be involved in how that money is spent. The other stroke of good fortune was that we had the great cinematographer Michael Bauhaus, who had shot a lot of movies and had done a John Sayles film called *Baby It's You*. We got along very well and he was very fast, to this day the fastest cinematographer that I have ever worked with. It was a very harmonious experience all around.

TELL ME ABOUT THE FIRST DAY.

It was magical. We were going to shoot a crucial scene outside with Darryl and Aidan on a ledge. The weather wasn't good. It kept snowing and we kept stopping, but it continued to snow and it was getting worse and worse. So finally we decided to shoot the whole thing in the snow, which was completely unplanned. Visually that scene turned out so well, and the snow was a real plus. So out of the jaws of defeat, and our frightened concern about the weather, came this thing that turned out to be golden. We were lucky for the rest of the shoot that way, and the continuity of weather matched. Having millions of dollars in a budget is one thing, but it's a very different number of millions if the weather doesn't cooperate, because you're eating up those millions in lost time. When you make a movie that has a lot of exterior shots, it really does matter what time of year you shoot. There are only six hours of usable light in a day in the winter as opposed to nine or more in the summer.

Everything else went smoothly for the most part. The only weird thing was that the editor I hired was cutting while we were shooting, and the studio understandably wanted to see the first scene cut together in order to find out if I knew what I was doing. So I'm shooting the film and not paying attention, and this guy cuts something and sends it to them. It was horrendous and it looked like junk. The studio got nervous and I went ballistic. I told them that I couldn't guarantee the film would make $100 million, but I knew that it would at least cut together.

I had to fire the editor after this happened. That is one of the worst experiences because you have to look that person in the eye and say, "You're fired," and no one likes that. But it was my ass on the line so I had no choice. I asked them to hire Al Magnoli, who had edited my student film but had never edited a feature before. They agreed to hire him for the time being and said they would hire someone else when the film was finished. He ended up editing the film himself. Once he got on board and did a recut of that first footage, the studio was quite satisfied.

WHAT HAPPENED WITH THE MOVIE?

What happened was very defined and it is in the archives. Dale Pollack, who was a writer for the *L.A. Times,* did an interview with me before the release of the film. It was all about how "hot" I was and stuff like that. The *Times* decided to hold the article until after the weekend that the film opened. The following Tuesday I opened the paper and there was a big headline that said, "When What's Hot Cools Down." I was enraged because their interview with me appeared as if I was talking to them after I knew that the film would be a flop. It was an absolute distortion of something and I had no recourse. The movie just didn't appeal to people, and it didn't do well at all. It tested through the roof and every indication was that it would be a commercial success. I remember getting my first taste of public promotion when there was a radio ticket giveaway. I remember the announcer reading about the film and saying they had tickets for a sneak preview for the film in a very sarcastic voice mocking the film. I called MGM and they were horrified too, because they were paying for this promotion and the people they were paying to promote it were dissing them. Now I think that they were mocking the genre, the pop teen thing. In making it I thought that I was going to transcend a genre and unfortunately it didn't work out that way. I remember years later when I was at NYU for a screening of a couple of my films, including *Reckless,* one guy said, "I really like how you stole the movie away from the script." I knew exactly what he meant. But I guess many other people didn't see that.

WERE YOU DEVASTATED?

I was devastated. I think that having this happen is a unique sort of self help because it's so fucking public. And also it depends on your expectations. The reviews were actually quite mixed. The first review was from the *Toronto Sun,* which gave it a rave and I thought, Man, we are off to the races. Then a bunch of reviews came in that weren't so complimentary. Looking back, *Reckless* got more good ones than it deserved. I remember where I was when I saw that headline in the *L.A. Times.* I was already at work on another film, and I was hardly down and out, but it didn't matter because it is all relative. You feel humiliated, publicly humiliated, and the flip side is that when it goes the other way and a film is successful it is one of the best moments you will ever have.

One thing I will say about that time is that I was incredibly cocky, and I remember that before the disaster I was complaining to Rick Nicita that I had too many things to deal with, too many offers coming in. That seems so ridiculous now. I remember it was once or twice a week that I had a call from Katzenberg, who would say he had a free moment and was just calling to see what was up. Later I thought, Foley, you fucking idiot, he had a free moment? He never had a free moment. He was doing his job and he is obviously very good at it because I really thought that he was my pal. When *Reckless* opened and didn't perform, he didn't seem to have any more free moments.

What's really weird is that no one ever tells you how they feel about your films. I've gotten personal notes from strangers as well as notes from people in the business just letting me know they saw something I did and liked it. It is just the sweetest thing that you can possibly get. Nobody ever does it, probably because they think you get deluged all the time with people telling you how wonderful you are. But that's never the case. Sometimes I meet somebody new and they know my film directing stuff and they never say a word about any of the films that I ever did. Finally they are drunk and something comes out about how good something is and I'm thinking, How come you never said anything before? I ran into Francis Ford Coppola in my student film days at a party and I mustered up the courage to tell him that I really liked *The Godfather*. I felt really embarrassed and awkward saying it but I remember his response exactly. He whispered, "Thanks." And he meant it.

After I finished *Reckless*, my life changed instantly. I was offered at least a hundred movies I didn't even have to have meetings to get. Unfortunately those offers stopped when *Reckless* finally came out.

BUT YOU ULTIMATELY GOT YOUR SECOND FILM?
Yes, I did, thank God. During the casting of *Reckless* I met Sean Penn. He didn't want to do the film and he really wasn't right for the part, but we became friends and kept in contact over the years, exchanging scripts periodically. He had a script called *At Close Range* that he asked me to direct, and I did. This was about a year after *Reckless* was finished. I think I was twenty-nine or thirty at the time. That performed much better and was received very well. After that, I didn't have to worry so much anymore.

TURNING TO THOSE PEOPLE WHO ARE TRYING TO FIND A WAY INTO THE INDUSTRY, HOW DOES ONE GO ABOUT BECOMING A DIRECTOR GIVEN THAT IT SEEMS SO HARD TO FIND A WAY TO EVEN GET A CHANCE TO PROVE YOUR CAPABILITIES?
There are three essential roads: having directed before, writing a brilliant and commercially viable script, or making a short film. No matter how good your short film is, it is going to be an uphill fight to direct your own script. If you write the script and it is sold and made into a film and it is successful commercially or with the critics, then you're in the position to write a second script and say, "I want to direct this," and your chances are much greater. If you are not a writer, then you have got to make as much film as

you possibly can, no matter what it is. You need to find a way to tell a story in a linear manner and to tell people a story that is familiar to them and that they can relate to so they don't have to make so much of a conceptual leap.

The way I got into the business was ultimately through connections and writing. I had had two development deals and I had written scripts, so I was someone of some relevance in the business. Even if those scripts weren't read, it didn't matter because they could see that I had been paid to write, that I had established a foothold. The next battle involves getting your script to the right person to read it. It's a very difficult thing that I believe is only achievable from political and personal manipulation and befriending somebody who knows somebody who knows somebody. There is no central script clearinghouse because the crush is too big, so there's no official place to send a script for a film for anyone to look at. Studios don't have departments of new people, and agencies don't really actively recruit new talent, so the only possible way is when a single human being, based on a friendship with somebody else, says to someone important, "Will you look at this film for me." Otherwise, it ain't gonna happen, and it's bizarre and totally nonlinear and again to me it seems that the unprepared cream will never rise to the top.

Many people ask me to read their scripts or watch their short films. I don't often do it, but if I meet someone who is a friend of a friend and that friend says, "Would you do me a favor and read this script?" I'm going to do it. If a junior agent calls and tells me that there is a script I can read that is much different than when someone higher up calls. One call from one agent who is high enough up and you go, "Yes, sir." It is just a mutual power thing because then you might do them a favor and you're gonna call them back and ask them for a favor, so I guess that's what creates the insularity, people only do for each other that which is beneficial to themselves through reciprocity. If you are outside the system, then the question is how can you pay back the favor? The only way to do that, of course, is through a personal connection that starts at all levels, from the bottom up.

Speaking articulately is very important. Before they read the script and before they look at the movie, executives will listen to you, and if you can spin something attractive about yourself and you are able to make a connection with that person, that is the first step in establishing a level of communication. If you can verbally communicate with the executives that is very key because that's what they do all day. That is their currency of exchange and you have to be able to talk to them and explain how you are going to make that film and make it better than anybody else. Anybody who is going to make a movie has got to communicate also with the actors to get them to that place where their performance fits the piece. The bottom line is that everything is based on this verbal communication that I have been talking about. I think maybe that's the part that people are not ready for and they fail to recognize its importance and impact. I remember talking to an agent about that very thing years ago. We were discussing a client of his who had made a brilliant film, but simply had such intense social anxiety that he could not function in a meeting. He could be in a very small group, but when he had to go to a meeting he was lost and his career suffered greatly from this. I learned that you have got to control the meeting without the executive thinking that you are doing it. I can't tell you how many times people have said that one director won over another because he had the most enthusiasm and passion for the movie. They get hired over people who are more talented, have more experience, and whose last films have made more money. Every executive wants to feel that somebody is going to make his or her movie and would die to do this. There is no other way to convey this than to tell the executives what they want to hear articulately and with passion and enthusiasm.

DO YOU THINK THAT THE GREAT NUMBER OF PEOPLE WHO RUSH TO TRY TO BECOME FILMMAKERS TODAY HAS MADE IT MORE DIFFICULT TO GET FILMS MADE?

I think that the bar can only be raised and that it all becomes relative with the numbers in that you still have to distinguish yourself. The expectations placed on a student film are definitely higher today than they were in my day, so the same competition is intensified. I sometimes see student films and I feel humiliated that they are so much more sophisticated than my own student films, both technically and conceptually. I believe that the reason to go to film school is to push your own limits and that of the medium itself. Now, because of digitization, one's imagination is expanded by what can be put on screen.

You have to also try to define for yourself who you are as an artist, and not present an image to outsiders but present a truth of what it is you do. You need to define your sensibility. I think that every filmmaker has to ask himself that question all the time. I don't think I can define what I actually do, but at least I can define what I want to do. I deal with psychological realism. More than anything else I tend to understand that that is where my heart is and that is what I do best. My best films are films that are based in that. *At Close Range, Glengarry Glen Ross*, and *After Dark, My Sweet* are among them. It is that psychological realism that is about moral ambiguity; I'm fascinated by that idea, that the truth in life is the existence of moral ambiguity: people want to murder the people they love, people want to do all kinds of strange things. This is what I was always attracted to and was why I was so seduced by the films of the seventies like *Serpico*. In a couple of reviews the critics mentioned that I was bravely trying to delve into moral ambiguity. It was very gratifying to me that people understood where I was coming from. Now in the current market of mass culture exploring that theme is the worst thing that you can possibly do.

My experience making *Who's That Girl?* was so important because it was so clearly not me and it showed in every way. It forced me to see what I can and cannot do. Being knocked on your ass like that pushes you to make better films that come from within, to explore those ideas that you hold within you, and to think about how to get that message across. You return to your strength, your center, and then you start looking back at the films that you like and you realize that there is a connection. I think that the best thing you can do is be known for what is truly you.

This whole process of breaking into the business is something that continues throughout your career. There is not a director alive who has not had to start over in one way or another and reconnect with the same questions and issues that he was dealing with at the start of his career. How do you reinvent yourself? How do you represent yourself? In my career I have had periods when I worked consistently and didn't have to find the work. I never had to go to meetings or meet anyone or work for anything. Then I would make a film that was not commercially successful and I would have to go back out there into the world of the executives and have meetings and sell myself just as I did in the beginning. That is hard work especially when over the years those executives have changed jobs so much that you don't have the connections with people that you once had. It is really like starting over when you put yourself in that place where the people you are talking with may or may not know who you are, and you have to figure out how to get up all that energy a second time around, all on a continuing basis.

There is a quote from someone in the French New Wave (I believe it was Godard) that I have taped to my computer that says, "The goal of making cinema is to show that which without you might never have been seen." I think that it is very important to know yourself and to ask yourself, What is it that I know that nobody else knows? Sell that and be aware of the customer you are selling it to. Really know who they are and what they are expecting so that what you are doing will be seen as truthful in the context in which it is delivered. But most importantly, I think that it is imperative that you know yourself.

Jake Kasdan | THE ZERO EFFECT

JAKE KASDAN *was born in Michigan in 1974. During his teenage years, he wrote and directed several plays, which he produced and opened in commercial theaters. After a year at Hampshire College, in Massachusetts, Kasdan dropped out of school to write a book about the making of his father's film,* Wyatt Earp. *Soon after that Kasdan began writing screenplays, ultimately producing the script to what would be his first feature:* The Zero Effect. *Kasdan is single and lives in Los Angeles.*

My mother is from Michigan and my father is from West Virginia. They met at the University of Michigan. My father worked in advertising after he graduated from school, but he wanted to try to get into the film business so my parents moved to Los Angeles. He worked in advertising during the day and wrote screenplays at night. He sold his first script when I was about six years old. I have one younger brother who works as a television writer. Right now he is working on the show "Dawson's Creek." Because my father was in the film business I was always on movie sets. Sometimes it would be for a couple of weeks and other times it was for an entire summer vacation. When he did *The Big Chill* we had a tutor and I was there for the whole shoot.

DID THAT AFFECT YOUR RELATIONSHIP WITH YOUR PEERS?

My good friends certainly knew all about it, but I didn't advertise it. I've never had it any other way so I don't really have much to compare it to. It was sort of like this cool thing and on some level it still is. Sometimes it was like, "Wow, your Dad wrote *The Empire Strikes Back.*"

I remember that certain movies were incredibly exciting when I was really young. I can recall seeing the first *Star Wars* when I was five. I remember the summer hits of my early childhood and I remember being on film sets when I was really young, so I already had an involved relationship with movies by the time I was six. I had this real awareness of how movies worked through the sets that I was indirectly involved with. I knew when I was really little that I wanted to make movies; I wanted to do what my dad did because it looked like fun.

DID YOU EVER CONSIDER DOING ANYTHING ELSE?

Intermittently throughout my adolescence I entertained thoughts of doing something else, but they were never really serious. Filmmaking was always what I was focused on. I started writing plays when I was in high school, and I concentrated on that for a few years. Dramatic writing and directing actors always seemed to be related interests of mine. I started seriously working at it by the age of sixteen and have continued working at it ever since. I just loved it. I was good at writing dialogue from the time I was really young and as I got older I began to learn everything else. I was good at making people laugh and it was easy for me to write stuff that was funny. At school I was always the last kid picked in sports; I had coordination problems and I never really excelled in anything. When I found writing it was the first time I felt like I was really good at something. How good I actually was is a trickier question, but I felt like I had the facility for it.

During high school I worked in the theater department writing and producing plays. I went to Beverly Hills High School for two years and then to a place called Windward for two years. At Beverly they had an incredibly intense drama department. It functioned almost like a professional program where you would work for hours and hours. It was crazy. We'd work about eight hours a night. It was like a full-time job outside of school and the department took it very seriously. They would put a lot of money into productions that they would put on in enormous theaters. In retrospect it seems a bit silly, but at the time it was a new world to step into so I was always around the theater. We did plays like *The Crucible,* by Arthur Miller, and other serious works. When I was fourteen I left Beverly Hills High and I started writing my own plays.

For the most part the plays were all written in the first person and the protagonist was always some minor variation of me, but slightly better looking and slightly cooler. The plays were relationship based and mostly dealt with family and friends. They were all comedies but they dealt with serious themes. The first play I wrote was about a bunch of kids and their high school love affairs. It was narrated by two hardboiled detectives, Raymond Chandler–like characters. It was very over the top and stylized.

I was definitely influenced by all the Arthur Miller and Peter Shaffer plays. In about six months I had read all of Shakespeare and all of John Patrick Shanley. I always kind of binge and read everything that somebody wrote so I can try to get to know him.

After a while, I started producing my own plays. I would rent a theater, cast my friends, rehearse for a few weeks, and then go out. I loved it. It was an incredible feeling and directing was almost like a revelation to me. This was also how I learned to work with actors. In my first plays I cast my friends from high school, but after a while I started branching out and I held auditions to find my actors. I did four plays over three years and by the time I produced the last one I had cast all my actors through the audition process. It was great for me to learn how to deal with actors on a more professional level.

After I graduated from high school in 1992, I went to Hampshire College. I hated it and I left before the end of the first semester. Hampshire is a great school in theory, but practically it just doesn't work. It is a very remote college located near Amherst, Massachusetts. It is an alternative school environment where the classes have no grades. It is a very new place so it's not particularly well endowed, and as a result it's very expensive to attend. There was also not much diversity in the student body. It just didn't work for me, so I left and went to UC Santa Cruz, which I liked much better, but also left after one year because my father had just begun to direct *Wyatt Earp.* I thought that I would go to the shoot with him with the intention of writing a book about the making of a film.

I decided that I would put together an incredibly in-depth record of how the film was made and how movies are made in general. I wrote about three hundred pages, but unfortunately when the film was released it was very poorly received. It was so unpleasant and horrifying that I put the book away and have never really finished it, although perhaps someday I will. But the experience was still very formative and a massive part of my education. It was a great lesson on how things work not only on a mechanical level, but also on a storytelling level, and how the storytelling relates to the mechanics. I was watching people at the top of their field at work making a huge beautiful movie. The unfortunate experience of having it die was also really educational.

I worked on *Wyatt Earp* for a while, and as a side wrote a promotional book for the film that I compiled and edited. It was really more of a fluff book, but it did come out. During this time I was still working on my plays. The last project I did was called *The Behavioral Patterns of Funny Man Tyler Hudson*. It was about a stand-up comic and his relationship with his girlfriend. His girlfriend leaves him and then he gets a new girl. The story deals with his relationships with a bouncer at his comedy club, his father, and his brother, who is an academic and a national Scrabble champion. Ultimately it was about a young man trying to figure out who he was. It was very personal and much more candid than any of the other things that I had written up to that point.

HOW DID PEOPLE RESPOND TO YOUR PLAYS?
People generally liked them. The reviews were really good and it was a great feeling to get such positive encouragement. That helped me to keep writing. Right around the time I finished *Tyler Hudson*, I felt like I needed to start thinking about screenplays. I knew Bill Pullman through my father because of *Wyatt Earp*, and he came to see the play. We had met on the set of *Wyatt Earp* and got along well, discovering that we had common interests. After Bill came to see the play he called me up to say that we should work on something together since he had just made a production deal and was trying to get some development going. He had a French movie based on a bizarre and wacky idea that he wanted me to adapt. Bill has very unconventional taste sometimes, but that is one of the reasons that we work well together. We were both really interested in behavioral drama, and a kind of quiet storytelling. I was twenty-one at that time and I was trying to figure out whether I should go back to school or keep writing. I decided that I should keep working and I thought that I would take a few months and try to write a script. I didn't want to do Bill's project and it wasn't really going to pay very much, so I decided that I should find a project that was a bit more personal and set about writing that.

WERE YOUR PARENTS SUPPORTIVE DURING THIS TIME?
They would have financially supported me, but they didn't really need to since my expenses were really low. I was living very happily and cheaply in a house in L.A. with five friends paying about $200 a month in rent. I had made a few thousand dollars doing the *Wyatt Earp* book, so that helped me through. I had very little money but I managed to make it last long enough so that I could work on my script. Unfortunately I couldn't finish it. I wasn't getting much reaction to it and I didn't know how to make it work.

Six months later I had the idea for *The Zero Effect* and I started writing it right away. I have always loved detective stories. I like reading them and I began to like writing them. I am attracted to the kind of storytelling epitomized by Arthur Conan Doyle's Sherlock Holmes stories and Raymond Chandler, and I knew that I wanted to write about an imperfect hero in the context of a detective story. I couldn't quite figure out how, so I started trying to extract some lessons from the failure of my first script. I knew that I wanted to write about a hero who had some real problems. I came up with the idea for a man who is the world's most accomplished private detective, but who is a profoundly disturbed recluse who has trouble even leaving his house. He is dealing with some very heavy emotional baggage. I conceived of the opening of the film where the scene of Ben Stiller praising the detective to Ryan O'Neal is intercut with Ben talking to his friend at a bar about what a catastrophe the guy is. He was describing him as a very dysfunctional genius. The contrast of him selling to a potential client and complaining to a friend about his boss felt like a scene that you would never expect to see in that type of story.

Part of my idea for the detective's isolation was born out of the fact that I had spent almost a year or more writing and it was a lonely and boring life. I was really young to have taken on that existence; I was just twenty-one and I was living in a run-down house spending all of my time writing. It wasn't a dark time for me, but it was definitely a time that many people can identify with after they finish college. You start thinking, What am I going to do with myself? Suddenly you have the responsibility of getting your life together and dealing with the reality that your decisions matter. Also, you have to get yourself together and go out and do something productive. As a writer you are constantly trying to push yourself to work. It is easy to sink into a state where you do nothing productive for several days. Thankfully there is a part of you that knows that in order to be productive in the world you have to get off your ass.

While I was experiencing all of that, I was also thinking about the Sherlock Holmes stuff. I had read a story called "The Scandal in Bohemia" that describes how Sherlock Holmes falls in love with a client. That felt to me to be the thematic heart of *The Zero Effect*. For my script I was more interested in the characters than in the story itself. Who was blackmailing who? Where were the keys to the safety deposit box? Those were important questions, but what really interested me was the idea of a guy who was a great observer of life but who was incapacitated and unable to participate. He found it easier to talk about things and think about things than to actually do things. He also had a great problem with intimacy and self-examination; he was always pretending to be someone else. Those are the things I was thinking about when I wrote the script.

I wake up early in the morning with the plan that I will start writing immediately. Then I put it off for the whole day and around eleven o'clock at night I start and I work all night. I try to wake up early the next day and the same thing happens. Ultimately I crank it out. I guess I find a balance between intense procrastination and the eventual work. Somehow I can't avoid it. It took me about six months to write *The Zero Effect* script.

After I finished it, I spent several months trying to get people interested in it. I met my agent in the course of that process. I had known him a little bit through the production of my plays (the agency helped me with them), but it was during the development of the script that we worked closer together. *The Zero Effect* script was well received by everyone who read it, but it took months to shop around. It was an unusual script and people were definitely interested, but we didn't have anyone saying, "Okay, we want to buy this and make it." I had somebody who wanted to buy it and have someone else direct it, but I wanted to direct it myself. There were also places that wanted me to develop the script for them.

I really wanted to direct the film so I was trying to find a producing partner who could get the money for me to make it. Eventually I hooked up with Lisa Henson and Janet Yang at Manifest Films. It was also around that time that I sent the script to Pullman. The previous year Bill had been in *Independence Day*, which was a big hit. He had a lot of power then. It was lucky timing that he was in a position where his involvement with the project might get it going. He had never been at that point in his career before. He was also my first choice for the detective, Daryl Zero. He's an amazing actor and this was the perfect moment for us to work together, so I sent it to him to see what he thought. After one week he committed. He realized how perfect the character was for him and what he could do with the part. He told me later that he initially didn't want to read the script because he was afraid he wouldn't like it. He was at a critical moment in his career, and he couldn't afford to screw around. But after he read it he said, "Let's do it."

Suddenly I had Bill Pullman and producers that were really excited about him. We decided that the best next step was to get another name actor attached to the project before we took it around to all the studios for funding. We all talked about who we wanted and everybody agreed on Ben Stiller. I had no relationship with him, but I was a huge fan. I thought he was great and that he would be hilarious alongside Bill, so we sent him the script. He was into it. The fact that the first two actors who read it said they would do it was really key to getting the project moving so quickly. By now we all felt that we had the goods, so we sent the project out to everyone in town. We released it on a Friday, which was a coordinated move to get bidders over the weekend. By Monday lunch, one studio had said yes, and a few hours later a second one had made a bid. Suddenly we had some power, because if you have two people bidding for an object then you can usually close a deal. When you leverage them against each other you can actually push the thing through.

WERE YOU CONCERNED ABOUT YOUR ABILITY TO MAKE A FEATURE?

I had never directed a film before. That was a stumbling block that made people a little nervous. But I had also convinced the actors to do the project, so I was released from a bit of people's skepticism. I feel that the big struggle was convincing Bill and Ben to come on board the project, and it was their confidence in me that made it happen. I should also say that in the pitch meetings there was always a time when they interviewed me for the directing position. I believed that I could do it and I believed that I could convince people that I could do it, so I persuaded them with my confidence. I believed that I was as qualified as anyone to direct my script and I knew I was the world's authority on *The Zero Effect* concept. It wasn't like God reached down from the heavens and said, "Now you are a movie director." I felt I had built and manufactured this thing and that I understood better than anybody how to get it right. I was ready to explain that to anyone who would listen.

The secret to directing is that no one can really tell whether you can do it or not until you have done it before. The truth is that people can't always do it, and that ruins a lot of movies. Everybody had questions that they asked me, but there was not necessarily a right answer to give. I would hear things like, "Who do you want to shoot the movie, and how do you see it being done?" or "How do you see your movie visually?" This has no specific answer. It was more about being persuasive and instilling confidence in them. I knew I wasn't being hired for my technical expertise. I was being hired for my expertise in telling a particular story. Obviously on a first film the crew knows more about the camera than you do.

HOW WAS THE PRODUCTION DEAL WORKED OUT AND WHAT WAS YOUR BUDGET?

Ultimately Castle Rock agreed to finance the film. The people at Castle Rock were the best people I have ever met in this business. It was incredibly good luck that they were interested in the project and let me do it. They were supportive believers in the movie and they ended up wanting to make it for more money than I was asking for, which was an unusual situation. Originally, when we sent it out, we said that we needed $5 million to make it. A large reason for this was that Bill and Ben were both willing to work for significantly reduced fees. But Castle Rock wanted to make it for more! This was for a variety of reasons, one of which was that they wanted it to have a certain larger-scale look to it so that they could release it in that way. The other reason was that because of a business arrangement they had, they needed to make a certain number of movies for a certain amount of money with very little room for movement. This was great news to us because it meant that we were going to have considerably more dough, and consequently more time and a better paid crew. I was happy with this arrangement, but I insisted that if we were going to increase the budget, then we had to increase the production value as well, and not just put the money into people's pockets. They were fine with this so that is what we did.

The budget ended up being around $12 million in the end. I had an almost criminally good experience because the guys at Castle Rock I was working for were really decent people. It was a small operation started by Martin Schaffer and Alan Horn. Alan is now the head of Warner Brothers. Martin was the president of the company and let me make my movie as I wanted. I was meticulous about who I wanted to hire and I knew what I was looking for in people. I had been around film sets when I was younger, so I knew what kinds of personalities I needed in different positions. Fortunately, I was able to hire a really interesting group of people who brought to the set hard-core production experience along with some really cool ideas. I had a great crew.

DID YOUR FATHER SERVE AS A MENTOR DURING THE PRODUCTION PROCESS?
He was very helpful and he has always been supportive of me. But I was preoccupied with the thought that maybe he shouldn't be too involved. We have a great relationship, but I didn't want him around while I was making the film, mostly because it was already hard enough to distance myself from his reputation and legacy without his physical presence on the set. I didn't want there to be any confusion about who was making the film. At times I got the sense that certain people thought I was unfit for the job, and having my father around would not have helped that situation. One thing that was helpful was that we were shooting in Portland, Oregon, which for Hollywood people is a pretty remote city. So there weren't many agents and studio people around while we were working, and I was left to make the film without much interference. I had great help from Jim Benke, who was my line producer, as well as from many other members of the crew. Ultimately though, I was the director. There is a lot of responsibility that comes with that title, as well as a huge manual labor dynamic that you can't ignore.

GIVEN THAT YOU WERE TWENTY-TWO AT THE TIME OF PRODUCTION, HOW DID YOU COMMAND THE RESPECT OF A MUCH OLDER CREW?
I never really felt that my age was an issue. If you treat people well and you seem to know what you are doing then they are really grateful and relieved.

They are used to working for people who don't know what they are doing most of the time. People are principally concerned with whether or not you are a decent human being, and whether you are efficient enough that they will get home at a decent hour. They want to feel confident that it won't be a nightmare to work for you because you waste time and are indecisive. I had some great people in key positions, including the set designer Gary Frucoff and my assistant director, Carey Dietrich. She is the one person I hired who had worked for my dad, which I believe makes me the only director ever who can say that he knew his first assistant director when he was eight. She is a really good friend and I loved working with her. Dick Pope was the cinematographer and he was incredible. The working environment was very fun and mellow, while also very focused. Bill and Ben were also a great combination and very exciting to work with.

We found the actress Kim Dickens through a grueling casting process where we saw at least two hundred women. I really don't like the casting process. I don't like the dynamic of reading and the amount of desperation that you see. It's not easy being an actor; in fact, it sucks. I was recently directing a television show called "Freaks and Geeks," where I was casting a bunch of thirteen-year-olds. That really put the process into perspective because you can see the disappointment and frustration really screwing these kids up. Then there is the occasional casting moment when you find someone who is fantastic, and that was what it was like with Kim. I was floored by her presence. She was quiet, interesting, real, sexy, and sweet, and I knew that she would be the lead.

The shoot was forty-four days. We ran only two days behind and we finished under budget for the production period.

TELL ME ABOUT THE EDITING AND TESTING PROCESS.

I had convinced the studio to hire a friend of mine as the editor, so I had a really great working relationship during that process. Again the studio pretty much stayed out of my hair until I was ready. When you're editing, you're on a certain financial schedule in terms of how long you've got everything for and when everything's supposed to be done. I had the full post period, which is a luxury these days when most people don't even have the union-mandated post period. There's a great crunch on postproduction in light of computer-editing; it makes things faster, but sometimes something gets lost along the way.

We worked like dogs over a ten-week period. I finished the thing and I finally showed it to the studio. It was about two hours long. I had been rigorous about getting it to there, which wasn't easy. I showed it to the studio, to Martin Schaffer, Alan Horn, and Rob Reiner (who is sort of the aesthetic godfather of Castle Rock), and they gave me a few notes of changes that they wanted to see. But they were really minimal, and they were generally happy with it. Their approach to the changes was really great, because they said, "Look, try our changes, and if you don't like them, don't use them." I did try them and they were great, so I kept them. That approach is great because it really takes the fight out of you—by giving you the freedom to explore, but not the obligation to change, they make the thing a better film.

The film went to a preview; it was terrible. The cards were terrible; the experience was terrible; the whole thing was a mess. I think that the process is not very good or particularly respected anymore though, because it doesn't make much sense. What you do is take a randomly recruited audience and let them see your film in a very strange context. Then you ask for note cards back. Previews are going out of style right now because everyone knows that not only is the process ridiculous, but that there's very little correlation between how the movie does and how the preview does. It's not a good predictor of commercial success. What the studios always say is that it helps them figure out how to market the film, where to buy the ad time, and stuff like that. So I'm on my way to the preview, and I drive up to the theater in Pasadena, and there's a line of people who'd been given free movie tickets composed mainly of sixteen-year-old hip-hop-styled kids. I knew before the film started that that kind of movie was just not what they were looking for. Daryl Zero is not a macho hero for a certain crowd, and so it was terrible. Martin Schaffer said to me afterward, "I knew it was gonna test badly because good movies test badly." Castle Rock was very good about it. All I really remember is how traumatic the experience was; it changes how you view the film forever, because you know that some people hate it.

After we finished the preview, I went back and did another cut of the film. I focused on responding to what I thought might have been some of the audience's problems, and when the cut was done we previewed it again. It played much better the second time around.

TELL ME ABOUT THE RELEASE OF *THE ZERO EFFECT*.

The reviews were very kind. Given what they can be, and given what they could've said about me because of my background, they were very respectful. People really liked it. Most reviews were positive and we only had a few bad ones. We opened in around one hundred screens. I spent a lot of time selling the film, traveling around the country doing press. It was very hard to get people to go. I don't know if there was a problem with the campaign or if people just didn't like the film, but we didn't really make much money. The film was just dropped, which happens all the time. We spent a hell of a lot of time selling it, but the materials just did not penetrate. We did very well in four cities, Los Angeles, Chicago, New York, and San Francisco, but we just didn't do anything anywhere else. The studio tried to make something of it, to go after it and not just cut their losses, but they just couldn't get people into the theaters.

The film ultimately did very well in the video rental market. Most of the movie-going audience today is very young, and video is the preferred way for adults over twenty-five to watch films. Everyone I run into now who saw it tells me that they saw it on video. And I always hear that people recommend it to others, tell their friends to rent and enjoy. I'm happy that it got out there eventually.

WHAT DO YOU THINK WAS ULTIMATELY RESPONSIBLE FOR GETTING THE FILM MADE?

I think the script. All of my experience has suggested that if you have a script that people are responding to extremely well, then you can get it made. But people have to really be freaking out over it; it can't just be okay. There are a million scripts out there in the world and most of them aren't that good. That's the tough part, making something that people really are moved by or that they like or whatever. If you have a great script, then you have something valuable. And you've got to stand by your work, just really stand behind it and keep pushing it out into the world so that people can see and respond to it.

These days, there are many other outlets for filmmaking. A good friend of mine just made a film on digital video for around $100,000. That movie did really well at Sundance, and then Artisan bought it and they are going to release it. The thing is that the movie is something that people can get passionate about. That's the kind of film you have to make if you want to be successful. You have to have material that people can get behind and really care about. Then you can convince the distributors to release it because they want to be on that train too, to be able to say that they were responsible for releasing some really cool new thing that lots of people were excited about. The challenge is creating the material. It's not an easy thing, and I haven't always been able to do it, but when you can do that, then you can do anything you want.

I really believe that the best way to get into the movie business is to write your way in. That's how I did it. It's very hard to make such an impression with a visual image that people feel that they desperately need to hire you as opposed to someone else who they already know. It's much easier to move people with writing because that's what they respond to. Of course it's not impossible to do it with a reel of work. It happens a lot. It never ceases to amaze me how many of these guys figure out how to scam someone into making a movie on the basis of a television commercial. That's awesome. If you can do that, God bless. I don't have whatever that gift is. I just don't think like that. I would have no idea how to do it. But I think that the best thing you can do ultimately is to have something that you control, that you own, that people want.

There are a lot of directors out there who make commercial films and who gear their whole approach toward making hits and working forever. That may work for them, but it's not really what interests me because the films don't interest me; they're only conceived in a commercial light. Since *Zero Effect* I have not made another movie, and there have been plenty of things that I could have done. Don't get me wrong, I'm very eager to make something else. I'm ready and hungry, but I haven't been able to find something that I'm mad for yet, so it puts the pressure on me to come up with something. The key to getting it done is to have a piece of material that you're willing to take to the grave. It would be false to imply, however, that after I wrote *Zero Effect* that the clouds parted and the sun shone upon me and I felt that the script in my hand was of divine making. That's not the case. If no one had wanted to make *Zero Effect* then I would've written another script. You just have to work on a movie that makes sense to you and that you desperately want to do. And if one doesn't work, keep trying.

HOW DO YOU HAVE PERSPECTIVE ON OLDER CHARACTERS GIVEN THAT YOU ARE SO YOUNG?
I feel like the philosophy that you have to live in order to write about your experience obviously has some truth. It's important to have a full, functional life and it does affect your ability to be creative. But I feel at the same time that people who say, "You must live a certain amount to tell a story" are generally not creative. The reality is that you have to do work in order to get good at your work and life happens to you regardless. If you don't die it happens. It's important not to be Daryl Zero and that is what *The Zero Effect* is about. It is about discovering that you need to participate in life and that the world happens to you however it happens, but that you can't control it and you certainly can't make it happen. When was the last time you thought, I'm gonna go out and live? The idea that the creative organism works with a stockpile of events filed away for later use is not something I subscribe to. I don't think that's how it works. My work is something that interacts with my life. It is an escape from my life and a reflection of my life. It is also a job.

HOW RELEVANT ARE CONNECTIONS AND AGENTS TO GETTING A FILM MADE?
It helps to be involved with good people, but that is really hard because there aren't that many. Sometimes people rely very heavily on networking, schmoozing, and the "who you know" theory. There are people who have a lot of success that way and they can talk their way into anything. People don't generally gravitate toward networkers like this though. People respond

to good work. How much does a good agent help? Sometimes a lot, and great stuff can happen if you have a relationship with an agent that is like a real partnership. I can tell you that all the connections in the world won't get something made. That I know from watching and from being around movies, as well as from being someone who knew people. There are many ways that people get into this business. You can say, "Obviously he was the guy who did this and he was the nephew of this guy or he was the friend of this guy," or whatever. The thing is that for every one of those people there are ten others who aren't making films. People are facilitated by and limited by their talent almost always. Of course, there are exceptions. There are a lot of untalented people out there and much of their success is due to the fact that they just work really hard. I know that I have always felt like I worked my ass off and I write like crazy. When other people are out doing things, I am home writing. I have sacrificed being a certain kind of person in order to be the kind of person I am. No one made me do it; I was ambitious and irrational and I wanted to be writing. I've been like that since I was really young. Instead of going out I preferred to stay home and write a play. This is partly egotistical and partly self-serving. But I do my work and that's how I've always thought of myself. If I were bad at it I wouldn't have been able to accomplish the things that I have.

DO YOU THINK THAT YOU GET THE SAME LEVERAGE IF YOU PURCHASE AN OPTION TO A BOOK AND WRITE A SCREENPLAY AROUND IT AS YOU DO IF YOU WRITE AN ORIGINAL SCREENPLAY?
If you option a book and own the rights to a successful book and write a good script around it, that can be irresistible to people. But there is nothing quite as simple as an original idea that you come up with yourself. That is the simple way to do it. The book option is tricky. What often happens is that you option a book for six months or for a year, which costs a lot of money, and nothing happens with it. At the end of the option period you no longer own the rights and then you have a script for something, but not the ability to use the underlying property. At this point you desperately need it so you find yourself in a screwy negotiating position.

WHAT DO YOU THINK ABOUT THE VALUE OF APPRENTICESHIP?
It's invaluable if you can figure out a way to do it. On some level I apprenticed with my father while I was growing up. Writing the book about *Wyatt Earp* was a certain kind of apprenticeship as well. I learned so much during that time and my whole language expanded. It was a great experience. I learned as much as I ever learned in my first week as a director. There is a huge learning curve to that job because you know so much more the second day than you did the first. However, getting a real apprenticeship is tough.

There is never going to be a shortage of people who want to direct films, and you are never going to get the job because a director desperately needs someone. If you want to get coffee for someone until you are eventually promoted to development, you can do that. But if you want to be an auteur film director, then it is a weird road. You don't work your way up through the career ranks to become a filmmaker. How many assistant directors have you ever heard of becoming a director? I don't think it is even an expectation. That's not to say that it doesn't ever happen, but it's rare. If you want to direct, then you need some way to convince people that you are the only one that can do the job and that you bring a unique perspective and insight to a particular project. That is something that is done by an artist, not a craftsman.

HOW WOULD YOU ADVISE SOMEONE INTERESTED IN BECOMING A DIRECTOR TO GO ABOUT IT?

Try to figure out a story that you want to tell. Don't overstress the importance of your project because people are not looking for a bible; they are looking for creative ideas. Think of five stories you want to tell and five kinds of movies you want to make. Look at the stuff you are interested in and write about that whatever it may be. Then ask yourself what is missing in your life that is provided by that thing you are interested in. What was enhanced in your life once that was there? What did it reveal to you about yourself? How did it facilitate what you became and how did it limit what you became? You can tell a story about dragons, but it can still be really personal. That was the big leap I took after my last play, before I wrote *The Zero Effect*. I didn't want to write about myself as me or as a standup comic or a professional baseball player. I wanted to write about myself as the world's greatest private detective. It wasn't me, but the heart of the character came from my personal experience. Writing about what you know can mean any number of things. You can write on an emotional level and you can write about what's important to you without writing literally about your own experiences. Find the allegory and the metaphor and write something. Look to all your favorite movies and see what they addressed. My advice is to come up with the script and either convince somebody to let you make it or make it yourself.

If you can think of anything else that makes you happy, do that instead, because this can be a very frustrating job, filled with anguish and despair. Trying to get it going sucks and it doesn't always work out. You have to chase this dream and to do that you have to create a piece of work that moves you. If you can do that, then it will probably move other people too.

WHY DO YOU MAKE FILMS?

Making films is all I have ever wanted to do. I love the idea of putting on a show. It is the best job there is and that is why so many people want to do it. I like the idea that I am able to express my ideas to others in the form of entertainment. Making films is about self-expression; you figure out who you are and then you find a way to communicate that and manifest your inner thoughts into something that hopefully endures. It's a fascinating process. I love the idea that I can make something from nothing.

While writing this book I tried to identify what made the filmmakers I interviewed successful in launching their careers. Not surprisingly, there were as many paths taken as there were directors interviewed. Still, I narrowed it down to five different roads: scriptwriting, making low-budget independent movies, working for a production company in order to network, directing television shows, and directing commercials and music videos.

By far the fastest and most commonly traveled road to feature-film directing is script writing. All of the directors interviewed in this book were at some level writers. Not all of them had their names on the script, but every director contributed to the creation of the source material. A common theme was the importance of the director as conceptualist from the film's beginnings. Many people bring scripts they have written and want to direct to possible funders, but few have something to say, and even fewer have something worth saying. Good ideas and good writing are the rarest of commodities. Everyone told me that if you can write scripts that contain a compelling and original story and that have more than a narrow appeal, you will find a market for your work and it will be produced. One of the additional benefits of "writing your way in" to the industry is that there is no capital investment except your own time. You need only paper, pencil, and talent and drive. If you can save up enough money to live on while you write, nothing can stop you but your own creative limitations.

Some filmmakers started as music video or commercial directors. There is a seemingly good logic to that approach: If you lack the life experience or creative drive necessary to create an appealing original script, working to master the technical craft of filmmaking is a useful interim task. But breaking into the music video or commercial business may be just as challenging as breaking into feature filmmaking; while the competition may not be as intense as it is for movie directing, it is still fierce. There are fewer people competing for music video or commercial directing spots than there are for feature films, but they are generally more capable specialists. These are people who are pursuing an obscure but highly rewarding and lucrative profession that they will fight hard to work in.

Moreover, there is no guarantee that a commercial director can successfully make the transition to feature director; the two are related, but not identical, jobs. Commercial and video directors usually tell an image-based story in a very short time period, and while learning to do this may be effective training for making features, it may also do one a disservice. Directors told me that the feature narrative requires a much more nuanced understanding of the principles of dramatic structure. However, Tamra Davis and Brett Ratner, as well as many others, have effectively leveraged their mastery of the video form into directing jobs. Those who went this road typically worked well with the visual image and were able to create a striking small-screen depiction of human emotion through innovative camera work and editing. The music video path continues to be accessible, although MTV, the largest exhibitor of music videos, has stopped focusing on them, instead programming their network with an emphasis on such reality-based shows as *The Real World* instead. As a result, there are fewer music video productions today, and the bar for producing them has been raised; record labels can no longer expect to get broad exposure from low-budget videos for small or mid-level musical acts and are now focused mainly on producing videos for their best-selling stars. Budgets have risen dramatically, resulting in far fewer slots for new directors. Although television advertising has not undergone a reduction in exhibition, but rather a marked increase, the stakes riding on a television commercial are so high that it is very difficult for a would-be director to persuade a national advertiser to entrust the millions of dollars worth of production value and air-time such a commercial to an unknown. However, the possibilities remain open, and video and commercial directing is still a viable road into the feature world, provided one remains focused on dramatic structure.

Some directors, like John Schlesinger and Edward Zwick, worked first in television production as directors, and later made the transition into feature filmmaking. But directing for TV is a highly competitive field with few new entrants, due largely to the scale and broad distribution of the programming. Advertisers pay the networks large amounts of money to push their product, and programming must be at the highest level of perceived excellence and broad appeal to achieve this goal. Those who made their entry into the film industry through television work largely did this by becoming television writers, and later made the move to directing. It is important to note that television directing is quite different from feature filmmaking; the role of the director is more that of an overseer, an executor of the producer's plan, and not that of a creative director or head conceptualist. The television director is much the less the creator of an idea than he is the one who runs with it.

A few of our directors started out by making a low-budget film, with friends' or family's money. This approach was, however, usually reserved for the creation of short films or projects worked on in school. None of the directors in this book financed a complete feature with their own money, although directors like Abel Ferrara and John Carpenter began projects that were ultimately cofinanced by outsiders with money for finishing costs that got their films theatrically distributed. Although the argument could be made that the funds required to make a theatrically viable film are too great for emerging directors to compile alone, for most filmed but unreleased low-budget movies the truth more likely lies with the insight offered by John Dahl: If a script is not exciting enough to elicit a good response from serious financing entities, then it is unlikely to merit being made into a film some other way. And unless you have money to burn, making your own feature film is an extremely high-risk investment with very low odds of being successful. This is true both because of the necessarily lower production value of a low-budget film and because of the lack of preexisting distribution agreements that will expose the film to a paying audience. There are, of course, exceptions to every rule and Neil LaBute is ours. *In the Company of Men* was shot for $25,000 (albeit postproduced and edited with a few hundred thousand more) and went on to receive substantial distribution and gross millions of dollars, establishing LaBute as a known director. In this way, LaBute's low-budget film, like John McNaughton's *Henry*, was used as a calling card to establish a name. It certainly worked.

Social relationships with movie industry players and famous actors were certainly helpful to many directors. All of the directors stressed the importance of working relationships and the fact that one relationship is always a door to another. The entertainment business and the film industry relies upon people as its product. Actors, writers, directors, and executives all trade in the currency of relationships. I heard often that no one in Hollywood likes to "tell you to go away" because they do not like to burn any bridges. It is very hard to know where the next talented director is going to come from, therefore the industry must remain open to new players as they emerge. But there is a wall around Hollywood that, to an outsider, can appear almost impregnable. Edward Zwick told us that he often felt like he was pressing his nose up against the glass, watching while his more successful friends quickly became powerful. However, with perseverance, charisma, and a healthy dose of arrogance, many directors leveraged their social relationships in the industry to help them get films made. Kris Isacsson got

Harvey Weinstein to read his script for his first feature, *Down to You,* through connections he made while working at Miramax. No one I spoke with was given a significant job on connections alone, but the combination of connections and merit proved to be very powerful.

Quite apart from the ways they became filmmakers, the directors interviewed share several personality traits. Drive is the number-one common attribute among our subjects. Many directors said that they felt a sense of compulsion throughout their lives, whether they were pursuing editing, directing, storyboarding, writing, or simply living. Many directors spoke of an inner voice that pushed them to create and to work continuously. They felt a sense that their work was never finished and that they would never get things just right, but that they had to keep creating new projects to try to attain perfection, even though it would forever elude them.

The directors were all resilient self-starters who refused to give up, even in the face of harsh criticism or against the toughest odds. Kim Peirce's struggle to develop her talent in spite of her financial difficulties and Tom DiCillo's ten-year push to get a feature off the ground while working as a house painter both epitomize a different, tough person who never took no for an answer. As Amy Heckerling said, "You may hear five hundred no's, but you only need one yes." The directors told me that persistence and time are the keys to success. The longer you try and the more you present your work to the buying public, the more likely you are to become successful. This is because a large part of getting recognized rests upon what our directors called the "luck" of being in the right place at the right time. But most directors believed that you make luck, that by constantly pushing your work into the world you expose yourself to those lucky opportunities and circumstances that would lead to a break.

Many of the directors I interviewed went to film school, and those who did not learned and developed their craft early on either by creating short films, working in the industry, or writing scripts. Not a single one of our interview subjects was promoted from within the industry, and every one thought that working for a producer or a studio had very little to do with securing directing work. Artists, not executives, direct movies, and what leads you to the directing profession is product and the ability to deliver it. However, the directors all advocated learning about filmmaking. Every one interviewed suggested reading as much as possible about movies and practicing filmmaking on today's inexpensive digital video cameras and editing systems.

Every director stressed the importance of the product. If you have any aspirations about making films, I was told, then you had better go out and make short ones right away. As Brett Ratner said, you may have the best connections in the world and meet people all the time, but if you have nothing to show them, then what good are those connections? You must have a film or a script in your hand, and that is something that you have to develop through study and hard work, and through reading and writing scripts, shooting short films, and making interesting projects that people want to see.

Using the twenty directors I interviewed as a sample, filmmakers are predominately white males who come from a middle- to upper-middle-class background. They grow up all over the United States, and at the time they make their first feature they are between the ages of twenty-eight and thirty-one. Their family is generally not in the film industry and some encounter slight resistance from their parents about becoming an "artist." They generally have little prior moviemaking experience but have a 25 percent chance of having done some theater work. Odds are even that they went to film school. They most likely made their way into the industry by writing screenplays, which is not surprising because all of the interview subjects studied writing in college and many concentrated on reading the great books and Aristotle's *Poetics*, as well as various texts on dramatic structure and theory.

Throughout the year that I have worked on this book I have made some strides in my own professional filmmaking career. Publishing this project was a fulfilling accomplishment, and the interaction with ICM and my agent there opened doors for me in getting my writing seen. My script-writing partner and I circulated two scripts through ICM and got some good feedback on them. We haven't sold anything, but we have gained a better sense of how agents evaluate creative submissions, and at least now we know where to find them. I also this year began a documentary film project about the pioneers of the computer operating system Linux and tried to raise some money to shoot that film. Although I was unable to get all of the funds I wanted for a feature-length movie, I did succeed in convincing two Fortune 1000 companies, Informix Software and IBM, to give me $15,000 and $30,000 grants, respectively, to shoot some industrial films for them that could be used as footage for my own project. I also bought a computer editing system (the cost of which I quickly paid back by renting it out to others), and having that kind of facility on-hand led to several jobs and some interesting collaborations with other people in the industry. During the course of postproduction on an independent television pilot I was hired to edit, I developed a meaningful friendship with another young director and shared creative ideas about how to approach the filmmaking process.

I believe that these accomplishments came from three things: hard work, perseverance, and some amount of talent. What the directors in this book said I have found to be quite true: While there is certainly no clear-cut path to feature filmmaking, it is energy, work, and an intense determination to succeed that propels people to the top.

I wish you the best of luck in your own efforts.

Nicholas Jarecki
May 2001

JOHN CARPENTER

Ghosts of Mars (2001)
Vampires (1998)
Escape from L.A. (1996)
In the Mouth of Madness (1995)
Village of the Damned (1995)
Body Bags (1993) (TV) (segments "The Gas Station," and "Hair")
Memoirs of an Invisible Man (1992)
They Live (1988)
Prince of Darkness (1987)
Big Trouble in Little China (1986)
Starman (1984)
Christine (1983)
The Thing (1982)
Escape from New York (1981)
The Fog (1980)
Elvis (1979) (TV)
Someone's Watching Me! (1978) (TV)
Halloween (1978)
Assault on Precinct 13 (1976)
Dark Star (1973)

JOHN DAHL

Joy Ride (2001)
Striking Back: A Jewish Commando's War Against the Nazis (1998)
Rounders (1998)
Unforgettable (1996)

The Last Seduction (1994)
Red Rock West (1992)
Kill Me Again (1989)

TAMRA DAVIS

What Are Friends For? (2001)
Skipped Parts (2000)
Half-Baked (1998)
Best Men (1997)
Billy Madison (1995)
No Alternative Girls (1994)
Bad Girls (1994) (uncredited)
CB4 (1993)
Guncrazy (1992)

TOM DICILLO

Double Whammy (2001)
The Real Blonde (1997)
Box of Moonlight (1996)
Living in Oblivion (1995)
Johnny Suede (1991)

PETER FARRELLY

Shallow Hal (2002)
Osmosis Jones (2001)
Me, Myself & Irene (2000)
There's Something About Mary (1998)
Kingpin (1996)
Dumb & Dumber (1994)

ABEL FERRARA

R-Xmas (2001)
New Rose Hotel (1998)
Subway Stories: Tales from the Underground (1997) (TV) (segment
"Love on the A Train")
The Blackout (1997)
California (1996)
The Funeral (1996)
The Addiction (1995)
Dangerous Game (1993)
Body Snatchers (1993)
Bad Lieutenant (1992)

King of New York (1990)
Cat Chaser (1989)
China Girl (1987)
Crime Story (1986) (TV)
The Gladiator (1986) (TV)
"Miami Vice" (1984), TV series (episode "The Dutch Oven," [1985])
Fear City (1984)
Ms. 45 (1981)
The Driller Killer (1979)

JAMES FOLEY
The Corruptor (1999)
"Gun" (1997/II), TV series
Fear (1996)
The Chamber (1996)
Two Bits (1995)
Glengarry Glen Ross (1992)
After Dark, My Sweet (1990)
"Twin Peaks" (1990), TV series
Who's That Girl? (1987)
At Close Range (1986)
Reckless (1984)

AMY HECKERLING
Loser (2000)
Clueless (1995)
Look Who's Talking Too (1990)
Look Who's Talking (1989)
European Vacation (1985)
Johnny Dangerously (1984)
Fast Times at Ridgemont High (1982)
Getting It Over With (1977) (short)

KRIS ISACSSON
Down to You (2000)
Man About Town (1996) (short)

JAKE KASDAN
"Undeclared" (2001), TV series
Orange County (2001)
Fresh Kills (2000)
"Grosse Pointe" (2000), TV series

"Freaks and Geeks" (1999), TV series (episodes "Pilot," "Beers and Weirs," "Noshing and Moshing," "Smooching and Mooching," "The Little Things")
Zero Effect (1998)

NEIL LABUTE
Possession (2001)
Bash: Latterday Plays (2000) (TV)
Nurse Betty (2000)
Your Friends & Neighbors (1998)
In the Company of Men (1997)

JOHN MCNAUGHTON
Speaking of Sex (2001)
Condo Painting (2000)
Lansky (1999) (TV)
Wild Things (1998)
Normal Life (1996)
Girls in Prison (1994) (TV)
Mad Dog and Glory (1993)
"Homicide: Life on the Street" (1993), TV series (episodes "A Many Splendored Thing," "A Model Citizen," "Partners," "Law and Disorder," "Stakeout")
Sex, Drugs, Rock & Roll (1991)
The Borrower (1991)
Henry: Portrait of a Serial Killer (1986)

VINCENZO NATALI
Cube (1997)
Elevated (1997), short

KIMBERLY PEIRCE
Boys Don't Cry (1999)
Boys Don't Cry (1995), short
The Last Good Breath (1994)

BRETT RATNER
Rush Hour 2 (2001)
The Family Man (2000)
Mariah #1's (1999) (V) (video "Heartbreaker")
Rush Hour (1998)
Money Talks (1997)
Whatever Happened to Mason Reese (1990) (short)

JOHN SCHLESINGER

The Next Best Thing (2000)
The Tale of Sweeney Todd (1998) (TV)
Eye for an Eye (1996)
Cold Comfort Farm (1995) (TV)
The Innocent (1993)
A Question of Attribution (1992)
Pacific Heights (1990)
Madame Sousatzka (1988)
The Believers (1987)
The Falcon and the Snowman (1984)
An Englishman Abroad (1983) (TV)
Separate Tables (1983) (TV)
Honky Tonk Freeway (1981)
Yanks (1979)
Marathon Man (1976)
The Day of the Locust (1975)
Visions of Eight (1973) (segment "The Longest")
Sunday, Bloody Sunday (1971)
Midnight Cowboy (1969)
Far from the Madding Crowd (1967)
Darling (1965)
Billy Liar (1963)
A Kind of Loving (1962)
Terminus (1961)
"Monitor" (1958), TV series

BARRY SONNENFELD

Men in Black 2 (2002)
"Tick, The" (2001), TV series
Big Trouble (2001)
Wild Wild West (1999)
"Maximum Bob" (1998), TV series
Men in Black (1997)
Get Shorty (1995)
For Love or Money (1993)
Addams Family Values (1993)
The Addams Family (1991)

JAMES TOBACK

Harvard Man (2001)
Love in Paris (1999)
Black and White (1999)

Two Girls and a Guy (1997)
The Big Bang (1989)
The Pick-up Artist (1987)
Exposed (1983)
Love and Money (1982)
Fingers (1978)

BEN YOUNGER
Boiler Room (2000)

EDWARD ZWICK
"Once and Again" (1999), TV series
The Siege (1998)
Courage Under Fire (1996)
Legends of the Fall (1994)
"My So-Called Life" (1994), TV series (episode "On the Wagon" [1994])
Leaving Normal (1992)
Glory (1989)
"thirtysomething" (1987), TV series
About Last Night... (1986)
Special Bulletin (1983) (TV) (as Ed Zwick)
Having It All (1982) (TV)
Paper Dolls (1982/I) (TV)
"Family" (1976), TV series

PHOTO CREDITS

005: EDWARD ZWICK *Photo by Dayna Taynon.*

022: BARRY SONNENFELD *Photo by Melinda Sue Gordon.*

033: JOHN SCHLESINGER *Photo courtesy of John Schlesinger.*

044: BEN YOUNGER *Photo by David Lee.*

058: KIMBERLY PEIRCE *Photo by Bill Matlock.*

075: VINCENZO NATALI *Photo courtesy of Vincenzo Natali.*

090: JOHN CARPENTER *Photo courtesy of John Carpenter / Paramount Pictures.*

097: KRIS ISACSSON *Photo courtesy of Kris Isacsson.*

114: ABEL FERRARA *Photo courtesy of AP/Wide World Photos.*

124: PETER FARRELLY *Photo courtesy of AP/Wide World Photos.*

142: AMY HECKERLING *Photo courtesy of Columbia Pictures, Inc. and SPE Finance LLC.*

157: JAMES TOBACK *Photo courtesy of AP/Wide World Photos.*

173: TAMRA DAVIS *Photo courtesy of Tamra Davis.*

190: JOHN MCNAUGHTON *Photo by Ron Batzdorff.*

202: NEIL LABUTE *Photo by Bruce Birmelin.*

214: TOM DICILLO *Photo by Richard Corman.*

231: JOHN DAHL *Photo courtesy of Regency Entertainment and Twentieth Century Fox Film Corporation.*

246: BRETT RATNER *Photo courtesy of Brett Ratner.*

257: JAMES FOLEY *Photo courtesy of James Foley.*

276: JAKE KASDAN *Photo by Gemma La Mana.*

317: NICHOLAS JARECKI *Photo by Ghislaine Maxwell.*

Since graduating from New York University's Tisch School of the Arts in 1999, Nicholas Jarecki has directed several short films and music videos, as well as a documentary about the building of a New York nightclub. He has also directed and produced television pieces for clients such as IBM and HBO. Currently at work on scriptwriting and directing projects, Jarecki lives in New York City.